LEGAL AUTHORITY BEYOND THE STATE

In recent decades, new international courts and other legal bodies have proliferated as international law has broadened beyond the fields of treaty law and diplomatic relations. This development has not only triggered debate about how authority may be held by institutions beyond the state, but has also thrown into question familiar models of authority found in legal and political philosophy. The essays in this book take a philosophical approach to these developments, debates and questions. In doing so, they seek to clarify the relevant issues underpinning, as well as develop possible solutions to, the problem of how legal authority may be constructed beyond the state.

PATRICK CAPPS is a Professor of International Law at the University of Bristol. He teaches in the areas of Public International Law and the Philosophy of Law. He has held visiting positions at the University of Melbourne, the University of Cambridge and the University of Copenhagen.

HENRIK PALMER OLSEN is a Professor of Jurisprudence at the Center of Excellence for International Courts (iCourts) at the University of Copenhagen. He is a leading expert in legal theory and has published foundational research within the areas of jurisprudence, the separation of powers and the relationship between institutional design and notions of justice, with a recent focus on international courts.

LEGAL AUTHORITY BEYOND THE STATE

Edited by

PATRICK CAPPS

University of Bristol

HENRIK PALMER OLSEN

University of Copenhagen

CAMBRIDGE
UNIVERSITY PRESS

CAMBRIDGE
UNIVERSITY PRESS

University Printing House, Cambridge CB2 8BS, United Kingdom

One Liberty Plaza, 20th Floor, New York, NY 10006, USA

477 Williamstown Road, Port Melbourne, VIC 3207, Australia

314–321, 3rd Floor, Plot 3, Splendor Forum, Jasola District Centre,
New Delhi – 110025, India

79 Anson Road, #06-04/06, Singapore 079906

Cambridge University Press is part of the University of Cambridge.

It furthers the University's mission by disseminating knowledge in the pursuit of
education, learning, and research at the highest international levels of excellence.

www.cambridge.org
Information on this title: www.cambridge.org/9781107190269
DOI: 10.1017/9781108100045

First published 2018

Printed in the United Kingdom by Clays, St Ives plc

A catalogue record for this publication is available from the British Library.

Library of Congress Cataloging-in-Publication Data
Names: Capps, Patrick, editor. | Olsen, Henrik Palmer, editor.
Title: Legal authority beyond the state / edited by Patrick Capps, University of Bristol;
Henrik Palmer Olsen, University of Copenhagen.
Description: Cambridge, United Kingdom; New York, NY:
Cambridge University Press, 2018. | Includes bibliographical references.
Identifiers: LCCN 2017053357 | ISBN 9781107190269 (hardback)
Subjects: LCSH: International law. | International courts. |
Jus cogens (International law) | BISAC: LAW / International.
Classification: LCC KZ3410.L437 2018 | DDC 341–dc23
LC record available at https://lccn.loc.gov/2017053357

ISBN 978-1-107-19026-9 Hardback

CONTENTS

CONTRIBUTORS

ALAN BRUDNER is Professor of Law and Albert Abel Chair Emeritus at the University of Toronto.

PATRICK CAPPS is Professor of International Law at the University of Bristol.

RICHARD COLLINS is Lecturer in International Law at University College Dublin.

ANDREAS FOLLESDAL is Professor of Political Philosophy at the Faculty of Law at the University of Oslo.

JOHN MARTIN GILLROY is Chair of the Department of Philosophy; Professor of Philosophy, International Law, and Public Policy; and Founding Director of the Environmental Policy Design Graduate Programs at Lehigh University, USA.

MARGARET MARTIN is Associate Professor at the Faculty of Law at Western University, Canada.

HENRIK PALMER OLSEN is Professor of Jurisprudence at the University of Copenhagen.

INGER-JOHANNE SAND is Professor of Public Law, Faculty of Law, at the University of Oslo.

INGO VENZKE is Associate Professor at the Department of International and European Law at the University of Amsterdam; Director, Amsterdam Centre for International Law.

ACKNOWLEDGEMENTS

The chapters that form this book have had a relatively long gestation. They were first presented at a conference held at the University of Copenhagen in December 2014. This was organized by Henrik Palmer Olsen and was funded by the iCourts Centre of Excellence at that university. The finished papers were then revisited at a workshop organized by Richard Collins and Henrik Palmer Olsen at University College Dublin (UCD) in January 2017. Alongside the contributors to this volume, we would like to thank the following colleagues: Başak Çali, Eoin Carolan, Maeve Cooke, Oran Doyle, Graham Finlay, James Gallen, Jakob v. H. Holtermann, Mattias Kumm, Mikael Rask Madsen, Rebecca Schmidt, Oisin Suttle and Chris Thornhill. In particular, we would like to also thank Mette Jarum (who helped organize the conference at the University of Copenhagen), Suzanne Darcy (who helped organize the workshop at UCD), and Matias Means, Julia Løcke and Reece Lewis (who provided research assistance). Finally, we would like to thank Stuart Toddington. Stuart has been involved in this project since its inception and has helped the production of this book in myriad important ways.

~

Introduction

PATRICK CAPPS AND HENRIK PALMER OLSEN

It is now an uncontentious observation about the very fabric of global society that international law can no longer be reduced to a conjunction of treaty law and diplomatic relations. This situation raises new and significant questions for those considering the authority of international, transnational and global law.[1] The authors of the chapters of this book aim to articulate and respond to these questions.

1 The Field of Contemporary Global Governance

The observation just made can be developed in at least two ways. In this section, we first set out some examples of how the validity of international law, and the authority of international courts, has extended beyond being merely a product of state will, and how this extension of authority has met resistance. Second, we then explain how this extension can be described as a form of autonomous *living international law*.

A   Growth and Resistance

The first example arises from the ongoing negotiations from 2017 between the United Kingdom (UK) and the European Union (EU) concerning the withdrawal of the UK from the EU. While the political and legal fallout from these negotiations will undoubtedly have significant legal, political and social implications for years, if not generations, one important early stumbling block in attempts to advance negotiations on a new association agreement between these parties is the question

---

[1] The literature surrounding the transformation of law beyond the state is considerable. See, for example, J. Klabbers, A. Peters and G. Ulfstein, *The Constitutionalization of International Law* (Oxford: Oxford University Press, 2009); M. Koskiennemi, *The Politics of International Law* (Oxford: Hart, 2011); J. L. Dunoff and J. P. Trachtmann, eds., *Ruling the World?: Constitutionalism, International Law, and Global Governance* (Cambridge: Cambridge University Press, 2009).

of what legal obligations the UK has accumulated towards the EU, and other EU member states, over the years and how those obligations can be withdrawn and replaced by new ones.[2] The complexity of these issues is immense because simple answers cannot be gleaned from the treaties alone; they are just as much concerned with practices, which are the product of decades of close economic, political and social cooperation and negotiation.

The second example is the rapid and recent growth and influence of international courts. Ninety per cent of the entire output of decisions from these institutions have been issued in the past two decades.[3] It is also now clear that international courts are becoming less arbitral and more genuinely judicial. These courts often have compulsory jurisdiction; allow litigants other than states to participate in, or even initiate, actions; and claim judicial authority to review state compliance with international rules.[4] There is, we observe, a general development of a form of judicial autonomy, by which we mean the willingness and ability of international courts to require states and other actors to comply with their judgments.[5]

There is resistance to the developments just outlined. One example is the Brighton Declaration (2012), which seeks to narrow the criteria of admissibility of the European Court of Human Rights with a view to return competences to states parties.[6] Further evidence of judicial retrenchment against international courts is to be found in the recent *Ajos* judgment of the Danish Supreme Court, which refused openly to follow a preliminary ruling from the Court of Justice of the European Union (CJEU).[7] This resistance reaches its current apotheosis with the UK's attempt to withdraw from the Union insofar as it is driven by discontent amongst British citizens that judges in the CJEU exert too much influence over the

---

[2] See 'Position Papers Transmitted to the EU27 on Article 50 Negotiations', European Commission, 29 May 2017, https://ec.europa.eu/commission/publications/draft-eu-position-papers-article-50-negotiations_en.

[3] Karen Alter, 'The New International Courts: A Bird's Eye View', Buffett Center for International and Comparative Studies Working Paper Series No. 09-001, 2009; and Karen Alter, *The New Terrain of International Law: Courts, Politics, Rights* (Princeton: Princeton University Press, 2014).

[4] See Alter, *New Terrain*; and, for an example, see *HM Treasury v. Ahmed* [2010] UKSC 2.

[5] Alter, *New Terrain*.

[6] See European Court of Human Rights, 'Brighton Declaration', High Level Conference on the Future of the European Court of Human Rights, Brighton, England, 19–20 April 2012, www.echr.coe.int/Documents/2012_Brighton_FinalDeclaration_ENG.pdf.

[7] See Judgment of 6 December 2016, DI som mandatar for Ajos A/S mod Boet efter A (sag nr. 15/2014).

interpretation of the content of EU law, and hence what obligations befall the UK. The same pattern also seems to be occurring outside Europe, as evidenced by the sustained critique by (often African) states and others of the International Criminal Court (ICC) who see it as being politically biased in its prosecution policy, or even being instrumental in exacerbating international crimes.[8] Proposals for the United States (US) to withdraw from the Paris Climate Agreement in June 2017 is further evidence of this retrenchment.

These examples give the impression of a fast-paced development in legal forms beyond the state, which runs simultaneously with political associations struggling to come to terms with this development. Traditional political associations – often converging on the sovereign state – are being asked to recognize that they are part of a broader global community, and from that emerges a need for the coordinated regulation of economic, political, environmental and technological developments. Often, though, this request is not being met because the forms of coordinated regulation that have emerged do not pay enough attention to, or may even alienate, the traditional political associations just mentioned. This is not simply a knee-jerk reaction to the forces of globalisation but is in part a plea by traditional political associations that when and where there is global or regional regulation, it must be responsive to the interests, needs and/or values of those it seeks to regulate.

B Living International Law

Another feature of the field of contemporary global governance is that it lacks systematically hierarchical relations,[9] which provides a stark and

---

[8] See Chapter 9 in this volume, M. Martin, 'The International Criminal Court: The New Leviathan?'; S. Nouwen and W. Werner, 'Doing Justice to the Political: The International Criminal Court in Uganda and Sudan', *European Journal of International Law* 21 (2011): 941–65; S. Kendall, 'Commodifying Global Justice: Economies of Accountability at the International Criminal Court', *Journal of International Criminal Justice* 13 (2015): 113–34.

[9] The wide and often uncoordinated spread of norms and institutions within international law has led some authors in the field to talk about the 'pluralistic' or 'fragmentary' character of contemporary international legality. See, for example, M. Koskenniemi, 'The Fate of International Law: Between Technique and Politics', *Modern Law Review* 70 (2007): 1–30; and N. Krisch, *Beyond Constitutionalism: The Pluralist Structure of Postnational Law* (Oxford: Oxford University Press, 2010). These authors accept the view that there is an increasing density of international legality but also remark on the relative absence of coordinatory mechanisms in international law. As a result, international law is seen as increasingly fragmented, regionalized and functionally divided.

immediate contrast with classical conceptions of the systematic unity of law found in many familiar philosophical accounts of international law.[10] This feature provides problems for theories of international legal authority. According to the familiar accounts just mentioned, systemic unity of the institutions that form global governance are understood to be initiated and regulated through multilateral treaties. At the heart of this reasoning reside two traditional legal principles. The first is the *ultra vires* doctrine, which states that a power that has been granted to an institution affords freedom to it to act within the boundary of that power, and not beyond it. Secondly, there is the *delegatus non potest delegare* principle, which (according to one version of it) prohibits delegation of legislative authority to another (non-legislative) branch of government. When brought together in the context of international law, it becomes clear that these principles support a static view[11] of international law; one that endorses domestic constitutionalism as fundamental to law, and which sees international law as emerging exclusively from agreements between states.

Our initial observations made in the previous sub-section suggest a *dynamic* or *evolutionary* conception of global governance. That is, a system of *living international law* seems to be emerging. This should not be confused with 'living law' in Ehrlich's sense of the term, which describes informal and private systems of rules beyond the state.[12] Living international law, instead, refers to a set of practices that have developed in and around existing treaty-based law. Part of this process is the maturation of international law – often through the work of international courts and other international bodies – who take it upon themselves to thicken the often thin content of posited treaty law. Conventions often under-specify the content of international law, and it is this under-specification that creates the normative space that is filled by the interpretative practices of international courts and bureaucracies.[13] These interpretative practices

---

[10] On this, see J. Kammerhofer and J. d'Aspremont, eds., *International Legal Positivism in a Postmodern World* (Cambridge: Cambridge University Press, 2014), ch. 1.

[11] What we here call the static conception of international law described in the text is the jurisprudential equivalent of what is known as the 'coexistence' or 'consent' theory in public international law.

[12] E. Ehrlich, *Fundamental Principles of the Sociology of Law* (1913; London: Transaction, 2001).

[13] See also A. von Bogdandy, M. Goldmann and I. Venzke, 'From Public International to International Public Law: Translating World Public Opinion into International Public Authority', *European Journal of International Law* 28 (2017): 115–45. They observe more generally in regards to the increasing complexity of the institutional setup in international law that 'in the attempt to cater to common interests, international law has developed a

establish what international law is taken to be, but they simultaneously raise questions of how the authority of law develops beyond the state. Officials cannot straightforwardly appeal to the texts of the treaties to claim authority; they must seek other grounds, such as an appeal to expertise; substantive justice, economic, political and social dynamics; or interpretive techniques drawn from domestic administrative law and so on.[14]

If a dynamic and evolving system of international living law is emerging, the actions or judgments produced by it cannot be explained as being authoritative according to the two principles just set out. Rather, the static conception of authority shuts down a full inquiry into the conceptual structure of the evolution and content of the actual processes of international organisations. Furthermore, it does not get close to allowing a full examination of the validity of the multifarious authority claims made by those occupying roles within newly evolving forms of global governance or, indeed, investigating their normative plausibility. One central aim of this book is to engage with the challenge of building – from various but closely related theoretical perspectives – a new jurisprudential understanding of the nature and plausibility of authority within contemporary international legality.

2   Ideas of Authority beyond the State

Without doubt, the reconciliation of forms of global governance just mentioned with democratic processes and other forms of accountability, within a dynamic and evolving system of international living law, remains an incredibly difficult problem to solve. This problem, though, is just one particularly modern expression of a more general problem of how authentic authority claims can be made by forms of global governance. We are not alone in seeing authority as a crucial entry point for understanding the complexity that surrounds contemporary international legal practices, and discussion of some related literature helps us locate the central methodological focus of this book.

---

sophisticated institutional structure that is hard to reconcile with ideas of horizontal relations based on (state) consent alone' (119).

[14] I. Venzke, *How Interpretation Makes International Law* (Oxford: Oxford University Press, 2012); and B. Kingsbury, 'The Concept of "Law" in Global Administrative Law', *European Journal of International Law* 20 (2009): 23–57.

A   Compliance and Authority

A special issue of *Law and Contemporary Problems* was issued in 2016 with the title 'The Variable Authority of International Courts'.[15] In their introduction to the issue, entitled 'How Context Shapes the Authority of International Courts', Karen Alter, Laurence Helfer and Mikael Rask Madsen set out their aim, which is to explain the relationship between *de jure* and *de facto* authority. *De jure* authority of international courts is understood by them to be the product of an act of delegation of competence by states to those courts, which establishes its jurisdiction. They then distinguish *de jure* authority from *de facto* authority, which is a form of compliance related agency that is studied as a matter of sociological fact. The special issue then explores and explains how various contextual factors influence the extent to which *de jure* legal mandates develop into various degrees of *de facto* authority within international courts. *De facto* authority is measured by examining the extent to which those whom the court seeks to regulate recognize (by their words, actions or both) that judgments of various international courts are legally binding.

From the perspective of legal philosophy, which is the focus of the present collection, the approach by Alter, Helfer and Madsen invites several important questions. The first question is whether what constitutes *de jure* authority can be dealt with as swiftly as Alter, Hefler and Madsen do. While the *content* of the obligations of states may be identified by state consent, does it also follow that consent establishes the *de jure* authority of the international court, where *de jure* authority is intended to establish conclusive reasons why a state should subordinate its will to the judgment of the court?

The answer to this problem advanced by Alter, Helfer and Madsen is, as has just been observed, to resort to an analysis of *de facto* authority: subjects, as a matter of sociological fact, sometimes accept the court as having normative authority.[16] However, this argument presupposes that consent is understood by subjects as a sufficient reason for them to subordinate their will to that of the official claiming *de jure* authority. This

---

[15] K. Alter, L. Helfer and M. Rask Madsen, eds., 'The Variable Authority of International Courts', *Law and Contemporary Problems* 79 (2016): 1–314.

[16] On this point, see H. Hart, *The Concept of Law* (Oxford: Clarendon Press, 1961). Also see L. Murphy, 'Law Beyond the State: Some Philosophical Questions', *European Journal of International Law* 28 (2017) 203-272 at 218-219.

presupposition is hard to sustain: factual *compliance* can be measured, but it cannot be assumed that compliance to a directive occurs *because* the court's subjects consider it as authoritative. Furthermore, it cannot be assumed that subjects consider the court authoritative *because* those subjects have given their consent. This is, as it happens, another way of stating the classic problem of identifying *opinio juris* (that 'States concerned must ... feel that they are conforming to what amounts to a legal obligation'[17]), which has preoccupied theorists of customary international law. But this issue also arises in relation to the authority of international courts that are established by treaty: a court's authority only arises to the extent that those subject to it believe it to have authority. This cannot be measured by observing individual examples of compliant behaviour in its subjects: Authority is not simply about obedience, as the fact of the latter has many different causes. Authority is a complex attitude by subjects towards an (in this case, international) institution that should involve a coherent and cohesive view of the legitimacy of obeying that institution; and such approach or attitude must be *built* and internalized over time. The theorizing of how authority is built by forms of global governance is a key theme of this book.[18]

B   Authority and Legitimacy

In this volume, we have not been prescriptive about how authority is to be defined. That said, in the previous sub-section, compliance is distinguished from authority, which is understood as a subjective belief on the part of the subject that he or she has an *obligation* to subordinate his or her will to that of various officials. This subject-orientated, but still empirical, conception of authority can be distinguished from a *claim* of authority made by a legal official. Raz, as is well known, regards that an essential feature of law is that those who apply it claim authority, which for him means that they claim that legal reasons are exclusionary reasons (and thus, they claim that the subject has sufficient reason to subordinate his or her will to that of the official).[19] Furthermore, the formal nature of a claim

---

[17] See *North Sea Continental Shelf*, ICJ Reports, 1969, para. 77; and G. Postema, 'Custom in International Law: A Normative Practice Account', in *The Nature of Customary Law*, ed. A. Perreau-Saussine and J. B. Murphy (Cambridge: Cambridge University Press, 2007), ch. 12.

[18] See especially the chapters in this volume by Alan Brudner, Henrik Palmer Olsen and Ingo Venzke.

[19] See J. Raz, *The Authority of Law* (Oxford: Clarendon Press, 1979), 29–31, ch. 2.

of authority of a legal official can be distinguished from inquiry into the authentic *sufficient reasons* why that claim is valid. The authentic reasons have sometimes been called 'legitimate authority'.

Obviously, there are many competing views on how legitimate authority can be justified. Notably, two of the leading arguments on legal authority reject the idea that legitimate authority arises from consent by states to international law. According to Raz's normal justification thesis (or, sometimes, condition) an authority claim by an official is justified (and legitimate authority genuinely arises) when to act in accordance with that official's directives would allow a person to better conform to the reasons that apply to him or her than to do otherwise. The official may, for example, have cognitive advantages (e.g., epistemic) over the subject, or the official may solve volitional defects (e.g., cultural prejudices) that arise if a person seeks to act upon their own subjective interpretation of their reasons.[20] Tasioulas gives a good example of a way by which the normal justification thesis can be fulfilled: 'Customary international law is a distillation of the time-tested collective wisdom of states, fruitfully drawing on their divergent cultural perspectives and historical experience in the resolution of common problems, thereby making it a more reliable guide to right reason than any other alternative.'[21]

From the perspective of the normal justification thesis, it is hard to see how the fact of consent by an effective state can in and of itself establish legitimate authority in international law. Consent by states to international law, from Raz's perspective, according to Tasioulas, can only have a 'derivative bearing' on justified authority: 'It is possible for A to have legitimate authority over B even if A's rule is neither consented to nor democratic; conversely, it is possible for B to consent to A's rule, or for A to rule democratically over B, without A's rule being legitimate.'[22] That said, consent by states may be part of a system which is instrumentally effective in establishing legal norms that are consistent with the requirements of the normal justification thesis (for example, it may lead to international laws that allow better conformity to relevant reasons). While this may be the case, it is far from settled that consent is sufficient to justify the authority of international courts.

---

[20] See J. Tasioulas, 'The Legitimacy of International Law', in *The Philosophy of International Law*, ed. S. Besson and J. Tasioulas (Oxford: Oxford University Press, 2010), 100–103.

[21] Ibid., 101.

[22] Ibid.

Another leading account of legitimate authority is given by democratic theorists, and they make a similar point about the consent-based theory of international authority. Kant, most notably, thought that the law of nations emerges from a non-coercive confederation of republican states but that it cannot exist in the relations between republican and non-republican states. By implication, international legal rules established by the consent of effective, but non-republican, states cannot obviously demand compliance as a matter of law.[23] By implication, any courts, or other forms of global governance, established by such rules cannot have legitimate authority.[24] A similar conclusion concerning the authority of international legality is reached by Thomas Christiano, a leading democratic theorist.[25]

If our initial observation (from Section 1) is correct – that international legality has now gone beyond simply a reflection of treaties, diplomacy and state practice – then it follows that new forms of international legality cannot have authority on the consent-based model. This evolution of international legality, when applied to our justified uneasiness with the consent-based model of legitimate authority itself, seems to fundamentally destabilize our familiar understandings of legal authority beyond the state. This is, in essence, the philosophical problem that the chapters in this book seek to address. Ultimately, our philosophical models of legitimate authority may be used to help build legal authority beyond the state, or to throw the authority of those who claim it into doubt, as living international law emerges.

3 Outline of the Book

Naturally, the chapters in this book touch in many different ways upon the themes just discussed. This said, let us conclude this introduction by describing the trajectory or narrative arc of the book. The first five

---

[23] The exception to this occurs when the content of that treaty is consistent with perfect moral duties. But if this is the case, then the state is only doing what it was morally obligated to do anyway. On this point, see P. Capps, 'Legal Idealism and Global Law', in *Ethical Rationalism and the Law*, ed. P. Capps and S. D. Pattinson (Oxford: Hart, 2017), ch. 12.

[24] P. Capps and J. Rivers, 'Kant's Concept of International Law', *Legal Theory* 16 (2010): 229–57.

[25] T. Christiano, 'Democratic Legitimacy and International Institutions', in *The Philosophy of International Law*, ed. S. Besson and J. Tasioulas (Oxford: Oxford University Press, 2010), ch. 5.

chapters by Brudner, Capps, Olsen, Venzke and Gillroy each focus on how and why authority can be built beyond the state.[26]

Alan Brudner's contribution, upon which some of the other contributions of this book rely, redeploys his 'career to authority', which he set out powerfully in *Constitutional Goods*,[27] to consider why states should treat attempts by international courts to enforce international human rights and international criminal law as authoritative. While some view the enforcement of international law as a threat to state sovereignty, Brudner regards it instead as the consummation of state sovereignty, and this explains precisely why international law should be treated as authoritative and interpretation of it by international courts as determinative. That is, international adjudicative institutions are a logical outcome of the evolution of domestic sovereignty from despotism to constitutionalism. To understand international legal authority in this way is to understand it as an aspect of the maturation of state sovereignty.

The chapters by Patrick Capps and Henrik Palmer Olsen then go on to argue that Brudner's 'career of authority' also has considerable use when considering the evolution of international legal institutions described in this introduction. That is, Brudner's claims not only relate to the reasons why states should regard international law and institutions as authoritative from the perspective of the evolution of state sovereignty; these contributors observe that the evolution of the authoritative governance structures of international institutions also seem to evolve according to Brudner's logic. Capps starts from the observation that a dense system of global administrative law has emerged over the last two decades. He then argues that the evolution of authority within global administrative law seems to match empirically the development of other primitive administrative systems, such as that in the early US, and that it is similar to Brudner's 'career of authority'. Capps's key claim is that the normative motor that drives the evolution of authority in global administration reflects what Kant called 'negative resistance' – that is, resistance *through* law – and this form of resistance is an expression of a duty of persons (whether officials, subjects or citizens) to live under legal institutions that allow them to relate to each other in a morally rightful way.

---

[26] We note that some of the material in this section is drawn from abstracts provided by the contributors of this book for the two conferences mentioned in Section 4.

[27] A. Brudner, *Constitutional Goods* (Oxford: Oxford University Press, 2004).

While Capps observes that a dense global administrative system has recently developed, so Olsen's contribution begins with the observation of the emergence of a dense international judicial system in the last few decades. These new and diverse international courts have become key drivers of the development of international legal norms, and Olsen's inquiry focuses on the problem of how the interpretative authority of international courts is first built, and then sustained, as those courts move beyond the rules and principles embedded in their constituent treaties. But when developing international law, it remains the case that international courts are politically situated in such a way that they are more sensitive to political pressure than domestic courts.

Olsen argues that for such courts, a special dilemma emerges: When international judges are attempting to optimize the protection of those values that are embedded in international law, but are coerced by the threat of having their institution removed (or significantly weakened) by powerful states removing their support for the institution, these judges are faced with a political challenge that cannot be fully circumscribed by either legal or moral reason. In order to save the institution's jurisdiction, or even existence, judges in these courts ultimately must choose between applying the law without consideration for subsequent political reactions to the result (thereby bringing their institution at risk of being removed or suspended) or adapting legal judgments to suit those member states that are threatening to weaken (or ultimately undermine) the entire institution. The existence of this dilemma shows how international courts operate in a universe in which international legal authority is more fragile than domestic legal authority. Olsen then argues that legal authority, which is presupposed by established mainstream legal philosophy, must be reconceptualized to consider the need to adjust legal reasoning to the expectations that strong political forces around these courts have of their institutional behaviour.

Ingo Venzke's chapter begins from a similar place to Olsen's, namely with the development of international law through interpretation by international courts. Venzke claims that the dynamics of the evolution of international law arise from the struggle between actors (who seek to have their claims about international law recognized) and their communicative environments. The capacity of actors to be recognized within their environments is explored through the lens of Venzke's key concept, called 'semantic authority'. Semantic authority captures the capacity of the individual actor to influence international legal discourse and is the basis of an understanding of the dynamics of the evolution of international legal authority.

John Martin Gillroy's chapter is a further attempt to explain how legal authority can be built beyond the state. He claims that underpinning contemporary international law is a tension between two concepts of international legality. The first is derived from David Hume's argument for social convention and links closely to the consent-based theory of international legal authority. The second is derived from Hegel's justification for law as a means for actualizing freedom through recognition. His analysis of the *Nuclear Weapons Advisory Opinion* is used to illustrate this tension. He then observes that there is a process by which the Humean conception of international law is challenged by the more critical Hegelian conception, and this process leads to the evolution of international legal authority.

Inger Johanne Sand's chapter reveals the landscape of contemporary global legality that has arisen from the evolutionary processes just described. For Sand, this landscape is one in which international law now goes way beyond its traditional 'static' sources. It is a living, breathing, dynamic and pluralistic system of norm production that is populated by networks of judges, diplomats and independent experts as much as by state representatives. Within this system, new forms of authority emerge, and these are charted. The problem that must be faced is that the norms resulting from this system are not obviously the product of democratic deliberation, and this chapter concludes with a call for a new justification of the authority of the legal landscape she describes.

The final three chapters, by Follesdal, Collins and Martin, engage in a philosophical analysis of international legal authority that is sceptical about many of the authority claims made within the international legal landscape, for which justification is sought in the earlier chapters in this book.

Andreas Follesdal asks the straightforward question: Why should the international actors who are described in earlier chapters give us reasons to act differently to the way we normally act? To answer this question, he resorts to Raz's normal justification thesis. In the context of international law and legal authority, Raz's thesis means that domestic legal institutions should defer to – for example – the judgments of international courts because those domestic institutions are more likely to act rightly by following those judgments than if they were to ignore them. Follesdal explains how the normal justification thesis works in international law, but he then considers some of the features of international courts that make Raz's thesis insufficient as an account of legitimate authority. He further identifies the circumstances under which domestic institutions would want to override judgments from international courts, thereby setting out the parameters for assessing when to expect support for resistance to the authority of international courts.

For Richard Collins, the formal consent-based account of the authority of international law should not be discarded; instead, it remains the most plausible justification for international legal authority. In terms of authority, the new forms of authority claims made by international lawyers are almost epiphenomenal and should not distract us from the genuine basis by which international law affords states pre-emptive reasons for action. Hence, we should be cautiously sceptical about these new forms. What is more, Collins argues, there are strong moral reasons for the formal consent-based view; in fact, it serves to ameliorate the problems of power imbalances that pervade international relations, not replicate them, as is often thought.

Margaret Martin sets out the reasons why she is sceptical of the authority claimed by the ICC. The ICC's claim to authority is fundamentally rooted in an appeal to state consent, fidelity to the wording of the statute of the ICC, the rule of law, and the protection of human dignity. As she documents, the claimed authority has been challenged because it is considered too political in terms of the cases it chooses to hear. More problematically, the Court may threaten to undermine local attempts to re-establish peace if it seeks to hold those, who are suspected of committing violations of international criminal law, too strictly to account. Provocatively, and possibly paradoxically, she turns to Hobbes to argue that a rational sovereign should not submit to the jurisdiction of the ICC because of the threats to peace that are sometimes implied by its attempt to administer international justice. Turning this around, if the ICC is to enhance its legitimacy, it should be sensitive to the consequences of a legally pristine judgment, especially in the lives of the vulnerable who are affected by these judgments. These claims are then illustrated by a discussion of the *Erdemović* judgment of the International Criminal Tribunal for the former Yugoslavia.

The traditional approach to authority, rooted in state consent, can no longer be used to explain the evolution of authority claims that are part and parcel of international living law. The chapters in this book seek to conceptualize international legal authority in new ways, so as to understand and criticize these authority claims.

1

The Evolution of Authority

ALAN BRUDNER*

Introduction

In *The Last Utopia*,[1] Samuel Moyn explains what he rightly considers the most important development in international law over the last three decades: the increased efficacy given *jus gentium* norms recognizing human rights. Several innovations make up this change, but the one that epitomizes it is the International Criminal Court (ICC) that sits in the Hague. Created by a multilateral treaty (the Rome Statute) in force since 2002, the ICC has a compulsory jurisdiction over state or organizational actors who commit crimes on a scale engaging the conscience of the global fraternity – over perpetrators of genocide, crimes against humanity, and war crimes. Though the court's jurisdiction is compulsory, its mandate is not unconditional. It takes hold only in the absence of domestic prosecution or if domestic prosecution is likely to be a sham.

The ICC's purpose is to fill two lacunae in the world's administration of penal justice. One is the erstwhile absence of a permanent and independent court to judge those accused of breaking the laws of war and peace applicable to sovereign states. *Ad hoc* tribunals have existed, but these were creatures of coteries of states – the Allied Powers of World War II or the UN Security Council – to which they were ostensibly tied. The other gap is internal to states. Many lack the politically independent legal system needed to hold state officials accountable for crimes committed against their own people. In both cases, the concern is impunity, but (some overlap aside) only the second absence creates impunity for

---

* This chapter folds into a larger project some material previously published in "Hegel and the Relation between Law and Justice" in *Hegel's Philosophy of Right*, ed. T. Brooks (Oxford: Wiley-Blackwell, 2012), 180–208. An expanded version of this chapter appears in *The Owl and the Rooster: Hegel's Transformative Political Science* (Cambridge: Cambridge University Press, 2017), chs. 6, 7.
[1] Samuel Moyn, *The Last Utopia* (Cambridge, MA: Belknap Press, 2010).

violations of human rights. The first creates impunity (except for retaliation) for violations of the rights of states as collective bodies.

My focus in this chapter is on the second lacuna and with what the ICC's filling it means for how we understand the idea of internal sovereignty. Two views seem possible. According to one, the ICC's jurisdiction reflects the idea that exercisers of sovereign authority can, juristically speaking, wrong their subjects and are legally accountable for their wrongs even if no domestic process exists to hold them responsible. That idea, set within the context of the history of political thought, is certainly an outlier. Locke and Achenwall aside, it is hard to think of any postmedieval political philosopher who espoused it.[2] On another view, nothing has changed in our conception of internal sovereignty. From a juristic standpoint, it remains true either that internal sovereigns (or those acting in their name) cannot wrong their subjects or that they are unaccountable for their wrongs, for if they were accountable to another, they would not be sovereign. What has changed is the finality of internal sovereignty. On this view, the ICC's jurisdiction reflects a social contract among peoples analogous to the hypothetical contract among individuals notionally establishing national authorities. By this contract, certain states have surrendered their legally bullet-proof internal sovereignties to the authority of a cosmopolitan right binding all states. That too would be a novel – indeed utopian – idea. It could be taken to foreshadow the end of the Westphalian system of sovereign states and the beginning of an international order based on an agreement among decent states to protect human rights against wicked ones.[3]

Moyn's explanation for the supranational protection of human rights tends to support the second view. He offers various historical and sociological reasons for the descent of transnational human rights norms from the ether of pious declaration to the terra firma of arrests, trials, and punishments. Most important for him is the rise – on the ashes of Cold War, state-supported ideologies – of borderless social movements devoted to human rights advocacy and organized in such nonstate bodies as Amnesty International and Human Rights Watch. That sort of

---

[2] Hobbes's sovereign can do iniquity but not injustice; Kant's can wrong its subjects but cannot be held accountable. See T. Hobbes, *Leviathan*, ed. Michael Oakeshott (Oxford: Blackwell, 1957), 115–16; I. Kant, *The Metaphysics of Morals*, in Kant, *Practical Philosophy*, trans. Mary Gregor (Cambridge: Cambridge University Press, 1996), 6:319. (Here I cite the volume and page numbers of the Prussian Academy edition of Kant's collected works. These numbers appear in the margins of the Gregor edition.)

[3] This is Rawls' view; see J. Rawls, *The Law of Peoples* (Cambridge, MA: Harvard University Press, 1999), 25–27, 59–88.

explanation has its place, but I won't engage Moyn's empirical hypothesis because I believe there is a deeper explanation for the phenomenon in question – one that supports the first view mentioned. The supranational protection of human rights has its determining cause, I'll argue, in the logical evolution of internal sovereignty, by which I mean the justified claim of some human being(s) coercively to rule a multitude of others. To understand the supranational enforcement of human rights historically and sociologically is to view it as a purely contingent phenomenon; but to understand its entailment by the internal logic of sovereign authority is to see its historical appearance as the happy realization of a juristic necessity.

Such an understanding at once elevates and humbles the kind of evolution the ICC reflects. On the one hand, it frees that change from dependence on state consent and gives it an *a priori* footing in practical reasoning about the nature of political authority. It thus gives practical reason's decisive *imprimatur* to a development over which one might otherwise waver between inconclusive thoughts pro and con. Shall we have state sovereignty with impunity for mass crimes or accountability with compromises of state sovereignty? Or shall we have a compromise solution that reflects ambivalence between these extremes?[4] The account given here dissolves the either/or, showing that accountability does not come at sovereignty's expense – that it reflects, rather, the perfection of *internal* sovereignty, on which unqualified *external* sovereignty depends. In a nutshell, rulers whose internal sovereignty is incomplete because lacking accountability to (hence endorsability by) independent subjects cannot claim unqualified external sovereignty; they can rightfully demand only that foreign actors respect the grade of internal sovereignty they have. So they cannot complain if, where no justification of their conduct to free subjects is possible (where sovereign immunity would once have been their only refuge), an international tribunal imposes the accountability requirement of their internal sovereignty that they fail to satisfy on their own. That idea elevates the ICC's authority in that it makes accountability for human rights violations an inherent requirement of internal sovereignty binding all state actors independently of their empirical consent. However,

---

[4] The Rome Statute manifests ambivalence. Its very name (*statute* rather than *convention*) reflects the court's compulsory jurisdiction (under the preconditions set out in Article 12) over officials of nonsignatory states. Yet only signatory states or those that have made a special agreement with the court are obligated to cooperate with the court. Since the court has no means of its own to collect evidence, arrest and detain, or secure the delivery of accused persons for trial, this means that the court's effective authority over a state depends on that state's consent.

this account of supra-state authority also humbles what it explains, for it *reduces* the enforcement of human rights at the international level to an epiphenomenon – a secondary effect – of sovereign authority's maturation at the municipal level. Basically, it says that international human rights law has no autonomous existence – that it is just the constitutional law of the most advanced internal sovereignties, those whose internal sovereignty is most complete. That understanding of the ICC assigns it a modest role in human rights protection. While amending the Westphalian conception of state sovereignty (showing that the equality of sovereigns is a perfectionist goal rather than an ahistorical fact), this account heads off any argument that the ICC portends the demise of state sovereignty as such or requires a notional contract among peoples to constitute a supranational authority to explain its compulsory jurisdiction.

1 Authority's Career

I begin from the idea that sovereign authority is a relational concept in that a claim of authority to rule people able to rule themselves must be capable of a validating recognition by a free subject. That is what distinguishes normative authority from purely factual force. Ruler and ruled are *parties* to sovereign authority. Validation, however, comes in different qualitative grades depending on how independent of the putative sovereign the subject is. The voluntary recognition of an unlimited despot by a servile subject does not confer the same quality of validation as the recognition of a constitutional ruler by an independent and equal subject. Nor, therefore, does it produce the same grade of authority. Servile recognition does, however, produce a partial or relative authority, because voluntary acceptance by the subject and deference to the subject's volition by the ruler distinguish the relationship from the sheer matter-of-fact subjugation by force from which normativity is absent. Such a relationship partakes to a minimal degree of an ideal form of recognition wherein the ruler's authority is perfectly validated by a subject whose full independence the ruler reciprocally guarantees. The particle of authority conferred by servile recognition correlates to a qualified duty not to resist the ruler except for the purpose of instituting a more validating kind of recognition.

We can thus speak of sovereign authority as having a career marked by developmental stages. Authority's career begins with someone's claiming a right to rule, climbs several plateaus at which the claim is progressively validated through its recognition by a subject whose freedom (in some sense) is reciprocally recognized by the ruler, and ends with its perfect validation by a fully independent subject equal to the ruler. The stages of authority may be called *de facto* authority, *de jure* authority, legitimate authority, constitutional authority, and just authority. If that ladder highlights important distinctions, then the customary division of authorities into *de facto* and legitimate is too simple.[5] Moreover, if, as I mean to show, authority's career concerns the logical development from germ to maturity of *valid* authority, then public lawyers err when they shunt the concepts legitimacy, constitutionalism, and justice from the juridical sphere to the sphere of the politically contestable.[6] The entire ladder would then constitute a juridical continuum, leaving for politics only Aristotelian *phronesis* – differences of judgment over what positive laws best embody constitutional justice.

As I use the term, *de facto* authority is authority constituted by the subject's voluntary acceptance of the ruler's claimed title to rule, whatever that title is. At this primitive stage, no law pertaining to authority constrains what the ruler may do or stops him from ruling through *ad hoc* decrees. *De jure* authority is a species of *de facto* authority where the ruler's deference to the subject's bare volition at the previous stage becomes deference to the subject's deliberative volition through rule by general laws by which the subject can guide itself. Here the ruler submits its authority claim to the subject's self-application of the ruler's laws to the subject's own conduct. Legitimate authority is that species of *de jure* authority in which the germ of ruler deference to subject autonomy present in *de jure* authority develops into a relation of mutual covenant; subjects acknowledge an obligation to submit on condition that the ruler acknowledge a duty to fulfill the autonomous purpose for which they submit, whatever that purpose is. Constitutional authority is that species of legitimate authority in which the idea of equality between ruler and ruled incipient at the previous stage is fulfilled in the idea of equal subjection of ruler and ruled to a conception of public reason all free subjects can accept. Here the ruled acknowledge a duty to submit on condition that the ruler acknowledge a duty to serve a specific purpose for their submission – namely, protecting

---

[5] Joseph Raz classifies authority as either *de facto* or legitimate; see J. Raz, *The Morality of Freedom* (Oxford: Clarendon Press, 1986), 26.

[6] Legal positivists generally include legality in practical authority but leave everything else on the continuum to moral controversy and politics. David Dyzenhaus includes legality and legitimacy but nothing else; see D. Dyzenhaus, *Legality and Legitimacy* (Oxford: Clarendon Press, 1997), ch. 5. Trevor Allan includes constitutionalism in general but not the ensemble of constitutional rights that perfects constitutionalism; see T. R. S. Allan, *Constitutional Justice* (Oxford: Oxford University Press, 2001), 25–29, 158–60, 232.

the subject's independence and therewith the subject's qualification to validate the ruler's claim of authority. Finally, just authority is that species of constitutional authority in which the rule of public reason is perfected under a comprehensive conception of public reason comprising the necessary and sufficient conditions of the subject's independence.

Accordingly, each stage of authority subsequent to the first is a species of its generic antecedent distinguished by its fulfilling a potential incipient at the previous stage and generating a new potential for the next to fulfill. Each stage before the last produces a relative authority limited by a permission to resist the ruler for the sole purpose of moving to a higher stage. Only just authority is absolute authority entailing an unqualified obligation to submit. Together, the stages comprise what can be called the juristic morality (or natural law) of sovereign authority.

What authority's career implies for this book's theme is the following. To each stage of sovereign authority belongs a corresponding *ius gentium* regulating authority. Because every case of relative authority mistakes itself for authority *simpliciter*, the law governing authority at each stage is equated with the whole natural law of authority, which law forms a part of the universal law of peoples. So a thin law of municipal authority correlates with a narrow conception of the *ius gentium* as regulating relations between sovereigns but not (or minimally) relations between sovereign and subject.[7] Here the root impediment to international law's protection of individuals is not the state's external sovereignty vis-à-vis foreign actors. It is rather the juristically untrammeled nature of internal sovereignty. The merely *de facto* or *de jure* sovereign owes no binding duty to its subjects that international law could recognize, let alone enforce. Furthermore, the ruler's untrammeled internal sovereignty (where this is equated with sovereignty as such) entails its unqualified external sovereignty vis-à-vis other states. Since the sovereign cannot do injustice within its domain, there is no juristic reason besides self-defense that could justify one sovereign's interfering with another. Here belongs the development-blind picture of equal and independent states assumed by Vattel and known as the Westphalian model.[8] Where internal sovereignty is equated with despotism, all sovereigns are equal.

---

[7] For the seventeenth-century separation of the *ius gentium* from the natural law pertaining to political authority, see S. Neff, *Justice among Nations* (Cambridge, MA: Harvard University Press, 2014), 151–78.

[8] E. de Vattel, *The Law of Nations*, ed. J. Chitty (Cambridge: Cambridge University Press, 2011), I, 4.

As we move from stage to stage, however, the natural law regulating municipal authority thickens, and so too, therefore, does the *ius gentium*. At the first stage of modern constitutionalism, for example, the sovereign owes a duty not to restrict unreasonably its subjects' liberty, though it remains the sole judge of whether a breach has occurred. Here, accordingly, the *ius gentium* declares a duty (in the Universal Declaration of Human Rights) but does not enforce an external judgment, just as domestic courts interpret statutes in accordance with common-law liberties but yield to the sovereign's contrary interpretation. So again, the basic impediment to supranational enforcement is not a state's external sovereignty but the absence in natural law (as so far unfolded) of sovereign accountability. The evolution culminates in the regime that perfects constitutionalism, where authority is recognized by a subject whose full independence the authority reciprocally recognizes through court-enforced guarantees of libertarian, egalitarian, and cultural rights. At this stage, the juristic necessity for the domestic enforcement of human rights against the ruler reveals itself, and with it, the necessity for supranational enforcement where domestic means are lacking. Domestic enforcement is thus the prior necessity, supranational enforcement a secondary one. International law merely responds to the internal juristic reality, or so I shall argue.

2   Preconstitutional Authorities

A   *The Problem of Political Authority*

An account of political authority must solve the problem of political authority. The problem can be set out as follows. To claim political authority is to claim a power to put people capable of self-rule under an obligation either to obey the claimant's commands or to submit to the application of his force. Let me roll that disjunctive obligation into one obligation to submit to the commander's will. Since a power to put others under an obligation is a good definition of a right, I'll say that a claim of political authority is a claim of right to coerce people capable of self-rule into obeying one's commands and to apply force if they disobey. Such a claim might be made by someone – an official – occupying a place in a chain of command, each placeholder claiming a right ultimately derived from that of the supreme commander, who is commanded by no one. The uncommanded commander is called the sovereign.

Of course, not all speakers in the imperative mood are commanders claiming a right to be obeyed or else. Robbers and extortionists make demands, but they do not command. Relying on unilateral fear rather than relational authority, they require *of* (de-mand) but not *with* (command). Because their success in obtaining compliance occurs from moment to moment, they cannot be said to rule those from whom they demand things, if by rule we understand an order that is stable over time. Robbers avail themselves of a power provided by nature that is also available to others against them. So they temporarily overpower, but they do not rule. Nor can their victims be said to obey them if by obedience we understand compliance from a conviction of duty. They comply, but they do not obey, or they refuse to comply and are at liberty to resist the consequence. By contrast, someone who commands in the context of ruling claims a right to coerce obedience. By commanding, he purports to put those whom he commands under an obligation to submit to his will, one that holds even if the commanded reasonably think that the command is foolish. This, however, raises a time-honored question. What transforms someone's subjective claim of right to coerce submission to his will into an objectively valid claim such that the subject has a valid obligation to submit to what is truly the command of a sovereign? What are the necessary and sufficient conditions of valid political authority?

B   De Facto *Authority*

A partial answer is one that H. L. A. Hart considered sufficient.[9] It is that the claim of authority must be recognized by at least some of those whom the ruler commands. The ruler must have subjects who accept the ruler's claim of right to rule them by accepting the grounds for that claim and by voluntarily obeying him for the reason that he (as they believe) satisfies those grounds. It is not enough that subjects habitually adhere to the ruler's directives. As Hart argued against Austin, even victims of extortionists might do that. They must obey *opinio juris* – from a belief that the ruler is entitled by some logically prior norm to rule them. This is so because, for a claim of authority to be valid, it must be spontaneously confirmed by the *other* over whom authority is claimed; otherwise, it remains a subjective claim asserted against the other – one lacking objective validation. It is not necessary to the existence of an authority that everyone over whom the ruler claims authority accepts his title to rule. Where *de*

[9] H. L. A. Hart, *The Concept of Law* (Oxford: Clarendon Press, 1961), ch. 4.

facto acceptance of title alone confirms authority, the ruler has no authority over those who reject his claim, but he exercises authority over those who do. Someone who interposed himself between a ruler and those who recognize his title would be an interloper relative to that relationship. So an authority, however fragile, exists.

Authority at its most fragile may be called *de facto* authority. Here the ruler's claim of authority is recognized by an ongoing factual acceptance of its authority and nothing more. It need not be validated by autonomous acceptance because at this point the ruler's subjects need not be autonomous agents who deliberatively set ends for themselves and who submit for self-interested reasons. They might submit from self-suppressive reasons – say, because they accept the ruler's claim that he is descended from the first patriarch and they are his children, or because they are awed by a warrior who seems godlike to them because he demonstrates an indifference to life without honor, while they remain sunk in life for its own sake. They might therefore submit to an authority that is unlimited by a duty to respect their autonomous (end-generating) agency, none having yet developed. In that case, the ruler could, without injustice to them, treat his subjects as instruments of his purposes and use them in any way he chooses. Consistent with *de facto* authority is the relation between a despot and his servants.

Let us assume that the despotic possibility to which *de facto* authority is open is the actual situation. We make this assumption because we want to begin at the beginning, logically speaking, and at its beginning, authority is *de facto* and nothing more. Authority that is *de facto* and nothing more is despotic because it defers to the subject's volition and nothing more. An authority of that kind owes no duty to its subjects beyond the duty to attract them rather than subdue them. We also want to begin with authority at its emptiest, normatively speaking, in order to see whether there is a logical momentum internal to authority driving it to acknowledge more robust constraints. Authority at its emptiest must defer to the subject's volition but not to its capacity for acting from ends it autonomously projects as distinct from those it picks up from the biosphere.

A despot is not necessarily a tyrant who rules solely in his particular self-interest; he might rule for the benefit, as he sees it, of his subjects. The distinguishing mark of this stage of authority, however, is that, while the ruled submit to the end-generating capacity of the ruler, the ruler recognizes no such capacity in the ruled, and so there is nothing beyond the subject's acceptance capable of limiting the ruler's authority.

Consequently, the ruler *cannot wrong* his subjects by subordinating them to his personal ends – by being a tyrant; that is what makes him a despot.

Though no human being is fit for serfdom, still, there is a particle of authority in the voluntary relation between a despot and his serfs. It consists in the subject's duty not to resist the despot until he develops an awareness of his own capacity to set ends for himself and can thus disobey on the principled ground of his unfitness for serfdom. He may not disobey merely to satisfy a contrary appetite. Moreover, this temporary duty to obey holds even if the despot is a tyrant. This is so because the despot's particle of authority issues from a voluntary acceptance of a claim of right, not from the ruler's virtue or service to a common good. That is to say, there is normativity here just because the despot-servant relation minimally partakes of the form of mutual recognition between free agents. One human being claims a right to rule others based on whatever ground (historically, patriarchy or valor) and attracts the allegiance of some. In that he attracts rather than overpowers, he defers to the subject's free volition. Deference to volition gives his claim a meager kind of validation, and so the despot has a weak authority irrespective of whether he rules solely in his own interest or for the benefit of the ruled. The despot's orders, therefore, also have a particle of authority irrespective of their content.

A despot may rule over servile subjects through administrative orders to do this or that and may settle their disputes through *ad hoc* judgments ungoverned by rules. The despot owes no duty to his subjects to rule through general laws, for the latter presuppose subjects with enough sense of their independence of mind to interpret the ruler's generalities and thoughtfully apply them to their own conduct; and yet the servile subject has no such sense of its independence. Not having manifested a capacity for authoring ends, subjects are not wronged by being ruled according to ends entirely external to them. But that is what rule by *ad hoc* orders is. Such orders call for mindless compliance in the service of another's ends, for there is no space for appropriating the command through interpretation – hence none for thoughtfully participating in their implementation.

In a world where despotic authority over servile subjects is the model of political authority (in the world before the Greco-Persian Wars), there is no common *ius gentium* pertaining to authority because there is no *ius* internal to any *gens*. Political authority is thought to be inherently unconstrained. There is no such law even in aspiration, not even one declaring a principle of legality. The merely *de facto* authority does no wrong by "punishing" without law and without process. He is bound by conscience not to treat his subjects cruelly, but his authority is independent of his goodness.

The fact that a relation between despot and serf is consistent with *de facto* authority shows that voluntary acceptance of title to rule cannot be a sufficient condition of valid authority. This is not because serfdom is morally wrong or because tyranny (a legal possibility under despotism) is morally bad. Rather, it is so for reasons internal to the relation of authority. A claim of authority can be independently validated by the addressee only if the addressee is an agent with a mind of its own – one to whose independent mind the claimant can submit for confirmation. A claim of authority cannot be satisfactorily validated by one whose mind is effaced in the ruler's, for such a being cannot deliver an independent validation.

C   De Jure *Authority*

De facto authority contains the seeds of its supersession in a kind of authority more adequate to the idea of a valid authority. By voluntarily acknowledging the title to rule of someone who acted from self-generated ends (e.g., honor), the subject manifested a potential for self-determination, for his recognition of the ruler's autonomy showed that autonomy was also nascent in him. Were the potential not in him, he could not have admired an exemplar to the point of acknowledging its right to rule him. Moreover, the subject's service for the despot actualized the subject's potential for self-determination, for he no longer worked to satisfy his natural needs but rather to serve an ego-ideal – a purpose independently set by the mind. Within despotic authority, accordingly, there develops a purposive agency in the subject to which the ruler can defer; and this potential for a more satisfactory validation of authority through autonomous acceptance by the ruled is actualized in *de jure* rule.

De jure authority perfects the potential for autonomous acceptance germinally contained in the servant's voluntary acceptance of *de facto* authority. *De jure* authority is a species of *de facto* authority distinguished by the ruler's ruling through general, prospective, knowable, and non-contradictory laws rather than through *ad hoc* orders and summary actions. In ruling only through general and published directives, the ruler defers to his subjects' purposive agency, for he now leaves room for their thoughtful self-execution of his commands. Directives published in general but clear terms and having only prospective force allow the subject to interpret the command and judge whether his planned conduct is permitted or forbidden by the rule. As a result, the subject acts not simply in obedience to the ruler's external ends but to the ruler's ends as interpreted by the subject and self-applied to his own conduct. In this way, the subject actively participates in the ruler's executive power, and the ruler obtains a more satisfying validation of his claim of authority. That claim is now validated by a thoughtful submission rather than a mindless one.

Correlative to a more satisfactory validation of authority is a stronger duty to obey. The serf's duty was conditional on a subjective condition – namely, his undeveloped capacity for autonomy – and so it could hardly be called a duty at all. As soon as he developed the capacity and was ready on that account to rise up, his duty ended. By contrast, the subject ruled by laws has a qualified *binding* duty to obey because his duty is conditional, not on what *he* chooses, but on the ruler's satisfying an objective condition for a verifiable authority claim. The ruler must rule through general, knowable, and clear laws. Provided it does so, the subject must obey unless resistance is for the purpose of instituting a further objective condition of valid authority. Accordingly, normativity has thickened on both sides of the relationship. Not only does the subject have a qualified duty to obey a ruler who observes the procedural constraints of legality; the ruler can now wrong its subjects by ruling outside of general and published laws or by applying force to them in the absence of a proven breach of law. Whether the ruler can be called to account for such wrongs is, however, another matter.

Here again the content of the ruler's laws is irrelevant to the ruler's *de jure* authority. The prince who rules through laws serving his selfish interests has an authority stronger than the benevolent despot just because his rule is accepted by autonomous subjects rather than by serfs. His *de jure* authority is simply a product of the grade of mutual recognition achieved in ruling through laws that subjects can interpret and apply to their own conduct; it has nothing to do with whether he rules tyrannically in his own interest or virtuously in his subjects' interest. A philosopher king who ruled for the common good through *ad hoc* decrees would not have an iota of right to be obeyed by free persons, whereas a tyrant who ruled in his own interest through general, knowable, and clear laws applied by subjects to their own conduct would have a partial authority (qualified by a right of resistance for the sole purpose of instituting a further condition of authority), and his subjects would have a duty correlative to that grade of authority.

In a world where *de jure* authority is the model of political authority (in the late Roman Empire), political authority is thought to be inherently hierarchical and unconstrained. Sovereigns unilaterally command subjects and are above the laws they will into being: the pleasure of the prince is the source of law.[10] Hence there is no *ius gentium* recognizing political rights of the subject, though the sovereign is bound by conscience and religion. This is not because lawyers are legal positivists who categorically separate law and morality but because they are natural lawyers who take a partial morality of authority for the whole morality of authority. So, there is a norm of the law of nations pertaining to authority, but it consists only of a principle of legality.[11] That norm is enforceable by subordinate magistrates, but only through the interpretation of statutes and the oversight of executive actions in accordance with a presumption that the sovereign means to rule through prospective and determinate laws by which subjects can regulate their conduct to conform to the sovereign's will. The principle of legality is not enforceable against the sovereign's clear will to deviate from it, because it was only for the sovereign's sake – for its more perfect sovereignty – that the principle was established. As there is no independent other who may demand that the principle be adhered to, there is no one to answer to for violating it. As a consequence, honoring legality may be ascribed, as it was by Justinian, to the "extraordinary liberality of our Imperial will," and what comes from generosity may go with impunity.[12] Accordingly, the law of peoples respecting the principle of legality can have no teeth against an internal sovereign who is *de jure* and nothing more.

Under *de jure* authority, there is a duty to submit to general and knowable laws, but that duty is qualified by a permission to resist the ruler for the sole purpose of instituting a further condition of valid authority. What is this condition?

In ruling through general laws, the merely *de jure* ruler defers to the autonomous agency of those who defer to its authority, and so there is a germ of reciprocity in the relation between ruler and ruled. But there is no developed reciprocity because, while the ruled defer to the ruler's legislative say-so, the ruler owes no duty to defer to the subject's independent

---

[10] *Digest*, bk. 1, t. 4.
[11] *Digest*, Prologue: "Therefore, since there is nothing to be found in all things so worthy of attention as the authority of the law, which properly regulates all affairs both divine and human, and expels all injustice; We have found the entire arrangement of the law which has come down to us from ... the times of Romulus to be so confused that it is extended to an infinite length and is not within the grasp of human capacity; and hence We were first induced to begin by examining what had been enacted by former most venerated princes, to ... make them more easily understood; to the end that being included in a single Code ... they may afford to all men the ready assistance of their true meaning."
[12] *Digest*, Prologue.

reasons for valuing legality or for submitting to the ruler's legislative will. Thus, while the ruler acknowledges a duty to rule by general laws, it acknowledges neither a duty to account to the ruled for a breach nor a duty to legislate exclusively for the sake of the interest the ruled had in accepting its authority. For the ruler who is *de jure* and nothing more, any such duty is one of virtue, the sanction of which is bad conscience, ill fame, damnation, and the like. It is not a juridical duty on whose performance the subject's duty to submit is conditional. Provided he does so under general laws, the prince may enrich himself at his subjects' expense. Hence submission is unilateral, authority hierarchical.

The want of full reciprocity under *de jure* authority constitutes an imperfection in the validation the prince receives for his authority claim. This is so because objective validation can come only from a subject who is independent of the authority-claimant, and yet where submission is unilateral, the subject gives up its independence – its liberty to rule itself – to the ruler's realized authority but is guaranteed nothing in satisfaction of its own self-interest. The ruled thus become unilaterally a means for the ruler. But authorization of rule by someone who treats himself solely as a means to the ruler's realized authority is not the independent authorization the ruler requires. It is still the authorization of a servile being incapable of delivering an objective validation.

This defect in *de jure* authority shows what a better authority is. A further desideratum (besides voluntary acceptance and rule through law) of valid authority is that the subject must retain in its submission to authority the independence *from* authority that qualifies it to give a validating recognition. The subject must accept the ruler's claim of authority to rule without losing the independence it had prior to acceptance. This, however, seems to require a contradiction. Submitting to authority just means giving up the liberty to act on one's independent judgment concerning matters on which authority has spoken. How then can one retain one's independence in submitting to authority? How can an authority acknowledge its subject's independence from authority and remain authoritative?

The contradiction dissolves once we notice a distinction. There is a difference between an authority's permitting its subjects to act on their independent judgment about matters on which it has ruled and its deferring to its subjects' independent reason for submitting unreservedly to its judgment. The former is incompatible with authority, but the latter is not. Accordingly, for an authority to be validated by the subject's autonomous submission, it must acknowledge a reciprocal duty to submit to its subject's autonomous agency by making the subject's own reason for submission the sole end of its rule. Submission must be mutual as between the parties to authority. In that way, each becomes a means for the other – the subject a means to the ruler's realized authority, the ruler a means for the subject's purpose in submitting to authority – but the independence of both is preserved by virtue of the reciprocity of submission. That ruler and ruled become at once end and means for the other is the condition for the subject's submission to the ruler being able to deliver an independent validation to the ruler's authority claim.

The requirement that submission be mutual entails that valid authority and correlative obligation are ultimately products of a covenant. This is not an empirical covenant, the legal force of which would presuppose the very sovereignty the covenant first establishes. Rather, it is an implicit or intellectual covenant (which at this stage, however, must borrow its particular content from the empirical values of the parties whose relationship the covenantal form governs) whereby subjects freely authorize the ruler to make laws for them in return for the ruler's pledge to rule solely for the sake of the subjects' interest in submitting to his rule. For validation to count, the subjects' submission to the ruler's say-so must be met by the ruler's submission to the reason for the subjects' submission, whatever that reason is. So authorities are as much servants as masters, and subjects are as much masters as servants. This marks the transition from merely *de jure* to legitimate authority.

D   Legitimate Authority

Legitimate authority is that species of *de jure* authority distinguished by a fully developed reciprocity in the relation between ruler and ruled. Legitimate authority perfects the germ of reciprocity incipient in *de jure* authority in that it is the product of an uncoerced covenant between ruler and ruled whereby subjects freely acknowledge the ruler's authority on condition that the ruler acknowledge a duty to serve its subjects' common purpose for accepting its rule. In this fully reciprocal relationship, there is also an equality between ruler and ruled, though only in germ. Both are equally ends for the other, but the ruler has no duty yet to share its ruling authority with its subjects. To be sure, the ruler is now accountable to them as a body, for the subjects have a power of oversight and deposition to enforce the covenant, and they may now demand legality for the sake of their own interest in security under laws they can know and answer to. Still, they have no right to self-rule, for this is what they surrendered in authorizing a sovereign. Thus authority remains hierarchical. The ruler commands; the subject obeys or else.[13]

Where authority is legitimate and nothing more, the common interest the ruler is duty-bound to serve is nonspecific. The subject is the author of particular ends, some of which many others share because they share a way of life or because the achievement of some ends – security of life, limb, and possessions, for example – is generally a precondition for everyone's achieving idiosyncratic ends. Where authority is merely legitimate, these shared material values are the only available source of a common interest for the sake of whose promotion the subjects submit to a ruler. Thus St. Augustine defines a republic as "an assemblage of reasonable beings bound together by common agreement as to the objects of their love."[14] They might love wealth, security, national honor, racial superiority, or whatever. Authority is legitimate if, and only if, the subjects freely submit to a ruler on condition that the ruler acknowledge a duty to promote the values the subjects commonly prize and for the sake of which they submit.

Also indeterminate is the composition of the group to whom the ruler is accountable. The subjects who share an interest requiring submission to a common authority for its satisfaction and who are conceived to have covenanted with the ruler may be all those subject to the ruler or only some. They may define themselves in whatever way they choose. If they are only some of the ruled, then rule is legitimate as between the parties to the covenant but only *de jure* as between the ruler and those excluded from the covenant. Legitimate rule is thus compatible with the tyrannical (self-interested) rule by the parties to the covenant over those excluded – for example, by those of noble birth over commoners, by property owners over the propertyless, or by one ethnic group over another. Accordingly, while normativity has thickened relative to merely *de jure* authority, it is still thin relative to just authority. A legitimate ruler may promote the interest of the part that authorizes it, and those subject to its rule do not necessarily have a duty to obey of equal strength. The dominated part may resist for the purpose of making their particular interests count for the ruler, whereas the domineering group may resist on the more onerous

---

[13] So, Grotius calls the relation between sovereign and subject one of preeminence, and the right pertaining to the relation is the "right of superiority." H. Grotius, *On the Law of War and Peace*, Book I, ch. 1, para. 3.

[14] *The City of God*, XIX, 24.

condition that their resistance aim at a revolution of a kind to be discussed shortly.

Under legitimate rule, the duty to obey is stronger than under merely *de jure* rule. This is so because we have here, for the first time, an authority claim that is autonomously validated by an independent end-for-itself. The ruler is duty bound to serve the shared interests of at least some of its subjects as the condition of their being able to deliver an independent validation. Because recognition is finally symmetrical, validation is authentic; and so the covenanting subject has an obligation to submit on condition that the ruler keep its pledge to rule through laws having nothing in view but the benefit of those with whom it covenanted.

In that sense, a strong political obligation is conditional on the ruler's laws' having a certain content. But observe that the content need not be that of justice. It suffices for legitimacy and for the obligation relative thereto that the content of laws be the shared values for the sake of which a self-defined group submits to a common ruler. And those values may be not only indifferent from the standpoint of justice but also antithetical to justice. They may be an interest in feudal privilege, in secure possession against the destitute, in religious orthodoxy against reformers, or in racial purity against the different. No doubt those excluded from the covenant have a weaker obligation to obey relative to *de jure* authority, one qualified by a right of resistance to compel a *de jure* ruler to take account of their interests. But the members of the in-group have an obligation to obey their legitimate ruler qualified only by a right of revolution for the sake of constitutional rule under a public reason all agents can accept.

In a world where legitimate authority is the model of authority (roughly Europe from the thirteenth to the seventeenth centuries), there are no civil or political "rights of man" held against the sovereign – not even declaratory ones. The sovereign now owes a duty to some or all of its subjects, to whom he or she is accountable for the failure to perform it. But the sovereign's duty is only to serve the interest of those – barons or *bourgeoisie* – who populate the implicit covenant and not to relinquish or divide the sovereignty on which those interests depend. Provided the ruler adheres to this duty, he cannot wrong the subjects. If peace and security are the reason for submission, the sovereign may, at its discretion, suppress free speech, association, and assembly for the sake of security; he may torture and detain or kill extralegally without doing injustice. As Hobbes argues, norms of legality and due process remain interpretive presumptions for subordinate magistrates – presumptions the sovereign may set aside on its unilateral judgment that civil peace requires it.[15] True, there remains a distinct moral standpoint from which the sovereign's arbitrary actions can be judged iniquitous; but as this standpoint lies outside the juristic morality of authority, its writ extends to admonition but not to rebellion. To this context, accordingly, belongs Bentham's motto of a good citizen: "To obey punctually; to censure freely."[16]

The law of peoples applying to merely legitimate sovereigns reflects this internal normative desert. It is restricted to the law for states in their relations *inter se*. The individual receives no protection from international law because he is juridically defenseless in municipal law. Rulers are legally immune for acts of state in the law *of* peoples because they are legally immune in the law *for each* people. Sovereigns are equal in international law because they are equally unlimited in municipal law. Since there are no legal duties apart from the covenant to bind the ruler, and since strangers to the covenant have no standing to judge whether it has been breached, there is no juristic reason (besides self-defense) to justify one sovereign's interfering with another. Hence the duty of states to respect each other's internal sovereignty is absolute. Only a *de facto* breakdown of the covenant leaving no clear internal sovereign can open the door.

However, legitimate authority is not the culmination of authority's career. While a notional covenant between ruler and ruled is a necessary condition of valid authority, it is not sufficient, for it is also necessary that the covenant be of a particular type – that the interest for the sake of which subjects submit to a ruler be a specific interest. This is so because the independent validation for an authority claim produced by all but one type of covenant is inherently unstable. Covenants between ruler and ruled that are unimpeachable as to their voluntariness and reciprocal benefit can reproduce *within the covenanting group itself* a condition of despotism over serfs in which the ruler fails to obtain recognition from independent ends. This means that legitimate authority can be criticized from within the juristic morality of authority itself, without invoking the (so far) external standard of justice.

The gap between legitimate and objectively valid authority is exemplified in the social contract described by Hobbes.[17] Under that

---

[15] Hobbes, *Leviathan*, 176–81.
[16] J. Bentham, *A Fragment on Government and an Introduction to the Principles of Morals and Legislation*, ed. W. Harrison (Oxford: Blackwell, 1967), 10.
[17] Hobbes, *Leviathan*, ch. 17.

covenant, a multitude of individuals surrender their precivic right to self-determination to the sovereign representative of a united body (a "commonwealth") on condition that the sovereign serve their fundamental interest in security of life, limb, and possessions by maintaining civil peace. As Hobbes argues, the sovereign's rule is legitimate because conditionally authorized by its subjects in return for the sovereign's securing the conditions of their felicity. But because individuals traded their independence and self-rule for security, the sovereign is a virtually untrammeled ruler who, as long as it keeps the peace and does not dissipate its sovereignty, cannot wrong its subjects; for when they alienated their right of self-determination to it, they authorized all its actions.[18] No doubt the subject may physically resist the sovereign's extralegal force (even legal force!) for the sake of the self-preservation he covenanted for; but he cannot legally enjoin the sovereign from crushing his puny resistance with all of Leviathan's might, and so he is totally exposed to the sovereign's caprice. Accordingly, this is a covenant through which the ruler *loses* the independent subject it needs to validate its authority.[19]

If covenants establishing legitimate authority can reproduce a relation between despot and serf, they can also produce a situation of no authority. This is so because, if a group of people constitute an authority for the sake of their particular interests and may withdraw their allegiance whenever they judge that the ruler has failed to protect those interests, then the subject has not unreservedly surrendered its private judgment about common matters to the ruler, and so the ruler is not a practical authority. It is unilaterally a servant of those with whom it covenanted. The feudal covenant between king and vassal is a case in point. Even if subjects constitute an authority for their common interest in adhering better to the norms of morality that apply to their conduct independently of authority, they do not constitute a practical authority if they reserve a liberty to disregard the law whenever they judge that their reason for submission does not apply.[20]

We can generalize from these examples in the following way. To the extent that the constituent covenant between ruler and ruled involves a trading of the subject's independence for the satisfaction of some interest other than independence, it either reinstates a despot-serf relation incapable of generating an objectively valid authority or else produces a

[18] Ibid., 112, 115–16.
[19] Grotius explicitly likens the relation between subjects and the sovereign they authorize to that of servitude to a master; see Grotius, *Law of War and Peace*, Book I, ch. 3, para. 8.
[20] Raz, *Morality of Freedom*, 68–69, 73.

situation of no authority. This defect in legitimate authority taken alone brings to sight a further desideratum of valid authority – one we might call (after its discoverer) the Rousseau factor. The covenant must have a specific content. In order for the subject to retain its independence in submitting to the ruler and for the ruler to remain an authority in being accountable to the judgment of the ruled, the ruler must rule, not in whatever material or moral interest the subject has in submission, but in the interest of the subject's independence itself. In that case, the subject recovers in a secure form the independence it possessed insecurely outside authority, and so it preserves in submission to rule its qualification to give an objective validation to the ruler's claim of authority. Correlatively, the ruler maintains its authority in becoming a means for the subject, for the ruler's authority is subservient to an ideal rather than an empirical will – to the will that wills independence from the arbitrary will of others. A ruler who rules for the sake of an ideal interest in independence rules under a public reason for rule that all independent subjects could accept as their own. To this public reason (and not to the empirically shared reason of his supporters) the authoritative ruler is answerable in the sense that any directive that is incompatible with the reason is denuded of authority – *ultra vires*. It is the mere demand of a natural person whose authority no independent subject can accept or (therefore) have an unqualified obligation to obey. With this step, we have entered the world of constitutional authority.

3 Constitutional Authority

A *The Concept of Constitutionalism*

Constitutionalism in general may be defined as that species of legitimate rule under which subjects are governed, not by natural persons factually accountable to them for failing to serve their empirically shared interests, but by office-holding representatives of a public reason all human beings could will as authoritative. By a public reason I mean a reason for submitting to rule that is universally and necessarily shared by beings possessed of certain natural capacities. Under ancient constitutionalism, the public reason for rule was to perfect humanity's political nature in active citizenship. Under modern (liberal) constitutionalism, the public reason for rule is a reason necessarily shared by beings possessed of a capacity for free choice and a potential for living out self-authored plans. That reason is their interest in securing the conditions for exercising the capacity and developing the potential – in short, for independence.

Political authority acknowledged for the sake of independence is constrained by the ruler's duty to respect the subject's independence, without which submission to authority would not yield a perfect validation of authority. So the duty is intrinsic to valid authority. The correlate of that duty is a political right in the subject – all subjects. This means that a constraint on rule for the sake of the subject's independence is an inherent right of *political* subjects – one that reflects a prior duty inherent in offices exercising political authority. It is not, if this account is correct, a right of humanity abstracted from subjection to particular sovereigns – of humanity in a transnational sphere. So, for example, a constitutional guarantee of free speech against the ruler or a guarantee against arbitrary detention or killing reflects an "inherent" right not because it actualizes a moral right of cosmopolitan humanity but because it perfects internal sovereignties, which are thus the real home and primary guarantors of human rights. Because the subject's continuing independence of the ruler qualifies it to validate a claim of authority through acceptance thereof, constitutional rights are complementary to valid political authority and constitutive of unqualified political obligation. To enforce them against the ruler is thus to fulfill, not to contradict, internal sovereignty. A *ius gentium* norm (such as the International Covenant on Civil and Political Rights) recognizing a right of free speech simply recognizes this internal juristic necessity.

Because it is only to the authority of a public reason that subjects can submit without losing the independence needed to validate authority, no natural person can have an absolutely valid authority over others. Only incumbents of offices executing the legal determinations of public reason and answerable to public reason through institutions (courts and parliaments) exercising powers of oversight may do so. In this way, constitutional authority realizes the equality between ruler and ruled implicit in the reciprocity of legitimate authority. Everyone is equally ruler because the public reason that is sovereign is everyone's reasonable will; everyone is equally subject because the ruler is himself subject to the public reason he represents. Here, instead of will ruling through law (*lex*), Law (*ius*) rules through will.

Where authority is constitutional rather than personal, the covenant between sovereign and subject is intellectual in content as well as in form; it need not fill in "the interest in submission" with the values of empirical parties. Given its postulated end of independence, the subject must submit to a lawgiver on condition that the lawgiver acknowledge a duty reciprocally to submit its commands to the impersonal test of self-imposability by an independent subject. An intellectual covenant with that content evinces the ideal form of mutual recognition. It is ideal in contrast to the deformed recognition of the indeterminate covenant because mutual recognition here preserves the subject's independence in submission to the ruler and the authority's independence in being a means for the ruled. Here, then, the product of mutual recognition is a valid authority. Worldly authorities are valid to a lower or higher grade of perfection (and political obligation is qualified or not by a limited permission to resist for the sake of moving to a higher grade) depending on the conditions necessary and sufficient for valid authority that they satisfy. Rulers who rule under a covenant of service to the ruled are stronger authorities than unlimited or merely *de jure* rulers; rulers who rule under a public reason all independent subjects could accept are authorities without qualification. So, *pace* Vattel, not all sovereigns are equal in authority; some are more perfectly sovereign than others. And while not all authority is just authority, only just authority is absolute authority.

Authority's development from despotism to constitutionalism is not the summit of its career. This is so because, while valid authority is constitutional rule under the public reason of guaranteeing independence, there are several conceptions of independence, each capable of informing constitutional order on its own. This plurality divides liberal constitutional thought into sects – libertarian, egalitarian, and communitarian – with counterparts in political parties in constitutional regimes throughout the world. The sects, however, are branches of one tree. All constrain rule by a public reason identified with, or inclusive of, the subject's independence, differing only in their understandings of what the right to independence means and what aspect of the subject – its will, moral conscience, or character – the quality of independence pertains to. For classical liberalism (which I will call libertarianism), the constitutional right to independence is the subject's permission to act pursuant to its freely chosen ends with no limit beyond the equal permission of others. For egalitarian liberalism, it is the right of equal citizens to self-rule and to shape their private lives in accordance with a self-formed conception of the good. For communitarian liberalism, it is the room that solidarities formed around national traditions are obliged to leave for individual characters freely to internalize (or not) their ways of life. This variety of conceptions of independence poses a problem for the possibility of constitutionalism as defined previously. The problem is that there exists a plurality of liberal conceptions of public reason such that the exclusive rule of one transforms public reason's rule into sectarian control, thereby subverting constitutionalism.

It might be thought that liberalism's fragmentation lies outside the focus of our interest – namely, the juristic morality of authority and whether it entails human rights enforceable against sovereigns, whether by domestic or international tribunals. Whatever the specific content of constitutional rights to independence, one might argue, their enforceability against rulers has been settled by the logical evolution of sovereign authority and its internal morality. The rest, one might say, is politics. On this view, the prescriptions flowing from the strictly juristic narrative seem straightforward. Set up the judicial machinery, both domestic and international, for enforcing constitutional rights; let political parties and states contend over what specific rights we have; let judges read into the general language of human rights charters their favorite conceptions of independence; and let the majority opinion prevail.

Alas, matters are not that simple. We'll see that each conception of liberal constitutionalism carries its own implications for the enforceability of human rights against sovereigns. One denies it, another affirms it, and a third, viewing human rights as embedded in a cultural ethos, conditions international enforcement on state consent. The question we must now ask is whether the juristic morality of authority is resourceful enough to guide us through this political thicket. Can it determine a solution to the political controversy within liberal constitutional thought? Has that morality exhausted itself in an indeterminate prescription for liberal constitutionalism or does it extend further to determine a specific content to liberal constitutionalism?

I argue that it extends further. We have come to the point in authority's career where we understand rule for the sake of the subject's independence as a requirement of an unqualifiedly valid political authority and obligation. It stands to reason, then, that the juristic morality of authority would encompass the necessary and sufficient conditions of independence. Rulers who secure only part of what is required for the subject's independence would attract a qualified obligation limited by a permission to resist for the sole purpose of securing a further requirement. Moreover, authority's internal morality has told us that authority is unqualifiedly valid only as the authority of a public reason all free subjects can accept. If, however, the rule of a particular conception of public reason singling out one ingredient of independence dissolves constitutional rule under public reason into despotic rule under a private reason, then that conception cannot be the one under which authority is unqualifiedly valid. Only the *conception* of public reason adequate to the *concept* of a public reason will fill the bill, and so the juristic morality of authority extends to that conception. This, then, is the path along which authority's evolution can continue. It develops toward the comprehensive conception of public reason encompassing the necessary and sufficient conditions of the subject's independence. So let us continue to follow authority's career through the stages of constitutionalism, and let us ask what natural (hence *ius gentium*) law of authority is generated at each stage.

B   *The Constitution of Liberty*

In the classical liberalism given exemplary expression by Kant, the solitary person is thought to be morally self-sufficient in the sense that it owes its right to respect to nothing beyond its innate free will. Put negatively, the human individual depends on no political body or deity for its dignity; rather, its dignity rests sufficiently on the unconditioned end-status involved in its capacity freely to posit ends. That is why the intellectual covenant forming a civil union is, for Kant, only a relative necessity – a necessity conditioned on the unavoidability of living in proximity with others. Were the earth a plane rather than a sphere (such that one could move away from others without at the same time drawing nearer to them), there would be no rational necessity for political association and no moral imperative to enter one. Accordingly, classical liberalism sees the human being as "naturally" solitary in the sense that no natural teleology moves him into political society. The individual need not *become* in a civic body the dignified end he potentially is, for he is already fully a dignified end by virtue of his free will. His state of nature is thus not a civic state but a state of mutual indifference and dissociation.

The dignity in free will entails that every person is at liberty to act on ends it freely chooses (no one may hinder it from doing so) to the maximum extent consistent with the equal liberty of others. In Kant's famous formula, "[a]ny action is right if it can coexist with everyone's freedom in accordance with a universal law."[21] Observe that this so-called axiom of right evinces the form of an ideal recognition. Each person is bound to suffer another's liberty only to an extent consistent with its remaining an independent end capable of validating the other's right-claim to liberty, hence only on condition that it can reciprocally bind others to suffer its liberty to an equal extent. Accordingly, the axiom of right exhibits the form of ideal recognition in the specific shape of mutual respect between

---

[21] Kant, *Metaphysics of Morals*, 6:230.

self-centered persons. Everyone may act self-interestedly within bounds consistent with the equal liberty and vulnerability of all.

For classical liberalism, coercive authority is justified only as specifying and enforcing this precivil axiom of right. In doing so, coercive authority remedies the defect in the axiom's natural authority stemming from the unilateralism of specification and judgment in the precivil condition. Because of this flaw, no one can wrong another, and so the person's innate right to be free of another's constraint is merely inchoate. For the sake of the right's realization, human beings must unite under a common authority that, by virtue of its impartial judgment and the assurance it gives of omnilateral obligation, brings a rightful condition into existence. That is classical liberalism's public reason for rule and obedience. It is to perfect both the natural authority of the axiom of right and the person's innate right to respect for its liberty. Of course, the rational necessity for globe-bound agents to unite under a common authority contradicts the claim that the human agent is morally self-sufficient, but of this contradiction classical liberalism is unaware.

In that public authority under the constitution of liberty is justified only as actualizing by its monopoly of force the axiom of right, those commands of the ruler are alone authoritative that specify and enforce the law enjoining mutual respect between persons or that create infrastructural supports for a rightful condition. Those that curtail liberty more than is necessary for equal liberty or that impose nonreciprocal obligations are devoid of authority. Here we see another instance of the ideal form of recognition – this time between ruler and ruled. By the terms of the libertarian covenant, the subject submits to rule under a public reason identified with guaranteeing mutual respect between free and equal persons; and the ruler reciprocally submits the validity of its commands to a test of acceptability by such persons. In that the ruler has a duty (going with its authority) to conform to that criterion, it wrongs its subjects by failing to do so. However, whether the ruler can be called to account for constitutional wrongs and whether subjects may resist the enforcement of wrongful commands is, for classical liberalism, a further question.

The constitution of liberty can be criticized in light of its own standards of rightful authority. That constitution reposes rightful authority on a public reason reconciling authority and independence. Yet libertarianism's public reason for rule and obedience is not sustainable as a public reason, nor is the axiom of right a constraint on rule sufficient for reconciling authority and independence. This is so because, if persons are thought to be morally self-sufficient, depending on no civic body for their dignity, then their critical reason will be entangled with their precivic right of unilateral judgment as to what constitutes a violation of the axiom of right. And so when, to cure the defect of the precivil state, they surrender their right of unilateral judgment to the public authority, they will also surrender their right to hold the public authority accountable to their critical reason for its constitutional wrongs; for such a right will appear as a revival of moral anarchy. They will therefore constitute a public authority that is once again unlimited in the sense that it will be unaccountable for breaches of its duty to rule solely for the sake of its subjects' independence.[22] It will have and acknowledge such a duty, but calling it to account will engage (or seem to) the very unilateral judgment that the civil condition was meant to overcome. So, while the ruler acknowledges a duty going with its authority to respect the subjects' independence, it acknowledges no duty to avoid being judge in its own cause as to whether it has conformed to its duty; it is supreme lawgiver and supreme court rolled into one. Put otherwise, the supreme commander has no duty to be right in determining whether its commands are consistent with the axiom of right, for it has a monopoly on authoritative judgment. Any authority to judge the rightness of its commands would contradict its supreme authority and place such authority in the judge, who would in turn be unaccountable. As a consequence, the ruler is once again an unlimited despot, and the subject has lost its independence in submission to rule. For its part, the public reason under which the supreme commander rules has collapsed into the private opinion of the commander. Constitutionalism has failed.

In a world where libertarian constitutionalism is the model of political authority (roughly from 1789 to 1945), the entrenchment of human rights in a supreme written law interpreted by a judiciary is optional. Since the sovereign is sole judge of whether its commands conform to public reason, there is no conceptual impetus to entrenchment. The issue thus falls to be decided on prudential grounds. The question is: in whose hands are constitutional rights safest – a representative assembly of the ruled or an elite judiciary? Where the choice is for the judiciary, it is thought that a despotism of judges is avoidable only if they interpret the written constitution as a positive statute of the founders, whose understanding of the entrenched rights (no matter how incoherent) is the key to their meaning. Thus constitutionalism dissolves into the despotism of the founders. Where the choice is for a parliament, constitutional rights remain

[22] Kant, *Metaphysics of Morals*, 6:319.

interpretive presumptions for subordinate courts, whose opinion that a statute conflicts with them yields to the legislature's contrary view. Here constitutionalism dissolves into the despotism of parliament.

The international situation simply reflects the domestic one. There is now a *ius gentium* norm acknowledging human rights, but the instruments recognizing them take the form of hortatory declarations unenforceable against internal sovereigns. This is not because states are externally sovereign in international law but because sovereigns are unaccountable according to the most advanced understanding of the natural law pertaining to their internal authority. It is now understood that internal sovereigns have a duty going with their authority to respect their subjects' independence, and so they can wrong their subjects by limiting their liberty excessively or by depriving them of liberty for the wrong reasons. But they cannot be called to account for their wrongs, for they are the sole judges of a violation. Here belongs the Kantian aspiration to a world confederacy under cosmopolitan right in order to remove the rule-of-law deficit (mistakenly) thought to be inherent in internal sovereignty.[23] Here too belong the Universal Declaration of Human Rights and the merely declaratory power of the International Court of Justice under the International Covenant on Civil and Political Rights. Human rights are paper tigers in international law because they are paper tigers in municipal law.

The failure of classical liberal constitutionalism teaches that a further desideratum of constitutionalism is that rulers be accountable for breaches of the public reason under which they claim to rule. Otherwise, they rule as natural persons with private opinions about their actions' legality, not as officers of a public reason all independent subjects can accept. Further, the logic that took us from moral anarchy to authorized despotism shows what must be rethought if rulers are to be accountable without their subjects' reverting to anarchy. In particular, the rational necessity for entering a civil condition shows that classical liberalism was mistaken to think that individual agents are morally self-sufficient – that they depend on nothing but their free wills for their dignity. Evidently, they require a civic union for their realized dignity. But then it was also a mistake to treat anarchy as humankind's natural condition and to measure rightful rule by whether it conforms to an axiom of right enjoining respect for the greatest possible liberty of atomistic and supposedly self-sufficient persons. The impossibility of rights without a common authority teaches that the normative benchmark is instead an ideal civic union guaranteeing everyone's independence

---

[23] Kant, *Metaphysics of Morals*, 6:355.

and of which all are equal and self-ruling members. Must we not regard such a union as the state natural to dignified beings rather than view as that state an anarchic condition that natural law precisely enjoins us to quit? If so, the argument for unlimited sovereignty never launches. If the justification of civil authority need not begin from rights to unilateralism in a precivil condition, then persons need not alienate their critical reason to an unlimited sovereign in order to establish the rule of law; for the link between critical reason and unilateral judgment (private reason) would be severed. The function of holding rulers accountable to the public reason for their rule could belong to organs of the civic body so structured by law as to be themselves independent organs of public reason.

C   The Constitution of Equality

With this arc of thought, we have moved to a new paradigm of constitutional rule. Here the public reason for rule and obedience is not to perfect a precivic duty of atomistic persons to respect each other's sphere of liberty. It is rather to enjoy a fair scheme of civic cooperation ordered to everyone's independence. The original position is not anarchy but an imaginary congress of disinterested thinkers charged with elaborating the principles of justice implicit in already going liberal orders. Here, accordingly, the meaning of independence can be disentangled from its narrow meaning for the atomistic persons of classical liberalism. It is not simply the free will's independence from others' coercive imposition of ends; it is also the economic independence that moral subjects require in order to shape their lives according to a deliberative conception of the good, and it is the political independence they gain through participation in law making and public administration. So, independence now has the richer meanings of private self-determination and democratic self-rule, of which the freedom of choice protected by negative rights is only a precondition.

So understood, independence is a human good, the enjoyment of which is faring well by an objective measure. And because classical liberalism recognized no universal human good promotable by authority, the emergence of such a good leads to a new covenant between authority and subject. The ruler's authority is conditional on its being under a positive duty to provide the conditions for all to become self-ruling citizens and self-authoring moral subjects – in other words, to promote the common welfare. Correlatively, subjects are entitled to these goods as a condition of retaining the moral independence that qualifies them to validate authority through obedience.

With the new covenant comes a new – let's call it the egalitarian – axiom of right. It is that rulers have a duty constitutive of their authority to provide their subjects with equal access to the means of self-rule and to show equal concern for their leading lives of their own authorship. Because, moreover, self-rule demands that the ruler be accountable for breaches of the new public reason, the ruler now has a duty to be right where a right answer exists and a duty to be reasonable where it does not. Accordingly, its commands must now be reviewed by independent and coordinate judges for consistency with *a priori* determinations of public reason; and they must be reviewed by representatives of the ruled for their reasonableness in implementing the common welfare. Sovereignty resides not in the legislative organ alone but solely in the public reason in which the governor-in-council, the representative assembly, and the judiciary are equal partners.

Whereas classical liberalism's constitution was the constitution of liberty, the new one is the constitution of equality. This is so because guaranteeing to everyone the conditions for self-rule and self-authorship requires eliminating the absolute disadvantages some face because of sheer bad luck and that result either in not having enough to sustain life or in having just enough to sustain life: low endowment, impoverished starting places, and interruption of income. It thus requires public redistributions of resources that reject as normative the historical and haphazard distributions resulting from subjects' having the maximum freedom of acquisition consistent with respect for free choice and established holdings. This means that, within the new constitutional order, classical liberalism's axiom of right is superseded. There is no longer a right regardless of its welfare consequences to the maximum liberty consistent with equal liberty, and so the public authority is not constrained by such a right. It may, for example, limit the kind of contract terms to which parties of unequal strength may voluntarily agree; it may impose a legal duty of care for a "neighbor's" welfare; and it may force someone to relinquish his peaceably acquired holdings so that others may have enough to support a life of self-authorship.

But further, there is not even a right to the maximum liberty consistent with equal self-rule and self-authorship – with the attainment of egalitarian goals. Such a right would imply an independent right to liberty, and yet for the constitution of equality, there is no such right.[24] This is

---

[24] R. Dworkin, *Taking Rights Seriously* (Cambridge, MA: Harvard University Press, 1977), 269.

because an independent right to liberty is so far enmeshed with the apolitical, atomistic conception of the person that the constitution of equality has surpassed in favor of a civic conception. Not yet free of that conception, the egalitarian constitution equates unreduced liberty with civically nonresponsible license, and so it recognizes no right to liberty apart from what fair terms of cooperation define. For it, there is only an equal entitlement to the conditions of self-authorship and self-rule, of which legal rights against interference with liberty are but one. Accordingly, the right to liberty is here mediated by an all-things-considered judgment as to what the common welfare requires; it does not exist separately. If we call classical liberalism's axiom of right $axiom_1$ and egalitarian liberalism's axiom of right $axiom_2$, we can say that the public authority is now constrained by a duty to specify and enforce $axiom_2$ but not $axiom_1$.

In a world where the constitution of equality is the model of political authority (roughly 1945 to the end of decolonization), the enforceability of human rights against the ruler is understood as a juristic necessity – a requirement of valid authority under public reason. There is thus a sudden proliferation of domestically entrenched bills of rights, whereas previously they were the exception. Right-infringing commands that a constitutional court deems unjustified by criteria indigenous to the constitution of equality are invalid irrespective of what the drafters of the constitutional document empirically intended or may be taken to have understood. Subjects need not obey them, and they may lawfully resist the ruler's attempt to enforce them in defiance of the court.

International law follows suit. Where no domestic means exist to call rulers to account for crimes committed against their subjects, an *ad hoc* international tribunal may be established to enforce the *ius gentium* norm of constitutional democracies. Because accountability is a juristic necessity, the tribunal's jurisdiction is compulsory; no prior consent is required. Sovereigns are no longer necessarily equal. Imperfect sovereigns of preconstitutional regimes are answerable to the demands of perfect sovereignty embodied in the public law of the best constitutional democracies. Thus, not only may an *ad hoc* international tribunal assert the human rights norms of constitutional democracy against the murderous officials of a despotic regime; a constitutional democracy may assert a universal jurisdiction to hold a foreign despot and his functionaries accountable for crimes against their people. Only constitutional democracies are equal. Among them, an international tribunal's jurisdiction is supplementary, and the enforceability of its judgments requires prior consent.[25]

We must now ask whether, taken by itself, the egalitarian constitution satisfies the form of an ideal recognition between ruler and subject such that the subject remains independent in submission to the ruler and the ruler remains independent in being a means for the ruled. We can see that, like the constitution of liberty, the egalitarian one produces an *instance* of ideal recognition in that it grounds political obligation in a reciprocal duty of concern for the subject's independence. But does it produce ideal recognition itself? We can also see that it produces something necessary for an ideal recognition, for it supplies the supremacy of public reason that, in the constitution of liberty, dissolved into the ruler's private reason. But does it produce what is sufficient for an ideal recognition?

To see that it does not, consider what follows from the fact that axiom$_2$ constrains the ruler but axiom$_1$ does not. Under the egalitarian constitution, the ruler has a duty of equal concern for everyone's capabilities for self-rule and self-authorship but no duty to respect individual liberty as a separate value. Thus there is no presumption in favor of liberty – no constitutional wrong in limiting liberty more than is necessary for achieving the ends of civic membership. But the right to liberty is the right of the discrete self – the self that is distinct from the civic body and its members. That self is not necessarily the atomistic free will of classical liberalism's state of anarchy; it might be the specific character in which a common way of life is individuated and who gives the common custom a distinctive interpretation and realization. In treating all entitlements of the subject as those of homogeneous citizens – as rights mediated by civic membership – the egalitarian constitution withholds recognition from the discrete self. But if the individual self is not a discrete end, then the civic body is the only end, to which the discrete self is once again unilaterally subordinate. And a civic body that is juxtaposed to a discrete self it subordinates and treats as right-less is a partisan body in relation to that self – in this case the partisan body of those who, under the constitution of liberty, would lack the means of economic independence.

Accordingly, the egalitarian constitution taken alone produces a despotism of the collective. The representative of that body cannot

---

[25] Thus the European Convention on Human Rights establishes a court whose jurisdiction is conditional on the exhaustion of domestic avenues and whose judgments of invalidity are binding only on signatories.

wrong the subject by limiting liberty more than is necessary for its egalitarian ends, by limiting liberty drastically for the sake of a marginal gain in equality that is small relative to the gain obtainable by a noninvasive option, or by taking private holdings for public ends without compensation. The subject recognizes the civic body as an end, but the civic body does not recognize the discrete person as an end. Yet from such a servile relationship no independent validation of authority can issue.

D   *The Communitarian Constitution*

The downfall of egalitarian constitutionalism teaches that the public reason for submission to authority must be to guarantee the independence of the subject considered as both a discrete agent and a civic member. *Both* must be understood here in the sense of "unison" rather than mere "togetherness;" for if human nature is sundered such that to be a citizen, one must lose one's individuality, and to be for oneself, one must be egocentric, then no possibility exists for a public reason encompassing the independence of both citizen and individual – hence none for constitutionalism in the strict sense. There can only be an eternal conflict (oscillation, negotiation) between the constitution of liberty and the constitution of equality and between the political moralities and parties that respectively champion them. So the new conception of public reason must involve a conceptual synthesis of civic member and discrete agent.

The communitarian constitution is ordered to such a conception. Here public reason is the mutual recognition of ruling representatives of a common way of life (ethos) and the individual character who freely makes it a way of *his* life. On the one hand, the community values the free volition and moral self-determination of the discrete subjects through whom the ethos flourishes in a profusion of interpretations; on the other, subjects conscientiously internalize and reproduce the ethos as the common good that ascribes importance to (hence dignifies) their individuality. Rulers are authoritative insofar as they acknowledge a duty to perpetuate the communal ethos under the constraint that the free agency and self-determination of its adherents be respected. Call that axiom$_3$. The ethos itself is indeterminate. It may be a folk culture, a particular religion, secularism, liberal capitalism, egalitarian liberalism, whatever.

Under the communitarian constitution, the basic freedoms the ruler is duty-bound to respect are those necessary for actualizing the ruling ethos. So freedom of conscience and expression are protected above general liberty because of the role they play in bringing the ethos to life.[26] Because the communitarian constitution protects the basic freedoms for the sake of the ruling ethos, it favors certain speech-contents over others, hence favors the adherent of the ruling ethos over the nonadherent – the insider over the outsider. Where the ethos is classical liberalism, expression antagonistic to that ethos (e.g., the promotion of communism) is vulnerable to prohibition if it presents an imminent danger to that ethos. Where the ethos is a particular religion, only religious expression that actualizes the communal ethos is protected; outsider religions fall into general liberty. In a secular ethos, religious expression as such is vulnerable to limitation if it is perceived as a threat to the dominant culture. Accordingly, in the communitarian constitution, we can no longer speak of human rights constraining the sovereign but only of the rights of Britons, Americans, West Europeans, and so on, who share a human rights tradition. Muslim citizens who dissent from that tradition's full content (e.g., from its egalitarianism) are in the same position as non-Muslim citizens of an Islamic constitutional republic – outside the communitarian covenant.

It would seem from the foregoing paragraph that the basic freedoms are protected under a communitarian constitution only where there is no need for protection, for the dominant cultural group has no reason to fear legal curbs on the propagation of its own values. This, however, is not exactly true. After all, to respect the free agency and moral self-determination of subjects for the sake of the ruling ethos is to risk disagreement with that ethos. Accordingly, some nonconforming expression must be tolerated by rulers so that the dominant ethos can be spontaneously confirmed as authoritative through conformist expression. Still, the duty to tolerate does not rule out limitation. There are ways for rulers to meet their obligation to perpetuate the public ethos while respecting their subjects' freedom to be different. They can outlaw nonconforming expression in public spaces while allowing them in private spaces, outlaw nonconforming expression in civil servants while allowing them in the private sector, or ban forms of expression perceived as threats to the ethos while allowing innocuous forms of nonconformism.

In a world where the communitarian constitution is the model of political authority (the contemporary world, it seems), all constitutional regimes are ethos regimes and all ethos regimes are on a level. All are equal expressions of the form of mutual recognition between ethos representatives and individual characters. So authority limited by human rights

---

[26] M. Moore, *Foundations of Liberalism* (Oxford: Clarendon Press, 1993), 191–92.

is authority limited by a human rights ethos. Such an authority is not superior to authority limited by a religious ethos of human inequality, for both are equally valid examples of the communitarian covenant and both create a division between insiders and outsiders. Non-Westerners say that constitutional authority limited by universal human rights is a European idea premised on rootless individualism, and Westerners are unable to answer – indeed, their best theorists now treat the egalitarian-liberal principles of constitutional law as derived from a "political" conception of justice defended as the best interpretation of the political culture of the West.

In this world, accordingly, the international enforcement of human rights belonging to the egalitarian-liberal ethos must depend on state consent, as it effectively does by virtue of Article 86 of the Rome Statute. As a practical matter, the ICC cannot execute its mandate to investigate and prosecute crimes committed by state actors against their own populations without the cooperation of the state in which the accused resides, and only parties to the Rome Statute are obliged to cooperate. The consent-based model is now explicable not in terms of the equality of legally untrammeled sovereigns but in terms of the equality of constitutional cultures. Where the communitarian constitution is taken for the whole natural law regulating the relationship between sovereign and subject, no norm of the *ius gentium* requires that a nonliberal ethos subordinate itself to a liberal one.

The communitarian constitution is a covenant exemplifying the form of an ideal recognition. Subjects acknowledge the authority of ethos representatives for the sake of the rational importance the ethos ascribes to their free interpretation of the ethos in their individual lives and characters. Reciprocally, ethos representatives defer to the free genius of their subjects for the sake of the spontaneous and individualized reproduction of ethos. But is this mutuality sufficient for valid authority? Do we have here an ideal recognition such that the public reason for rule and obedience survives deference to the subject and the subject's independence survives submission to the ruler?

The answer is obviously no. In that the way of life toward which the communitarian constitution is ordered is conceptually undetermined, it is opaque to intellect. Ethos is simply the custom that is there and that has been for as long as anyone can remember. As a consequence, the public reason of the communitarian constitution is hostage to a requirement of empirical unanimity. As soon as one subject asserts her difference, the public reason becomes a parochial one. Subjects who identify with the now dominant ethos have an independence-based reason to accept the authority of ethos representatives, but the different do not. Their submission (for whatever reason) entails a loss of independence, for their moral independence is tolerated within limits, not positively valued, and the limits are drawn by what is good for others. Thus, the ethos ruler is a despot vis-à-vis them. He cannot wrong the different by limiting their conscientious expression for the sake of the customs of the same. But then the ethos ruler has lost the independent subject required to validate its authority. Because that authority can be validated by some but not by others, constitutional rule has dissolved into ethnocultural chauvinism.

4 Just Authority

The breakdown of communitarian constitutionalism reveals a further desideratum of an ideal recognition between authority and subject. There must somehow be a covenant of mutual recognition between the representatives of a common way of life and the outsider. Outsiders must acknowledge the authority of a way of life that values their outsider status, and the political community must defer to the outsider's independence for the sake of its validation as the individual's natural end. This, however, sounds impossibly paradoxical. What sort of communal way of life can defer to the outsider for confirmation of its natural authority?

The answer lies behind us – along the road already travelled and in the constitutional orders sojourned in. As before, the way forward is to reflect on the failures of the past, but this time on the past conceived as a logically continuous narrative about the solitary self's education to the political ground of its fulfilled independence and about the ruler's education to the full conditions of its valid authority. The community that engages the outsider as an equal partner comprises in logical sequence all instances of the ideal form of recognition produced by the *apolitical* (atomistic) individual as it journeys from presumed self-sufficiency to the constitution of liberty to the constitution of equality to the communitarian constitution to the comprehensive constitution sufficient for independence. Through this *curriculum*, the community ordered by the comprehensive constitution – the constitution embracing the previous three as distinctive parts of a whole – is validated as the independence seeker's final end by one who initially claims independence outside community. Reciprocally, that community values the outsider's moral independence as that through which its end-status is confirmed by an independent adversary. Let me call the way of life instituted by the covenant between the political community and the outsider the life of the dialogical community.

This way of life is no longer an indeterminate ethos. It has a specific, intellectual content comprising the three conceptions of public reason connected by the logic of their transitions, along with their respective constitutional paradigms and axioms of right. Together, the three constitutions generate the totality of constraints on rule necessary and sufficient for reconciling authority and independence – hence for valid authority and unqualified obligation. This totality is the full content of human rights complementary to perfect political authority. Its constituent elements are: the classical liberal axiom of right enjoining public respect for the maximum liberty consistent with equal liberty and so recognizing the individual's independent worth as a *free will*; the egalitarian liberal axiom of right, enjoining equal public concern for the individual's self-rule and self-authorship and so recognizing the individual's moral independence as a *self-determining conscience*; and the ethos community's axiom of right, enjoining public respect for cultural communities viewed as sources of worth for *specific characters*. Accordingly, the dialogical community is the one sufficient for reconciling authority with the independence of the *whole* subject – the subject clothed with all logically possible layers of concreteness, from extreme generality (free will) to generality determined (autonomous conscience) to extreme determinacy (specific character). This means that no logically possible construal of subject independence is left unrecognized by the representative of the common life of free individuals. Having for that reason an intellectual content endorsable by all liberal sects, the dialogical community is the inclusive community – philosophically diverse, yet unified. Neither a politically dominant cultural community nor a borderless thought-entity abstracted from cultures, it is the rational community sufficient for human independence – one that embraces and constrains the many cultures within its borders in which specific characters obtain rational importance.

In the dialogical community, all superseded conceptions of public reason are recovered, albeit demoted from sovereign conceptions to constituent ones. All are thought-stages in the apolitical self's education to the ground of its independent worth in the dialogical community and, correlatively, in the validation of that community as the final end of the worth-seeking self. As the subject learns by grades the full meaning of independence, political authority gains the fully independent subject it requires as a validating partner. Concomitantly, the subject gains a polity that acknowledges an obligation to guarantee all ingredients of its independence as a duty constitutive of fully valid authority. As grades of thought equally necessary to the subject's education to independence, the three conceptions of public reason are included as equal phases of one development, but also as equal examples of the one encompassing archetype of ideal recognition between whole and phase, the whole respecting the phase's integrity as a constitutional *Gestalt*, the phase acknowledging itself as a phase of the whole. Accordingly, the public reason alone absolutely entitled to that name is the developmental process itself, understood in its logical continuity. It is the ensemble of fallen conceptions of public reason connected by the logic by which the whole came to sight and by which the fallen are raised to required stages in learning what public reason is. What public lawyers call the sovereignty of law is finally the sovereignty of public reason specified in this way.

5 International Law Implications

In a world where the model of domestic authority is constitutional authority under the conception of public reason adequate to the concept thereof, how would international human rights law change?

One change would fortify the ICC's compulsory jurisdiction with a duty on states under investigation to cooperate with the court's prosecution of their nationals whether or not they are signatories of the Rome Statute or have agreed to cooperate. If, by virtue of authority's internal morality, state actors are accountable for domestic crimes independently of their consent, then their home states cannot remain at liberty to frustrate the ICC's investigative and prosecutorial efforts if they are unwilling to act on their own. But what about the scope of compulsory jurisdiction itself? Would it change?

A Why only Mass Atrocities?

One might think that in a world where just authority is the model of authority, international law would give the ICC a much broader jurisdiction than it now has. Under the Rome Statute, the court's jurisdiction extends only to "the most serious crimes of concern to the international community" – crimes against humanity, genocide, war crimes, and the crime of aggression. I'll leave aside aggression and war crimes because they come under the law regulating the interaction between states, whereas my object is the law regulating the relation between sovereign and subject. So, of all the criminal wrongs that state actors can commit against those subject to their authority, only crimes against humanity and genocide fall within the ICC's jurisdiction. On the account given here, by contrast, that jurisdiction seems logically to extend to any coercive act of an official lacking justification by constitutionally tested legal authority where no prospect of domestic accountability (say, because the judiciary is vulnerable to political interference) exists. So even an arrest without probable cause would seem to qualify. From our point of view, the limitation of the ICC's jurisdiction to so-called international crimes seems incoherent, but this only makes our point of view seem eccentric.

The apparent discrepancy between the ICC's actual jurisdiction and the one our account seems to require might suggest the superiority of John Rawls's account of the same matters. For Rawls, the human rights enforced by international law form a subset of the rights protected by constitutional democracies.[27] They are rights that any decent people would recognize. One might say that they form a Noachide code for the modern world – one to which even nonliberal legal systems could assent. The advantage of this account is that it explains the limitation of the ICC's jurisdiction to crimes amounting to atrocities. Some might argue that it also makes human rights more properly transnational – not simply the rights of constitutional democracies but rights recognizable by both constitutional democracies and what Rawls calls decent hierarchical societies. The downside, however, is that peoples who fail to meet the decency bar are given no reason for accepting the law of peoples, which is nonetheless said to be binding on them. Indeed, they are excluded from the society of peoples, whose law is thus unilaterally applied to them – a stunning departure from justice as fairness.[28]

The account of human rights given here has no need of a Noachide code because it has no need of a hypothetical contract to which all decent peoples could assent. All who claim sovereign authority are *a priori* answerable to its full internal morality, and so no state, however barbaric, is subject to an external law. But without the idea of a Noachide code, how do we generate the restrictions on the ICC's jurisdiction contained in the Rome Statute and that seem appropriate to an international tribunal? In

---

[27] Rawls, *Law of Peoples*, 78–81.
[28] Rawls's decency bar is high enough to exclude many current members of the United Nations, including Iran and Egypt. It requires constitutional protection of cultural minorities, consultative rights for all major groups in society, and recognition for rights of conscience; see Rawls, *Law of Peoples*, 64–78.

particular, how do we limit jurisdiction to crimes against humanity and genocide?

The statute defines crimes against humanity by a set of three limitations. First, only a short list of crimes (such as murder, mass extermination, enslavement, rape, torture, apartheid) qualifies. Second, a crime on this list is a crime against humanity only if committed as part of a widespread or systematic attack on a civilian population. So there must be a series of wrongful acts targeting a multitude. Third, even these are crimes against humanity only if committed "pursuant to a state or organizational policy." The crime of genocide is separate from crimes against humanity, which are crimes against individual members of a population. It consists of actions destructive of an ethnic, religious, or racial entity with intent to destroy. Let's see how well the restrictions on jurisdiction generated by our account match up with the statute's.

On our account, the ICC's jurisdiction takes hold at the final stage of internal sovereignty's logical development toward completion. Its jurisdiction is in that sense relative, and the object of its relative jurisdiction is crimes hitherto sheltered under sovereign authority – under the idea that the internal sovereign cannot do injustice or, if it can, is inherently unaccountable for injustice. Until now, the bar to international criminal jurisdiction has not been *justification* by sovereign authority but sovereign *immunity*. Therefore, the relative jurisdiction logically covers only those wrongs that cannot be defended otherwise than by a claim of sovereign immunity – that cannot, in other words, be justified. So, it is not enough that an official commit an act that, while *prima facie* wrong, *can* be justified by legal authority (an arrest, say) but was unjustified in this case (he arrested without probable cause), and there is no prospect for domestic accountability. In that case, the issue is whether this *prima facie* wrong action was or was not justified in the circumstances by constitutional authority, and that is a matter for the ordinary criminal law. It is for a domestic court alone to judge whether the action can be subsumed to the public justification for the official's use of force – let us say, the need to actualize the sovereign's monopoly of coercion. To hold otherwise – to say that a foreign tribunal may judge an official's claim of justified force on the merits – is to state a maxim incompatible with the internal sovereignty of states even if no process for official accounting exists. This is so because it belongs to the internal sovereign to *apply* its sovereignty to particular cases, and so if no means for asserting sovereignty over wayward officials exist, this is a weakness of internal sovereignty for the internal sovereign to cure. Here an international tribunal's intervention would usurp the domestic government's exclusive authority to enforce the sovereignty in whose name it acts.

Different is the case where an *unjustifiable* wrong seeks refuge under the claim that those exercising sovereignty cannot do injustice or are inherently unaccountable for injustices. Here either a domestic or an international court may take jurisdiction – a domestic court because authority's internal morality says that there is no such refuge, an international court because sovereigns invoking nothing but their majesties are the proper subjects of international law. The domestic court takes priority, however, because the international jurisdiction reflects the self-limitation of internal sovereignty rather than its surrender. All this, by the way, fits the positive law. The Rome Statute establishes a complementary jurisdiction over the crimes it selects for last-resort international jurisdiction.

If the proper object of international criminal jurisdiction is the set of crimes for which sovereign immunity is the only conceivable defense, then to define the jurisdiction, one would first ask what wrongs can never be justified such that only sovereignty could conceivably shelter them. That would give us the Rome Statute's short list of crimes that can be crimes against humanity. Some wrongs – murder, rape – can never be justified because they contain absence of justification in their definitions. Others – mass extermination, mass deportation, apartheid, genocide – can never be justified because there are no circumstances that could justify them. So, what is the legally relevant category to which the crimes on the Rome Statute's short list belong? Is it the most serious crimes of concern to the international community as a whole? No. Is it wrongs that even nonliberal but decent peoples would recognize? No. It is wrongs impossible to justify.

Secondly, having settled on a list of wrongs that can never be justified, one would then require that the unjustifiable wrongs be putative acts of sovereignty or acts of state, for to these alone would the old doctrine of sovereign immunity have applied. But acts of state are acts done pursuant to a reason of state or to a general policy, and so we arrive at the limitation that the unjustified wrongs be committed pursuant to a state policy or to a policy of an organization seeking sovereignty and justifying its actions by the supposed justness of its claim to sovereignty. Third, a wrong impossible to justify that serves a general policy or reason of state must, by virtue of its generality, implicate a multitude rather than a singular; and so we derive a requirement that the crime potentially be part of a widespread or systematic attack on a civilian population. This is not an exact fit with the Rome Statute, but I believe it is close enough and conforms to what a reasonable international jurisdiction would be. So we arrive at a suitably limited international criminal jurisdiction without recourse to the idea of a contract among members of an exclusive club of decent peoples to accept a modern version of a Noachide code.

B   On Justified Intervention

In a world where the model of authority is just authority, the now fledgling doctrine of humanitarian intervention would become firmly established, though not on the grounds typically invoked. Absolute internal authority (there is no permission to resist, period) entails unqualified external sovereignty, for, absent aggression, there can be no juristic permission for one sovereign's interfering with another's unqualified authority. However, "absolute" can be understood in two different senses. It can mean legally untrammeled or legally full. Where authority is legally untrammeled, the ruler cannot wrong his subjects, who are thus at his mercy; where authority is legally full, the ruler is legally constrained such that no further constraints are needed to ensure that the ruler's authority is recognized by independent and equal subjects. In 1648 (when the Peace of Westphalia was signed), absolute authority meant legally untrammeled authority.[29] As a consequence, every internal sovereign was conceived as a despot equal to every other, hence entitled to exclude every other from interference with its internal rule.

However, once sovereign authority is perfected in the state that perfects constitutionalism, it is understood that absolute authority is restricted to *perfect* authorities – those recognized by subjects whose full independence is reciprocally recognized. Now rulers at preconstitutional stages have but a relative internal authority and, correspondingly, a qualified external sovereignty. So not all sovereigns are equal. Only sovereigns whose internal authority is perfect can have an external sovereignty that is unqualified; for what other sovereigns must recognize is just the internal sovereignty, such as it is. So, if subjects may legally resist a despot for the purpose of instituting a constitutional regime, then other states may intervene to protect them against the despot's illegal repression. If a supranational court may punish a criminal despot after the fact, then other states may protect his subjects during the fact. It is not that they have a legal *duty* to intervene in order to realize cosmopolitan human rights. It

---

[29] Grotius defines sovereign power as power "whose actions are not subject to the control of any other etc. so as to be annulled by the pleasure of any other will." Grotius, *Law of War and Peace*, Book I, ch. 3, para. 7.

is rather that there is no legal impediment to third parties' performing an obligation springing from humanitarian morality (so no juristic wrong in discharging a moral duty to rescue).[30] Only a state whose internal authority is absolute can have an external sovereignty that is absolute, and only just states have an internal authority that is absolute. Thus, only in a world where all domestic authorities conform to the ideal form of mutual recognition can we speak of external relations between absolutely independent and equal states. The Westphalian idea is a goal.

6   The Last Utopia?

Many see in the ICC and the doctrine of humanitarian intervention evidence of the passing of the Westphalian system of sovereign states toward a new international order. Rawls, for example, sees these innovations as products of a distinct law of peoples posing external limits on internal sovereignty.[31] Others see them as means by which international law manages the pathologies of a system of sovereign states the law otherwise validates – pathologies presumably curable only in a world without sovereigns.[32]

If the account given here is correct, then these views are mistaken. Humanitarian interventions in defense of human rights as well as the ICC's compulsory jurisdiction enforce sovereignty's internal limits; they do not curb despotic sovereignty from outside. They thus signify the passing only of a certain conception of the Westphalian idea – one according to which a state's unqualified external sovereignty is independent of the stage of maturity of its internal sovereignty. They are not evidence of the transience of state sovereignty as such. Just domestic authorities are unqualifiedly sovereign both internally and externally, for there is no juristic reason for resistance to, or intervention in, a just state. Nor is the international protection of human rights explicable in terms of the

---

[30] A state asserting universal jurisdiction to prosecute foreign state actors for international crimes committed outside its territory raises other issues. That such a doctrine was recognized in the Eichmann and Pinochet cases reflects a growing awareness that not all sovereigns are equal. But though not all sovereigns are equal, it is a further question whether one state may set *itself* up as competent to judge another. If it could, then Syria could have prosecuted Saddam Hussein for crimes committed against his people.

[31] Rawls, *Law of Peoples*, 26–27.

[32] C. Beitz, *The Idea of Human Rights* (Oxford: Oxford University Press, 2009), 129; P. Macklem, *The Sovereignty of Human Rights* (Oxford: Oxford University Press, 2015), 31–50.

pathologies of state sovereignty; on the contrary, it reflects the maturation of domestic sovereignty in the well-ordered constitutional state.

If the Westphalian order is a goal, then it must be judged in its perfect, not in its underdeveloped, forms. So whether or not that order is a final goal depends on whether a society of sovereign states, all of which have perfected constitutionalism, would satisfy all the requirements of human dignity or whether there would be need for a more comprehensive political association of which states are constituent units. That in turn depends on whether perpetual peace is required for human dignity and, if so, whether perpetual peace is obtainable only in a world state. While those questions go beyond this chapter's scope, allow me a closing thought to which the chapter's argument leads.

Let us say that human dignity requires perpetual peace because a state of incipient war threatens the domestic institutions in which dignity is realized. Assuredly, one way to achieve perpetual peace is to abolish the "other" in a union of states, but that is not the only way. Another is to preserve the other while abolishing the other as enemy. A society of sovereign states is necessarily a state of incipient war only if the other must be an incipient enemy. But the other must be an incipient enemy only for states that require the other to be an enemy for the purpose of bonding subjects to their sovereigns. Such are preconstitutional authorities, which, except during war, rule externally over passive subjects. Where, however, authority is endorsed by active citizens whose civic-mindedness is nurtured by an acknowledged duty on authority to respect and promote all dimensions of their independence, enemies are no longer necessary for internal sovereignty. Hence we can expect that a society of perfect sovereigns would abolish the state of incipient war just as effectively as would a world state. The first path ends in a peace without the self-determination of states that, but for the state of incipient war, are comprehensive associations sufficient for dignity. The second ends in peace with self-determination. Might not the last utopia be a world of perfectly sovereign states?

2

The Evolution of Global Authority

PATRICK CAPPS*

Jerry Mashaw writes the following about the birth of administrative law in the early years of the United States:

> Imagine the development of administrative law as a waltz, a three-step pattern repeated over and over again. First, something happens in the world. Second, public policy makers identify that happening as a problem, or an opportunity, and initiate new forms of governmental action to take advantage or to remedy the new situation. Third, these new forms of action generate anxieties about the direction and control of public power. Means are thus sought to make the new initiative fit within existing understandings of what it means to be accountable to law.[1]

I quote this passage because Mashaw's three steps can be said to more or less describe the process of evolution, in the last few decades, of what has come to be known as Global Administrative Law.[2] Thus, Global Administrative Law is the latest example of a 'pattern repeated over and over again' in the evolution of primitive administrative systems.

In his third step, Mashaw is really concerned with how emerging administrative systems can justify the authority they claim to order human conduct, as well as the duties and acts of coercion they seek to impose. The familiar concern is that without such a justification, it is difficult to distinguish such systems from organized, but ultimately arbitrary, coercion. This concern is considered in this chapter in the context of global

---

* Thanks to Henrik Palmer Olsen, Julian Rivers and Ingo Venzke for reading earlier drafts of this chapter.
[1] J. L. Mashaw, 'Recovering American Administrative Law: Federalist Foundations, 1787–1801', *Yale Law Journal* 115 (2006): 1256–1344, esp. 1337.
[2] In this chapter, I use the term 'global administration' to refer to the range of forms of governance that have developed globally, which are described in later sections. When these forms of global administration have authority to govern, they are forms of 'global administrative law'. In the literature on this subject, though, Global Administrative Law is a term used to describe both global administration and global administrative law as I have used them, and when referring to this literature, I use the term Global Administrative Law.

administration. In this context it is acute because the ways of governing adopted by global administrative bodies do not seem to correspond to with our familiar understanding of governmental authority, let alone a more stringent republican concept of authority, which is employed in what follows. This concern then becomes a question about how persons should rationally respond when subjected to regulation by global administrative bodies that fail to live up to (and are imperfect relative to) these concepts of authority. Both Kant's and Brudner's work on authority, in related ways, offer an answer. Their work can be used to defend the claim that there is a *pro tanto* duty to comply with imperfect global administrative bodies but that this duty is one part of a dialectic of authority: there is a duty to obey, but also a permission to resist when to do so is likely to move a particular global administrative body further towards an ideal form of authority. At least for Kant, within this dialectic, the permission to resist is 'negative' in that it must be done lawfully, or through legal means. A vital aspect of this process is the *entangling* of new administrative forms within existing forms of legal accountability. Just as the process maps onto the steps of Mashaw's waltz, there are also some high-profile examples of this entangling occurring in global administration. Entanglement, as a form of negative resistance, is a process which has the potential to drive the evolution of global administrative law to higher levels of authority.

1 Global Administration

According to those who study it, global administrative law consists of various bodies that seek to regulate particular transnational activities. It does make sense to distinguish *public* administrative bodies that are created by treaties between effective states (e.g., the United Nations), or through intergovernmental networks of domestic regulators (e.g., the European Systemic Risk Board [ESRB][3]), from *private* administrative bodies that are created by non-state actors such as a group of companies in a particular sector of the global economy (e.g., GLOBALG.A.P. or the Forestry Stewardship Council [FSC]). While the UN Security Council is probably fairly familiar, the private bodies just mentioned are likely to not be. GLOBALG.A.P. is a private-sector body whose membership is dominated by European producers and retailers of agricultural produce and which

---

[3] The ESRB was established by the European Commission (in light of a report by the Larosière Group) to coordinate the policies of various bodies (for example, EU states and their central banks) to help ameliorate the risks of another global banking crisis.

sets ostensibly voluntary standards for the safety certification of agricultural production processes around the world. The FSC was set up by various participants in the forestry industry to collectively set standards and principles on the sustainable development of the global forestry industry and regulate it through a certification process. As Mashaw suggests in relation to the development of the administrative system in the early US, the bodies just mentioned are the result of the mobilisation of political and economic power to solve joint coordination problems or to regulate the distribution of important public goods. Here are three further important features of global administrative bodies.

First, there is no doubt that bodies like these now form a dense system of global administration. According to the Union of International Associations, there are around 7,000 intergovernmental organisations and more than 40,000 non-governmental bodies.[4] Aalberts estimates that there are now more than 16,000 international organisations.[5] Thus, global governance is here, but it is not a hierarchical federal global order rooted on the will of sovereign states or built on substantive values such as human dignity, as would fit the aspirations of self-styled cosmopolitans. Instead, it is disorganized and often instituted by and directed towards the interests of private actors, alongside states.[6]

Second, it is now clear that the global administrative bodies just mentioned do order coercively whether public or private in the sense given above. This claim can be supported in a number of ways, but it is useful to point out initially that legal pluralists[7] and realists[8] realized long ago that legal science cannot plausibly place *a priori* limits on its object of inquiry so as to be only concerned with those forms of coercive ordering connected to states and the will of states. Underpinning the pluralist's and

---

[4] *Yearbook of International Organizations: Guide to Global and Civil Society Networks App* 1 (2004–5): 2914.

[5] T. Aalberts, *Constructing Sovereignty between Politics and Law* (London: Routledge, 2012).

[6] Recent work has begun to explore how non-state forms of global governance have, through history, existed alongside the interstate system. Often, these forms of global governance have been hidden from view because of our preoccupation with the interstate system. See, e.g., L. Benton and L. Ford, *Rage for Order: The British Empire and the Origins of International Law, 1800–1850* (Cambridge, MA: Harvard University Press, 2016). Global administrative law is an emerging form of global governance that we are luckily able to study during its formative years.

[7] See, for example, S. Roberts, 'After Government? On Representing Law without the State', *Modern Law Review* 68 (2005): 1–24.

[8] K. Llewellyn, 'What Price Contract? An Essay in Perspective', *Yale Law Journal* 40 (1931): 704–51, esp. 731; R. Hale, 'Our Equivocal Constitutional Guarantees', *Columbia Law Review* 39 (1939): 563–94, esp. 578–79.

realist's claim is a republican sentiment[9] that state and non-state bodies alike can coerce in the sense that they can dominate – by restricting freedom of choice of – the will of those subject to those acts of coercion.

A *prima facie* example of coercion by private bodies is where states contract with private companies to perform military and security functions on their behalf.[10] This example is illustrative but possibly problematic because it is well-established that the activities of such companies would fall under the responsibility of the contracting state under customary international law.[11] A better but less well-known example is the private agency called World Check (which is owned by Thompson Reuters). This body consolidates, and charges for access to, various blacklists of those suspected of various financial crimes (including funding terrorism). The banking industry uses information purchased from bodies such as World Check in its attempt to fulfil its due-diligence obligations under domestic regulatory statutes. As a result, listing can lead to a significant restriction of access to financial products, that are vital if one wishes to lead a viable life in a modern Western state, for listed persons. Quoting Dick Marty, Marieke de Goede argues that listing in this way can be a form of 'civilian death penalty'.[12] Similarly, the refusal to embrace GLOBALG.A.P.'s certification programme will result in suppliers of agricultural produce being *de facto* frozen out of major economic markets, which can result in significant economic harm.[13] In sum, the idea that listing or denial of access to markets are non-coercive seems fanciful. Rather, listing or denial of access is a way by which these bodies are able to dominate the will by restricting the freedom of choice of those who the listing bodies seek to regulate. Failure to comply can lead to serious harms to the well-being or freedom of those caught by the attempts at regulation by these bodies. As

---

[9] See F. Neuhouser, *Rousseau's Theodicy of Self-Love: Evil, Rationality, and the Drive for Recognition* (Oxford: Oxford University Press, 2008); P. Pettit, *Republicanism: A Theory of Freedom and Government* (Oxford: Oxford University Press, 1999).

[10] E. Krahmann, *States, Citizens and the Privatization of Security* (Cambridge: Cambridge University Press, 2010).

[11] See articles 5 and 8 of the Articles on the Responsibility of States for Internationally Wrongful Acts (2001).

[12] M. de Goede, *Speculative Security: The Politics of Pursuing Terrorist Monies* (Minneapolis: University of Minnesota Press, 2012), xxviii. Also see M. de Goede and G. Sullivan, 'The Politics of Security Listing', *Environment and Planning D: Society and Space* 34 (2016): 67–88.

[13] N. Hachez and J. Wouters, 'A Glimpse at the Democratic Legitimacy of Private Standards: Assessing the Public Accountability of GLOBALG.A.P.', *Journal of International Economic Law* 14 (2011): 677–710.

Justice Owen Roberts said in *United States v. Butler,* 'the asserted power of choice [to comply or not] is illusory'.[14] Without a valid justification of its authority, coercion by global administration is no more than an example of the arbitrary exercise of power. Thus, a third feature of global administration is that it attempts to justify authority in a variety of ways that often appeal to justifications frequently deployed in developed legal orders: global administrative bodies have adopted Mashaw's 'existing understandings of what it means to be accountable to law'. Here are two ways by which this has occurred.

A first way is the development within many global administrative bodies of constitutive rules and statements of purpose, internal accountability structures, or systems of internal oversight. These are often similar to those found in the administrative systems of developed legal orders. For example, the FSC claims to be committed to normative values such as participation rights and transparency. It has a general assembly with six hundred members divided into three chambers, which collectively determine policy. Participants in the forestry industry can both participate in the standard setting in the general assembly and seek certification from the FSC. Expert certifiers, who are approved by the FSC, accredit participants. There is a complaints system, and there must be a published explanation of the decision by the certifier.[15]

A second way that global administrative bodies are rendered accountable to law is by becoming entangled with other established legal forms. The *Kadi*[16] cases are perhaps the most famous recent examples of this. Here the listing of someone suspected of financing terrorism by the Security Council Sanctions Committee was resisted by various European courts, and this has, in turn, and in part, led to reform of the Sanctions Committee.[17] The corruption charges laid against Fédération Internationale de Football Association (FIFA)[18] officials by US federal prosecutors is another example of how global administration becomes entangled with established legal forms.

---

[14] *United States v. Butler,* 297 U.S. 1 (1936).

[15] E. Meidinger, 'The Administrative Law of Global Private-Public Regulation: The Case of Forestry', *European Journal of International Law* 17 (2006): 47–87.

[16] Case C-402/05 P and C-415/05 P, *Kadi and Al Barakaat International Foundation v. Council and Commission* (2008), ECR I-6351.

[17] See the following, and see also G. Sullivan and M. de Goede, 'Between Law and the Exception: The UN1267 Ombudsperson as a Hybrid Model of Legal Expertise', *Leiden Journal of International Law* 26 (2013): 833–54.

[18] FIFA governs world football but is a private association registered under the Swiss Civil Code.

2   Ways of Governing and Authority

A   *Ways of Governing*

The point just made, and the examples used to illustrate it, show that global administrative bodies have developed various *ways of governing*. What I mean by this in general is close to one of Hart's key claims[19] – in the context of global law, to create a global administrative body is to *institute* a distinctive social practice governed by constitutive rules and principles that determine how the body is to govern. It is as well to also point out here, echoing Fuller,[20] that when such bodies regulate, those regulated – as well as, for example, those states or companies that create the body – expect that the bodies regulating should abide by the rules that constitute them.[21] That is, there are those who have an interest in ensuring that global administrative bodies stick to the rules. So the act of creation of a global administrative body is to create a set of constitutive rules and principles to which that body is expected to conform. Answers to questions of authority emerge from an analysis of these *ways of governing*.

Each global administrative body has a unique way of governing. Thus empirically, the landscape is highly complex, and this makes generalisation difficult. One method used to generalize about legal forms is developed by Max Weber, and his approach is borrowed here. In brief, Weber

---

[19] H. L. A. Hart, *The Concept of Law* (Oxford: Clarendon Press, 1961). See also Chapter 3 in this volume, Henrik Palmer Olsen, 'International Courts and the Building of Legal Authority beyond the State'.

[20] L. L. Fuller, *The Morality of Law*, rev. ed. (New Haven: Yale University Press, 1969); and see K. Rundle, *Forms Liberate: Reclaiming the Jurisprudence of Lon L. Fuller* (Oxford: Hart, 2012).

[21] This said, oversight by states is, according to Stone Sweet and Brunell, often absent in global administration. They have shown that, practically, its exercise of power by forms of global administration constituted by treaties has not been challenged by states (which would be the key institutions which could hold global administrative bodies to account) *ex post* against either constitutive treaty norms or principles such as rationality or proportionality. Moreover, 'no important ruling on treaty interpretation by these courts has ever been overridden by states through treaty revision.' That is, the negotiation process by which treaties are ratified can be seen on the positivist model as a means by which publicly constituted global administration can be legitimately afforded powers *ex ante*, but the *ex post* powers implied by the positivist model are neither institutionalized nor exercised by states. See A. Stone Sweet and T. Brunell, 'Trustee Courts and the Judicialization of International Regimes: The Politics of Majoritarian Activism in the European Convention on Human Rights, the European Union, and the World Trade Organization', *Journal of Law and Courts* 1 (2013): 61–88.

developed four categories of legal thought, which were based on the formal or substantive characteristics of the legal forms he studied, on the
one hand, and, on the other, on the rational and irrational features of
these legal forms.[22] He then was able to show how these categories of legal
thought describe the dominant form of 'legal technique'[23] found in various
societies and sketched historically significant moves from one category to
another, focusing especially on the development of formal rational law in
the West. My suggestion is that something similar can be developed to
generalize about the dominant categories of ways of governing found in
global administrative law. To keep matters straightforward, my attempt
at generalisation will focus on *ex ante* constraints on the production of
directives.

Echoing Weber, the categories of ways of governing in global administrative law form a typology based around two axes. These axes are based
on the republican/non-republican and positivist/non-positivist attributes
of a way of governing. Republican ways of governing are attentive to the
subjective views of those regulated by a global administrative body in the
process of directive formation. Ideally, that body's attentiveness just mentioned will take the form of equal and meaningful participation rights
for persons in that process.[24] Non-republican ways of governing do not
attend, either directly or indirectly, to the subjective views of those they
coerce. Non-republican ways of governing, however, may appeal to the
interests of some or all those affected or the expertise of officials in working out how those interests are realized. Positivist ways of governing allow
states, and not individual persons, to directly determine the content of
directives. Non-positivist ways of governing allow direct participation by
relevant individual persons in the process of directive creation. Thus,

Republican positivism	Republican non-positivism
Non-republican positivism	Non-republican non-positivism

Although each global administrative body may exhibit a number of
ways of governing within this chart (just as Weber understood that a legal
order may reflect different categories of legal thought simultaneously),

---

[22] M. Weber, *Economy and Society*, ed. G. Roth and C. Wittich (Berkeley: University of
California Press, 1978), 654.

[23] Ibid.

[24] The possibility that these axes are scalar (e.g., a body can be more or less republican) will
not be considered here.

the chart does allow us to describe various ways of governing in global administrative law:

Republican positivism. The content of directives is determined by unanimous or majoritarian consent by *republican states* within the decision-making structures of global administrative bodies. The will of citizens within republican states is mediated by their state, as an agent of those citizens, in the decision-making processes of the global administrative body. The Council of the European Union would be the closest example of this way of governing, and an idealized version of this way of governing is set out, I believe, by Kant.[25]

Non-republican positivism. Directives are created by (often unanimous) consent of *effective states* within a global administrative body. The classical international legal positivist position is illustrative of this way of governing, and this position would be exemplified by a conference leading to the establishment of a multilateral treaty or, perhaps, the UN General Assembly (although its resolutions are not generally understood to be legally binding in and of themselves).

Republican non-positivism. Directives are established by a way of governing that takes *direct* account of the subjective views of those affected by acts in accordance with that directive. In this quadrant would fall some of the ways of governing exhibited by the FSC and GLOBALG.A.P., described above, as well as Interpol or the International Seabed Authority.[26] That said, participatory rights in these bodies tend to be restricted to a fairly narrow constituency and are not afforded to all those subject to regulation (i.e., affected) by these bodies.[27]

Non-republican non-positivism. Bodies in this quadrant govern in a way that does not take account of the subjective will of states or individual persons. However, they may take account of the interests of all or some of those affected by the acts of a body and may seek to claim authority on epistemic grounds.[28] For example, the members of the Legal and

---

[25] P. Capps and J. Rivers, 'Kant's Concept of International Law', *Legal Theory* 16 (2010): 229.

[26] B. Schöndorf-Haubold, 'The Administration of Information in International Administrative Law: The Example of Interpol', *German Law Journal* 9 (2008): 1719–52; R. Wolfrum, 'Legitimacy of International Law and the Exercise of Administrative Functions: The Example of the International Seabed Authority, the International Maritime Organisation (IMO) and the International Fisheries Organizations', *German Law Journal* 9 (2008): 2039–59.

[27] See the following and also, importantly, R. E. Goodin, 'Enfranchising All Affected Interests, and Its Alternatives', *Philosophy and Public Affairs* 35 (2007): 40–68.

[28] A claim of epistemic authority, as Shapiro puts it, is where the official claims to know 'more about a subject than one does'. If this is the case, 'it makes good sense to defer to that

Technical Commission of the International Seabed Authority hold their position due to their expertise in technical, economic or legal matters relating to ocean mining. Into this quadrant also fall completely despotic or autocratic forms of global administration, of which it is difficult to think of a clear example.

Although we know actual bodies are much more complex than these four ways of governing, they do allow us to map how various bodies adopt particular ways of governing at a particular time. While this categorisation of these four ways allows descriptive generalisation of the complex landscape of global regulation, it does little more. However, more can be said about the evolution, and authoritative character, of these ways of governing.

B   The Process of Evolution of Ways of Governing

Although this will be examined in more detail in the sections that follow, there is a sense that there is an empirical move from positivist and non-republican ways of governing towards more non-positivist and republican forms. Speculatively, the effective state as constituent power and decision maker seems to be becoming less relevant to ways of governing in global administration. This may be partly because global administration is becoming more 'autonomous' and 'dynamic' as officials within global administrative bodies take a primary role in the interpretation of constituent rules originally established by states.[29] Also, and as described previously, it may be that global administration is now often private and not rooted on state consent or administered by, or with the input of, state officials. Once detached from state consent, officials undertaking ways of governing appeal to new authoritative grounds. As the paternalism that is implied by leaving the complex balancing of competing interests to experts is difficult to justify to those coerced by them, we have seen forms of accountability emerge which take direct account of the views of at least some of those affected by the global administrative body.

---

person's judgment; by doing so, one will do better than if one relied on one's own judgment'. See S. Shapiro, 'Authority', in *The Oxford Handbook of Jurisprudence*, ed. J. Coleman and S. Shapiro (Oxford: Oxford University Press: 2002), 382–439; and H. Hurd, 'Challenging Authority', *Yale Law Journal* 101 (1991): 1611–77.

[29] See Chapter 4 in this volume, I. Venzke, 'Semantic Authority, Legal Change and the Dynamics of International Law'; and Olsen, 'International Courts'.

While this simple description of a trend seems intuitively plausible, we do not yet have an explanation of the *process* by which it occurs. To assist an attempt to provide such an explanation, it might be surmised that we can once again return to Weber's categories of legal thought. Indeed, Weber discussed how 'legal techniques' evolve from primitive to advanced forms. He argued that it was possible to use his categories to describe historically dominant trends, especially with regard to the development of formal rational law in the West. He wrote:

> The formal qualities of the law emerge as follows: arising in primitive legal procedure from a combination of magically conditioned formalism and irrationality conditioned by revelation, they proceed to increasingly specialized juridical and logical rationality and systematization, sometimes passing through the detour of theocratically or patrimonially conditioned substantive and informal expediency. Finally, they assume, at least from an external viewpoint, an increasingly logical sublimation and deductive rigor and develop and increasingly rational technique in procedure.[30]

Weber, although, immediately qualifies his claim by the caveats that 'we here are only concerned with the most general lines of development'[31] and that 'in historical reality the theoretically constructed stages of rationalisation have not everywhere followed in the sequence which we have just outlined.'[32] Furthermore, he considers the causal processes by which legal forms become more rational and formal are 'multiple' but only outlines a few suggestions about why this might have occurred. Although tremendously insightful in many ways, these suggestions fall short of a systematic explanation of how this process, by which legal forms evolve, operates.[33] Can something more systematic be said about this process in global administration? My claim is that a systematic explanation of evolution is on offer. To begin to substantiate this claim, a concept of authority is needed to form a focal point from which this trajectory can be explained.

---

[30] Weber, *Economy and Society*, 882.
[31] Ibid.
[32] Ibid.
[33] See ibid., 883:

> 'We shall not be troubled either by the multiplicity of causes for the particular type and degree of rationalization that a given law has actually assumed ... We shall only recall that the great differences in the line of development have been essentially influenced, first, by the diversity of political power relationships, which, for reasons to be discussed later, have resulted in very different degrees of power for the imperium vis-à-vis the powers of the kinship groups, the folk community, and the status groups; second, by the relations between the theocratic and the secular powers; and, third, by the differences in the

C   Ways of Governing and the Focal Point of Authority

Fairly obviously, the way in which a global administrative body governs is relevant to the normative question of whether it has *authority* to govern. A particular justification of authority leads us to conclusions about whether a global administrative body is rightly able to impose duties or has warrant to coerce. For example, if we take a democratic justification of authority, the way of governing exhibited by the commission of the International Seabed Authority just mentioned (which I have suggested reflects non-republican non-positivism) would appear normatively problematic.[34] By contrast, those who adopt a Razian justification of authority would be more likely to consider the same commission authoritative.[35] If one adopts the traditional concept of authority adopted by international lawyers (rooted in the consent of effective states), the Security Council has authority to require states to restore international peace and security because it is a way of governing that exhibits non-republican positivism (although questions of *vires* remain). However, the FSC and GLOBALG.A.P. (both of which are established by private industry) would not have authority. From the perspective non-republican positivism, while the internal deliberative procedures adopted by the FSC and GLOBALG.A.P may give these bodies an air of administrative rigour, they are better understood as a sort of cartel which uses the economic clout of its members to push around economically and organisationally weak producers of timber or agricultural produce.

D   Authority

Continuing this line of argument, the ways of governing just set out may be justified by a republican conception of authority, which is developed by Kant and others.[36] For this republican concept of authority, officials have authority to coerce to the extent that they have a moral warrant to do so. A moral warrant arises when the official's act of coercion is consistent

structure of the [strata of] "legal notables" significantly for the development of a given law, differences which were also largely dependent upon political factors.'

[34]   That the members of the commission of the International Seabed Authority are elected on the grounds of expertise obviously muddies my argument.

[35]   See, e.g., J. Tasioulas, 'The Legitimacy of International Law', in *The Philosophy of International Law*, ed. S. Besson and J. Tasioulas (Oxford: Oxford University Press, 2010), ch. 4.

[36]   See, e.g., T. Christiano, 'Kant's Moral Concept of International Law', *Journal of Political Philosophy* 12 (2004): 266–90; and P. Capps and J. Rivers, Kant's Moral Concept of Law (unpublished manuscript, 2017).

with the moral duties each person has to respect the dignity of others, which means that others are not to be treated as a means to the fulfilment of each person's purposes.

Authority arises in two circumstances. First, officials have moral authority when applying directives that logically follow from the perfect moral duties or innate rights those subject to that directive possess. When these directives[37] are imposed, the act of legislating for the directive adds no new reasons for persons: they have a categorical obligation to act morally and rationally cannot complain if they are coerced (using proportionate force[38]) to do so. Although as a matter of fact there will be some who disagree with the content of this form of law within a morally diverse society, there is a right answer which can be found from an analysis of the requirements of moral duty. Officials who are experts should, in principle, be able to determine what perfect duties or innate rights require of persons in complex factual situations, and in such cases, it is rational for those subject to these officials to *defer* to their expertise. These expert officials have, in principle, *epistemic authority in personam*, and this justifies their attempts to govern.

Second, in cases of moral optionality and moral disagreement, a warrant to coerce in accordance with a directive arises when each person subject to it has equal political rights[39] to influence its content. The political

---

[37] Such laws are 'obligatory *a priori* by reason even without external law-giving'. See I. Kant, *The Metaphysics of Morals*, trans. M. Gregor (Cambridge: Cambridge University Press, 1991), 6: 224. I refer to Kant's works as found in the Academy edition of the *Gesammmelte Schriften* and cite the volume and page number.

[38] See M. Willaschek, 'Which Imperatives for Right? On the Non-prescriptive Character of Juridical Law in Kant's Metaphysics of Morals', in *Kant's Metaphysics of Morals: Interpretative Essays*, ed. M. Timmons (Oxford: Oxford University Press, 2002), ch. 3.

[39] For Kant, the creation of law must conform to four constraints. The first constraint, which has already been discussed, is that legislation cannot be inconsistent with perfect moral duties (e.g., 6:371, 6:315, 19:594–95; 5:155–57). The second constraint is 'lawful consent' to legislation. Thirdly, each citizen must have 'civil equality': law making should not recognize 'among the people any superior with the moral capacity to bind him as a matter of right in a way that he could not in turn bind the other'. Jointly lawful consent and civil equality are the basis for political rights that allow each citizen to have an equal chance to influence the content of laws and, by implication, requires the rejection of all forms of government based on unequal allocation of these political rights (such as aristocratic government). Fourthly, the 'the attribute of civil independence, of owning his existence and preservation to his own rights and powers as a member of the commonwealth, not to the choice of another among the people' requires that each citizen must be able to participate as a moral, motivated, purposive agent without suffering unjustified hindrances from other members. Citizens should have legally enforceable rights that express the four constraints just set out against the institutions that govern their conduct, such as the state (6:313–14).

rights just mentioned establish the conditions by which freedom can be exercised within a political community. If an official does not take equal account of the will of *all* persons subject to that legislation, that official, by implication, subordinates the will of those without those political rights to those that have them. And this subordination constitutes a failure to recognize fellow community members as free and responsible persons capable of exercising choice. Officials have *political authority* to impose such laws if they respect these constraints.

State institutions that enforce either of these two types of directive are republican in the sense that they establish the conditions by which persons (as citizens) can both relate to others in a non-dominating way and have freedom themselves. A person, now a citizen of a republican state, has sufficient reason to subordinate his or her own unilateral will to state institutions, which issue these directives because it is the only way his or her freedom of choice can be aligned with the freedom of choice of others.

Against this concept of authority, two features of the complex and unique global administrative bodies that exist empirically can be identified. The first is that because many of these bodies are established to respond to global coordination problems, which concern the balancing of complex competing interests over which there are significant disagreements, their directives are likely to be only able to appeal to the second ground just set out, and thus authority arises because bodies afford equal political rights to those persons affected by their directives. Second, these bodies are unlikely to have authority on this account because they fail to afford those political rights to those subject to their directives. Richard Stewart makes this point convincingly in his argument that the ways of governing by many global administrative bodies leads to a disregard of the interests and voice of many of those who are coerced by them.[40] Stewart discusses two forms of disregard. First, he shows how substantive harms are caused to objective 'interests and concerns' (against standards that are articulated by the major human rights treaties) of weaker and poorly organized political and economic groups. Second, Stewart argues that global administration tends to be accountable to the most powerful states and economic actors and is not accountable to weakly organized and less powerful states and political and economic groups, who may be significantly affected by decisions of global administration. For these two

---

[40] R. Stewart, 'Remedying Disregard in Global Regulatory Governance: Accountability, Participation, and Responsiveness', *American Journal of International Law* 108 (2014): 211–70.

reasons, global administrative bodies fail generally to issue authoritative directives. So while some bodies do make efforts to be accountable to at least some of those affected by their attempts at regulation, and they are sometimes respectful of or constrained by fundamental human or political participation rights, it is unlikely that the ways of governance adopted by global administrative bodies will be authoritative against the stringent concept of republican authority set out in this sub-section.

3   Negative Resistance and the Career of Authority

The comments made about the evolutionary trajectory of global administration can be held against the concept of authority just set out to suggest two conclusions. First, global administration seems to be evolving in a direction that is towards the republican concept of authority. Second, it would be churlish to suggest that global administrative bodies govern in a way that is consonant with that concept for reasons given by Stewart, so we must conclude that until they do so, they are not authoritative. Instead, we might conclude that while the establishment of an authoritative global administration is a rational aspiration for practically rational persons and would demand their obedience, it remains a relatively distant ideal, and in the meantime, there are (at best) merely prudential obligations to comply with its directives.[41]

I do not think the presupposition that underpins these conclusions – which is that the institutions that govern us have authority because they correspond pristinely to a demanding concept of authority, or they do not – must be accepted. Instead, practical reason does tell us more about how we should respond to such imperfect institutional forms. There are two sources for this argument. The first is Kant's argument in support of *negative resistance* and the second is Alan Brudner's idea of the *career of authority*.

A   Negative Resistance

Kant distinguishes between what he called *active* resistance, which is impermissible, and *negative* resistance, which is permissible.[42] Active

---

[41] See Chapter 7 in this volume, Andreas Follesdal, 'The Legitimate Authority of International Courts and Its Limits: A Challenge to Raz's Service Conception?'; and I. Hurd, 'The International Rule of Law: Law and the Limits of Politics', *Ethics and International Affairs* 28 (2014): 39–51.

[42] Kant, *Metaphysics of Morals*, 6:322.

resistance is refusal to comply with the law with the aim of dismantling a 'defective'[43] constitutional arrangement and reconstituting a new one. The example he gives of negative resistance is 'a *refusal* of the people (in parliament) to accede to every demand the government puts forth as necessary for administering the state'.[44] That is, the resistance through the legislative authority, which 'can only belong to the united will of the people',[45] is the constitutionally valid means by which a community can challenge the demands of the executive power. What Kant means here, I think, is that negative resistance, which has the aim of perfecting the authoritative credentials of the state, describes challenges to the exercise of power that are *absorbed* within the institutional structure – that is, the constitutional arrangements in relation to the separation of powers – of the state.[46] Put in the language used in this chapter, once a way of governing is established, resistance is to be conducted through lawful means: legal challenge and political pressure. It should not be conducted through revolution and conflict.

B   *The Career of Authority*

I believe a similar idea is explored by Alan Brudner in both his chapter in this volume and in also in *Constitutional Goods*.[47] His idea is that there are 'grades of authority', some of which are merely 'justified', while one is 'fully justified'. Although Hegelian in inspiration, 'fully justified', or 'true', authority for Brudner is close (in at least form) to the republican concept of authority advanced in this chapter.[48] Lower grades of authority are distinctive forms of authority that contain within them a *particle* of true

---

[43] Ibid., 6:322.
[44] Ibid., 6:322.
[45] Ibid., 6:314.
[46] See the following and ibid., 6:321–22.
[47] A. Brudner, *Constitutional Goods* (Oxford: Oxford University Press, 2004).
[48] No doubt, Brudner would consider that the Kantian conception of authority is only partial in that it is a form of classical liberalism that does not incorporate the egalitarian and communitarian aspects of independence that inform a just constitutional order. Therefore, he might claim that the correlation made in the text is inappropriate. I believe that Kant's position is actually closer to Brudner's view. Kant argues that while there are certain inviolable perfect duties (which can be articulated as rights), agents have moral discretion (which should be articulated by democratic institutions at the level of a community) and a right to civil independence (which corresponds to the material conditions by which persons have the capacity to act as free citizens of a state). Perfect duty, moral discretion and civil independence, I believe, are held in relation in a just state. This parallels Brudner's claim.

authority. There remains a duty to comply with 'lower grades' of authority because they exhibit this particle of authority.

One example of a lower grade of authority is an official who governs in accordance with rules and not merely whims. Brudner's view is that by governing in accordance with rules, the official exhibits a thin form of respect for the autonomy of the subject. This is the particle of authority which gives the subject a duty to comply.[49] There are higher grades of authority that are contained within each lower grade. This, then, gives rise to his *career of authority*:

De facto authority. This is essentially the *ad hoc* decrees of a ruler.

De jure authority. This 'is a species of *de facto* authority where the ruler's deference to the subject's bare volition at the previous stage becomes deference to the subject's deliberative volition through rule by general laws by which the subject can guide himself. Here the ruler submits his authority claim to the subject's self-application of the ruler's laws to its own conduct.'[50]

Legitimate authority. This is 'that species of *de jure* authority in which the germ of ruler deference to subject autonomy present in *de jure* authority develops into a relation of mutual covenant; subjects acknowledge an obligation to submit on condition that the ruler acknowledge a duty to fulfil the autonomous purpose for which they submit, whatever that purpose is.'[51]

Constitutional authority. This is a 'species of legitimate authority in which the idea of equality between ruler and ruled incipient at the previous stage is fulfilled in the idea of equal subjection of ruler and ruled to a conception of public reason all free subjects can accept. Here the ruled acknowledge a duty to submit on condition that the ruler acknowledge a duty to serve a specific purpose for their submission, namely, protecting the subject's independence and therewith the subject's qualification to validate the ruler's claim of authority.'[52]

Just authority. This is a 'species of constitutional authority in which the rule of public reason is perfected under a comprehensive conception of public reason comprising the necessary and sufficient conditions of the subject's independence.'[53]

---

[49] This is not too far from a normative version of the authority claim made by the legal official in Hart, *Concept of Law*.

[50] See Chapter 1 in this volume, A. Brudner, 'The Evolution of Authority', p. 18.

[51] Ibid., p. 18.

[52] Ibid., pp. 18–19.

[53] Ibid., p. 19.

Thus, Brudner's career of authority moves beyond the binary distinction mentioned previously. Instead, each grade of authority describes a form of relationship between the official and the subject in which both seek, as members of the same society, to afford some respect to each other *qua* official and subject. Lower grades of authority are ones in which the official affords little respect to the objective interests and subjective views of the subject, but there is *some* respect afforded by the official to the subject, and this respect should be reciprocated by a duty to comply with the official's directives.

Brudner's argument appears *prima facie* problematic for the following reason. He has established that there are various forms of authority – all but one of which are imperfect – but all are a sufficient ground upon which to base a duty to comply. What practical or theoretical work, then, does the career of authority do except to lower the bar by which bodies claiming authority should be considered by persons to actually have justified authority? Brudner's answer is that there is a permission to resist an imperfect form of authority if that resistance is instrumentally likely to succeed moving the relevant way of governing to a higher level of authority. Specifically,

> each stage subsequent to the first is a species of its generic antecedent distinguished by its fulfilling a potential incipient at the previous stage and generating a new potential for the next to fulfil. Each stage before the last produces a relative authority limited by a permission to resist the ruler for the sole purpose of moving to a higher stage. Only just authority is absolute authority entailing an unqualified obligation to submit. Together, the stages comprise what can be called the juristic morality (or natural law) of sovereign authority.[54]

But how is this dialectic between a duty to obey and permission to resist an authority played out? It would seem that if there is a permission to resist – that is, to be determined by the unilateral choice of the subject – then it is unclear whether the duty to obey is actually a duty: the idea of a 'relative authority' seems to be a contradiction in terms.[55] The answer to

[54] Ibid.
[55] This said, it could be that an authority could exist between an official and one person for various reasons but not exist between another person and official in a different situation. This is, after all, the basis of jurisdiction. More than this, though, it could be that an official has *de facto* authority with regard to one person and legitimate authority with regard to another (see note 76, below). The term 'relative authority' is a term used and developed in a related but different context by N. Roughan in her book *Authorities* (Oxford: Oxford University Press, 2013).

this question emerges from a claim just made: both the official's and subject's are rationally committed to a joint project to institute true authority. So to resist imperfect forms of authority in all circumstances is to pull the whole joint project down, which is instrumentally irrational given the official and subjects shared rational aim to institute just authority. However, to resist only where resistance will lead to an authority claim closer to just authority is to take instrumentally rational action to achieve the end of that joint project.

This argument clarifies Kant's claim that active resistance is impermissible but negative resistance is permissible. For Kant, all persons, whether officials or citizens, have a moral duty to will the institutionalisation of perfect, or just, authority. As it is for Brudner, active resistance is to tear down a community's imperfect attempt to achieve this, and this is why it is morally impermissible. However, negative resistance is an attempt to perfect an imperfect authority and so is permissible.

Practically, and to return to the question at hand, what precisely is negative resistance? We have already sketched Kant's view, which focuses on the separation of powers within primitive states, but he also writes,

> A change in a (defective) constitution, which may certainly be necessary at times, can therefore be carried out only through *reform* by the sovereign itself, but not by the people, and therefore not by revolution ... In what is called a limited constitution, the constitution contains a provision that the people can legally *resist* the executive authority and its representative (the minister) by means of its representatives (in parliament).[56]

Thus, for Kant, the dialectic between the duty to comply and negative resistance is articulated as various legal rights and freedoms within a state constitution that allow challenge to the state's various attempts to exercise power over citizens, and are necessary to perfect a defective constitution.[57]

---

[56] Kant, *Metaphysics of Morals*, 6:321–22.

[57] In his posthumous writing on international law, Dworkin develops a theory of the evolution of international law that resembles the claims made by Kant and Brudner. Dworkin begins by specifying the values – such as a commitment to human dignity and democratic values – that a just international order should adhere to. For Dworkin, there are a number of imaginary or real systems of international law that could reasonably ensure a just world order of states. He then expounds the principle of salience, which is described in the following way: 'If a significant number of states, encompassing a significant population, has developed an agreed code of practice, either by treaty or by other form of coordination, then other states have at least a prima facie duty to subscribe to that practice as well, with the important proviso that this duty holds only if a more general practice to that effect, expanded in that way, would improve the legitimacy of the subscribing states and the international order as a whole.' Dworkin's view is that states have a duty to comply with international law except when not complying will lead to an improvement of the legitimacy of the

C *The Career of Authority and Global Administration*

With the dialectic between the duty to obey and the permission to resist imperfect authorities in place, we can return to global administration. The first point to make is that the career of authority offered by Brudner provides a possible basis for the missing process, which explains how global administrative law evolves in the way it appears to. That is, the trajectory of development in global administrative law, which was sketched previously, from positivist and non-republican ways of governing to republican, and non-positivist, forms, seems to resemble the trajectory of the career of authority. Although the two schemas do not tie up perfectly, forms of non-republican non-positivism (e.g., epistemic authority) may be close to *de facto* authority in many examples, while non-republican positivism (e.g., the interstate system) is close to *de jure* (i.e. rule-based) authority. Moreover, once public global institutions adopt interpretative practices that cannot be derived from treaties, or when private global institutions emerge, they seem to begin to reflect aspects of republican non-positivist forms of governance. For example, the ESRB, established by the European Commission to oversee the mitigation of systemic risk with the EU financial system, now seeks to be directly accountable to key players within that financial system.[58] That said, as Willem Buiter points out, the ESRB's understanding of what a key player is, is very limited.[59] Something very similar can be said in relation to the way of governing adopted by GLOBALG.A.P and the FSC.

These bodies, which echo republican non-positivist forms of governing, may be most plausibly considered a form of 'legitimate authority' according to Brudner's career of authority. For GLOBALG.A.P., at least some of those subject to its way of governance are in a mutual covenant with it. On the basis of this covenant, GLOBALG.A.P. has a 'duty to fulfil

---

international legal order, which resembles the claims made by Kant and Brudner discussed in the text. See R. Dworkin, 'A New Philosophy for International Law', *Philosophy and Public Affairs* 41 (2013): 2–30, esp. 19.

[58] Its internal structure comprises sixty-five members, thirty-seven with voting rights, among whom are the governors of the twenty-seven EU state central banks, president and vice-president of the ECB, a member of the European Commission and the chairpersons of three other European supervisory authorities. In its annual reports, the ESRB takes care to explain how it is to be accountable and transparent. Commentators have worried that it is not accountable in the right way because its decision-making bodies do not represent those whom its recommendations affect.

[59] See the Treasury Committee's Opinion on Proposals for European Financial Supervision (Sixteenth Report of Session 2008–9), Ev 25.

the autonomous purpose for which' it submits.[60] GLOBALG.A.P. does pursue, on the basis of a covenant that establishes a comprehensive rule-based and principled regulatory system, the legitimate aim of global food safety. For the reasons offered by Brudner, there appears to be a duty for those subject to GLOBALG.A.P.'s attempts at regulation to obey it.

This said, while GLOBALG.A.P. it is attentive to the voice of *some* of those affected by its decisions, it is well acknowledged that it also disregards the voices of many (e.g., poor farmers in the poorer parts of the world). Furthermore, it prioritizes the interests of Western consumers and food producers. Surely GLOBALG.A.P. cannot be said to be a legitimate authority with regard to those disregarded by it? At a general level, Brudner explores the implications of this problem in his chapter in this book. He writes, using the example of feudal privilege (which is quite a good way of describing the limited forms of accountability exhibited by some global administrative bodies), that with regard to some persons, a body might be legitimate (the 'in-group'), and for others, *de jure* (i.e. rule-governed) authority. Authority arises bilaterally, by which I mean that the authority claim of a global administrative body can differ depending on the extent to which each subject to that body is recognized as having a genuine say in how it governs. It is for this reason that those 'excluded from the covenant have a weaker obligation to obey' and may resist 'to compel a *de jure* ruler to take account of their interests'.[61] Such resistance is justified for those subject to GLOBALG.A.P's directives, but not given a say in how it governs, to the extent that it will result in a higher grade of authority being achieved. Furthermore, it has been argued that this dialectic between the duty to obey and the permission to resist plays out through negative resistance: resistance within, and through, the law.

This can play out in at least four ways. First, accreditation by GLOBALG.A.P. is formally voluntary, so refusal to comply with GLOBALG.A.P. could be a legal form of resistance. That said, and as set out earlier, this may lead to substantive harms to food producers. Second, political or economic pressure may be mustered to *reform* or reconstitute global administrative bodies such as GLOBALG.A.P. so that they become more responsive to those disregarded by them. The treaty-making process could be an important way by which political power could develop (perhaps from the existing institutions of GLOBALG.A.P.) a system of global

---

[60] See Brudner, 'Evolution of Authority'.
[61] Ibid.

food safety that is at a higher grade of authority. But it is not the only way by which reform can take place. Other methods would be, for instance, for food producers in the economically poor parts of the world to form a union that can represent their interests, or for their interests to be supported by NGOs. Third, various forms of pressure could be placed at the national or international level to induce political institutions to pass legislation that can protect weaker parties not represented by GLOBALG.A.P. for reasons that would be similar to the rationale for consumer protection regulation. Fourth, domestic, transnational or international law – public and private – remedies could be sought (perhaps, most obviously, through competition law). These four possibilities are forms of permitted resistance because each is an instrumentally rational attempt to move GLOBALG.A.P. to a higher level of authority.

What is offered by this argument is an explanation of what practical reason requires of us when we are faced, as we clearly are, by the development of the dense and coercive system of global governance, which was described in Section 1 of this chapter. The global administrative bodies that claim authority over us should be obeyed except when negative or lawful resistance in one of the four forms just set out is likely to move those bodies to higher levels of authority. These forms of resistance are emerging as a feature of global administration and provide, I believe, the motor that drives the process by which the ways of governing adopted by global administration evolves from positivist and non-republican forms to more republican and non-positivist forms. Let me give some examples of how negative, or lawful, resistance leads to the evolution of global administrative law by looking at the idea of entanglement between it and existing legal forms.

D   Entanglement among Existing Legal Forms as a Form of Negative Resistance

In his analysis of the development of administrative law in the early days of the US (cited in the introduction to this chapter), Mashaw argues that there was little provision for the legal regulation of administrative agencies in the US constitution. Instead, a system of administration developed around that time that did not resemble the hierarchically organized system we associate with the modern US. While administrative agencies emerged to deal with various pervasive coordination problems or to pursue collective goods, these new agencies had to be made to 'fit within existing understandings of what it means to be accountable to law'.[62] This was done by irregularly *entangling* these new agencies with existing bodies of law (e.g., criminal, property, contract and tort law).

Specifically, Mashaw identifies two important, but related, ways in which the regulation of the administrative system developed. First, in the early Republic, the administrative system and its power to exercise discretion were not only established through legislation but also through contractual relations between individuals, often with expertise or local standing, and the state. Second, controls over those with administrative roles had their basis in law in various ways. One example is that the delegation of powers to officials by legislation could be a defence against common-law actions or criminal-law charges. Sometimes governance was achieved by the state to provide, through legislation, economic incentives for performance of duties by administrative officers.[63] These examples of entanglement with existing legal forms illustrate a crucial mechanism by which early US administrative agencies were able to fit 'within existing understandings of what it means to be accountable to law'.[64] These mechanisms were the real foundations of the modern administrative state in the United States. But what is noticeable is that what Mashaw is describing here is what was described earlier as being lawful resistance, or resistance *through* law, which serves to elevate US administrative agencies to a higher level of authority. If Mashaw is right, and from the theoretical perspective outlined in this chapter, then this entanglement with existing legal forms is a normative motor by which the higher grades of authority emerge within administrative systems.

These forms of legal entanglement in the early US are instructive for our analysis of the process of evolution of global administration. Negative resistance has been, for example, undertaken by litigants appealing to existing legal structures – that arise from the structural couplings between a range of global administrative bodies – with a view to block coercive acts that arise from the institutions that exhibit lower grades of authority. The most famous examples of blocking are the exercise of review powers by the United Kingdom's Supreme Court in *A v. HM Treasury*,[65] the courts of the European Union in the *Kadi* judgments[66] and the European

---

[62] Mashaw, 'Recovering American Administrative Law', 1337.
[63] For example, the treasurer of the Bank of the US was required to pay a $50,000 bond on taking office. See Mashaw, 'Recovering American Administrative Law'.
[64] Mashaw, 'Recovering American Administrative Law', 1337.
[65] *HM Treasury v. Ahmed* (2010), UKSC 2.
[66] 1 Case C-402/05 P and C-415/05 P, *Kadi and Al Barakaat International Foundation v. Council and Commission* (2008), ECR I-6351.

Court of Human Rights in *Nada*.[67] In each judgment, those listed by the Security Council were ultimately successful in the sense that the courts felt compelled to declare the implementation by states of orders freezing their assets made by the UN 1267 Sanctions Committee illegal. Because of the possibility that these judgments would create large holes in the sanctions net, pressure was put on the Sanctions Committee to become more attentive to the procedural rights of those listed.[68] Consequently, there is now an ombudsperson for the 1267 Sanctions Committee who can be petitioned by those whose assets have been frozen and who can recommend delisting. This said, the powers of the ombudsperson to garner evidence by which to make recommendations are distant relations of the forms of judicial review we find in states with developed legal orders.[69] An obvious further example of this process of entanglement between existing legal forms and private global administrative bodies are the fraud, money laundering and racketeering charges made against FIFA officials by US prosecutors.

Negative resistance has also occurred by the application of political pressure to reform private bodies. In response to concerns by NGOs about the considerable power exercised by GLOBALG.A.P. over poor farmers, it has recently appointed 'the ambassador of smallholders'.[70] That said, this ambassador has no voting power, and this is one reason why Hachez and Wouters argue that its provision 'does not place stakeholders from developing countries on an equal footing with their western counterparts and does not ensure inclusive and egalitarian participation meeting the (deliberative) democratic standard'.[71] Therefore, there are examples of how negative, or lawful, resistance to global administrative law occurs and how it holds the possibility of moving it to higher grades of authority. This, I believe, is the normative motor that drives the development – Mashaw's three-step waltz – of primitive administrative legal orders.

---

[67] *Case of Nada v. Switzerland* (Application no. 10593/08) (2012), European Court of Human Rights.
[68] See D. Hovell, 'Kadi: King-Slayer or King-Maker? The Shifting Allocation of Decision-Making Power between the UN Security Council and Courts', *Modern Law Review* 79 (2016): 147–82; and C. Murphy, 'The Dynamics of Transnational Counter-terrorism Law: Towards a Methodology, Map, and Critique', in *Constitutionalism across Borders in the Struggle against Terrorism*, ed. F. Fabbrini and V. Jackson (London: Edward Elgar, 2016), 78–97.
[69] Sullivan and de Goede, 'Between Law and the Exception', 833.
[70] Hachez and Wouters, 'Glimpse at the Democratic Legitimacy', 703.
[71] Ibid.

4 Conclusion

In the last few decades, a new form of coercive ordering has emerged at the global level, and this is called global administrative law. Although its claims to authority are imperfect, the ways of governing of most global administrative bodies contains within them a particle of authority against a familiar and persuasive republican concept of authority and this gives rise to a duty to comply. However, the duty to comply with imperfect or lower grades of authority is one side of a dialectic, the other side of which is a permission to resist imperfect ways of governing. Resistance is only permitted when to do so will move a global administrative body to a higher grade of authority and should be negative, or lawful, resistance. In the development of primitive administrative orders – such as global administration – resistance to achieve a higher grade is in part achieved through the entangling of new administrative forms with existing legal forms. This entangling is occurring in global administration and is an important motor for its evolution.

3

International Courts and the Building of Legal Authority beyond the State

Introduction

One of the most important transformational processes in law and governance since the fall of the Berlin Wall in 1989 has been the significantly increased importance of international law in international and domestic governance in the form of an intensified juridification of international relations – both public and private – and a steadily growing population of increasingly active international courts.[1] In the longer historical perspective, international relations has mostly been troublesome, and the most recent political developments in our time strongly signal a re-emerging nationalism,[2] which does not bode well for close international collaboration. In this light, the developments in international law and politics may, on the one hand, be viewed as exceptional and may now be slowing down to a more 'normal' level. On the other hand, internationalisation in economics, culture, social relations and so on does not seem to be waning in the long run. Consequently, it is unlikely that the accompanying need for regulation beyond the nation-state should suddenly diminish or disappear. It is therefore urgent to understand how law operates in an international environment. At its most fundamental, this is a question of how legal authority is established and exercised beyond the state.

* This research is funded by the Danish National Research Foundation Grant no. DNRF105 and conducted under the auspices of iCourts, the Danish National Research Foundation's Centre of Excellence for International Courts.
[1] For the most elaborate explanation of this, see K. Alter, *The New Terrain of International Law: Courts, Politics, Rights* (Princeton: Princeton University Press, 2014).
[2] For example, the election in the US of Donald Trump on a mostly nationalistic agenda, Britain's exit from the EU and nationalistic political parties on the rise in many countries in Europe.

In this chapter, I will discuss a small fragment of this larger question. My focus will be on international courts and their relation to law and politics and the question of how legal authority is established for international courts in this field. In discussing this relationship, I initially inquire into a controversy over the correct way to theorize authority and more precisely over whether there is a conceptual connection between legitimacy and authority or whether this connection is only contingent. Recent scholarship has attempted to approach authority as a value-neutral concept that can be made the object of a purely empirical inquiry.[3] I address the assumptions behind this approach and the accompanying critique of linking authority to legitimacy, which is driving the argument for a value-neutral conceptualization of authority. My conclusion is that the arguments in favour of value neutrality are not entirely convincing. Although value-neutral empirical studies are helpful in measuring one dimension of authority, there remains a value-laden component that relates to the normativity of authority understood as the authorized, and hence implicitly rightful, exercise of social power.[4]

Following this analysis, in Section 2 I consider whether legal authority of international courts can be gained through recourse to a view that law constitutes an exclusive, autonomous sphere of reasoning and that legal decision making is therefore somehow detached from or untainted by politics. In analysing the specific political context in which international courts operate, I argue that these courts must to some degree act in a politically diplomatic way because of the need to have their decisions accepted by other (domestic as well as international) institutions. Simultaneously, however, this politic must be articulated through legal reasoning for the court to retain its authority.

International courts need to reach out to what Karen Alter has called 'compliance partners'[5] (i.e., those persons/institutions whose agency is either helpful for – or necessary to – promoting compliance with the jurisprudence of international courts). By linking this observation to the type of law, which Günther Teubner has called 'reflexive',[6] I point out that successful international courts are characterized by their ability to build

---

[3] See the discussion of the work of Alter, Helfer and Madsen in Section 1.
[4] At the end of this chapter, I show how international courts attain this normative authority through their role as institutions that perform a function of critical validation of the political power exercised by sovereign states. I explain this via the theory of 'the career of authority' as developed by Alan Brudner, 'The Evolution of Authority', ch. 1 of this volume.
[5] Alter, New Terrain.
[6] See G. Teubner, 'Substantive and Reflexive Elements in Modern Law', Law and Society Review 17 (1983): 239–86.

consideration of the need for compliance into their choice of legal interpretation when making decisions. Following on from this, I argue, based
on an empirical study by Alec Stone Sweet and Thomas L. Brunell, that
international courts at their best use this reflexivity to operate as so-called
trustee courts.[7]

Finally, I conclude by showing how Stone Sweet and Brunell's empirical findings about trustee courts fit with Alan Brudner's notion of just
authority.[8] Ultimately, my argument is that long-term operational success
of international courts requires the pursuit of a kind of judicial politics
that render such courts legitimate in the sense described by Brudner –
that is, as institutions that help complete the justification of domestic
political authority.

1   Theorizing Authority: Facts and Values

The concepts of authority and legitimacy have been seen to be closely
related at least since Thomas Hobbes argued that any sovereign with the
capacity to maintain peace and public order and thereby retain a civil society was immediately legitimate by virtue of doing so and therefore ought
to be obeyed. It is also characteristic that the entries on both 'authority'
and 'political legitimacy' in the well-regarded *Stanford Encyclopedia of
Philosophy* discuss the relationship between these two concepts. Both
accounts, written by Tom Christiano and Fabienne Peter, respectively,
emphasize that there is no agreement among scholars about the precise
definition of the terms, and the two authors themselves seem to approach
the relationship between these concepts in different ways.

In some important recent literature on authority and international
courts, there is a tendency to try to strictly separate legitimacy from
authority by clearly distinguishing between *de facto* authority and legitimate authority. In their work from 2013, Birgit Peters and Johan Schaffer
argue that many attempts to conceptualize authority do so by connecting it so closely to legitimacy that 'legitimate authority' becomes a tautol-
ogy: if it is not legitimate, then it is not authoritative. This, according to
Peters and Schaffer, is problematic because it makes it difficult to criticize

---

[7] A. Stone Sweet and T. Brunell, 'Trustee Courts and the Judicialization of International
Regimes: The Politics of Majoritarian Activism in the ECHR, the EU, and the WTO', *Journal
of Law and Courts* 1 (2013): 61–88, esp. 64.
[8] See Brudner, 'Evolution of Authority'.

authorities for being illegitimate, and they therefore endorse divorcing authority from legitimacy. The authors say,

> Embedding legitimacy in the definition of authority may be both analytically and empirically problematic, especially if you want to theorize how international authority relates to resistance, mobilization and contestation … First, if legitimacy and authority are two sides of a coin, then the more authority an institution has, the more legitimate it must be. This runs counter to experience: sometimes institutions acquire authority over new issues without necessarily being seen as more legitimate by all actors. Second, the [conflation of authority and legitimacy] seems to deny the existence of illegitimate authority – which might seem troubling for both normative and conceptual reasons.[9]

There is much to agree with here, and others have endorsed this separation of normative justification and factual authority.[10] This, however, also produces problems at a conceptual level.

Fabienne Peter writes in her entry, 'Authority stands for a right to rule – a right to issue commands and, possibly, to enforce these commands using coercive power.'[11] This perception of what authority means can be traced back at least as far as Hobbes. On this view, then, an institution has authority if its use of force is legitimate. If it is illegitimate, it loses authority. Alter, Helfer and Madsen (referring, among others, to Peters and Schaffer) argue that an institution can retain authority without being legitimate. Alter, Helfer and Madsen put forward three reasons why authority and legitimacy should be separated. First, they contend that international courts (ICs) have an express legal competence usually based on a consensual act of delegation from states. But is a competence derived from a consensual act not a legitimate ground for ruling? If anything, this fact may justify that ICs have legitimacy by virtue of this consensual act; wherefore it is not necessary to inquire *further* into their legitimacy when one aims – as Alter, Helfer and Madsen do – to study the extent to which various groups and institutions accept ICs as authoritative. This consent, as they correctly point out, only provides *de jure* authority, not *de facto* authority – that is, it provides authority on paper but not in action. But the

---

[9] B. Peters and J. K. Schaffer, 'The Turn to Authority beyond States', *Transnational Legal Theory* 4 (2013): 315–35, esp. 316.

[10] See, for example, K. J. Alter, L. R. Helfer and M. R. Madsen, 'How Context Shapes the Authority of International Courts', *Law & Contemporary Problems* 79 (2016): 1–36, who quote the same passage (7).

[11] See P. Fabienne, 'Political Legitimacy', ed. E. N. Zalta, *Stanford Encyclopedia of Philosophy*, April 29, 2010, last modified April 24, 2017, https://plato.stanford.edu/entries/legitimacy/.

distinction between *de jure* and *de facto* is not overlapping with the distinction between consensual and non-consensual (act of delegation). In other words, if the formal *de jure* consent Alter, Helfer and Madsen refer to is not truly consensual in the sense of being a voluntary and informed act of accession, then it could be argued that what they refer to as *de facto* authority would instead be more appropriately conceptualized as an act of political power through which some government has been pressurized into signing an act of delegation. In such cases, it is difficult to see why compliance should be described as an act of accepting the authority of the international court and not as an act of submitting to political force. Their argument does not, in other words, establish that in *describing* authority, we *must* equate the formal *de jure* act of delegation with the existence of a voluntary and informed consent. Once we let go of this assumption, it becomes obvious that what Alter, Helfer and Madsen call *de facto* authority is not necessarily authority but could be viewed instead as various acts of compliance. For acts of compliance to be seen as acts of yielding to the authority of an international court, there must be some kind of evidence supporting that the compliant behaviour is indeed based on a view that the legal form through which the court has obtained its right to rule is also truly valid.

By starting from and taking for granted the *de jure* authority of international courts and then moving on to examine the *de facto* authority of these courts in terms of the extent to which the decisions of that court enjoys support and is embedded in actual socio-political agency, Alter, Helfer and Madsen introduce a conceptual bias to their empirical study. This is because they omit from their study the possibility that the agency through which this support and embedment takes place is driven by political submission of weaker states to a regime that these states do not genuinely accept as valid. The authors' very notion of authority prevents this inquiry from being relevant to their study.

Alter, Helfer and Madsen's second argument is restricted to simply setting out the aim of their inquiry. They say that they seek 'a straightforward and measurable yardstick to evaluate how a range of contextual factors shapes de facto authority of ICs via an analysis of audiences' practices toward ICs'.[12] This is fair enough. They wish to create a ground for empirically measuring what they call the '*de facto* authority'. But this is no conceptual argument, either; it is a stipulated delimitation of the concept of authority, tailored to the purposes of carrying out a specific

---

[12]   Alter, Helfer and Madsen, 'Context Shapes', 6

empirical study. Obviously, an empirical study of authority needs a concept of authority that lends itself to empirical studies, but having already settled on a specific methodology and then tailoring a concept to fit that study does not settle the conceptual dispute over how authority is best understood. It merely shows why the method that the authors have opted for cannot be reconciled with a normatively infused concept.

Third, in endorsing the argument from Peters and Schaffer, Alter, Helfer and Madsen say that the conceptual separation of legitimacy from authority makes it possible to see that an IC 'can do everything normative theorists might expect of a legitimate international judicial body and still not have authority in fact'.[13] What this means is that an IC can have formal legitimacy authority but still have no authority in fact, by which they mean that the IC has no cases, state parties do not comply with the IC's rulings or a similar kind of scenario. As I shall argue, this is an important insight that actually has normative ramifications. What Alter, Helfer and Madsen also say, however, is that 'the converse scenario – authority in fact, without normative legitimacy – is also possible'.[14] This is much more controversial, for it raises the following question: On what grounds does the authority of an illegitimate institution rest? My point here is that the authors do not identify any of the international courts they investigate as illegitimate; therefore, they never make any concrete claims about the authority of illegitimate institutions.

Peters and Schaffer are also troubled about how to descriptively handle the notion of 'illegitimate authority'. If legitimacy is tied closely to authority, then that seems to deny the existence of illegitimate authority. They seem to think that this makes it somehow impossible to put forward a critique of an institution, for if an institution has authority, it is legitimate. This is a misunderstanding. The very point of tying authority to legitimacy is precisely to normatively deny authority to the institution when it ceases to be legitimate. Peters and Schaffer, then, confuse the idea of a necessary *conceptual* connection between legitimacy and authority with the contingent *empirical* connection between authority and legitimacy. This is not to limit the scope of sociological or socio-legal inquiry but to apply a methodology of concept formation to one's theoretical apparatus and use this consistently to categorize what one empirically finds.

From this, I draw the conclusion that despite these recent attempts to separate legitimacy from authority, there still do not exist arguments that

---

[13] Ibid.
[14] Ibid.

have been entirely persuasive in settling the conceptual issues involved in defining the relationship between them. There remains some conceptual ambiguity in the field, even in the work of those who carefully try to explicate what they mean by authority. I do not take this to be a mark of academic inattention; rather, I think that the ambiguity stems from the nature of social life itself. Authority and legitimacy are complex concepts with long histories, and their roles in the organization of social life cannot be easily compressed to fit into a well-defined empirical study – even one that is as comprehensive and careful as the one carried out by Alter, Helfer and Madsen. The attempt to do so – and indeed the study by Alter, Helfer and Madsen, and others of a number of ICs and of how various compliance groups react to and support or disavow these ICs – is an impressive effort that reveals a lot about the authority of ICs.

The rest of this chapter could be seen as complementary to these studies, since the focus is on how *de facto* compliance relates to the issue of legal authority beyond the state in a more normative sense. Seen as a whole, I argue that international courts that are successful in maintaining an active jurisprudence and an active debate about the role of the court in the international community will gain authority by engaging in a practice of mutual validation, which involves the international court in question and the member states under its jurisdiction.

2 International Courts: Seeking Approval and Compliance through Strategic Interpretation

One of, if not *the* most debated issues in jurisprudence is over the relationship between law and morality. Proponents of legal positivism and legal idealism have for long disputed what the relationship is between legal and moral reason. More specifically, they have debated whether there is a necessary conceptual relationship between law and morality. Is law, properly understood, the morally justified use of force? Or is legal reason a specific and distinct form of practical reason that exists and can be exercised without presupposing any form of moral justification in relation to the use of force that is the consequence of legal decision making? This debate, to a large degree, resembles the debate over the relationship between authority and legitimacy.[15]

---

[15] See previous section in this chapter and also see Chapter 7 in this volume, A. Follesdal, 'The Legitimate Authority of International Courts and Its Limits: A Challenge to Raz's Service Conception?'; and Chapter 9 in this volume, M. Martin, 'The International Criminal Court: The New Leviathan?'

This classic debate has been fought out in the discipline of general jurisprudence, and so the debate has been conceptual and not attached to any
specific legal systems. Arguments have been taken to apply universally to
any jurisdiction, whether Danish law, English law, German law and so on.
However, it seems that this debate has been constructed almost exclusively –
perhaps unconsciously – with domestic law as the archetype of what a legal
system is. Very rarely, if ever, have examples or problems related to international law and/or international courts taken centre stage in the debates
in general jurisprudence. On the contrary, to the extent that international
law has been considered, the main question has been – as also expressed by
H. L. A. Hart in 1961 in *The Concept of Law* – whether international law
should be considered to be law at all.[16]

Today, there do not seem to be many who would contend that international law is not really law. Indeed, the turn towards an increased nationalistic orientation in politics I mentioned in the introduction seems to confirm
that international law is indeed law. If it was not, there would be no need to
act politically to try to remove it.

But while international law is law, it is also distinct from domestic law in
many ways. One important dimension of this follows from the emergence
of international courts and their role in regard to institutionalizing international law. In this section, I focus on how the political context of international courts differs from that of domestic courts and how that influences the
way international courts operate.

One basic and initial observation in regard to international courts
is that they are not part of a more traditional constitutional setup that
involves the distribution and separation of (what, from a domestic
constitutional viewpoint, is perceived as the totality of legal) powers.
International courts are established by international treaty, not by a constitutional event, and as a general principle, any state is free to withdraw
from the jurisdiction of an international court whenever it so wishes.[17]

---

[16] See M. Payandeh, 'The Concept of International Law in the Jurisprudence of H.L.A. Hart',
The European Journal of International Law 21 (2011): 967–91 for an analysis of Hart's view
of international law. See also P. Capps, *Human Dignity and the Foundations of International
Law* (Oxford: Hart, 2009), ch. 3.

[17] This could be said to follow from the principle of state sovereignty: just as states are free
to enter into treaties with other states, they are also free to sign out of such agreements.
Moreover, some courts are made operational only on a principle of voluntary jurisdiction,
which means that courts will only have the competence to adjudicate a conflict between
two states if both states accept that the court be granted competence to rule in the individual case at hand.

Moreover, most international courts have subject-specific competences (e.g., human rights, trade or regulating the sea), and although each must apply general international law, each court is not part of a systematic, hierarchically coordinated system of judicial institutions.[18] Furthermore, there is no centralized international enforcement system that ensures that decisions by international courts will be complied with (although states can enforce judgments and are even required to in some conditions).[19]

So while domestic courts are part of an existing constitutional system in which there is a background expectation (and legal duty) on the executive to enforce decisions from the domestic court, international courts need to rely on states to accept their jurisdictional competences. What is more, they also have to offer enforcement and implementation measures in a complex and sometimes legally fragmented context of international law more broadly.

Domestic courts are embedded in a political and legal context that generally presupposes and ensures a commitment to the rule of law.[20] International courts do not operate in quite the same context. International law surely is law, and international courts surely are an integrated part of the legal enterprise, but reasonable assumptions about how domestic courts operate in a domestic system of law cannot be directly transferred to international courts. Nor should one be led to believe that such assumptions will automatically be equally applicable to international courts generally or to any one specific international court. Instead, it should be noted that international law is a young phenomenon compared to state legal orders and that it is only very recently that international courts emerged as an integrated part of the structure of international law. As a sign of this youth, even the most established international courts cannot automatically expect full compliance from member states in the same way domestic courts can. International courts, then, rely to a much

---

[18] This situation is often referred to as the fragmentation of international law, a phenomenon that has given rise to much concern. See, for example, the International Law Commission's report from 2006, 'Fragmentation of International Law: Difficulties Arising from the Diversification and Expansion of International Law', Report of the Study Group of the International Law Commission, UN Doc. A/CN.4/L.682, Geneva, 13 April 2006. http://legal.un.org/ilc/documentation/english/a_cn4_l682.pdf

[19] See Payandeh, 'Concept of International Law', for a further discussion of this.

[20] The rule of law is of course a complex notion, but see T. Bingham, *The Rule of Law* (London: Penguin, 2011), for an accessible yet nuanced and serious account of what that notion entails.

larger extent than domestic courts on the political willingness of states to submit to their decisions. States do not automatically accept and implement the decisions in quite the same way they would for decisions from domestic courts.[21] As a consequence, ICs must actively attempt to leverage acceptance from states. Or rather, they must attempt to leverage support either from agents within a given state or, as Karen Alter explains, by appealing to political actors outside the state to pressure governments to comply: 'International judges may not be able to call upon centralized tools of coercion to enforce their rulings, but they can often call upon legal and political actors around the world to pressure governments to respect international law as defined by IC rulings.'[22]

---

[21] As an illustration of this claim, one could point to the reception of decisions from the ECtHR, whose judgments are undoubtedly legally binding on member states according to the convention. (Article 46 of the convention requires states to 'abide by the final judgment of the Court in any case where they are parties'.) Still the UK – acting through its Supreme Court – nevertheless openly declares that ECtHR decisions may be challenged when the Supreme Court finds that they do not sufficiently appreciate or accommodate particular aspects of UK's legal practices (*in casu* criminal procedure). See 'Relationship with the European Court of Human Rights', The Supreme Court and Europe, www.supremecourt .uk/about/the-supreme-court-and-europe.html. What this means is that the highest judicial authority in the UK considers itself competent to 'decline to follow' decisions by an international court (*in casu* ECtHR). According to s.2(1) of the Human Rights Act passed in 1998 by the UK Parliament, UK courts are required to take account of any relevant Strasbourg judgments or opinions when determining a question in connection with the convention rights, but decisions of the ECtHR are not binding in the strict sense of the word. For a discussion of the extent to which lower UK courts may depart from precedents set by higher UK courts when such precedents are clearly at odds with ECtHR practice, see S. D. Pattinson, 'The Human Rights Act and the Doctrine of Precedent', *Legal Studies* 35 (2015): 142–64. The example given here is not unusual. For a long time in the EU, it has been the case that both the Court of Justice of the European Union (CJEU) and member states' supreme courts have, each within their own jurisdiction and from their own point of view, declared themselves as the highest judicial authority with respect to the applicability of EU law. See the *Costa v. Enel* and *Simmenthal* decisions by the CJEU (formerly ECJ) and, for example, decisions by the German Constitutional Court in the so-called Solange cases, most recently the *Brunner* case (also referred to as the *Maastricht* case and as *Solange III*), BVerfGE 89, 155. In a more open example of political discontent, the Zimbabwean government in 2008 'declined to follow' the landmark decision of the South African Development Community (SADC) Tribunal in the *Campbell* case (*Campbell and others v. Zimbabwe*, Case No. SADC [T] 2/2007, 28 November 2008) and instead mobilized resistance towards the court in the governments of neighbouring countries, leading to the suspension of the court in 2010. Most recently, the Danish Supreme Court, in the so-called *Ajos* case, has openly refused to follow a CJEU ruling, which it has described as *ultra vires*. See M. R. Madsen, H. P. Olsen and U. Sadl, 'Competing Supremacies and Clashing Institutional Rationalities: The Danish Supreme Court's Decision in the Ajos Case and the National Limits of Judicial Cooperation', *European Law Journal* 17 (2017): 140–50.

[22] Alter, *New Terrain*, 10.

Making their judgments widely available, writing press releases, publishing annual reports, and so on are all methods ICs can use to make their activities visible, thereby activating the international environment – for example, NGOs and international organisations – by appealing to respect for the rule of law. Importantly, the same strategy can be applied to ICs' relationships with domestic agents: 'The problem for ICs is that governments can choose not to comply, defending noncompliance as consistent with the domestic rule of law. Moreover, domestic populations may actually prefer noncompliance with international agreements. But where domestic actors are unhappy about government violations of international agreements, and even where populations are mostly indifferent, ICs can work with domestic and transnational interlocutors to either orchestrate compliance or construct counter-pressures that alter the political balance in favour of policies that better cohere with international legal obligations.'[23] Karen Alter refers to those domestic agents who collaborate with ICs in leveraging acceptance for IC rulings as 'compliance partners.'

But relying on compliance partners *after* a judgment has been made is not the only course of action available to ICs. And noncompliance is not the only problem international courts can face. ICs may face the harder problem of open threats to their existence. Decisions that governments find very controversial and problematic can lead to direct political opposition and attempts to remove the court.[24] In order to avoid such a situation, an international court may think about how states will react to its decisions *before* making them. Doing so may involve adjusting its legal reasoning to the political preferences of the states on whose support it depend for its continued existence. The judges of an IC may therefore have to either apply the law in its pure form to the legal problem they have been asked to rule on and disregard the political consequences of their ruling; or they can seek to cater their legal judgments to the political demands of the states when they perceive that such an action is necessary to avoid retaliation and disbandment, and thereby can make it generally acceptable for states to not adhere to their rulings. Both of these options threatens to undermine a strict version of the rule of law (either through a politicisation of judicial decision making or a disregard for the legal regime set up around the IC in question).[25]

---

[23] Ibid., 20.
[24] See H. P. Olsen, 'Fidelity to International Law: On International Law and Politics', *Ethical Rationalism and the Law*, ed. in P. Capps and S. D. Pattinson (Oxford: Hart, 2017).
[25] Olsen, 'Fidelity to International Law'.

Handling this kind of dilemma, I suggest, requires a form of reflexive law. This is a form of law that allows judges to be responsive to inputs from those subject to legal regulation. It is this reflexive rationale that underpins a judicial strategy that makes it possible for ICs to build and sustain the trust that is necessary for the courts to become institutions in their own right – that is, to become authoritative legal institutions beyond the state. Legal authority on this view is both normative and factual: it is normative because it is embedded in an ethos of rule of law, which it aims to uphold under challenging circumstances; it is factual because in doing so, it constantly negotiates political support for itself. The IC will gain authority beyond the state when it succeeds in sustaining its own life as an institution with a rationale that aims at implementing the treaty complex that has brought it to life. Legal authority beyond the state, then, is achieved when the rationale of an international court is normatively embedded in a rule of law ethos and when, simultaneously, the court is successful in achieving state support for that role. Or to put it more succinctly, it is precisely the sensitivity to politics *per se* that allows an IC to transcend the political and build its own specific interpretations of what international law requires, thereby becoming a legal authority beyond the state.[26]

This view of how ICs practice international law resonates with the theoretically more general notion of 'reflexive law' that was developed in an article published in *Law and Society Review* in 1983 by Günther Teubner.[27] Although not aimed at explaining international law or international courts – his article addresses features of reflexivity in contemporary forms of law (sometimes described by the author as emerging features) drawn from examples in domestic law (e.g., labour law; consumer law) – the notion of reflexivity in law as set out in this general theory fits well with the explanation I have just given. Teubner states that reflexive law is a type of law that is characterized mainly by (1) focusing on controlling self-regulation as opposed to regulating directly through substantive intervention and (2) being procedure oriented rather than rule or purpose oriented.[28] The European Court of Human Rights (ECtHR) may immediately appear as regulating directly (e.g., setting up requirements for states that they must allow their citizens freedom of speech on sensitive political

---

[26] See also H. P. Olsen, 'International Courts and the Doctrinal Channels of Legal Diplomacy', *Transnational Legal Theory* 6 (2015): 661–80.
[27] See G. Teubner, 'Substantive and Reflexive Elements in Modern Law', *Law and Society Review* 17 (1983): 239–86.
[28] Ibid., 257, table 1.

and religious issues) and being purpose oriented (the purpose here being the pursuit of fundamental political freedom and equality for all citizens in the member-states). However, the political and institutional context of the court, makes it clear that it is operating much more on the reflexive law model. Focusing on self-regulation, for example, is a predominant feature of the way the court communicates with compliance partners. As has been showed in previous research, the courts uses instruments such as a policy of variable intensity of review to promote self-regulation mechanisms.[29] Also with regards to the characteristic of focusing on pro-cedure, it has long been acknowledged that the court has been leading a 'proceduralization of substantive rights' policy, which is designed to move the focus away from difficult issues of attending to and balancing delicate fundamental rights problems to a focus on the issue of what procedures states may engage with in order to secure proper attention to and action for protecting fundamental rights in a way that conforms with the con-vention requirements.[30]

Teubner, in drawing a larger theoretical picture, boils the vision of the role of the legal order under a reflexive law regime down to the follow-ing: 'Law realizes its own reflexive orientation insofar as it provides the structural premises for reflexive processes in other social subsystems.'[31] While this is written in the context of broader social theory derived from Jürgen Habermas (on legitimation crisis) and Niklas Luhmann (on autopoietic subsystems), it is not difficult to see that this works well as a description of how the ECtHR's judgments establish reflexive processes in the intersection between domestic politics and international and domes-tic law (via compliance partners).

This kind of reflexivity promotes precisely the kind of sensitivity to compliance partners that is necessary for an international court to obtain a large degree of de facto authority as defined by Alter, Helfer and Madsen.[32] Simultaneously, this reflexive approach to international law, as it seeks to promote compliance with international law in(side) domestic

---

[29] H. P. Olsen 'International courts and the doctrinal channels of legal diplomacy', *Transnational Legal Theory*, 6: 3–4, (2015) 661–680; J. Rivers, 'Proportionality and Variable Intensity of Review', *Cambridge Law Journal* 65 (2006): 174–207; L. Helfer, 'Redesigning the European Court of Human Rights: Embeddedness as a Deep Structural Principle of the European Human Rights Regime', *European Journal of International Law* 19 (2008): 125–59.

[30] See, for example, J. Christoffersen, *Fair Balance: A Study of Proportionality, Subsidiarity and Primarity in the European Convention on Human Rights* (Leiden: Martinus Nijhoff, 2009).

[31] Teubner, 'Substantive and Reflexive Elements', 275.

[32] See Section 1 in this chapter.

political communities, often achieves *normative* authority. The very same processes that are used to leverage compliance are what promotes normative acceptance of the role of the court.

In the following and concluding sections, I shall show how empirical findings about the capacity of ICs to operate as international legal authorities, square with the normative role these institutions, when at their best, can have in creating justified legal authority.

3   International Trustee Courts and Just Authority

In international relations theory, it is customary to model the relationship between international agencies and states along the lines of a principal-agent model. In this model, states are principals that decide to delegate some of their powers to international agencies, which are then perceived as agents of the states. Agents carry out the will of their principals because their principals (the states) will disempower them if they act in contravention of their principals' interests. This model has been used numerous times to explain the behaviour of international agencies, including international courts.[33] In line with both positivistic conceptions of law and rational choice theory, this invites an image of international law as one of contractual interaction among states. Accordingly, states will pursue their own interests vis-à-vis other states, and sometimes they will do so through the means of agreements with other states. International law in this view, then, consists of contracts between states, and the role of international courts is to adjudicate conflicts on the basis of the common contractual will of states as set out in international treaties.[34] Decisions that involve customary international law amount to more or less the same thing, except in this case, the treaty is unwritten: it emerges from common state practice and a common, subjective attitude towards this practice.

This simple image of international law takes state action as the primary source of law and adjudication. Such an image corresponds well with the emergence of international law as portrayed by Koskenniemi in *The Gentle*

---

[33] See, for example, Carruba et al., 'Judicial Behavior under Political Constraints: Evidence from the European Court of Justice', *American Political Science Review* 102 (2008): 435.

[34] See also, for example, Article 31 of the Vienna Convention of the Law of Treaties, which sets out a principle for the interpretation of treaties that resembles principles of interpretation in contract law. Decisions that involve customary international law amount to more or less the same thing, except in this case, the treaty is unwritten: it emerges from common state practice and a common subjective attitude towards this practice.

Civilizer of Nations from the politics of diplomatic relations.[35] It does not, however, correspond particularly well with more contemporary practices and understandings of international law,[36] and especially not with the new regime of international law,[37] in which international courts and the adjudicative activity surrounding them have built rather dense legal practices in some areas of law.[38] This development has resulted in a situation where the identification of the social practices addressed by international legal regulation can no longer be narrowly identified with the expressions of

[35] See, for example, Koskenniemi's description of Lauterpacht's reaction to his predecessors' perception of doctrine in international law, which Lauterpacht sees as partly responsible for the international development that led to the First World War. Koskenniemi writes, 'Lauterpacht's early work is written in the form of a doctrinal polemic against a voluntarist and state-centered "positivism," castigated as the main obstacle on the way to universal legal organization ... In order to constrain politics, one had to develop better doctrines. The problem, Lauterpacht held, was the low level of ambition in pre-war doctrine; its readiness to compromise with aggressive nationalism and to leave a large field of activity – such as the right to wage war – outside legal regulation. Lauterpacht's constructive work was directly aimed at such self-amputation.' M. Koskenniemi, *The Gentle Civilizer of Nations* (Cambridge: Cambridge University Press, 2001), 363. The 'low level of ambition' identified by Lauterpacht in the work of his predecessors should be assessed, however, in the light of tradition. As D. Armitage explains in *Foundations of Modern International Thought* (Cambridge: Cambridge University Press, 2013), legal thinking since Hobbes has been so closely identified with the state and the idea of sovereignty that international relations could not, for a long time, be considered as legal in any positivistic sense. For international law to be law in the positivistic sense required decoupling of the state from the concept of law in order to sustain the proposition that international relations could have the character of law (international law). The 'self-amputation' Lauterpacht refers to is therefore not an accurate metaphor – those early writers did not have a body from which they could amputate anything. Instead, they were involved in attempting to build that body.

[36] For a contemporary view on how non-state actors are participating in international law practices, see, for example, J. d'Aspremont, ed., *Participants in the International Legal System: Multiple Perspectives on Non-state Actors in International Law* (London: Routledge, 2012). For a contemporary view on the relationship between international law and domestic law and politics, see Alter, *New Terrain*.

[37] See Alter, *New Terrain*.

[38] Benedict Kingsbury observes that there is an uneven judicialization of international law. See B. Kingsbury, 'International Courts: Uneven Judicialization in Global Order', in *Cambridge Companion to International Law*, ed. J. Crawford and M. Koskenniemi (Cambridge: Cambridge University Press, 2011). As a response to Kingsbury, it is worth noting that despite this unevenness, some legal fields, which have been the objects of intense judicialization, have legal as well as political consequences beyond the immediate scope of those fields. Hence human rights jurisprudence has become important for many issues in criminal law, administrative law and even welfare law. Furthermore, case law from regional human rights courts (e.g., the ECtHR) seems to become increasingly important at other human rights courts around the world.

governing elites in official documents.[39] What this means more concretely is that the meaning of international law cannot be reduced to, or controlled by, governments. International institutions such as international courts are participating in interpretive processes whereby they provide autonomous input to the meaning of a particular rule of international law at a given time in a given context.[40] This new situation raises the question of how normative authority can be both factually sustained and normatively justified.

Almost all theories on the justification of public power take as their starting point the ability of rational agents to voluntarily enter into covenants, whereby they agree to protection from the vicissitudes in life in return for some submission to public authority. Many if not all of these theories ultimately seek to justify the authority of the modern state by appealing to some version of democracy and human rights welded together in a foundational constitution that enjoys popular support. States may be more or less perfect in realizing the full justificatory potential in this. Elections may be flawed, human rights might not be respected to the fullest extent and so on. And in states where citizens are not protected by their public authorities, those authorities might ultimately be considered as unjustified and hence not authorities at all.

On this classic normative view, authority is closely connected to justification. No justification means no authority, and hence no legitimate basis. In this situation, individuals remain individuals – they will not be able to occupy offices, since no such offices can truly exist without justification.

In his contribution to this book, Alan Brudner outlines what he calls the career of authority. He describes the evolution from the most basic to the most advanced and freedom-enhancing forms of authority one can imagine. In analysing the various forms of authority-based relationships between ruler and ruled, he distinguishes between *de facto* authority, *de jure* authority, *legitimate* authority, *constitutional* authority and finally *just* authority. It is specifically in relation to the latter and penultimate form of authority that Brudner discusses the role of international law and international legal institutions (more specifically, he focuses on the International

[39] Jutta Brunée and Stephen J. Toope, *Legitimacy and Legality in International Law* (Cambridge: Cambridge University Press, 2010), 56.
[40] See J. Merrills, 'International Adjudication and Autonomy', in *International Organizations and the Idea of Autonomy: Institutional Independence in the International Legal Order*, ed. R. Collins and N. D. White (New York: Routledge, 2011); See also I. Venzke, *How Interpretation Makes International Law* (Oxford: Oxford University Press, 2012).

Criminal Court [ICC]) in relation to the classic perception of sovereign states as the embodiment of public authority. Brudner writes,

> Many see in the ICC and the doctrine of humanitarian intervention as evidence of the passing of the Westphalian system of sovereign states toward a new international order. Rawls, for example, sees these innovations as products of a distinct law of peoples posing external limits on internal sovereignty. Others see them as means by which international law manages the pathologies of a system of sovereign states the law otherwise validates – pathologies presumably curable only in a world without sovereigns ... If the account given here is correct, then these views are mistaken. Humanitarian interventions in defence of human rights as well as the ICC's compulsory jurisdiction enforce sovereignty's internal limits; they do not curb despotic sovereignty from outside. They thus signify the passing only of a certain conception of the Westphalian idea – one according to which a state's unqualified external sovereignty is independent of the stage of maturity of its internal sovereignty. They are not evidence of the transience of state sovereignty as such. Just domestic authorities are unqualifiedly sovereign both internally and externally, for there is no juristic reason for resistance to, or intervention in, a just state. Nor is the international protection of human rights explicable in terms of the pathologies of state sovereignty; on the contrary, it reflects the maturation of domestic sovereignty in the well-ordered constitutional state.[41]

More generally, Brudner's convincing argument is that international checks on the behaviour of individuals – whether citizens or officials – serve the purpose of upholding and perfecting state sovereignty. International law should not be viewed as an intrusion into domestic legal orders but as a necessary validation exercise of the authority of those orders. I can think of no better way to explain this than through another quote from Brudner's chapter in this book. In reading it, it will be useful to think of 'the outsider' as an international institution inhabited by individuals that do not (necessarily) belong to the community in which the public authority we discuss (i.e., state sovereignty) is situated. Brudner explains,

> The breakdown of communitarian constitutionalism reveals a further desideratum of an ideal recognition between authority and subject. There must somehow be a covenant of mutual recognition between the representatives of a common way of life and the outsider. Outsiders must acknowledge the authority of a way of life that values their outsider status, and the political community must defer to the outsider's independence for the sake of its validation as the individual's natural end. This, however,

sounds impossibly paradoxical. What sort of communal way of life can defer to the outsider for confirmation of its natural authority? ... The answer lies behind us – along the road already travelled and in the constitutional orders sojourned in. As before, the way forward is to reflect on the failures of the past, but this time on the past conceived as a logically continuous narrative about the solitary self's education to the political ground of its fulfilled independence and about the ruler's education to the full conditions of it valid authority. The community that engages the outsider as an equal partner comprises in logical sequence all instances of the ideal form of recognition produced by the *apolitical* (atomistic) individual as it journeys from presumed self-sufficiency to the constitution of liberty to the constitution of equality to the ethos constitution to the comprehensive constitution sufficient for independence. Through this *curriculum*, the community ordered by the comprehensive constitution – the constitution embracing the previous three as distinctive parts of a whole – is validated as the independence-seeker's final end by one who initially claims independence outside community. Reciprocally, that community values the outsider's moral independence as that through which its end-status is confirmed by an independent adversary. Let me call the way of life instituted by the covenant between the political community and the outsider the life of the dialogical community.[42]

Public authority in the form of state sovereignty is then ultimately validated by its capacity to engage with international institutions, and those international courts in turn similarly gain authority (beyond the state) by *their* capacity to communicate with sovereigns.

This resonates well with Hart's critique of what may be called the sovereignty-based objection to international law.[43] This objection is fuelled by the idea that a state cannot be sovereign and be bound by law at the same time. This assumed inconsistency is based on the supposition that the sovereign is, by definition, above the law. Hart rejects this assumption in his critique of Austin in the introductory chapters of *The Concept of Law* (by showing that 'the sovereign' is also subject to law) and then applies this insight in the context of international law. Following Hart's critique, and resonating with Brudner's arguments, one can agree that sovereignty exists only within the limits of international law and only to the extent that the rules of international law, when applied reflexively (see Section 2), validate state sovereignty. Hart's and Brudner's analyses, in other words, converge in an attempt to set valid law above political domination, or in Brudner's terminology, just authority above lower forms of

---

[42] Ibid., 48–49.
[43] See H. L. A. Hart, *The Concept of Law* (1961; Oxford: Oxford University Press, 2012), 220ff.

authority. Ultimately, therefore, international law is not only a matter for states. International law seeks to regulate state behaviour for the purposes of facilitating diplomatic comity among ruling elites and (increasingly) enhancing the explicit and implicit values that attach *to* human civility *for* the benefit of civil society. Interestingly, this view of what *justifies* the role of international law has recently been found to also factually sustain the support for and hence the continued existence of international courts.

Some of the most recent research on international courts confirms that they do in fact operate successfully by functioning as institutions that validate state sovereignty by reflexively examining domestic law. In their study of majoritarian activism[44] in three international courts, Stone Sweet and Brunell conclude, among other things, that decisions in these courts (which they call 'trustee courts'[45]) are based not only on state preferences but also on 'relevant social beliefs and practices as they evolve'[46] and that these courts manage to base their decisions on such broader bases because they engage in dialogue with the regime's beneficiaries.[47]

Trustee courts can escape submission to narrow government interests and instead engage more broadly with the regime of values they are set up to protect and relate those values to the underlying interests of citizens' social beliefs and practices because these courts are tasked with the job of

[44] Majoritarian activism is a term that is coined by Miguel Maduro, former general advocate at the CJEU and, at the time of this writing, professor at the European University Institute. See M. P. Maduro, *We, the Court: The European Court of Justice and the European Economic Constitution* (Portland, OR: Hart, 1998). The term refers to the disposition of judges to produce rulings that reflect outcomes that states might adopt under majoritarian, but not unanimity, decision rules. According to Stone Sweet and Brunell, 'The strategy helps these courts manage judicialization, mitigate the legitimacy problems associated with judicial lawmaking under supremacy, and render efforts at curbing the growth of their authority improbable or ineffective'. Stone Sweet and Brunell, 'Trustee Courts', 64.

[45] Trustee courts are defined as courts that operate 'in an unusually permissive zone of discretion', which 'is determined by the sum of competences explicitly delegated to a court and possessed as a result of its own lawmaking, minus the sum of control instruments available for use by the principals [in a principal-agent relationship] to override the court or to curb it in other ways' (Stone Sweet and Brunell, 'Trustee Courts', 65). In line with what I suggested previously, Stone Sweet and Brunell explain that many constitutional courts have an exceptional position within political polities, which allows them to legitimately overturn legislative acts, thereby creating a difficult obstacle for governments who must carry out constitutional revisions in order to pass the legislative act in question.

[46] Ibid., 86.

[47] Ibid. Beneficiaries are those who benefit from human rights protection (ECtHR), free movement (EU) and trade liberalization (WTO). Dialogue is made possible through adjudicative processes in which the parties and the court collaborate in collecting information about relevant social and legal practices in the member states.

applying and interpreting legal norms. It is precisely in their exercise of this capacity that courts get involved in the politics of legal diplomacy I have outlined in the previous sections.

Stone Sweet and Brunell explain that a trustee court can only emerge if states accept that legal meaning is (at least partly) constructed through adjudication. This entails that states must be willing to accept that the legal meaning of terms and distinctions in international law may evolve over time and that this evolution may be determined by international courts. Furthermore, if this is accepted, it entails that states must be willing to use prior decisions from the courts in their legal reasoning in present cases.[48] For this situation to occur, the court must build a relationship of trust with state governments. Only if states trust that international courts will apply the law responsibly and in good faith will these courts be able to develop the authority necessary to become trustee courts.

Building such trust and authority cannot be done in an instant or be established by a single decision. Instead, an international court must build authority and acceptance over time, by gradually making decisions that give them increased influence. When successful, trustee courts meet the aspirations of congruence and legal rationality in the broadest sense, thereby helping states become the best version of themselves.

4 Conclusion

I began this chapter with a description of the current trend towards an increasing nationalism in politics. I end with the observation that international law is perhaps the best instrument available to temper and validate national sovereignty. Our world is not a flat surface that extends into an infinite space. It is round and interrelated in more ways that we can immediately see from the viewpoint of one individual or one state. Such a world needs global governance, but we do not have a global government and it seems unlikely that we will ever get one. But the need for governance persists. The best anyone can do is to assemble what bits and pieces of knowledge we have about law, politics and society and merge these fragments into an attempt at conceptualizing some sustainable form of global governance.

Assembling the inputs from what I consider to be among the best scholarship in the field, I have attempted to outline how insights from

---

[48] K. Pelc, 'The Politics of Precedent in International Law: A Social Network Application', *American Political Science Review* 108 (2014): 547–64.

sociology- and political science–driven analyses of the authority of international courts can be married to the more normative approach associated with jurisprudence and legal science (or some specific strands of these), producing important new insights. The result of this examination shows that there is a precarious but valuable relationship between sovereign states and international law.

By analysing this relationship through the prism of international courts and their role in sustaining international law, I hope to have contributed to the foundation of practical knowledge that will be useful for future deliberation in regard to establishing good global governance.

4

Semantic Authority, Legal Change and the Dynamics of International Law

INGO VENZKE*

Introduction

The Achilles' heel of large parts of international legal theory and doctrine is its surprisingly static view of international law. That rather static view, I submit, is the product of a twofold mythical imagery. First, lawmaking is pictured to be a matter of sources. The law springs from dark and hidden places into daylight in an act of natural production. Second, interpretations of the law downstream are understood as an act of consumption and use. Legal doctrine further distinguishes between, on the one hand, applying the law where it is clear for everyone to see and, on the other, acts of interpretation where the waters are muddy. In the latter case of interpretation, it is necessary to first dry up the law that had been enacted earlier to then apply it. The act of interpretation turns out to looks like an act of archaeology – of recovery rather than creation. Changes in the law are confined to changes that come about through the sources of law, not through interpretation. While there may be some dynamism in the law as a result, it is rather limited. With cumbersome processes of treaty making and changes in customary law at glacial speed, international law seems to be rather static. But that view from large parts of theory and doctrine is at odds with the reality of legal change.

Of course, there are many exceptions to such a static view of international law that confines the creation of law to that one-time act when, at its source, the law sees the light of day. And in present legal theory, the understanding is indeed rare that the act of interpretations only unearths

* This is a revised version of an article under the same title published in *No Foundations: An Interdisciplinary Journal of Law and Justice* 12 (2015): 24–44. I am grateful to the participants of the workshop on 'International Jurisprudence: Rethinking the Concept of Law', at iCourts, Copenhagen, December 2014, and especially to this volume's editors, for their valuable comments.

the law that is already out there, ready to be discovered and used. The jurisgenerative, lawmaking side of interpretation is widely recognized. But that recognition is only the beginning. It continues to stir controversies and it comes with profound challenges that branch out into three sets of questions: normative, sociological and doctrinal.

First, it is not convincing to recognize the lawmaking side of legal practice and to simply call every act that contributes to the making of law a source of law. It does not follow from the recognition of judicial lawmaking, for example, that the decisions of international courts and tribunals should be understood as sources of law. The theory and doctrine of sources is part of a normative construction. Sources doctrine distributes blessings. What kinds of acts and whose acts should be allowed to serve as a basis for claims about (il)legality, formally speaking? In international law, the close connection between sources doctrine and ideas about legitimate order is clear to see in the interactions between nationalism and mainstream positivism, which promises to tie international law to the state as the exclusive reference point for legitimate order. If either that promise does not hold or the foundation of nationalism is shaking, what should stand in its place? One can simply not draw normative conclusions from the mere recognition of factors that are influential in shaping international law.

Second, concerning the sociological set of questions, it might be possible to understand and describe legal change and dynamics without getting into questions about normative foundations – for example, judicial decisions have an effect on the development of the law and serve as reference points in legal arguments, not unlike international treaties, despite the uncertainties as to whether judicial decisions should be treated as legal sources of law. It might be that legal practice shapes rules of recognition. That has been H. L. A. Hart's prominent proposition. But that proposal seems to overlook the fact that the social practice is also shaped by normative considerations. Any attempt at making sense of it is bound to buy into one or another idea of legitimate order. There is a tangible resistance to recognizing a legal act – an international judicial decision, to stick to that example – as a source of law even if legal practice fights about its meaning as if that decision had the same legal status as the distant treaty that formally serves as the basis for claims about (il)legality. Such resistance only makes sense in light of the normative retardation that fights against the swift resignation to sociological facts. It is thus not so much that sociological inquiry can push the normative set of questions aside, even if it can contextually inform them. Rather, the sociological set of questions opens other promising inquiries. Above all, it centres normative questions on an assessment of who enjoys authority over what the law says and what it is that sustains this authority.

Third, the doctrinal set of questions is traditionally placed at the intersections between normative and descriptive claims. This is what makes doctrine so weak and so strong, so vulnerable and so resistant.[1] It can be discarded by suggesting that its view of things is either unjust or out of touch with reality. For example, 'The nation-state has long lost its innocence and other actors, such as international organizations, should be recognized as lawmaking subjects', or, 'It is artificial to deny that international judicial decisions are, in fact, a source of law'. Conversely, both normative theory and sociological observation can support legal doctrine. For instance, 'Governments, at least those democratically accountable, are the most legitimate actors on the international plane and international law should thus be tied to their input. International agreements should form the basis of claims about (il)legality, not the decisions of a group of international judges', or 'Even if judges make law, the way they do so differs from treaty making. Legal discourse also treats a judicial precedent differently from a treaty provision.' At the junctures between normative theory and sociological observation, issues of legal doctrine include questions about how to legally frame the power that an actor exercises in making law that is not captured in the imagery of sources doctrine or of interpretation.

In this chapter, I wish to further develop the concept of semantic authority in response to the observation that many actors impact the dynamic development of international law through their practice. I build on an understanding of semantic authority as actors' capacity to find recognition for their claims about international law and to establish reference points for legal discourse that other actors can hardly escape.[2] The concept, I submit, has the potential of capturing sociological insight. Rather than immediately conveying a normative judgment, it (re)directs attention and guides normative inquiry. The understanding of authority here is one that stands in the tradition of public authority,

---

[1] Thus it is at this juncture between fact and norm that Jürgen Habermas sets up the concept of *Rechtsgeltung*, of legal *validity*. J. Habermas, *Between Facts and Norms: Contributions to a Discourse Theory of Law and Democracy* (Cambridge: Polity Press, 1996), 28–41.

[2] I. Venzke, 'Between Power and Persuasion: On International Institutions' Authority in Making Law', *Transnational Legal Theory* 4 (2013): 354–73.

öffentliche Gewalt or *puissance publique* – authority as capacity, not as a normative reason for action.[3] At the same time, my choice is for the concept of authority rather than power or violence – authority as a capacity that requires legitimacy. This chapter's primary ambition, in other words, is to offer sociological reflection to support normative inquiries into the legitimacy of international lawmaking.

The notion of semantic authority highlights the dynamics of international law against the backdrop of an otherwise rather static picture. It adds dynamism in distinct ways. First of all, it is attuned to thinking of international legal practice as a jurisgenerative process, a communicative practice in which actors struggle for the law and make law.[4] Second, semantic authority certainly shifts. At its core, it is sustained by a social expectation that a legal argument somehow needs to deal with it. Semantic authority is the product of dynamics in which one actor might evoke it and another cannot get away from it. It is thanks to the twofold move from sources to communicative practice, on the one hand, and from rules that allocate legal competences to shifting semantic authority, on the other, that international law appears in a much more dynamic and realistic light. All this becomes clearer in light of a brief set of examples that paints the scenery of semantic authority and of a dynamic international law (Section 1).

In what follows, I will develop and support the thesis that international law is best understood as the product of communicative processes in which different actors with varying degrees of semantic authority struggle for the law. For that purpose, I will summarily review the shift from sources toward communicative practices and highlight how existing approaches in this vein have understood legal dynamics. I argue for a conception of lawmaking in communicative practice that transcends divides between actor-centred and structural approaches. It is precisely the relationship between actors and their strategic environment that contains the dynamics for change (Section 2). Moving on from the shift toward lawmaking in communicative practice, I zoom in on the dynamic construction of authority, focusing on how it is produced in legal discourse. The argument continues to be embedded in an understanding of lawmaking in communicative practice and thus focuses from among the many factors that shape authority on those that connect to the language of international law

---

[3] A. von Bogdandy, M. Goldmann and I. Venzke, 'From Public International Law to International Public Law: Translating World Public Opinion into International Public Authority', *European Journal of International Law* 28 (2017): 115–45.

[4] R. M. Cover, 'Nomos and Narrative', *Harvard Law Review* 97 (1983): 4–68, esp. 11–16.

itself. How does that language sustain the authority that contributes to its change (Section 3)? The conclusions move from these points of sociological reflection to the normative implications. I will clarify how exactly the next steps have a normative purport and which directions they might take (Section 4).

1   An Exemplary, Scenic Overview

Many contemporary theories approach international law with a shift in emphasis from the sources of law toward the communicative practices in which a plethora of actors use, claim and speak international law. The scenery is not that of legal sources and the state actors that the received wisdom of sources doctrine accentuates; the scenery is characterized by a notable increase in forms of law, in the nature legal instruments and in the scope of relevant actors. A brief set of examples may clarify this point of departure. To first illustrate why thinking about international law has moved from sources to communicative practices, one may consider the distinction between 'combatants' and 'civilians', which lies at the core of international humanitarian law and appears, among other places, in many different provisions of the 1949 Geneva Conventions. In order to 'know the law' it is necessary to ask what it means to be a combatant or a civilian. That answer cannot be gleaned from the text itself but needs to be sought in legal practice. The meaning of the terms does not lie in or behind the text of the Geneva Conventions; it is the product of communicative practices that uses these terms.[5] These practices are not limited to state representatives who sign international treaties but include the opinions of military advisers, cases from domestic courts, the jurisprudence of international (criminal) courts and tribunals, statements of the International Committee of the Red Cross (ICRC), interventions by nongovernmental organizations (NGOs) such as Human Rights Watch, as well as the arguments of prominent legal scholars.[6]

---

[5] The deeper theoretical underpinnings are those of the linguistic turn, developments in hermeneutics and semantic pragmatism, most of which follows on the heels of Ludwig Wittgenstein's resonating observation that 'the meaning of a word is its use in language'. L. Wittgenstein, *Philosophical Investigations*, trans. G. E. M. Anscombe (Oxford: Blackwell, 1958), 43.

[6] See, in detail, I. Venzke, 'Legal Contestation about "Enemy Combatants": On the Exercise of Power in Legal Interpretation', *Journal of International Law & International Relations* 5 (2009): 155–84.

The extent to which any one of those actors contributes to the making of international (humanitarian) law by shaping what either *combatant* or *civilian* means depends on his semantic authority – the capacity to establish reference points for legal discourse that other actors can hardly escape. Whether he enjoys such authority, and to what degree he enjoys it, in turn depends on myriad factors. Those factors may still be grouped in the classic tripartite division of any authority's legitimacy bases, connecting to (legal) rationality, tradition or personal and institutional esteem.[7] Semantic authority, like the law that it shapes, is a product of struggle. It is clear to see how actors try their best to nourish their own authority, sustain the authority of likeminded actors and aim at destabilizing the authority of others. Not only does the law change through the practice of its use; semantic authority is negotiated simultaneously. Jean Combacau and Serge Sur write lucidly in their general treatise on international law: 'Controversies regarding interpretation would not be so strong if they did not translate into a battle for mastering the legal system, which turns the interpretative process into a variant of the battle for the law.'[8]

Semantic authority rests on a belief that needs to be fought for and gained. Military advisors might thus seek to embolden or to undermine the ICRC. The ICRC relies and lends authority to domestic court decisions. Scholars rely on international jurisprudence, and international jurisprudence relies on domestic courts and so on. Those interactions not only shape the law but also negotiate each actor's semantic authority.

As further examples from the scenery of dynamic international law, a couple of specific cases from international trade law are illustrative. When China joined the World Trade Organisation (WTO) in 2001, it had made, among other things, a commitment to liberalizing trade in 'sound recording distribution services'. Does this commitment also extend to distribution by electronic means? A panel found that it did. On appeal, China argued that the scope of its commitments could not simply increase due to 'temporal variations in language'.[9] The Appellate

---

[7] M. Weber, *Economy and Society* (Berkeley: University of California Press, 1978), 36–38.

[8] J. Combacau, S. Sur and S. Sir, *Droit International Public* (Paris: Montchrestien, 2010), 172, quoted in English translation in J. M. Sorel and V. B. Eveno, 'Article 31', in *The Vienna Conventions on the Law of Treaties: A Commentary*, ed. O. Corten and P. Klein (Oxford: Oxford University Press, 2011), 804–37, esp. 806.

[9] Appellate Body Report, *China: Publications and Audiovisual Products*, WT/DS363/AB/R, 21 December 2009, para. 47.

Body disagreed and held that the terms were 'sufficiently generic that what they apply to may change over time'.[10] The Appellate Body decided a concrete case *inter partes*, but its interpretation will carry onward and instruct future practices.[11]

It would be next to impossible to understand international trade law were it not for the thicket of case law. Struggles over how earlier decisions are interpreted oftentimes gloss over the treaty language that is otherwise supposed to sustain the judgement of legality on its own. That the treaty language on justifying trade restrictions because they 'relate to' the conservation of exhaustible natural resources, for instance, has largely been forgotten in the sense that the legal discourse has come to turn on whether such measures 'are primarily aimed at' that objective.[12] The terms 'exhaustible natural resources', in turn, are shaped by the Appellate Body with reference to many international legal instruments so as to support an evolutionary interpretation.[13]

2   Lawmaking in Communicative Practice

In this section, I will briefly discuss two prominent angles from which the communicative practice of international lawmaking has been approached.[14] The first is actor centred and includes the legacies of legal realism, the New Haven School and its progeny (Subsection A). The second is centred on structures and comes in the form of systems theory (Subsection B). In their outlooks, the image of international law was certainly set into motion. But they have either one-sidedly emphasized the choice and impact of the actor to the detriment of legal structures or, conversely, lost all sight of any specific actor in communicative lawmaking. Their summary discussion paves the way toward developing an understanding of semantic authority that purports to transcend that divide (Subsection C).

---

[10] Ibid., para. 396.
[11] According to the Appellate Body, its reports create 'legitimate expectations' among WTO members so that panels are expected to follow its precedents. Appellate Body Report, *Japan: Taxes on Alcoholic Beverages*, WT/DS8, 10 & 11/AB/R, 4 October 1996, 14.
[12] Appellate Body Report, *US: Shrimp*, WT/DS48/ABR, 12 October 1998, para. 136.
[13] Ibid., para. 130.
[14] Here I draw on I. Venzke, *How Interpretation Makes International Law: On Semantic Change and Normative Twists* (Oxford: Oxford University Press, 2012), 29–37.

A The Impetus of Actors

Early American realists already articulated a view of law not as rules but as process, not as 'law in the books' but as 'law in action'.[15] Holmes's emphasis on prophecies about what courts do already goes a long way toward understanding lawmaking in a communicative perspective, where some actors – courts, in the context of Holmes's argument – are more powerful than others.[16] The agenda was precisely to shift attention from sources and rules to practice and process.

Taking their cues from early realists, the founding fathers of the New Haven School of international law were, first of all, most outspoken about their disdain for thinking of international law in terms of formal sources.[17] They foreshadowed theoretical developments that place emphasis on how the law changes through practice. International law, Myres McDougal already found, should be 'regarded not as mere rules but as a whole *process* of authoritative decisions in the world arena'.[18] He and his colleagues spelled out a view on international law that a substantive overarching morality toward which all efforts should be directed – that is, the protection of human dignity.[19] The view was decidedly functionalist, as international law should be practiced to serve that end.

Michael Reisman takes the view a step further.[20] He argues that scholarly teachings and judgments had set up the myth that international law could be found by looking at what Article 38 of the International Court of Justice (ICJ) Statute claims to be the sources of all law. The model of positivism, he contends, is distorting precisely because it holds that law is made by the legislator.[21] He maintains instead that international law

[15] See also R. Pound, 'Law in Books and Law in Action', *American Law Review* 44 (1910): 12–36.

[16] O. W. Holmes, 'The Path of the Law', *Harvard Law Review* 10 (1897): 457–78.

[17] See, generally, G. J. H. Van Hoof, *Rethinking the Sources of International Law* (Deventer: Kluwer, 1983), 39–44; M. Koskenniemi, *The Gentle Civilizer of Nations* (Cambridge: Cambridge University Press, 2001), 474–80.

[18] M. S. McDougal, *Studies in World Public Order* (New Haven: Yale University Press 1960), 169. Also see R. Higgins, 'Policy Considerations and the International Judicial Process', *International and Comparative Law Quarterly* 17 (1968): 58–84 ('international law is a continuing process of authoritative decisions').

[19] M. S. McDougal, 'International Law, Power, and Policy: A Contemporary Conception', *Recueil des Cours* 82 (1954): 137–259.

[20] M. Reisman, 'International Lawmaking: A Process of Communication', *American Society of International Law Proceedings* 75 (1981): 101–20.

[21] Ibid., 107.

emerges from the myriad legal communications that a plethora of actors utter every day. Given that the international legal process is no longer dominated by governments alone, Reisman finds that newly generated legal norms can conflict with norms that others might find with a formalist look at traditional sources of the law. His process-oriented view of international law transcends formalism and claims to be in a position of granting humanitarian concerns, voiced by a wide range of actors in international political discourse, a legal status even if they conflict with norms that have a formal pedigree in the sources of law.[22] Humanitarianism is construed as a social fact. It amounts to a point of reference for normative judgment and for legal argument with a certain distance to positive legal provisions that might be spelled out in the United Nations (UN) Charter, for instance.[23] It is clear to see in this approach the recognition of communicative lawmaking that unfolds under the spell of a plethora of different actors.

The theory of transnational legal process (TLP), a spin-off from New Haven, borrows the concept of jurisgenesis from the work of Robert Cover to look at the law-generating interactions among a multitude of actors.[24] Yet it does not share the earlier New Haven School's conviction in an overarching end of human dignity that can offer guidance. Paul Schiff Berman's approach stands in this tradition, focusing on the contestation among interpretative communities that 'do create law and do give meaning to law through their narratives and precepts'.[25] This opens the door to sketching law as existing in numerous coexisting, competing and overlapping normative universes. Cover did not engage in debates of legal pluralism, but his work certainly lends itself in support of pluralist conceptions of law when he writes that 'all collective behaviour entailing systematic understandings of our commitments to future worlds [can lay] equal claim to the word "law"'.[26] Law is not tied to recognized sources

---

[22] See I. Venzke and J. Von Bernstorff, 'Ethos, Ethics, and Morality in International Relations', in *Max Planck Encyclopedia of Public International Law*, ed. R. Wolfrum (Oxford: Oxford University Press, 2010).

[23] M. Reisman, 'Unilateral Action and the Transformations of the World Constitutive Process: The Special Problem of Humanitarian Intervention', *European Journal of International Law* 11 (2000): 3–18.

[24] H. H. Koh, 'Transnational Legal Process', *Nebraska Law Review* 75 (1996): 181–207.

[25] P. S. Berman, 'A Pluralist Approach to International Law', *Yale Journal of International Law* 32 (2007): 301–29. See also P. S. Berman, *Global Legal Pluralism* (Cambridge: Cambridge University Press, 2014).

[26] R. M. Cover, 'The Folktales of Justice: Tales of Jurisdiction', *Capital University Law Review* 14 (1985): 179–203, esp. 181.

but emerges from social interaction among a variety of actors, including multinational corporations, NGOs, international organizations, terrorist networks, media and in special circumstances, individuals. There is no centralized process of lawmaking or a single unified body of international law. Instead, there are multiple normative communities that generate their own legal norms. The grand picture is one of global legal pluralism.[27]

B   *The Logic of Legal Arguments*

The theoretical framework of systems theory paints a similar picture of lawmaking in communicative processes. It takes many of its cues from Eugen Ehrlich, one of the founding figures in sociological jurisprudence who inspired the free law movement, on which American legal realism also relied. Ehrlich opined in 1903 that 'the modern dogmatic legal science, that is inclined to first investigate the intention of the legislature what concerns any legal norm, has never considered sufficiently that the meaning that the law actually gains in life depends much more on its interpretation and on the persons who are called upon to deal with it'.[28]

But it sets itself apart from policy-oriented jurisprudence à la New Haven by understanding legal practice as a distinct enterprise that cannot be reduced to the exercise of power or the pursuit of values or as expressions of culture. It recognizes that speaking the language of the law compels actors to use a certain code of legality. It critiques external perspectives on legal practice for reducing that practice to the logics of other systems such as the political, economic or cultural systems. Legal practice, in its view, then becomes indistinguishable – for instance, politics by other means.[29]

According to systems theory, law is an autopoietic subsystem of society that encompasses all communications containing claims about (il)legality.[30] *Autopoiesis* roughly means self-reproduction. Niklas Luhmann introduced the concept in order to grasp the features of social systems and suggest that communications within any single system can only operate by reference to communications of that same system – legal claims have to

---

[27] Berman, 'A Pluralist Approach', 301–29. See also B. de Sousa Santos, *Toward a New Legal Common Sense* (Evanston: Northwestern University Press, 2002).

[28] E. Ehrlich, *Freie Rechtsfindung und freie Rechtswissenschaft* (Leipzig: C. L. Hirschfeld, 1903), available at http://www.gleichsatz.de/b-u-t/can/rec/ehrlich1frei.html, my translation.

[29] A. Fischer-Lescano and P. Liste, 'Völkerrechtspolitik. Zu Trennung und Verknüpfung von Politik und Recht der Weltgesellschaft', *Zeitschrift für Internationale Beziehungen* 12 (2005): 209–49.

[30] N. Luhmann, *Das Recht der Gesellschaft* (Frankfurt am Main: Suhrkamp, 1993), ch. 2.

refer to legal claims in order to be valid legal claims.[31] The test for knowing what amounts to a valid claim in (international) law cannot be based on an idea of sources or on pedigree. It must refer to legal practice itself.[32]

C   Dynamic Developments

(1)   Actors in Legal Practice

The critiques of policy-oriented jurisprudence à la New Haven have cen-tred, among other things, on its difficulty, or unwillingness, to account for law as a genuine field of practice that is structured by demands of action unlike that of politics, economics or morality. The critique is that making a legal claim, even vesting policy preferences in the mantle of the law, faces constraints that come with the choice for the language of law. That language has argumentative traditions, standards of validity and demands of practice that render some claims more likely to be accepted than oth-ers. Some claims might be impossible to be made at all or, if made, sound ridiculous or plainly wrong. Systems theory takes that critique on board and abstracts from any specific actor and interests that might be expressed in legal interpretations. Instead, it looks at communicative operations whose writers or speakers remain in the dark.

When it comes to the dynamics of international law, views in the trad-ition of legal realism and the New Haven School see dynamism through an emphasis on the actors in processes of continuous decision making. Systems theory, on the other hand, sees dynamism through the lens of evolution: The law adapts in an evolutionary fashion to changes in its environment. Actors and policies cannot bear on the law in any direct fashion. But the process is one of natural selection according to the logic of the law.[33] Luhmann thus goes to great lengths to formulate a theory of legal evolution. He thereby replaces the mystique of sources with yet another metaphor – the evolution of law – that distances the law from human action to no lesser degree.[34]

---

[31] Luhmann, *Das Recht der Gesellschaft*, 98; see further G. Teubner, *Law as an Autopoietic System* (Oxford: Blackwell, 1993).

[32] N. Luhmann, *Law as a Social System* (Oxford: Oxford University Press, 2004), 128. ('Validity is nothing but the symbol for the nexus that is part and parcel of all legal opera-tions. It cannot be validated point by point but only recursively, that is, by recourse to valid law. Validity achieves connectivity in the system.')

[33] Luhmann, *Das Recht der Gesellschaft*, 239–96.

[34] Luhmann duly notes that thinking of legal change in terms of evolution only makes good sense if the legal system is operationally closed – that is, political operations do not have an immediate impact on legal communications. See Luhmann, *Das Recht der Gesellschaft*, 257.

(2) The Evolution of Law

Luhmann is not alone in understanding legal change in evolutionary terms. Even Hans Kelsen opted for this imagery and developed an evolutionary theory of international law, which was based on his idea of a 'biogenetic law'.[35] Scholarly literature generally offers many spirited uses of the concept of evolution just as well.[36] In judicial practice, it is above all the European Court of Human Rights (ECtHR) that has embraced the notion of 'evolutive interpretation' as a common *topos* in its judgments.[37] The ICJ has likewise, though with less frequency, spoken about the evolution of international law.[38] And the WTO Appellate Body has found, for example, that the expression 'exhaustibly natural resources' is evolutionary by definition.[39] In *China: Publications and Audiovisual Products*, the panel further held that China's schedule entry should be interpreted in an evolutionary fashion.[40] In short, it is rather common to understand developments in law and language as evolution.

Linguistic theory also seems to support such an understanding of legal change. Alterations in language, according to linguist Rudi Keller, is the unintended by-product of myriad intentional actions.[41] But for an evolutionary explanation to be adequate, he notes, three conditions have to be met. The process must not be analysed in light of a given goal or endpoint (this precludes any talk of evolution *toward* anything) and must be a cumulative process involving numerous individuals and knowing no

---

[35] H. Kelsen, *Law and Peace in International Relations* (Cambridge, MA: Harvard University Press 1942), 148–49; see further C. Jabloner, 'Verrechtlichung und Rechtsdynamik', *Zeitschrift für öffentliches Recht* 54 (1999): 261–78.
[36] See, for example, A. Anghie, 'The Evolution of International Law: Colonial and Postcolonial Realities', *Third World Quarterly* 27 (2006): 739–53; E. Benvenisti and G. W. Downs, 'National Courts, Domestic Democracy, and the Evolution of International Law', *European Journal of International Law* 20 (2009): 59–72; R. Kolb, 'Repères historiques dans l'évolution de l'occupation de guerre', *The Global Community: Yearbook of International Law and Jurisprudence* 1 (2007): 65–102; N. Schrijver, *The Evolution of Sustainable Development in International Law: Inception, Meaning and Status* (Leiden: Nijhoff, 2008).
[37] See, with further references, E. Bjorge, *The Evolutionary Interpretation of Treaties* (Oxford: Oxford University Press, 2014).
[38] *Aegean Sea Continental Shelf (Greece v. Turkey)*, [1978], ICJ Reports, 3, para. 77; *Dispute Regarding Navigational and Related Rights (Costa Rica v. Nicaragua)*, [2009], para. 65. Also compare the *dictum* in *Legal Consequences for States of the Continuing Presence of South Africa in Namibia (South West Africa) notwithstanding Security Council Resolution 276 (1970)* [1971] Advisory Opinion, ICJ Reports, 16, para. 53.
[39] Appellate Body Report, *United States: Import Prohibition of Certain Shrimp and Shrimp Like Products*, WT/DS58/AB/R, 6 November 1998, paras. 127–31.
[40] See Appellate Body Report, *China: Publications and Audiovisual Products*, para. 47.
[41] R. Keller, *Sprachwandel* (Tübingen: Francke, 2003), 93.

single author. In addition, the dynamics of the process must be based on a combination of variation and selection.[42] This fits well with central tenets of systems theory.[43] However, Keller is enormously cautious and notes with reference to his colleague Eugeniu Coșeriu that human sciences will eventually have to find their own concept to replace the notion of evolution in order to explain legal dynamics.[44] Coșeriu notably warned that nothing could impact language that does not pass through the speakers' freedom and intelligence.[45] He thus brings intention and will back into the equation.

(3)   Change through Practice

Competition between agency-centred and structural explanations flares up again in the discussion of the concept of evolution. Sure enough, no single interpretation can by and for itself be transformative: claims to the law need to find acceptance within a community of interpreters. The concept of evolution highlights environmental (structural) conditions that drive selection processes and impact particular interpretations' chances of success. Yet with this focus, it blends out any bearing of particular actors on those same conditions. In legal interpretation, actors engage in a struggle for the law with the decided interest of finding acceptance for their claims. They seek to influence what is considered (il)legal. Some actors possess immense resources that they are willing to put to use in those semantic struggles. Like any language, the language of international law is a social, not a natural product.[46] While the concept of evolution recalls that no single act of interpretation generates meaning, it unduly abstracts from the capacities of specific actors and from the politics that are at work within processes of change.[47]

---

[42] Ibid., 191–96. Luhmann has aptly noted that the concept of evolution precludes predictions in Luhmann, *Das Recht der Gesellschaft*, 296. This fitting insight is certainly not widely heeded.

[43] Luhmann, *Das Recht der Gesellschaft*, 277.

[44] E. Coșeriu, *Synchronie, Diachronie und Geschichte. Das Problem des Sprachwandels* (München: Wilhelm Fink Verlag, 1974), 154.

[45] Ibid., 169.

[46] See P. Bourdieu, 'Authorized Language: The Social Conditions for the Effectiveness of Ritual Discourse', in *Language and Symbolic Power*, by P. Bourdieu, trans. G. Raymond and M. Adamson (Cambridge, MA: Harvard University Press, 1999). On the (mis)use of the metaphor of the language of international law see I. Venzke, 'Is Interpretation in International Law a Game?', in *Interpretation in International Law*, ed. A. Bianchi et al. (Oxford: Oxford University Press, 2015).

[47] See also the critique by Rudolf von Jhering of Friedrich Carl von Savigny's historical school of law for its romantic idea that lawmaking dynamics unfold in an inward and natural

With regard to understanding legal dynamics in terms of evolution, Max Weber's insights continue to be pertinent. Writing about legal change by way of changes in consensual meaning, he observed, 'The mere *change of external conditions* is neither sufficient nor necessary to explain the changes in "consensual understandings". The really decisive element has always been *a new line of conduct* which then results either in a change of the meaning of existing rules of law or in the creation of new rules of law.'[48]

It is a lasting task for international legal theory to develop an account of legal change and lawmaking that captures legal interpretation as a distinct enterprise that is not reduced to politics, morality or culture, on the one hand, and maintains, on the other, a grasp on those actual lines of conduct. I suggest that a renewed conception of practice helps meet that challenge.

Whereas the concept of practice used to be closely linked to strong structuralist positions, Maurice Merleau-Ponty brought life and agency into it.[49] He conceived practice as historically situated speaking, thinking and acting. Practice was not the embodiment of (material) structures but the acting of *living* persons.[50] Pierre Bourdieu was then still more blunt in his critique of structuralist abstractions from agency: they blunder into the trap of equating what they see as objective observation (unburdened with dealings of living persons) with the view that actors themselves have of their practice.[51] Social actors tend to be ignored where they should be included as a constitutive element of the social world.[52] On the contrary,

---

process. R. v. Jhering, *Der Kampf um's Recht* (1913; Frankfurt am Main: Klostermann, 1948), 65–70.

[48] Weber, *Economy and Society*, 755.

[49] See 'praxis' in *Handbuch Philosophischer Grundbegriffe*, vol. 2 (München: Verlag Karl Alber Freiburg, 2011), 1131. For a renewed appreciation of the concept, see T. R. Schatzki, 'Introduction: Practice Theory', in *The Practice Turn in Contemporary Theory*, ed. T. R. Schatzki, K. Knorr Cetina and E. von Savigny (London: Routledge, 2001), 1–14.

[50] M. Merleau-Ponty, *Die Abenteuer der Dialektik* (Frankfurt am Main: Suhrkamp, 1968), 62–63; *cf.* C. Taylor, 'To Follow a Rule ...' in *Bourdieu: Critical Perspectives*, ed. C. Calhoun, E. LiPuma, and M. Postone (Chicago: University of Chicago Press, 1993), 45–60, esp. 49 (on the commonalities between Merleau-Ponty and Wittgenstein with regard to their understanding of actors as engaged in practices – as beings who act in and on the world).

[51] P. Bourdieu, *Sozialer Sinn. Kritik der theoretischen Vernunft* (Frankfurt am Main: Suhrkamp, 1987), 56. See in further detail Y. Dezalay and M. R. Madsen, 'The Force of Law and Lawyers: Pierre Bourdieu and the Reflexive Sociology of Law', *Annual Review of Law and Social Science* 8 (2012): 433–52.

[52] This critique may also very well be directed at strong variants of ideal political theory. See R. Geuss, *Philosophy and Real Politics* (Princeton: Princeton University Press, 2008).

however, only taking account of practice without any critical detachment or understanding of structural predispositions would fall for an unbroken subjectivism. Sociological insight would be impossible. In other words, factors that explain a person's behaviour (her claims about international law) should not be equated with the reasons for action that actors themselves see or make explicit.[53]

An understanding of international law as a practice is attuned to the actors who struggle for the law to pull it onto their side.[54] And it places emphasis on the fact that the struggle is one that takes place within a structured context – a strategic environment that is international law and much else. Such structural conditions for the semantic struggle can frequently amount to a constraint while being a product of that same struggle. A product of a social process that stretches over time, international law does not easily bow to the whim of any single actor or to the impulse of any single moment. And yet, gradual change still depends on 'new lines of conduct' – on the actors that carry it along.

Not many approaches to international law take this step toward articulating how the law relates to its lawyers, how the strategic environment relates to the people who live in it. Few approaches take their cues from the idea that sociology contains a well-received suggestion: actors and structures are co-constitutive; one cannot do without the other. Actors keep structures alive and structures shape actors.[55] When it comes to international law, that co-constitution contains the forces of dynamism.[56] If that is so, then the received terminology of the co-constitution might turn out to stand in the way. It suggests the ordered settlement of a constitution. It suggests closure. But the relationship between the structure of the law and the people that inhibit it, who use it and shape it, is not settled. It is unstable and dynamic. Of course, a constitution can and probably should be thought of as a living constitution. But it might be better to drop that

---

[53] See P. Bourdieu, *Entwurf einer Theorie der Praxis* (Frankfurt am Main: Suhrkamp, 1996). Of course, the agency–structure divide reverberates in his concepts of 'habitus' and 'field'. For legal practice, see P. Bourdieu, 'The Force of Law: Toward a Sociology of the Juridical Field', *Hastings Law Journal* 38 (1987): 814–53.

[54] See also in this vein, M. Koskenniemi, 'Between Commitment and Cynicism: Outline for a Theory of International Law as Practice', in *Collection of Essays by Legal Advisers of States, Legal Advisers of International Organizations and Practitioners in the Field of International Law*, ed. United Nations (New York: United Nations Publication, 1999), 523. ('International Law is what international lawyers do and how they think.')

[55] A. Giddens, *Central Problems in Social Theory: Action, Structure and Contradiction in Social Analysis* (London: Macmillan, 1979).

[56] Similarly, see Dezalay and Madsen, 'The Force of Law'.

terminology and think of the relationship between international law and its lawyers as both symbiotic and antagonistic. The concept of semantic authority not only builds on the idea of communicative lawmaking to stay attuned to the dynamics of international law and to capture the authority of specific actors; it also emphasizes that this authority is one that largely depends on how an actor's claim about international law links up with that language of international law. In other words, from the myriad factors that shape, tug and pull on any specific actor's authority, semantic authority focuses on those elements of authority that lie on the level of communication. Many different factors certainly sustain an actor's capacity to find recognition for claims about international law and establish reference points for legal discourse. They range from the appearance of rationality and such things as the use of wise words, via esteem and the reverence paid to successful operators in the law, to tradition and the fact of having been right in the past.[57] They include such things as having the right pedigree of education, having practices in the right places or having a sufficiently prestigious university affiliation.[58] For institutional and state actors, the size of GDP or military prowess may be considered. All of that matters to varying degrees for an actor's semantic authority. In the following section, I wish to focus on elements of communication: How does (the language of) international law sustain the authority that changes it?

3 Semantic Authority

Semantic authority is a specific form of power. It is generally sustained by a social expectation – an expectation that an actor at least refers to and deals with a specific claim in the international legal discourse. To pick up the introductory example of the Appellate Body, this actor enjoys semantic authority in international trade law because every actor who makes a claim is expected to do so in close engagement with the Appellate Body's earlier decisions. That expectation is something that the Appellate Body

---

[57] For a reconstruction of sources of authority in the International Court of Justice, see G. Hernandez, *The International Court of Justice and the Judicial Function* (Oxford: Oxford University Press, 2014).

[58] P. Bourdieu, *The Logic of Practice* (Stanford: Stanford University Press, 1992), 171–82. In detail for the field of commercial arbitration, see Y. Dezalay and B. G. Garth, *Dealing in Virtue: International Commercial Arbitration and the Construction of a Transnational Legal Order* (Princeton: Princeton University Press, 1998).

itself can foster – for instance, by giving its reports strong precedential force. Its authority also leans on common sentiments, such as like cases are decided alike. Its authority is furthermore linked to incentives structures, such as winning a case and therefore choosing a litigation strategy that is likely to be successful (i.e., vesting claims in the Appellate Body's preferred hermeneutics, picking up its earlier decisions and hints, spinning them rather than suggesting that they were wrong, etc.).

This section focuses on how international law feeds and possibly sustains actors' semantic authority, or that authority which changes and makes that same international law. It might be that semantic authority is a specific form of persuasive authority (Subsection A), but that notion fails to offer an account of what authority might mean if it needs to be persuasive. Similarly, it cannot be that an actor enjoys semantic authority because it is in some sense right – unless, that is, the assessment of rightness receives a pragmatic twist. The language of international law notably allows semantic authority to hide (Subsection B). As a matter of fact, actors' semantic authority seems to be at its strongest when it is not recognized. The prevailing social expectations within any specific community ultimately shape their authority as well as the ways in which they might effectively hide it (Subsection C).

A   Persuasive Authority?

Claims to the law might be authoritative simply because they are persuasive. When discussing the role of judicial precedents, for example, a number of international courts and tribunals are happy to say that earlier decisions have persuasive authority: they should be taken into consideration to the extent that they are convincing.[59] In the *dictum* of the Permanent Court of International Justice, earlier decisions should be taken into account if 'the Court sees no reason to depart from a construction which clearly flows from the previous judgments the reasoning of which it still regards as sound'.[60] When it comes to domestic courts and their treatment of claims to international law, they likewise resort to such views. Examples include the treatment of legal instruments of the UN

---

[59] See, for example, *ADC Affiliate Limited and ADC and ADMC Management Limited v. Republic of Hungary*, ICSID Case No. ARB/03/16, Award, 2 October 2006, para. 293.
[60] *Case of the Readaptation of the Mavrommatis Jerusalem Concessions (Jurisdiction), Greece v. Britain*, Judgment, 10 October 1927, para. 43.

High Commissioner for Refugees (UNHCR) – its Guidelines of Refugee Protection.[61]

While widespread, such reasoning is ambiguous at best. Above all, it remains utterly unclear what authority means in instances where authority relies on persuasion. The notion of persuasive authority is at odds with the strong argument that authority needs to be distinguished not only from coercion but also from persuasion. It is in this regard that Hannah Arendt wrote sweepingly that 'where arguments are used, authority is left in abeyance'.[62] H. L. A. Hart translated this aspect of authority into legal scholarship with the notion of content-independent reasons, or reasons that derive from the intention of the person or institution having authority and not from an assessment of their contents.[63] If authorities had to persuade and convince in order to be taken into consideration, they would cease to be authorities. It is a constitutive feature of authority that it persists even in the absence of agreement.[64]

Ideas on persuasive authority seem to be at their strongest in comparative law and with regard to the use of foreign judicial decisions arguably providing a repository of good reasons.[65] But the notion fails to offer an answer for what authority might mean if arguments were simply persuasive. It might be similar to the epistemic authority of experts, the typical example being medical doctors or other experts. But the understanding of authority then is certainly a distinct one and arguably not a strong one – what is the difference between epistemic authority and expertise?[66]

---

[61] See, with references to domestic court practice, Venzke, *How Interpretation Makes International Law*, 117–32.

[62] H. Arendt, 'What Is Authority?', in *Between Past and Future*, ed. H. Arendt and J. Kohn (New York: Penguin, 2006), 92. See also T. Hobbes, *De Cive* (Whitefish: Kessinger, 2004), 115 (noting no less drastically that a 'command is a precept in which the cause of the obedience depends on the will of the commander' and 'the will stand[s] for a reason').

[63] H. L. A Hart, *Essays on Bentham* (Oxford: Oxford University Press, 1983), 254–55; S. Sciaraffa, 'On Content-Independent Reasons: It's Not in the Name', *Law and Philosophy* 28 (2009): 233–60.

[64] S. J. Shapiro, 'Authority', in *The Oxford Handbook of Jurisprudence and Philosophy of Law*, ed. J. L Coleman, K. E. Himma, and S. J. Shapiro (Oxford: Oxford University Press, 2004), 382–83 (authority then is either pernicious or otiose).

[65] H. P. Glenn, 'Persuasive Authority', *McGill Law Journal* 32 (1986–87): 261–98; C. Flanders, 'Toward a Theory of Persuasive Authority', *Oklahoma Law Review* 62 (2009): 55–88.

[66] See also F. Schauer, 'Authority and Authorities', *Virginia Law Review* 94 (2008): 1931, 1940–1952; N. Jansen, *The Making of Legal Authority* (Oxford: Oxford University Press, 2010).

The notion of persuasive authority is part of a tradition that thinks of authority not as a factual capacity (of finding recognition for claims) but as a reason for action. The prevailing question in that tradition is why an actor (Y) should do what somebody else (X) says. Well, because X enjoys authority over Y. Y recognizes that X's reasons are better (Y is persuaded) or Y recognizes that X is in a better position to decide (Y defers judgment). When it comes to international legal practice, it strikes me that such authority is a truly rare phenomenon. In any event, it would be at odds with an understanding of that practice as a veritable struggle for the law. When an actor refers to a report of the Appellate Body in his legal argument, it is because it suits him, not because he is persuaded by it or because he defers judgment on the matter to the Appellate Body.

More generally, it seems that the notion of persuasive authority reflects the struggle of legal doctrine to come to terms with the use of ubiquitous 'authorities' that impact the development of the law even if they are nonbinding and do not fit within the orthodox ordering of sources doctrine. Alas, the concept of persuasive authority does not offer the easy way out of this quandary that some authors wish it did.[67] Similarly, it is not very helpful to think of an actor's semantic authority as sustained by the fact that her claims are right unless the assessment of rightness receives a pragmatic twist.

All actors in the struggle for the law might of course claim that they are right. The fact that they typically do not do so, at least not explicitly, suggests that this would add next to nothing. In cases of any controversy, it seems futile and plainly meaningless to claim that one is right as the whole practice is competing claims to rightness. Or, in other words, to present and establish claims in international law as the right ones is simply the aim of the game.[68] The assessment of what amounts to a right legal claim is a pragmatic one that leans on the views of other actors in the game. Rightness, to be sure, cannot be judged against the yardstick of the law.[69] The law provides the battleground for competing claims about what is a right claim.

---

[67] M. Torrance, 'Persuasive Authority beyond the State: A Theoretical Analysis of Transnational Corporate Social Responsibility Norms as Legal Reasons within Positive Legal Systems', *German Law Journal* 12 (2011): 1573–1636.

[68] D. Peat and M. Windsor, 'Playing the Game of Interpretation: On Meaning and Metaphor in International Law', in *Interpretation in International Law*, M. Windsor, A. Bianchi and D. Peat (Eds.) (Oxford: Oxford University Press, 2015).

[69] For further details, see Venzke, 'Interpretation in International Law'.

B Subservient Authority

It seems that an actor's semantic authority can be most effective if he takes himself out of the game and instead presents himself as a handmaiden of other authorities.[70] In the struggle for international law, the prevailing sentiment that distributes authority continues to be legalism flanked by formalism – the belief that rightness is a matter of following the rules of the law.[71] To be influential, the actor needs to hide. In the words of Kevin Spacey in *Usual Suspects*, 'the greatest trick the Devil ever pulled was convincing the world he didn't exist'.[72] The language of the law allows actors to do precisely that, to hide. As Bourdieu observed, 'the ritual that is designed to intensify the authority of the act of interpretation … adds to the collective work of sublimation designed to attest that the decision expresses not the will or the world-view of the judge but the will of the law or the legislature (*voluntas legis* or *legislatoris*)'.[73]

In the language of international law, participants in the legal discourse typically point to treaties or customary international law as the basis for their claims. As the scenery of a dynamic international law has suggested, there are other reference points, such as international judicial decisions or instruments of international institutions. Even if judicial decisions have built up a body of case law that largely glosses over the treaty texts, they first operated on precisely that basis. There are notable exceptions, however. In some instances, claims were not at all supported by the 'will of the laws or of the legislature' but by references to substantive justice or to community values. A noteworthy example may be one of the first decisions of the International Tribunal for the Law of the Sea (ITLOS), in which it assumed jurisdiction 'in the interest of justice'.[74]

In any event, actors in the communicative practice of international law typically present themselves as subservient to other masters or ends: the

---

[70] Shai Dothan offers the alternative, largely complementary account, of how a court can build up authority by visibly getting away with interpretations that are recognized as expansive. See S. Dothan, *Reputation and Judicial Tactics: A Theory of National and International Courts* (Cambridge: Cambridge University Press, 2015).

[71] See, seminally, J. N. Shklar, *Legalism* (Cambridge, MA: Harvard University Press, 1964).

[72] Paraphrasing Charles Baudelaire, 'The Generous Gambler': 'My dear brethren, do not ever forget, when you hear the progress of lights praised, that the loveliest trick of the Devil is to persuade you that he does not exist!' See 'Devil', Wikiquote, last modified June 22, 2017, http://en.wikiquote.org/wiki/Devil.

[73] Bourdieu, 'Force of Law', 814–53, esp. 828.

[74] ITLOS, *St. Vincent and the Grenadines v. Guinea*, No. 2, Judgment on the Merits 1999, para. 73.

law, state governments, the world community or justice, above all. The law rules, not the actors who are bound by it. If the law runs out in its rule, so to speak, then other resources have to come in, such as the parties' intentions or justice. The variety of the masters or ends, which actors may invoke, is reflected in the way they speak and craft their claims. A sociolinguistic approach to legal reasoning helps to better understand the resources of semantic authority. Such an approach serves the interest of understanding the ways in which actors seek semantic authority by speaking in a way that resonates with relevant peers and audiences.[75] The point is to understand claims within the international legal discourse not as structured by a given language that is international law but as communicative practices in which actors gain authority by striking the right chords within their communities and, at the same time, perpetuate the underlying value and knowledge systems of those communities.[76]

C   The Dynamics of Social Expectations

Semantic authority is, above all, the product of discursive construction. It is a product of discursive practices in a dynamic context that exceeds dyadic relationships picturing one actor in authority over another.[77] What sustains the authority is not individual recognition in the specific case of its exercise but its social recognition – a social belief in its legitimacy, which, as Luhmann argued, 'does precisely not rest ... on convictions for which one is personally responsible, but to the contrary on social climate'.[78] In Richard Flathman's words, 'shared values and beliefs' are constitutive of authority, and those shared underpinnings are shaped and upheld in discursive practices.[79] In this sense, as Bruce Lincoln also concurs, authority is based on 'culturally and historically conditioned expectations'.[80]

[75] L. Baum, *Judges and Their Audiences: A Perspective on Judicial Behavior* (Princeton: Princeton University Press, 2006).
[76] M. A. K. Halliday, *Language as a Social Semiotic: The Social Interpretation of Language and Meaning* (Baltimore: University Park Press, 1978), 2; M. A. K. Halliday and R. Hasan, *Language, Context, and Text: Aspects of Language in a Social-Semiotic Perspective* (Oxford: Oxford University Press, 1989), 16–24.
[77] For a well-developed argument in this vein, see R. E. Flathman, *The Practice of Political Authority: Authority and the Authoritative* (Chicago: University of Chicago Press, 1980).
[78] N. Luhmann, *Legitimation durch Verfahren* (Frankfurt: Suhrkamp, 1983), 34.
[79] Flathman, *Practice of Political Authority*, 26.
[80] B. Lincoln, *Authority: Construction and Corrosion* (Chicago: University of Chicago Press, 1991), 116.

The dynamic expectations that underpin any semantic authority, once more, hinge on many factors. Above all, it seems that they hinge on past practices. How well does a claim about the law in the present fit with past claims? Being tied to the past, semantic authority might suggest everything but dynamism, but that is not the case. On the contrary, it emphasizes incremental processes of constructing both authority and law. The use of precedents, gain, illustrates this argument. The WTO Appellate Body's authority *and* the development of international trade law received a push when the Appellate Body found that its earlier decisions 'create legitimate expectations ... and, therefore, should be taken into account where they are relevant to any dispute'.[81] The fact that actors in the marketplace, public officials and participants of the legal discourse generally shape their expectations and legal arguments around earlier decisions sustains the Appellate Body's semantic authority.

What is more, the Appellate Body picks up on an apparent fact – namely, that its reports create legitimate expectations. Actors already do converge around its reports, and therefore it is only proper that panels take them into consideration. The consequence of this finding is, of course, that actors take the reports into consideration even more so. The Appellate Body found further support for its position, adding yet more force to its precedents, when it stressed 'the importance of consistency and stability' in interpretation. It emphasized that its findings are clarifications of the law and, as such, are not limited to the specific case. When it critiqued a panel for failing to follow its earlier reports, it stated that it was 'deeply concerned about the Panel's decision to depart from well-established Appellate Body jurisprudence clarifying the interpretation of the same legal issues. The Panel's approach has serious implications for the proper functioning of the WTO dispute settlement system'.[82] Similar patterns can be found to varying degrees within other judicial institutions.[83]

---

[81] On strategies and patterns, see Chapter 3 in this volume, H. P. Olsen, 'International Courts and the Building of Legal Authority beyond the State'; Appellate Body Report, *Japan: Taxes on Alcoholic Beverages*, 14; Appellate Body Report, *Zeroing in Anti-Dumping Measures Involving Products from Korea*, WT/DS402/R, 18 January 2011, para. 7.6.

[82] Appellate Body Report, *United States: Final Anti-Dumping Measures on Stainless Steel from Mexico*, WT/DS344/AB/R, 30 April 2008, paras. 161–62; Appellate Body Report, *United States: Continued Existence and Application of Zeroing Methodology* WT/DS350/AB/R, 4 February 2009, paras. 362–65.

[83] ICTY, *Prosecutor v Aleksovski*, para. 113; cf. *Prosecutor v Kupreckic*, IT-95-16-T, Judgment, 14 January 2000, para. 540. See also M. Swart, 'Judicial Lawmaking at the Ad Hoc Tribunals: The Creative Use of the Sources of International Law and "Adventurous Interpretation"', *Zeitschrift für ausländisches öffentliches Recht und Völkerrecht* 70 (2010): 459; H. P. Olsen and S. Toddington, 'The End of an Era: Static and Dynamic

An actor enjoys semantic authority, as in the example of Appellate Body reports, if not everything can be made of its claims. Semantic authority is a form of power precisely because it precludes some courses of action or interpretation in the future. An act of lawmaking amounts to a constraint in the future. There would be no force of the past or of the law if everything could be made of it. Only if claims about the law carry content and constrain can they reach into the future and make law. Their constraint, semantic pragmatism suggests, stems from legal practice itself: authority in lawmaking is constrained and can constrain – is tied to the past and can reach into the future – because it is tied down by the future that looks back to see how any use relates to the past.[84]

The practical construction of semantic authority does not take place at the international level alone. When it comes to the claims of international institutions such as courts or tribunals, it matters in which way they are received on other, supranational or domestic, levels of governance. First of all, domestic constitutional provisions that recognize the applicability of international law and, by extension, the use of international decisions that interpret it might be read as express delegations of authority to international actors. But again, a lot turns on interpretative practices, even in the by and large exceptional case that the domestic legal order grants international decisions direct effect. Domestic cases relating to international decisions have precedential effects on domestic systems. If domestic courts, for example, hold other domestic actors to international commitments as interpreted by international institutions, they would certainly contribute to such international institutions' authority. Many domestic legal systems thus require that domestic actors take international judicial decisions into account under certain circumstances.

To offer but one prominent example from the field of human rights, the semantic authority of the ECtHR received a boost when the German Constitutional Court held that domestic fundamental guarantees need to be interpreted in light of its jurisprudence.[85] One reading of this example might suggest that the ECtHR's authority took a blow because its

---

Interpretation in International Courts', *International Criminal Law Review* 14 (2014): 1–26. Similarly, ECtHR, *Ireland v United Kingdom*, Judgment of 18 January 1978, Series A, No. 25, para. 154.

[84] R. Brandom, 'Some Pragmatist Themes in Hegel's Idealism: Negotiation and Administration in Hegel's Account of the Structure and Content of Conceptual Norms', *European Journal of Philosophy* 7 (1999): 164–89; M. Winkler, 'Die Normativität des Praktischen', *Juristenzeitung* 64 (2009): 821.

[85] German Federal Constitutional Court, *Görgülü*, 2 BvR 1481/04, 14 October 2004.

decisions were not given direct effect or otherwise enjoyed the force to be determinative of the outcome (*in casu* whether the claimant was entitled to see and care for his son).[86] That is a matter of enforcement and compliance, and indirect effects can, in any event, go a long way. What concerns the development of international human rights law within the 'European public order', is that the obligation 'to take into account' has more pronounced effects because it extends beyond cases to which the respective government has been a party.

Semantic authority is thus not well understood along the traditional lines of a command that demands obedience. Rather, it connects to Roman law practices, where the *auctoritas* of the Senate was distinguished from the *potestas* of the magistrates. While it did not impact the validity of the magistrate's acts if they went against the advice of the Senate or lacked the Senate's consent, such acts were without authority and politically frail. According to Theodor Mommsen, '*auctoritas* was more than a piece of advice and less than a command – a piece of advice that cannot easily be disregarded'.[87]

4   Conclusions and Normative Implications

This chapter began with the recognition that international lawmaking unfolds in a practice of struggling for the law. Practice sets international lawmaking into motion. Recognizing the lawmaking side of using international law, of speaking its language, however, is only the beginning. Normative, sociological and doctrinal sets of questions follow. In this chapter, I have tried to present lawmaking as a practice. This view transcends divergent approaches that either zoom in on policy-oriented actors and then lose a grip on the contextual constraints that come with speaking the language of international law or that stay attuned to those constraints by blending out the actors in the process. Whereas the former would see actors and their preferences as origins of change and dynamism, the latter would abstract from those actors and understand change in terms of evolution. Conversely, understanding lawmaking and legal dynamics through the lens of communicative practice suggests that it is precisely the relationship between actors and their strategic environment that contains the dynamics for change.

---

[86]   Ibid.
[87]   T. Mommsen, *Römisches Staatsrecht*, vol. 3 (Cambridge: Cambridge University Press, 2010), 1028. See also T. Eschenburg, *Über Autorität* (Frankfurt: Suhrkamp, 1969), 23–24.

The concept of semantic authority attempts to capture those actors who are influential in processes of communicative lawmaking. My argument is embedded in an understanding of lawmaking in communicative practice as it draws out actors' semantic authority precisely in the way in which semantic authority connects to the international law it shapes. It is by highlighting the dynamic construction of such authority that a second level of dynamism is introduced: the law is a product of practice, as is the semantic authority of the actors that contribute to its making. Actors struggle for the law in the law and in interaction with other authorities, trying to undermine some and support others.

My ambition in this chapter has primarily been one of sociological reflection to inform practice about itself. This goal serves the normative project that underpins sources doctrine: Who should have what say in the making of international law? The concept of semantic authority offers an anchor of normative inquiry in this sense. Who has what authority? Is that authority well justified? It will not be enough to point out that semantic authority hinges on acceptance, that it is fragile or that it needs to be gained and that it can be lost.[88] It is true that unlike instruments of violence, authority cannot be stored up and kept in stock to be employed in cases of dwindling support.[89] But this fragility far from undoes the understanding of semantic authority as a species of power – the power to make law through interpretation. And as such, it makes a fine target for inquiry and critique.

---

[88] When semantic authority amounts to an exercise of international public authority, it will need to live up to standards of democratic legitimacy. For the argument as it pertains to international courts, see in detail A. von Bogdandy and I. Venzke, *In Whose Name? A Public Law Theory of International Adjudication* (Oxford: Oxford University Press, 2014).

[89] H. Arendt, *Human Condition* (Chicago: University of Chicago Press, 1958), 200.

5

Practical Reason and Authority beyond the State

JOHN MARTIN GILLROY

The Philosophical Essence of Authority

Authority involves more than empirical practice. It is not just in the decisions of courts or the stipulations of treaties. It is an inherently philosophical concept. Essentially, authority, defined as the ability of law to elicit cooperation through the effective imposition of duties or powers,[1] has saliency to the degree that it is persuasive to those upon whom it is exercised. This persuasiveness is conditioned by how well the logic of the law-seeking authority maps onto one's understanding of what is reasonable – that is, what is concurrent with practical reason as a lawful expression of moral agency. Concurrence is justification, and justification is a prerequisite to the successful exercise of authority.

My purpose in this chapter is to suggest that arguments for transnational authority require, first, an understanding of how practical reason has evolved as a foundation of international law and, second, an understanding of what definitions of authority have salience. Treating authority as a philosophical concept, we must consider both the superstructure of the positive law and the substructure, or logic, of philosophical premises that define both sovereign and transnational authority.

Considering its superstructure, I will begin with the premise that the international legal system is made up of two kinds of law-seeking authority. These have traditionally been defined as the *voluntary* and the *necessary* law.[2] Alexander Orakhelashvili has described this landscape in terms of the tension between *jus dispositivum* and *jus cogens*, and I will

[1] B. Çali, *The Authority of International Law: Obedience, Respect, and Rebuttal* (Oxford: Oxford University Press, 2015), 11.
[2] E. de Vattel, *The Law of Nations*, ed. B. Kapossy and R. Whitmore (Indianapolis: Liberty Fund, 2008), §§ 7, 27.

adopt his vocabulary.[3] Considering substructure, I will argue that each type of law has a distinct philosophical foundation yielding a different justification for authority. *Jus dispositivum* arises from an idea of practical reason based on the value of social *process*, or collective action, as an end-in-itself, while *jus cogens* finds its essence in practical reason defined through *critical principle* – that is, principle based on reflective or critical reason, challenging social stability in the name of individual right.

These two dialectically engaged sets of philosophical premises will be considered to exist concurrently, as overlapping fields of philosophical reasons for the acceptance of authority by the agents involved. Although concurrent, because *jus dispositivum* predates *jus cogens*, it will be argued that the modern international legal system, at its origin, was primarily process based and that it is only in more recent times that critical *public order principles* have gained salience in an attempt to establish balance with process.[4] If this is the case, authority will be subject to the essential dialectic of *process⇄principle*[5] as these terms are previously defined. This core dialectic will also render two distinct but interdependent stages of international legal practice that authority beyond the state must navigate: a *Stage-I Procedural-Legal-System* and the progressive codification of critical principles anticipating the transition to a *Stage-II Critical-Legal-System*.[6]

To give philosophical content to this two-stage model – that is, to find philosophical premises for practical reason that logically and morally substantiate legal practice – I will begin with the philosophical method of R. G. Collingwood.[7] He contends that issues of practical reason can be understood by deciphering the essential metaphysics of absolute and relative presuppositions inherent in a particular philosophical argument as arranged on a dialectically evolving scale of forms. He argues that practical reason begins in the *utility* of cooperation itself and then evolves to a more essential focus on law and *right* as reflected in the requirements of reason to empower the person.[8] Therefore, the original organization of the

---

[3] A. Orakhelashvili, *Peremptory Norms in International Law* (Oxford: Oxford University Press, 2006), ch. 2.

[4] Ibid., ch. 5.

[5] I have picked this symbol to represent the dialectic interaction of concepts. The arrows represent influence; the bars, resistance to that influence.

[6] J. M. Gillroy, *An Evolutionary Paradigm for International Law: Philosophical Method, David Hume and the Essence of Sovereignty* (New York: Palgrave Macmillan, 2013), ch. 3.

[7] R. G. Collingwood, *An Essay on Metaphysics* (Oxford: Clarendon Press, 1940); R. G. Collingwood, *An Essay on Philosophical Method* (Oxford: Clarendon Press, 1933).

[8] R. G. Collingwood, *The New Leviathan or Man, Society, Civilization & Barbarism* (Oxford: Clarendon Press, 1942), 104–25.

international legal system as an expression of practical reason, or Stage-I, will emphasize *utility* that will cause the *process⇆principle* dialectic to be weighted to the former term, limiting authority beyond the state in the name of *jus dispositivum* and the stable international order of sovereign states it protects. But because the scale of forms is dialectic, we should also expect that the rise of principle will initiate momentum toward a Stage-II international legal system, where the counter-pressure of critical reason sanctions authority beyond the state in the name of *jus cogens*.

In order to provide detailed sets of philosophical premises for these two definitions of practical reason, I will utilize *Philosophical-Policy & Legal Design* (PPLD)[9], which is my technique for translating whole philosophical systems into legal-policy paradigms for the more comprehensive[10] analysis of contemporary practice and the synthesis of arguments for change. I propose that the Stage-I system is best illuminated through the application of David Hume's Philosophical-Policy Paradigm as a field of practice marked by the dominance of *process* over *principle*, where social convention provides the groundwork for the authority of *jus dispositivum* and *Lotus*[11] sovereignty. Meanwhile, the argument for balancing process with principle, necessary for the salience of authority beyond the state, is best represented by G. W. F. Hegel's Philosophical-Policy Paradigm. Hegel's philosophical argument, with its emphasis on freedom as the predominant imperative for law, provides a more essential justification for moving into a Stage-II international legal system. Here the rise of public order, or critical *jus cogens* principle, not only challenges *jus dispositivum* and *Lotus* sovereignty but transcends it in defence of right in law. Overall, the tension between *jus dispositivum* and *jus cogens* will be understood as two distinct definitions of practical reason supporting two dialectically engaged philosophical characterizations of authority.

To test my contention that practical reason illuminates the philosophical foundation of authority beyond the state, I shall utilize the International Court of Justice (ICJ) decision on the *Legality of Nuclear Weapons*. This

---

[9] J. M. Gillroy, *Justice & Nature: Kantian Philosophy, Environmental Policy & the Law* (Washington, DC: Georgetown University Press, 2000); J. M. Gillroy, 'Justice-as-Sovereignty: David Hume and the Origins of International Law', *The British Year Book of International Law* 78 (2008): 429–79; J. M. Gillroy, 'Philosophical-Policy & International Dispute Settlement: Process⇆Principle and the Ascendance of the WTO's Concept of Justice', *Journal of International Dispute Settlement* 53 (2012): 59–73.

[10] By *comprehensive*, I mean an application of not just what a philosopher specifically writes, in this case, about international law but what his or her greater logic of concepts about humanity, law and the foundations of practical reason and choice imply for the contemporary subject at hand.

[11] *S.S. Lotus (France v Turkey)* [1927], P.C.I.J. (ser. A) No. 10 (Sept. 7), A10.

case is important not because of the finding itself but because of the mental gymnastics of the court that has confused commentators and caused controversy.[12] I contend that this judgment can be better understood as an example of the court's effort, within the context of a transition between a Stage-I and Stage-II international legal system, to awkwardly juggle two dialectically engaged conceptions of practical reason, each with its own distinct claim to authority.

1 The Superstructure of International Legal Practice

In 1996, in an advisory opinion for the United Nations (UN) General Assembly (analysed in Section 5), the ICJ refused to declare the use of nuclear weapons illegal.[13] This conclusion was reached despite a review of international law that emphasized essential harms to humanity and nature and the violations of rights considered from within the law of armed conflict, humanitarian law and the international law of the environment. The inability of the ICJ to promote essential values over state sovereignty is not new. In 1951, the ICJ allowed states to enter reservations to the Genocide Treaty.[14] In 1966, it refused to intercede on behalf of the people of Southwest Africa to stop the imposition of apartheid by their trustee, the South African government.[15]

From the perspective of authority as practical reason, the aforementioned judgements can be argued to be evidence for the court's assumption that the practice of international law elevates previously codified principle, treaty and customary international law[16] as *jus dispositivum* over its other component: critical *public order principles*. However, increasingly, the legal system has recognized an international public policy process to integrate these principles, providing both an inventory of competitive norms and arguments for legal change, as well as a valid evolutionary process to progressively codify or update empirical practice with new *jus cogens* imperatives. This policy, or 'public order process', begins with the assumption that 'public policy is a concept derived from law not from politics'[17] and posits that international tribunals, including the ICJ, have

---

[12] L. B. d. Chazournes and P. Sands, eds., *International Law, the International Court of Justice and Nuclear Weapons* (Cambridge: Cambridge University Press, 1999).

[13] *S.S. Lotus (France v Turkey)*, A10; *Legality of the Threat or Use of Nuclear Weapons* [1996], Advisory Opinion, ICJ Reports at 226.

[14] *Reservations to the Convention on Genocide* [1951], Advisory Opinion, ICJ Reports 15.

[15] *South West Africa* [1966], Second Phase, Judgment, ICJ Reports 6.

[16] Statute of the ICJ, Article 38.

[17] Orakhelashvili, *Peremptory Norms*, 12.

recognized that international law is more than those rules and norms existing in blackletter law but includes 'generally recognized principles of morality which are not necessarily part of positive law'.[18]

Traditionally, the public policy process integrates the three sources of law to form two strata of legal rules: *jus dispositivum* and *jus cogens*. The former, translated from the Latin as 'law subject to the dispensation of the parties', is defined through the voluntary law of treaty and custom. *Jus dispositivum* means 'the law adopted by consent'. This category of international law consists of rules derived from the reciprocal relations of states, founded on their self-interest. It is a body of permissive and voluntary international law created, more or less, at a state's discretion, where all states hold sovereign equality.[19] Therefore, *jus dispositivum* binds only those states consenting to be governed by it. Within this category of the law, states may derogate from the rules, while sources of law that are of more recent origin are generally accepted as more authoritative, and specific rules (i.e., *lex specialis*), take precedence over general rules (i.e., *legi generalis*).

Jus cogens is the superior strata of the positive law that contains not only peremptory principle but *erga omnes* obligations.[20] It translates as 'compelling law' and these 'necessary' rules 'are not just binding but operate in an absolute and unconditional way'.[21] These are peremptory principles and, unlike positive-consensual law (*jus dispositivum*), are positive law that is non-derogable and not subject to considerations of state consent. These norms are characterized by the absolute value of their inherent content and exist to protect individual and community interests that are transcendent of the interests of the state.[22] *Erga omnes* obligation creates international standing that permits state action on behalf of international society, while 'the absolute nature of *jus cogens* makes irrelevant the pleas of reciprocity and circumstances precluding wrongfulness, such as necessity'.[23] International law has codified prohibitions against genocide, slavery and aggressive warfare as *jus cogens* and freedom of the seas with

---

[18] *Kuwait Air Corp.* [2001], 116 International Law Reports 571; H. J. Musielak and K. Schurig, eds., *Festschrift für Gerhard Kegel* (Berlin: Kohlhammer, 1987), 326.

[19] E. de Vattel, *The Law of Nations*, §§ 16, 27, 86.

[20] M. Ragazzi, *The Concept of International Obligations* Erga Omnes (Oxford: Oxford University Press, 1997), ch. 3; C. Tams, *Enforcing Obligations* Erga Omnes *in International Law* (Cambridge: Cambridge University Press, 2005), ch. 4.

[21] Orakhelashvili, *Peremptory Norms*, 67.

[22] P. Capps, *Human Dignity and the Foundations of International Law* (Oxford: Hart, 2009), 15, 19.

[23] Orakhelashvili, *Peremptory Norms*, 69.

the obligation to inhibit piracy as *erga omnes* obligations. These precepts, as codified in the Vienna Convention on the Law of Treaties[24] (which is declaratory of custom) and in critical ICJ cases like *Barcelona Traction*,[25] possess a higher status than *jus dispositivum* in juridical reasoning. Once a value becomes a rule or obligation under *jus cogens* or *erga omnes*, it cannot legally accommodate a state opting-out or derogating through private agreements, domestic statutes or bi- or multilateral treaties.[26]

Overall, international law has been slow to integrate these peremptory norms and obligations, which are produced by the public-order process and require transcendence of the state. Consequently, *obiter dicta* in the ICJ opinion for the *Barcelona Traction* case limits these norms to banning slavery, the slave trade, genocide, torture and piracy. However, within the public-order process, *jus cogens* and *erga omnes* are now understood to encompass a wider field of 'essential' legal concerns,[27] including a prohibition on the use of force, self-defence, self-determination, fundamental human rights and the basic principles of both humanitarian and international environmental law.[28] But if this is so, then in the ICJ's *Advisory Opinion on the Legality of Nuclear Weapons*, the court's examination of humanitarian and environmental law should have generated critical *jus cogens* principles[29] that, when judged against a state's use of nuclear weapons, would prove peremptory of that practice.

But even with a complete examination of all of the customary and treaty law relevant to these areas of practice, the court could find nothing to make the use of nuclear weapons illegal. In fact, *Nuclear Weapons* supports the argument that the number of these 'right-to-force' precepts has not been significantly enlarged since their inception within customary international law in the nineteenth century, when the *erga omnes* obligation to prosecute piracy and the *jus cogens* rules against slavery and the slave trade were codified as peremptory.

Empirically, one can argue that the court was simply applying the law. In addition, one could contend that the expansion of the authority of

---

[24] Vienna Convention on the Law of Treaties, Articles 53, 64. See also Articles 40–48 of the Articles on State Responsibility, which takes the idea of *jus cogens* as a basis for invalidating treaties in Article 59 of Vienna Convention on the Law of Treaties.
[25] *Barcelona Traction, Light and Power Company Limited* [1970], Judgment, ICJ Reports 3.
[26] Tams, *Enforcing Obligations*, 151, 306.
[27] J. Crawford, *The Creation of States in International Law*, 2nd ed. (Oxford: Oxford University Press, 2007), 81.
[28] Orakhelashvili, *Peremptory Norms*, ch. 2.
[29] On this, see *Gabčíkovo-Nagymaros Project (Hungary/Slovakia)* [1997], Judgment, ICJ Reports 7.

peremptory norms is controversial and that reasonable argument differs on where the line between *jus dispositivum* and *jus cogens* is, or ought to be, drawn. But this simply begs the question of why the international legal system, in practice, is not quick to recognize basic critical principles that have all the reasonable characteristics for peremptory status.

To explain this reluctance within the legal system by simply saying that power and interest conspire against an enlargement of *jus cogens* principles and *erga omnes* obligations, or that this is simply the way the positive law of nations works, is inadequate. Such logic indulges what Diderot defined as 'the sophism of the ephemeral', or what Allott calls 'the disempowering idea that what happens to exist now is inevitable and permanent'.[30] In order to transcend the ephemeral, one must elaborate the essential logic of philosophical argument at the foundation of both *jus dispositivum* and *jus cogens*. To accomplish this task in a systematic and rigorous manner, I will utilize PPLD, which transforms selected philosophical sets of premises about practical reason and human agency into paradigms for policy and legal design.

The result, detailed in the next two sections, is that the PPLD of David Hume best illuminates the origin and evolution of practice as *jus dispositivum*, while G. W. F. Hegel's Philosophical-Policy best elucidates the character of *jus cogens*. These paradigms, summarized in Figure 1, will be explained in some detail in order to allow the reader to fully grasp the distinctive and essential philosophical character of each of the two types of authority competing for the court's attention in the *Nuclear Weapons* case.

2   Deciphering the Essence of Sovereign Authority through PPLD: Hume's Philosophical-Policy and *Jus Dispositivum*

To produce a PPLD paradigm of practical reason for application to the law, I first utilize Collingwood's philosophical method to decipher the metaphysical structure of the philosopher's argument and its evolving scale of forms.[31] Collingwood posits that this structure contains an *absolute presupposition* and a series of *relative presuppositions*.[32] The absolute presupposition is a precept that drives, or provides the ultimate imperative for, the philosophical argument as a whole. The relative presuppositions are concepts that are instrumental, either positively in terms of making

---

[30] P. Allott, *The Health of Nations* (Cambridge: Cambridge University Press, 2002), 154.
[31] Collingwood, *Essay on Philosophical Method*, pt. 3.
[32] Collingwood, *Essay on Metaphysics*, ch. 5.

PHILOSOPHICAL METHOD APPLIED TO THE
ARGUMENT OF DAVID HUME TO RENDER HIS PPLD

Metaphysics =	Absolute Presupposition = Passion For A Stable Social Order. Relative Presuppositions = Scarcity, Limited Generosity, & Equality

Scale of Forms = Levels of Sanction To Correspond With The Growing Size and Complexity of Society
Approbation ⟹ *Process-Norm of Justice* ⟹ *Governance* in Political Society

HUME'S PPLD

Core Dialectic = *Process⇄Principle*

The Individual *Passion⇄Reason*	Collective Action *Utility⇄Right*	Role Of The State *Passive⇄Active*
Agent motivated by the *passion* for a stable social order challenged by the circumstances of justice.	Need to stabilize property through approbation, then justice and then government to maintain *public utility* in the face of any demands from *private right*	A *passive* state that empowers preexisting social convention through law in the name of social stability

Policy/Law Operating Imperative = Justice-As-Convention
{*Justice-As-Sovereignty*}

PHILOSOPHICAL METHOD APPLIED TO THE ARGUMENT OF
G.W.F. HEGEL TO RENDER HIS PPLD

Metaphysics =	Absolute Presupposition = Reason Made Concrete In The World Relative Presuppositions = Thinking, Legal and Historical Agency

Scale of Forms = Dialectic Progressions In The Pattern—*Simple* Unity⇄Opposition⟹*Complex Unity*.
Making Reason Concrete Through The Dialectic Progression:
Thinking Agency⇄Legal Agency⟹Historical Agency

HEGEL'S PPLD

Core Dialectic = *Process⇄Principle*

The Individual *Passion⇄Reason*	Collective Action *Utility⇄Right*	Role Of The State *Passive⇄Active*
A self-conscious and potentially moral agent motivated to use reason to overcome their animal passions	The Assurance of essential individual *right* as moral will in the face of the threat from arbitrary will as mere *utility*	An *active* state codifying law to empower the process of recognition and make individual right or freedom concrete in political life

Policy/Law Operating Imperative = Freedom Through Recognition

Figure 1 Philosophical-Policy and Legal Design: Hume's and Hegel's Arguments

the absolute presupposition real in the world, or negatively in presenting those obstacles to its realization that must be overcome.

The absolute presupposition of Hume's philosophical argument, on which the rest of his logic of concepts is built, is the *human passion for a stable social order*.[33] Fundamentally, Hume's concept of law focuses on the effect of context or circumstance on the individual and the requirements for collective action needed to establish a stable, certain and ordered existence that defines practical reason as social utility.[34] This passion, however, is impeded in creating order, by empirical 'scarcity' and 'equality' that combined with the idea of limited generosity, are Hume's 'circumstances of justice.'[35] These circumstances are Hume's relative presuppositions, or the conditions necessitating the creation of justice through law to ensure social stability.

Next, an evolving scale of forms is identified within Hume's concept of law. This is rendered when the dialectic balances between the relative presuppositions of an argument cause corresponding changes in the surface practice of the law, creating a dynamic context for human practical reason. Hume's scale of forms is defined in the progressive levels of sanctions necessary to counter the circumstances of justice and maintain stability as society grows larger and more complex. These sanctions begin with the *approbation* of others; moving on to *justice*[36] in the form of a social convention, or process-norm, that establishes a moral standard for each stable social equilibrium and finally legal *governance* within a political society though contract-by-convention.

The moral core of this evolution of sanctions is in the rise and empowerment of *social convention*.[37] Conventions are not customs[38] but those socially efficacious and unconsciously learned rules that set the parameters of agency, stabilizing social order. The further growth and universal spread of convention as accepted authority is dependent on consensus

---

[33] D. Hume, *A Treatise of Human Nature*, ed. L. A. Selby-Bigge and P. H. Nidditch, 5th. ed. (Oxford: Oxford University Press, 1978), 485–86, 497, 526, 543.

[34] S. Buckle, *Natural Law and the Theory of Property: Grotius to Hume* (Oxford: Oxford University Press, 1991); Gillroy, *Evolutionary Paradigm*, ch. 1.

[35] Hume, *Treatise of Human Nature*, 447–88.

[36] Ibid., 491.

[37] Ibid., 496–98.

[38] Unlike the standard positivist assumptions about custom adopted by H. L. A. Hart, *The Concept of Law* (Oxford: Clarendon Press, 1961), social convention is efficacious, endowed with an internal moral quality and generates the essential tension between process-principle that engages the validity of the law and its moral authority in a dialectic between procedural and substantive rules, respectively. See Gillroy, *Evolutionary Paradigm*, 73–82.

over an equilibrium and process-norm that provides a moral focus for just order, adding moral obligation to human agency through the 'artificial' maxim of justice. Here the dialectical interdependence between the empirical and the normative dimensions of justice become critical to the establishment and persistence of authority in society. Specifically, morality, through a sympathy for the general interest, lends approbation and obligation to empirical authority that supports society and denies it to that which challenges the status-quo, threatening social disintegration. Morality is a necessary foundation and reinforcement of one's *sense of justice* and empowers a public consensus for the utility[39] of society that further realigns self-interest to collective ends.

The last stage of Hume's scale of forms is governance. Hume's initial contention that society can and does establish itself with the process norm of 'Justice-As-Convention' alone, and without formal institutional governance, is based on the premise that society remains homogeneous, small and simple.[40] With increasing social complexity, Hume's 'political society' finds its genesis in the conscious reconfirmation of personal utility in the collective interest through codified law based on pre-existing social convention.[41]

Taking Hume's metaphysics and scale of forms as a point of departure, PPLD next requires that a specific legal-policy paradigm be deciphered. The paradigm makes the philosopher's metaphysics accessible for contemporary policy and legal analysis by exposing the essential dialectic structure of practical reason as defined by the philosopher's fundamental assumptions about the *individual*, how we act *collectively* and the proper role of *state* authority.

I have determined that the dialectic structure of practical reason, within the context of law and policy, begins with the tension between *process↔principle*.[42] This dialectic represents the essential tension between a definition of morality as *process*, making a stable social order an end-in-itself, and *critical principle*, which offers a definition of morality as reason-based right applied independent of context and pertaining to the status of

---

[39] In the *Treatise*, utility begins with self-interest but finds expression only in the collective good. See Hume, *Treatise of Human Nature*, 472. In the *Enquiries*, he begins with the case for the utility of social convention and ends with its relationship to self-love. See D. Hume, *An Enquiry Concerning the Principles of Morals*, ed. L. A. Selby-Bigge and P. H. Nidditch, 3rd ed. (Oxford: Oxford University Press, 1975), 174.

[40] Hume, *Treatise of Human Nature*, 499.

[41] Ibid., 538.

[42] Gillroy, *Evolutionary Paradigm*, ch. 1.

the person. This dialectic structure also acknowledges that while critical principle is required to protect the legal status of humanity as an end-in-itself, it inevitably disrupts the pre-existing process of social cooperation. The *Process↔Principle* dialectic is broken down across the three fundamental assumptions of a PPLD through a series of component dialectics. For the *individual*, it is the balance between *Passion↔Reason*. Assuming that human agency is a struggle between the comparative influence of passion and reason to determine human agency, which is given more weight by the philosophical argument, and why? The next fundamental assumption defines the *collective action* problem and focuses on the sub-dialectic of *Utility↔Right*. One asks how the transition from individual choice to collective outcomes balances the influence of the collective *utility* of social stability (*Process*) against individual *right* (*Critical Principle*). Lastly, the *role of the state* is deciphered in the tension between an *Active State↔Passive State*. An *Active State* is charged with not only the protection of a private sphere but the regulation of process in the name of principle. The active state both supports the negative freedom of the person and the empowerment of their positive freedom or moral agency in the world. By contrast, a *Passive State* exists primarily to provide the legal background conditions of civil life where negative freedom of process is protected against the disruptive quality of critical principle.

Applied to international law, Hume's PPLD emphasizes social stability, the first component of the *process↔principle* dialectic. Here the individual's practical reasoning is defined in terms of human agency arising from the influence of *passion* over *reason* (where reason is but passion's 'slave'[43]). The collective action problem emphasizes social *utility* over an independent idea of legal *right*, and the role of the state promotes a *passive* governance structure emphasizing the authority of pre-existing social convention in codified law.[44]

Hume describes the individual in terms of the passion of 'fellow-feeling', or sympathy.[45] However, he also acknowledges that sympathy struggles with self-interest, the balance between them being defined as 'limited generosity'.[46] One of the circumstances of justice, limited generosity must be supported in the struggle to successfully achieve and maintain collective action. The role of the state is to provide the ultimate sanction toward

[43] Hume, *Treatise of Human Nature*, 415.
[44] Gillroy, *Evolutionary Paradigm*, ch. 4.
[45] Hume, *Treatise of Human Nature*, 470, 472, 478, 484.
[46] Ibid., 487–88.

this end: a formal legal system. By reinforcing the authority of established social conventions, Hume's passive state – codifying the pre-existing process-norm of justice – provides a cumulative and more powerful authority over individual cooperation on Hume's scale of forms.[47]

Lastly, within the structure of PPLD, these fundamental assumptions render an *operating imperative* for policy and legal decision making that operationalizes Hume's absolute presupposition in practice. Within the context of international law, the demands of a passion for a stable global-social order create the *operating imperative* of *Justice-As-Sovereignty*.[48] Sovereignty is the social convention that defines justice as a process-norm securing the reciprocal cooperation of states and the stability of property in transnational legal practice.[49] Justice-As-Sovereignty has authority by the fact that, for Hume, a process that stabilizes property achieves a consensus that justice-as-convention is meant to represent and defend. Here, the *process* of cooperation is both the *means* to, and the *ends* of, justice itself.

For Hume's philosophical-policy, justice is order, or the stable coordination of human interaction, where one's sympathy to fundamental social interests requires an additional level of sanction to persist. Justice is also that pattern of allocation and distribution that solves the collective action problem and assures a stable international order. In effect, as the passion for order evolves and overlaps with the circumstances of the empirical world of international relations, Justice-As-Sovereignty is a means for legally incorporating new social facts over time while primarily protecting pre-established international coordination.[50]

In this way, Hume provides a philosophical argument for *practical reason as utility*, which describes the origin of international law in a procedural process–oriented (Stage-I)[51] legal system. Here, the process-norm of Justice-As-Sovereignty solves an international version of a Lewis coordination game[52] that secures the reciprocal cooperation of states at the

---

[47] Ibid., 543.
[48] Gillroy, 'Justice-As-Sovereignty', pt. 4; Gillroy, *Evolutionary Paradigm*, ch. 2.
[49] Gillroy, *Evolutionary Paradigm*, ch. 2.
[50] Hume, *Treatise of Human Nature*, 567–69.
[51] Gillroy, *Evolutionary Paradigm*, 130ff.
[52] A Lewis coordination game describes a cooperative strategic interaction where the two self-interested players (row and column) prefer joint to independent decision making. The motivation of the players is to conform to the predominant pattern of behaviour, which may arise without conscious choice. Here, knowledge that all other players will choose a specific strategy to cooperate is enough incentive for any other player to choose an identical strategy; all a new player needs to know is on which of the two preferentially indifferent equilibria – around what latent norm – the cooperation is taking place.

Westphalian equilibrium.[53] Justice-As-Sovereignty compensates for the circumstances of justice through a rule of recognition defined by mutually agreed 'effective control' of territory, thus stabilizing the interaction of states within a primarily voluntary legal system.[54] This idea of justice becomes the standard of legitimacy in a passive-prohibitory system of practice based on the sovereign authority of *jus dispositivum*.[55]

However, the dialectic structure of process-principle suggests that law seeking to transcend Justice-As-Sovereignty and the restrictive character of social convention in the name of critical principle will require a distinct PPLD. In order to justify the authority for making human freedom real in the world through *jus cogens*, a philosophical foundation for *practical reason as right*, derived from Hegel's philosophy, will now be proffered.

3   The Essence of Authority beyond the State: Hegel's Philosophical Policy and *Jus Cogens*[56]

To decipher Hegel's PPLD, philosophical method requires us to identify his metaphysics and scale of forms. This means, first, that we examine not just Hegel's *Philosophy of Right* for his argument about law but his entire exegesis and decipher its macro-argument that sets the foundation for the specific evolution of transnational authority in law and policy. Beginning in the *Logic*, we shall use Hegel's technique of dialectic progression to reveal not only his scale of forms but his absolute and relative presuppositions that drive this evolution of concepts from the *Logic* through the *Philosophy of Mind* and into the realm of the *Philosophy of Right*.

For our purposes, the core logical point of departure for Hegel is the idea of *being*[57] and how this idea eventually generates right, states and their international relations.[58] Specifically, the ability to reason practically

Gillroy, 'Justice-As-Sovereignty', 443; and see D. Lewis, *Conventions: A Philosophical Study* (Oxford: Wiley-Blackwell, 2002).
[53] Gillroy, *Evolutionary Paradigm*, 33–34.
[54] Gillroy, 'Justice-As-Sovereignty', 441–53; Gillroy, *Evolutionary Paradigm*, 29–33.
[55] Gillroy, 'Philosophical-Policy', 59–63; Gillroy, 'Justice-As-Sovereignty', 429–79.
[56] While only English translations of Hegel's work appear in these footnotes, all references were first drawn from: G. W. F. Hegel, *Werke in 20 Bänden mit Registerband* (Frankfurt: Surkamp, 1986).
[57] G. W. F. Hegel, *Science of Logic*, trans. A. V. Millers (London: George Allen & Unwin, 1976), 50, 58.
[58] G. W. F. Hegel, *Encyclopedia of Philosophical Science V3: Philosophy of Mind*, trans. W. Wallace and A. V. Wallace, introduction and commentary by M. Inwood (Oxford: Oxford University Press, 2007), § 408.

starts, logically, when subjective *Being* (one's consciousness), which is the same as nothing, confronts its objective *Essence* (self-consciousness) and, in this dialectic progression (Being⟷Essence⇒Concept), converts nothing into something: a *concept* (i.e., *reason*).[59] Reason then seeks its full expression in the world through human agency as this agency grasps the *Idea of Freedom*[60] and, through it, makes *Reason concrete in the world*,[61] providing the absolute presupposition of Hegel's philosophical argument.[62]

Through PPLD, three types of agency can be deciphered from Hegel's argument. While practical reason begins as *Thinking Agency*, in its confrontation with the ongoing evolution of dialectic progressions[63] – toward law and the state – it becomes more complex. The reasoning person must allow what Hegel calls his or her 'subjective spirit' to confront the objective world and dialectically render the absolute form of the concept of reason in the idea of freedom.[64] In this process, one becomes, in addition to a thinking agent, a 'legal and an historical agent'.[65] While *Thinking Agency* focuses on freedom as self-conscious thought and provides the most foundational manifestation of practical reason,[66] this simplicity is made concrete in the objective socio-political context of *Legal Agency* and creates the path of a greater 'world spirit' through *Historical Agency*.[67] These types of agency become the relative presuppositions through which reason is made concrete in the world.

As the types of agency express reason through freedom, their progress is driven by the *process of recognition*.[68] For Hegel, human freedom can

---

[59] Ibid., § 417.

[60] G. W. F. Hegel, *The Philosophy of History*, trans. J. Sibree (New York: Dover Publications, 1956), 19.

[61] Hegel, *Philosophy of Mind*, §§ 382, 385.

[62] Ibid., §§ 379, 381.

[63] I have deciphered a seven-step scale of forms for Hegel's argument from the foundation of the Logic through the Phenomenology of Mind and into Political Right and World Spirit. These I have summarized in terms of agency for the purposes of this essay. A full exposition must await my forthcoming book., see J. M. Gillroy, *The Assent of Public Order Principles in International Law: Philosophical Method, G. W.F. Hegel & Legal Right through Recognition* (New York: Palgrave Macmillan, forthcoming).

[64] G. W. F. Hegel, *Encyclopedia of Philosophical Science: V1 Logic*, trans. W. Wallace (Oxford: Oxford University Press, 1975), §§ 236–44.

[65] Hegel, *Philosophy of History*, xxix, 9, 22.

[66] Hegel, *Philosophy of Mind*, §§ 381, 385.

[67] Hegel, *Philosophy of History*, 76; G. W. F. Hegel, *Outlines of the Philosophy of Right*, trans. T. M. Knox and S. Houlgate (Oxford: Oxford University Press, 2008), §§ 21, 29; Hegel, *Philosophy of Mind*, § 444.

[68] Hegel, *Philosophy of Mind*, §§ 425, 431; Hegel, *Philosophy of Right*, § 4.

only be realized by the person in the mutual recognition of that freedom between moral agents. Hegel's thinking individual,[69] therefore, is argued to be a conscious agent seeking a more complex moral agency who uses reason to overcome his or her baser passions through recognition of, and by, others. Overall, the process of recognition, as mediated by law in the dialectic interaction of Thinking, Legal and Historical Agency creates an ever more perfect concrete reality of freedom through right, which PPLD reveals as Hegel's scale of forms.[70]

Hegel, unlike Kant, requires that moral agency be concrete and not merely metaphysical.[71] For its full expression, *Thinking Agency* must transit the process of recognition by others to find, first, one's private place in the community, and second, their public place within a People. This is achieved through *Legal Agency*, which assures the status of individual right in the progressive expression of thought through the legal-institutional transformation of individuals into families, then into members of civil-economic society and, finally, as citizens within an active state. For Hegel, the active state and its constituent People exists within a greater context of *Historical Agency*, where abstract individual right becomes moral right within a community and then ethical life as a citizen.[72]

This scale of forms for recognition is defined by distinct logical, practical steps, each step more perfect or absolute than its predecessor. The recognition process refines practical reason by progressively resolving the dialectic contradictions of Thinking, Legal and Historical Agency. Hegel argues that, upon first confrontation with an 'other', the human predisposition is to consume it. However, when the confrontation is with another human being, the reaction progresses to struggle, killing, enslavement and then finally reconciliation in mutual freedom through right-in-law. As these progressive steps are traversed, practical reason becomes more concrete, with fewer internal contradictions.[73]

Translated through PPLD, Hegel's metaphysics and scale of forms redefines the core *process↔principle* dialectic through fundamental assumptions for law that rebalance the pre-existing dominance of process with the rise of critical principle and provides a new standard for authority. In terms of the individual, *reason* is promoted over the 'animal' *passions*, the

---

[69] Hegel, *Philosophy of Right*, § 5, preface.
[70] Hegel, *Philosophy of Mind*, §§ 474, 481.
[71] Ibid., § 484.
[72] Hegel, *Philosophy of Right*, §§ 340, 342; Hegel, *Philosophy of History*, 59.
[73] Hegel, *Philosophy of Mind*, § 549.

collective action problem is reoriented to the needs of *right* over *utility* and through law, the role of the state becomes *active* to the end of implementing those critical principles connected to the freedom of the person. This renders the *operating imperative* of *Freedom-Through-Recognition* and justifies that legal authority necessary to make freedom real within the human context, whatever that may entail.[74]

Hegel's logic of practical reason as it renders the sovereign state is not controversial. But using his philosophical logic of concepts to transcend the sovereign state in terms of justification for transnational law is indeed controversial. This transition, however, is more feasible if we consider Hegel through the lens of philosophical method and PPLD. This shifts one's focus, first from the *Philosophy of Right* to Hegel's greater philosophical argument, and second from the state as an end-in-itself to the more essential progress and ongoing demands of Freedom–Through–Recognition as a policy-legal imperative.

Applied to international law, Hegel's operating imperative of Freedom-Through-Recognition, if it is to be made concrete in the authority of both municipal and international law, must first address the pre-existence of the Stage-I international legal system as described by Hume's PPLD. Here the process's principle dialectic is significantly weighted toward process, where principle is only acknowledged to the degree it is contextual to Justice-As-Sovereignty. Consequently, the necessary imperative of reason to establish the authority of right independent of, and overriding the pre-established authority of social convention, meets resistance in both the institutions created for the stability of the status-quo, and the conscious and unconscious predispositions of those assigned to empower these governance structures.

Hegel, like Hume, requires a social order as an ethical prerequisite for the freedom of the person. Specifically, Hegel uses the imperative of freedom to establish a state providing ethical life for a People. For Hume, the process of stable collective action is the end-in-itself; for Hegel, this social order is merely the point of departure for the rise of critical principle from the imperative of Freedom-Through-Recognition. Within Hegel's PPLD, this operating imperative for policy requires a focus on an ongoing scale, or dialectic progression, of forms, where states evolve over time toward their full legitimacy.[75] The scale of forms constantly evolves because one's subjective freedom continues to be negated by the objective world

---

[74] Hegel, *Philosophy of Right*, § 331; Hegel, *Philosophy of History*, 38, 59.
[75] Hegel, *Philosophy of History*, 59, 64–65, 78–79, 417.

of others and then transformed into further iterations of the 'absolute'.[76] These 'moments' of relative progress within the evolving concrete reality of history[77] persistently challenge human practical reason to both create and use legal authority to implement the changing ends of freedom.

In terms of the authority of transnational law, PPLD suggests that the most important 'moment', or Hegelian dialectic progression, is when the process of recognition transforms the *abstract right* of the person, as negated by convention and social *morality*, restoring the balance between process↔principle in the *ethical life* of a People. This state-based *Sittlichkeit* solves the collective action problem though the imperatives of an active state, which establish the authority of right-in-law to the empowerment of the person and to the detriment of social conventions that obstruct the full manifestation and evolution of human reason in the world. This creates the tension between the authority of pre-existing convention and the rising authority of critical principle in law at the core of the transition between what I have defined as a Stage-I utility-based definition of practical reason and a Stage-II definition based in right.

Many interpreters of Hegel would maintain that this empowerment of freedom only concerns the internal absolute sovereignty of the state where its international relations are simple and therefore of little interest. But this conclusion overlooks the full complexity of Hegel's dialectic scale of forms and the imperative of freedom that drives it. When Hegel's entire argument is examined through the lens of PPLD, it is not the state but his absolute presupposition as represented by the operating imperative of Freedom-Through-Recognition that takes precedence in defining legal authority. Here, three specific components of his argument offer new possibilities for the justification of transnational authority: (1) the role or scope of philosophy in deciphering the absolute; (2) the international manifestation of the process of recognition; and (3) the inherent and necessary steps of that dialectic process.

First, Hegel limits the task of philosophy to the retrospective analysis of the path of dialectic progression made evident in the historical record. Hegel's 'owl of Minerva' flies 'at dusk'[78] and is charged with interpreting the past within the context of the present with an eye to deciphering

---

[76] The Hegelian word *absolute* has many meanings and can be used as an adjective or a noun. Here I assume that the absolute is a modifier of a particular moment in law that perfects the moment before in terms of a closer integration of the concept of reason with reality, in the concrete idea of freedom.

[77] Hegel, *Philosophy of History*, 78–79, 417.

[78] Hegel, *Philosophy of Right*, preface.

those trends, in making reason concrete through freedom, that will continue into the future. In 1817, international law was primarily a system of
moral norms, an undeveloped system of *jus dispositivum* predominantly
dependent on the will of independent states or Justice-As-Sovereignty.[79]
At that time, the historical progression toward the modern European definition of ethical life for a People, secured by the legitimate state, dominated the trends of history and therefore Hegel's philosophical argument.
However, while the ethical life of a People within the state was all that
the imperative of Freedom-Through-Recognition needed to consider
then, the much more fully developed international legal system of 2017
requires reassessment of the requirements of this imperative.

PPLD also illuminates a second component of Hegel's argument, namely
the ongoing process of recognition. He contends that for the state, the process of recognition has two manifestations: *internal* sovereignty and *external* sovereignty.[80] Hegel emphasizes the former but considers the latter,
concerning an international law of Peoples, as an essential dimension of
what he calls the 'absolute majesty of the ethical totality'.[81] Hegel also argues
that the process of recognition that changes mere agency in the person into
a more sophisticated moral agency through recognition is also a factor in
transforming the simple state into the legitimate state.[82] States have authority
through their recognition by other states. Freedom-Through-Recognition
is an imperative of the state in international relations, as it is the imperative of the person in society. As Hegel argues, 'Without inter-state relations
[*Verhältnis*] a state can no more be an actual individual [*Individuum*] than
a mere individual [*der Einzelne*] can be an actual person.'[83]

While the state is in some ways not a private person,[84] Hegel uses the
two German variations of the word *individual* for the evolution of both
the person and the state in terms of recognition. Both evolve from a
mere agent (*der Einzelne*) with an arbitrary will into a moral-legitimate
agent having integrated the subjective and objective into the absolute
(*Individuum*). The state must pass through 'successive phases of Spirit …
into a … universal Spirit … a self-comprehending *totality*'.[85]

---

[79] Ibid., § 333.
[80] Ibid., §§ 321ff.
[81] G. W. F. Hegel, *Natural Law*, trans. T. M. Knox (Philadelphia: University of Pennsylvania
Press, 1975), § 477.
[82] Hegel, *Philosophy of Right*, § 331; Hegel, *Philosophy of History*, 78–79, 417.
[83] Hegel, *Philosophy of Right*, § 331.
[84] Ibid., § 330.
[85] Hegel, *Philosophy of History*, 78.

The third component of Hegel's greater argument, brought into relief by PPLD, concerns the steps in the recognition process.[86] In 1817, Hegel is presented with a context in which two distinct Peoples with two distinct definitions of ethical life within the state – what he describes as 'two rights' – either peacefully grant recognition to one another or go to war.[87] As with the person, the subjective state is confronted with an objective international system that presents war as the primary means for the recognition of its particular definition of the absolute manifestation of the idea of freedom. Consequently, Hegel argues for the moral status of conflict between concepts of ethical life as the primary international means of prosecuting the process of recognition between states. But in the process of recognition, as applied to the person, the 'struggle to the death' is only the most primitive step. The enslavement of the other and then, finally, reconciliation and right-through-law are more advanced steps.[88]

Assuming that Freedom-Through-Recognition for the state will follow much the same logical pattern of evolution as it does for the person, we should be able to examine the last two hundred years of state development in terms of how the dialectic of internal↔external sovereignty[89] has made the more advanced stages of the process of recognition real in legal practice. If authority in law and policy is considered in terms of the tension between two distinct but interdependent definitions of practical reason, this evolution can be charted by deciphering the various points of balance between the process-driven law of *jus dispositivum* and the imperatives of critical public order principles, or *jus cogens*.

This task is too extensive for this chapter.[90] Nevertheless, PPLD provides some insight into what new demands the imperatives of Freedom-Through-Recognition might make on the Hegelian state, namely what role authority beyond the state will take within an international legal system that has added right in law to war as a means of empowering the progress of reason in the world.

First and foremost, Hegel's dialectic of internal↔external sovereignty will have to expand from a strictly internal focus on right as a balance of stable collective action and individual status within a People to an external focus on the comparative development and authority of ethical life for all

---

[86] Hegel, *Philosophy of Mind*, §§ 430–35; G. W. F. Hegel, *The Phenomenology of Spirit*, trans. W. Wallace and A. V. Miller (Oxford: Oxford University Press, 1977), 178–95.
[87] Hegel, *Philosophy of Right*, § 334.
[88] Ibid., §§ 36–38.
[89] Ibid., § 321.
[90] See my forthcoming book, Gillroy, *Assent of Public Order Principles*.

persons. This will redefine the legitimacy of the state based on the demands of international right and transnational law. When does its legitimacy as an 'actual' *Individuum* require the state to rebalance its internal⇌external sovereignty in order to acknowledge the transnational authority of critical *jus cogens* principles for the sake of Freedom-Through-Recognition?

Next, if the contemporary international system is in transformation between a Stage-I and Stage-II concept of practical reason, we should expect that the bias of the legal system toward established authority as social convention, and the process-norm of Justice-As-Sovereignty, will be increasingly challenged by the rise of critical principle related to the imperative of Freedom-Through-Recognition. This means that public-order principles and their promotion to *jus cogens* status becomes a core issue of international law as public right. This is because public-order principles represent the transnational authority of that critical law necessary to the person as a human being rather than as a citizen of a state. Internal sovereignty is no longer absolute but must more fully entertain the consideration of when and where authority beyond the state is necessary. The authority of *jus cogens*, built on Hegel's absolute presupposition of making reason concrete in the world through its Idea of Freedom, requires nothing less.

Overall, the role of the state, as a dimension of Hegel's PPLD, becomes more complex. Considerations like sovereign intervention now must weigh the empowerment of freedom in the self-determination of all Peoples against any sovereign priorities, in addition to humanitarian considerations. The legitimate state will no longer be judged primarily in terms of its effective control of territory; instead, it will acquire a responsibility to cooperate in the progressive codification of critical principle, encouraging the freedom of humans as historical agents both within its boundaries and beyond. The requirements of becoming a moral agent (*Individuum*), for both the individual and the state, will transcend the competence of sovereign authority alone.

This potential transition away from Justice-As-Sovereignty challenges us to reconsider the role of the active Hegelian state. Now charged with assessing self-conscious freedom in ethical life as a matter of the progressive transnational refinement of the process of recognition, the state emphasizes external rather than internal sovereignty. In a juxtaposition of Hume's and Hegel's PPLDs, this tension becomes the foremost dialectic of modern international dispute settlement and the test of legitimate authority beyond the state.[91]

---

[91] While Hegel puts the future beyond the realm of philosophical judgment, we may anticipate the necessary adjustments of state function given the necessity of authority beyond

This juxtaposition also illuminates the surface distinction between the sovereign authority of *jus dispositivum* and the transnational authority of *jus cogens*. The literature on public-order principles says little about the moral origins of each of these categories of law or the particulars of their dynamics. However, with PPLD, this changes.

If the authority of *jus dispositivum* is now characterized as codified law drawn from those social conventions that originally established social stability and the cooperative equilibrium of the international community, then Hume's PPLD offers a normative grounding that explains both their conscious and unconscious power to influence legal practice.

If *jus cogens* is characterized through Hegel's PPLD as having its philosophical roots not in convention but in the transnational authority of critical principle, then it becomes both more morally definitive and comprehensive. *Jus cogens* is now morally defined in terms of reasoned reflection on the requirements of right necessary to protect and empower Freedom-Through-Recognition. This means that public-order principles are not just those precepts that have peremptory status in law but all critical principles seeking such status.

If *jus dispositivum* has its normative core in the process of cooperation as an end-in-itself, while *jus cogens* finds its imperative in protecting and empowering free persons, then we can expect that *jus cogens* is inherently disruptive of *jus dispositivum*. Also, since social convention has its origin in unconscious human interactions that predate positive law, while *jus cogens* depends on codification and a conscious policy infrastructure to debate and formally adopt critical principle, we can assume that the authority of *jus dispositivum* has pride of place. Within the normative structure of the international legal system, its original institutions would have been created solely for the protection and persistence of these social conventions in law.

Thus, *jus dispositivum* and its sovereign authority would not only be entrenched and difficult to change; its institutions and practice would try to co-opt any challenges by critical principles rather than acknowledge them as having a distinct normative essence and source of authority. This frames the history of international law as one of dynamic interaction between a conventional first stage of process and order and an impending second stage where critical principle struggles to establish itself, and the authority of individual right, within the transnational legal context.

---

its sovereignty, as he anticipated Freedom-Through-Recognition as expressed through Peoples within the ethical life of the State, which took until the late nineteenth century to find its full expression in Europe.

4   The Case as Analysed by PPLD

The *Advisory Opinion on the Legality of Nuclear Weapons* was fundamentally controversial. Perhaps not since the *South West Africa* Cases of
1966 has there been a more divided reaction to the resulting opinion. My
analysis will focus on three specific dimensions of this controversy: *Lotus*
as a normative-legal standard used throughout the case, the idea that the
court came to its conclusion because of worries about a *non liquet*, and
finally, the use of *necessity and proportionality* within the law of armed
conflict to ultimately settle this case.

A   *Retreat to* Lotus?

The authority of Justice-As-Sovereignty, the operating imperative of
Hume's PPLD, considers any pre-existing social convention related to
the international system to be determinative of policy unless a compelling reason can be argued for amending it. Therefore, in the dialectic of
process↔principle, process is considered prior to, and determinative of,
the challenge of principle.

As previously noted, social conventions are not customs but unconsciously learned rules that set the parameters of action in terms of the
requirements of justice, thereby stabilizing social order. An unconscious
predisposition toward the authority and persistence of established social
convention provides a bulwark of law against change from critical principle. The authority of pre-existing social conventions becomes engrained
through codification, and these standards are applied without excessive
reflection, adding to the stability of the social order. This engrained quality makes their codification in law primarily a process of establishing
a general permission for learned and established patterns of behaviour.

Applying Hume's PPLD, international legal practice ought to be biased
toward the process side of its dialectic with critical principle. This bias has
both conscious and unconscious roots and makes any suggestion of critical principle in law inherently suspect. This bias also codifies its first formal law on an established system of practice where the agency of states is
presumed to be supportive of social stability. International law is then created as a system regulated by the process-norm of Justice-As-Sovereignty,
where specific regulations or prohibitions on the conventional behaviour
of that practice are limited only to those which are necessary to maintain
a stable international equilibrium over time. Therefore, the process -norm

of Justice-As-Sovereignty[92] should regulate a system of law where the established practices of state are allowed unless specifically prohibited. This definition of sovereignty was definitively stated in 1927 within the context of the *Lotus* case: [93] 'International law governs relations between independent States. The rules of law binding upon States therefore emanate from their own free will. Restrictions upon the independence of States cannot therefore be presumed.'[94]

The complicated decision of the majority in *Nuclear Weapons* takes place within a more developed international legal system than that which existed when the Permanent Court of International Justice (PCIJ) decided the *Lotus* case. As PPLD shows, they are in fact dealing with two dialectically engaged ideas of authority, indicated by the rise of public-order principles in an effort to balance process with critical principle. However, recognizing the ingrained status of laws codified with a foundation in social convention, we might also expect that, other things being equal, policy and legal choice will cling to the authority of a known and stable certainty of process unless the demands of critical principle become overwhelming.

It should not be surprising, then, that the first major decision of the court was to redefine the case's question in terms of the authority of Justice-As-Sovereignty. In the first procedural decision, the judges decided to switch the question from whether international law existed that would *permit* the use of nuclear weapons to a search for a specific '*prohibition*' against the use of such weapons. In this choice, the subject of illegality for nuclear weapons was recognized as a potential critical principle seeking a prohibition. Meanwhile, this reconceptualization of the argument – a direct application of the *Lotus* case in defence of established/ingrained practice – relies on the underlying assumption that the legal burden of proof lies with those who would prohibit a state's actions

---

[92] Gillroy, 'Justice-As-Sovereignty', 429–79.
[93] This case is about a collision at sea that caused death and the arrest and trial of a French ship's officer for manslaughter. The issue of criminal jurisdiction was first settled in terms of humanitarian law in time of war in Article 11 of the 1958 Geneva Convention on the High Seas but only settled in terms of peacetime in Article 97 of the United Nations Convention on the Law of the Sea, which allowed the ship's flag to determine jurisdiction. However, this case remains critical to international law in terms of its making the law a system of prohibitions where a state, because of its sovereignty, must only refrain from action if a specific rule prohibits it.
[94] *S.S. Lotus (Fr. v. Turk.)*, A10, 18.

within a convention-based international system of *jus dispositivum*. In its advisory opinion, the ICJ argues:

> The use of the word 'permitted' in the question put by the General Assembly was criticized before the Court by certain States on the ground that this implied that the threat or use of nuclear weapons would only be permissible if authorization could be found in a treaty provision or in customary international law. Such a starting point, those States submitted, was incompatible with the very basis of international law, which rests upon the principles of sovereignty and consent ... contrary to what was implied by use of the word 'permitted'. States are free to threaten or use nuclear weapons unless it can be shown that they are bound not to do so by reference to a prohibition in either treaty law or customary international law. Support for this contention was found in dicta of the Permanent Court of International Justice in the 'Lotus' case ... [citing Nicaragua Judgment, paragraph 269] 'in international law there are no rules, other than such rules as may be accepted by the States concerned, by treaty or otherwise, whereby the level of armaments of a sovereign State can be limited.'[95]

While the original question was changed through the authority of the *Lotus* definition of Justice-As-Sovereignty, the need to change it may indicate that critical principle has more status as law than it did in 1927. This potentially increased status becomes the core of Judge Weeramantry's dissent:

> It would have been furthest from the mind of the Court deciding that case that its dictum ... would be used in an attempt to negate all that the humanitarian laws of war had built up – for the interpretation now sought to be given to the 'Lotus' case is nothing less than that it overrides even such well-entrenched principles as the Martens clause, which expressly provides that its humanitarian principles would apply 'in cases not included in the Regulations adopted by them' ... In the half century that has elapsed since the 'Lotus' case, it is quite evident that international law – and the law relating to humanitarian conduct in war – have developed considerably, imposing additional restrictions on state sovereignty over and above those that existed at the time of the 'Lotus' case ... This Court cannot in 1996 construe 'Lotus' so narrowly as to take the law backward in time even beyond the Martens clause.[96]

Weeramantry's dissent acknowledges the predominance of social convention from *Lotus* and that this system pre-dates the rise of concerns more associated with reason, right and a more active international legal system.

---

[95] *Legality of the Threat or Use of Nuclear Weapons* 226, § 21.
[96] Ibid., dissenting judgment of Weeramantry, § 9.

But he contends that the progress of authority from critical principle over process has already succeeded in transcending *Lotus*. He argues, in effect, that a Stage-II international legal system exists where critical principle has balanced process. Specifically citing what he perceives as the depth and complexity of humanitarian law, focusing specifically on the Martens Clause,[97] he argues that the evolution of the 'laws of humanity', which he characterizes as based in what PPLD would call the authority of critical principle and Freedom-Through-Recognition, have established obligations to right within the core of international law that transcend process.

Weeramantry's argument shows that he recognizes the importance of the authority of critical principle, but the fact that it is written in dissent demonstrates that it has not yet established itself to the degree necessary to transcend the ingrained predisposition toward the authority of Justice-As-Sovereignty. Weeramantry's puzzlement as to why the court would revert to the *Lotus* case eases if one understands the choice involved as one of protecting the authority of social conventions of property stabilization that pre-date formal law within the international legal system. He argues that the authority of critical principles of right, which would further restrict sovereignty, is 'evident' within the context of international law. However, the depth of conscious and unconscious obligation that the law codified from the legacy of social convention still has is not acknowledged in his dissent. He also fully appreciates neither the inherently disruptive quality of *jus cogens* nor the fact that to fully integrate, it requires that a distinct definition of authority be accepted.

From the standpoint of Hume's PPLD, the process-norm of Justice-As-Sovereignty, as the core of the law of *jus dispositivum*, arises from the conventions stabilizing the effective sovereign control of property. This provides a powerful and entrenched philosophical foundation for the authority of *process* over any peremptory *critical principle* that might eventually restrict it. The prohibitory system of law thus established holds priority as the definition of practical reason for both one's unconscious understanding of stability in the system and in the conscious choices that arbitrate when the authority of critical principle is robust enough to both challenge and transcend conventional-sovereign process.

---

[97] The Martens Clause is the humanitarian foundation for the laws of armed conflict since its first appearance in the preamble to the 1899 Hague Convention (II) with respect to the laws and customs of war on land: 'Populations and belligerents remain under the protection and empire of the principles of international law, as they result from the usages established between civilized nations, from the laws of humanity and the requirements of the public conscience'.

B   Non Liquet *or the Challenge of Critical Principle?*

The *Lotus* case is an omnipresent point of contention. The fact that it is debated is telling of the rise of public-order principles, or critical principles of right, within the context of a Stage-I international legal system. If the authority of *jus dispositivum* as the representative of process and social convention were still completely dominant, as it had been previously, and more so after the 1927 case, then the assumption of the court would have been that the 'so-called residual negative principle, which says that whatever is not prohibited is permitted' is the only law.[98] Instead, the relative weight of *Lotus* sovereignty given the growing legal demands of critical principle and right in law became a central controversy of the case.

One purpose for deriving policy paradigms from distinctive philosophical arguments for practical reason is to offer a better understanding of the essential principles, dialectics and philosophical foundations of the law. This then allows us to highlight misunderstandings and confusions in surface practice. PPLD, for example, provides insight into both the moral foundations of the *Lotus* case and its status as law for the court.

Specifically, Hume's PPLD allows us to reframe *Lotus* as the codification of social convention at the origin of the modern system of international legal practice. *Lotus* can no longer be described as anachronistic law devoid of authority but becomes the natural point of departure for any consideration of legal change.[99] Justice-As-Sovereignty represents those fundamental values that established the baseline moral equilibrium of the international legal system. Any challenge to this baseline would be resisted in the name of the prior stability and security of the system's status-quo and authority. In addition, process must anticipate the inevitable rise and growing challenge of principle because they are dialectically interdependent. This dialectic interdependence also indicates that each has a distinct philosophical foundation, where principle is inherently disruptive to status-quo process.

The dilemma created by the court's inability to ignore the growing status of humanitarian and environmental law, combined with its unwillingness

---

[98] D. Bodansky, '*Non Liquet* and the Incompleteness of International Law', in *International Law, the International Court of Justice and Nuclear Weapons*, ed. L. de Chazournes and P. Sands (Cambridge: Cambridge University Press, 1999), 160.

[99] G. Verdirame, 'A Normative Theory of Sovereignty Transfers', *Stanford Journal of International Law* 49 (2013): 371–424.

to significantly confront the *Lotus* equilibrium, creates the basis for the misidentified issue of *non liquet*.

If the system of established *jus dispositivum* as represented in the process-norm of Justice-As-Sovereignty were unchallenged, then the system of prohibitions would also be unchallenged. And within a system of prohibitions, the law is not there to regulate but to empower social convention or previously established practice in law. This type of legal system maintains itself by having limited reach, only extended after the lengthy acceptance of new practice over time, so a *non liquet* is not an issue.

For a *non liquet*[100] to be an issue, two things must be present. First, there must be a more advanced system of authoritative rules from both process and principle, both prohibitions and permissions, where the law is encouraged to extend conventional practice so that 'its rules cover a wider and wider array of actions'.[101] The gap between where we want the authority of law to stretch and how far it has extended creates the space for a *non liquet*. Second, within PPLD, a *non liquet* means that it is critical principle/right pressing the case for expansion of the law. Since *jus dispositivum* predates the rise of critical principle, anything that can be accommodated by process alone is duly integrated by social convention and creates no *non liquet*. Justice-As-Sovereignty, however, cannot simply expand to include *jus cogens* but must create space for its distinct definition of authority. This creates the possibility for a *non liquet*.

A richer philosophical environment allows the process's principle dialectic to be more fully engaged. Only when authority as critical principle pushes Justice-As-Sovereignty beyond the conventional evolution of practice can 'some actions ... not be covered by either a prohibitory or a permissive rule':[102] 'A finding of *non liquet* presumes that the issue is one that international law ought to govern ... a legal question ... what gives rise to a *non liquet* is the existence of a gap or indeterminacy *within* international law'.[103]

That *non liquet* becomes an issue in this case suggests that a richer space for the authority of critical principle is perceived to exist. This potential gap cannot be filled by the authority of sovereign process and *jus dispositivum*, but neither does the court allow *jus cogens* to properly fill it.

---

[100]   Ibid., 153.
[101]   Ibid., 163.
[102]   Ibid.
[103]   Ibid., 157.

In the decades since *Lotus*, the authority of critical principle and the imperative of Freedom-Through-Recognition in legal argument have advanced to challenge Justice-As-Sovereignty and partially rebalance the process-principle dialectic. In addition to the progress of human rights law, established by both treaty and the UN Charter, humanitarian law has been more thoroughly codified.[104] International environmental law, seeking to protect the integrity of nature, has also been incorporated in treaty, principle and custom. Most critically, the ideas of *erga omnes* obligations, containing the seeds of universal jurisdiction, and *jus cogens* critical principles, as the most important class of pre-emptive norms or substantive moral principles of law, are codified in case law and treaty, respectively.[105]

This evolution of critical principle in law is evident because while a survey of humanitarian and environmental law by the court did not find the prohibitory rule necessary to make nuclear weapons illegal within *jus dispositivum*, it did produce an acknowledgement by the court that critical principle had authority enough to impose certain 'obligations' on a state within the conventional system of law. For example, within the law of environmental protection, 'the Court thus finds that while the existing international law relating to the protection and safeguarding of the environment does not specifically prohibit the use of nuclear weapons, it indicates important environmental factors that are properly to be taken into account'.[106]

But if PPLD is correct, to fully acknowledge an obligation to critical principle is also to acknowledge it as *jus cogens* and peremptory in regard to Justice-As-Sovereignty. However, the court specifically declined to consider *jus cogens* within the case. Reasoning that *jus cogens* was a matter of 'legal character' and that the General Assembly in its petition did 'not raise the question of the character of the humanitarian law which would apply to the use of nuclear weapons', the court saw 'no need ... to pronounce on this matter'.[107]

The petition of the General Assembly notwithstanding, illuminating the case with PPLD allows one to see that it is not that no law, or a gap

---

[104] That is, humanitarian principles originally confined to the context of armed conflict have been increasingly accepted to apply independent of declared civil or interstate war as they enter the realm of customary and treaty law that transcends the original circumstances of the Geneva Conventions.

[105] Tams, *Enforcing Obligations*; Ragazzi, *Concept of International Obligations*, ch. 3.

[106] *Legality of the Threat or Use of Nuclear Weapons* 226, § 33.

[107] Ibid., § 83.

in the law, exists but that two dialectically engaged and distinct ideas of authority are competing for recognition. To accept humanitarian and environmental law in terms of its true character in relation to nuclear weapons (as critical legal principle) gives it authority beyond the state, requiring that Justice-As-Sovereignty yield security of process in favour of the authority and rational necessity of principle. Since the court had already established *Lotus* as the standard but found no distinct prohibition in humanitarian or environmental law to satisfy it, it proceeded to acknowledge the authority of the significant body of humanitarian and environmental law that existed without granting it the authority of legal-critical principle.

In effect, the court needed to de-fang critical principle by co-opting it into the service of Justice-As-Sovereignty. In doing so, the court created a perceived gap between the requirements of authority and the extent of the positive law, which could be seen as a *non liquet*. This was done by taking a critical principle that is claiming authority beyond the state that requires *jus cogens* status and instead defining it through *jus dispositivum* and sovereign authority.

PPLD shows that the core dialectic of process-principle has ramifications for the definition of a 'principle' within the international legal system that is demonstrated in this case. Justice-As-Sovereignty requires that certain principles be established as a basis for rules that support social convention and its status as a process-norm. These principles derive their meanings from social convention and are therefore *contextual principles* that structure process, creating social stability.[108]

In this way, the core dialectic illuminates two definitions of principle. If they are independent of social convention and necessary or essential to humanity in the person, they are *critical principles*. If they are completely dependent on social convention, they are *contextual principles*. This dichotomy further suggests that any principle could be based in either foundation. For example, the idea of human dignity can be regarded as an either contextual or critical principle. Based on Hume's PPLD, a contextual principle acquires its meaning from the social circumstances around which the stable society is formed. It is defined, externally to the individual, by social convention and requires that the dignity of the person be judged collectively. As a critical principle, within Hegel's PPLD, dignity is defined by self-consciousness and the requirements of reason and individual freedom independent of context or the social conventions

---

[108] Gillroy, *Evolutionary Paradigm*, 82ff.

involved. It is defined internally, by the ability of the person to maintain a higher-order moral control of his or her life in the face of social pressure.[109]

PPLD suggests that the way a principle is defined is important to the manner by which the philosophical argument for authority relates to both the definition of justice and the practice of the law – that is, to its success. To treat a critical principle as contextual, or vice versa, may create a *non liquet*. If the principle seeking authority comes from the passions and defends process and social convention, then it is adequately justified by the authority of Justice-As-Sovereignty and the practice of *jus dispositivum*. But if the principle is a product of reflective reason on the freedom of the person, independent of context, then it requires authority beyond the state and the peremptory status of *jus cogens*. These connections are especially pertinent for an international legal system making a transition from Stage-I to Stage-II.

In Stage-I, the balance of process⸱principle within the core dialectic defines justice as simultaneously an empirical condition of stable coordination and a normative imperative to maintain that equilibrium. Hume's argument for the authority of justice[110] creates a synthesis where process and its contextual principles outweigh any pre-emptive definition of Freedom-Through-Recognition. But Hume's PPLD promotes the passions over reason without eliminating the latter as a part of human nature. Within a legal context, this empowers process and contextual principle over peremptory law and critical principle without denying the existence of the latter in shaping the process norm of justice. For Hume's PPLD, the stability of the Stage-I process of collective action is paramount. But it must strategically accommodate the rising claims of critical principle, represented by Hegel's PPLD for a Stage-II international legal system, without allowing Justice-As-Sovereignty to be destroyed.

Treating critical principle as contextual is one tactical solution to this dilemma. In effect, the court addressed the challenge of humanitarian and environmental law in terms of principle contextual to the process norm of Justice-As-Sovereignty, not in terms of their true philosophical foundation in the authority of right and critical principle:[111]

---

[109] Jane Austin's heroines are driven by this dialectic. See, especially, the struggle against social convention undertaken by Anne Elliot in J. Austen, *Persuasion*, World Classics vol. 356 (Oxford: Oxford University Press, 1975).

[110] Hume, *Treatise of Human Nature*, 472, 480, 497.

[111] Guglielmo Verdirame has noticed this pattern in the way courts adjudicate human rights cases, especially in their inappropriate use of proportionality. See G. Verdirame, 'Rescuing Human Rights from Proportionality', in *Philosophical Foundations of Human Rights*, ed. R. Cruft, S. M. Liao and M. Renzo (Oxford: Oxford University Press, 2014), 341–60.

The extensive codification of humanitarian law and the extent of the accession to the resultant treaties, as well as the fact that the denunciation clauses that existed in the codification instruments have never been used, have provided the international community with a corpus of treaty rules the great majority of which had already become customary and which reflected the most universally recognized humanitarian principles. These rules indicate the normal conduct and behaviour expected of States.[112]

In effect, this is not a case of *non liquet*; it is a case of trying to co-opt critical principle under the authority of social convention. The court acknowledges humanitarian and environmental principles within existing law. The problem for them was in codifying their unique authority as critical principles, which would have required the transcendence of process and a violation of *Lotus*. The intuition of *non liquet* comes from the perception that these principles have a distinct authority that is weightier than the court acknowledges and therefore should have been decisive. The denial of the distinct authority of critical principle, and the knowledge that the sovereign authority of *jus dispositivum* is inadequate to establish critical principle in transnational law, suggests that a *non liquet* may exist.

The 'gap', however, was not in the law but in the court's failure to appreciate that there were two distinct concepts of authority involved in this decision. By treating critical principle under the authority of *jus dispositivum* rather than the proper authority of *jus cogens*, the court created the impression that no proper authority existed, which is the definition of *non liquet*.

C   Contextualizing Critical Principle: Necessity and Proportionality in Nuclear War?

Using one definition of authority when another is required confounds and confuses our understanding and application of practical reason. The court's strategy of contextualizing critical principle leads it to a justification of nuclear weapons use that contorts the logic of sovereign authority. In its use of the law of armed conflict to decide the case, it is argued that there could not be a ban on the use of nuclear weapons because there remains the possibility that a sovereign state, faced with the spectre of being annihilated by nuclear weapons, might have to use them to annihilate an opponent. This logic is aided by the court's reliance on the pre-existing contextual interpretation of the principle of self-defence under

---

[112] *Legality of the Threat or Use of Nuclear Weapons* 226, § 82.

the law of armed conflict: 'The Court cannot lose sight of the fundamental right of every State to survival, and thus its right to resort to self-defense, in accordance with Article 51 of the Charter, when its survival is at stake.'[113]

To further specify the context of this 'use', the court relied on the precepts of necessity and proportionality. PPLD suggests that it is only appropriate to apply the tests of necessity and proportionality to contextual, not critical, principle. Critical principle, by definition, has inherent necessity that makes proportionality irrelevant. Specifically, a pre-emptive norm contains its own moral causality and is never measured continuously but discreetly; it either exists (e.g., within the law) or it does not. For example, if self-defence were a critical principle in the mind of the court, then it would lead the judges to hold that the tests of necessity and proportionality would not be appropriate, as the right would apply to all recognized agents within the legal system regardless of time or context.[114] As a principle contextual to sovereignty, it pertains only to the state and in terms of the specifics of circumstance as contained within *jus dispositivum*. Here, in order to maintain conventional practice and a stable social order, context would require that force be used only when necessary and then in proportion to the force incurred.

Although there may be a predisposition to think of self-defence as a critical principle, grounded in Freedom-Through-Recognition and *jus cogens*, the fact that these conditioning tests are applied is evidence that the court is defining self-defence in terms of what Hume's concept of law recognizes as a contextual principle. For the court, self-defence is subject to consent and the voluntary rules of social convention within a law of *jus dispositivum*. Using the contextual principle of self-defence, the majority produces a finding that circumstances do exist in which a state's use of nuclear weapons is legally justified.

Overall, the court found that there is no direct prohibition on the use of nuclear weapons. Within PPLD, this suggests that the authority of Justice-As-Sovereignty and the established conventional equilibrium continues to dominate the process-principle dialectic. The court partially recognizes

---

[113] Ibid., § 96.
[114] Because of the inherent *necessity* of critical principle, *proportionality* is never appropriate to the decision whether to violate or apply *jus cogens*. Proportionality, however, may be part of the subsequent decision on what policy is appropriate to that application or violation. Here the court is applying proportionality to the decision to use nuclear weapons (the first of the two choice situations), which is only appropriate for contextual principle. The character of critical principle must be distinguished from its application. See Verdirame, 'Rescuing Human Rights'.

the body of humanitarian and environmental law, but only as contextual principle that does not endanger the equilibrium established by Justice-As-Sovereignty. By not recognizing the unique authority of critical principle, the court contorted the logic of the law of sovereign authority, as well as Article 51 of the charter, to create the legality of a pre-emptive nuclear strike in self-defence.

5 Conclusion

Jus dispositivum and *jus cogens* are based on distinct definitions of authority, one protecting Justice-As-Sovereignty, and the other empowering Freedom-Through-Recognition and authority beyond the state. To establish authority beyond the state requires that the true status of critical public-order principles be acknowledged, as they cannot be adequately instituted within the scope of sovereign authority.

Sovereign authority is defined within the context of *jus dispositivum*, or that specific law that is derived from the process of international cooperation as an end-in-itself. This philosophical foundation is illuminated by Hume's PPLD, which demonstrates that the authority of law based in social convention will be antithetical to any law from critical principle. *Jus dispositivum* and *jus cogens* are not just distinct kinds of law; they have dialectically opposed and definitive philosophical assumptions and structures. When law seeks to replace the utility of convention with right for individual freedom, each compromises its effectiveness to be improperly categorized as the other.

PPLD suggests that we are confronted with an international legal system with two dialectically engaged imperatives, each with its own philosophical justification and specific requirements, based on either the persistence of Justice-As-Sovereignty or the oncoming demands of Freedom-Through-Recognition. Specifically, the international legal system is in transition between Stage-I and Stage-II, rebalancing the process-principle dialectic.

Within this context, the core dialectic of process-principle is being played out on an evolving scale of forms that dictates the terms of the balance between them. The power of pre-existing convention forms an unconscious bias for the authority of a formal law of *jus dispositivum*. This stable equilibrium, maintained by the process-norm of Justice-As-Sovereignty, is ingrained in the basic assumptions of a stable international system. While the legal system also provides institutional context for the consideration of the demands of Freedom-Through-Recognition, as represented in *jus cogens* law, such critical principles will be perceived as dialectically opposite and disruptive to the established coordination of the international system.

To recognize a public-order rule as peremptory is to give it authority beyond the state. This will be resisted in deference to the practical reason of established authority as sovereign law. Consequently, codifying critical principle to rebalance its dialectic with the bulwark of process and establish its unique authority will be difficult. Because principle in law can be either contextual or critical, those responsible for the security of the existing system will attempt to fit these extra-sovereign imperatives into an existing framework of *jus dispositivum*. While such a classification will seem to be less disruptive to the present equilibrium, the peremptory quality of freedom, or right in law, will be lost. In addition, the misclassification will seem counterintuitive, spurring syntactic gymnastics and perceptions of gaps in authority or *non liquet*.

If the components of the process-principle dialectic have distinct and opposite philosophical foundations, and if the practical reason of critical principle is to vindicate the freedom of the individual through right in law, the predisposition to deprive right in law of its philosophical foundation in critical principle must be overcome. Only then will it be effective in protecting and empowering right as authority beyond the state.

6

Varieties of Authority in International Law

State Consent, International Organisations, Courts, Experts and Citizens

INGER-JOHANNE SAND

Introduction: Legal Authority and International Law

Definitions of law and its legitimacy in modern societies have been closely linked to definitions of rights and legal authority. Self-determination of individuals and states is a hallmark of the legitimacy of law and legal authority. Individuals, corporations and associations have the authority to speak for themselves based on their autonomy, human rights and contractual rights. Sovereign democratic nation-states and elected state officials have the authority to act on behalf of their peoples based on democratic and rule-of-law constitutions. Democratically enacted legislation and higher-court adjudication are the primary expressions of the legal authority of states.[1] Over the last fifty years, however, modern democratic states have expanded and dispersed their executive branches in ways that have created different forms of delegated, autonomous and hybrid legal authority. Privately owned corporations have in parallel developed complex and dispersed corporate constructions of authority. International law has based its authority on treaties resulting from voluntary cooperation and consent of sovereign states and on principles of customary law, but it is now experiencing similar forms of differentiation as domestic law in the expression of legal authority. Vital aspects of international law and how it operates are changing, with consequences for its legal authority and legitimacy.

First, international law is now regulating new areas such as human rights, competition, environmental protection, biotechnology, intellectual property rights, health and parts of criminal law that have previously

---

[1] J. Habermas, 'Postscript', in *Between Facts and Norms*, trans. William Rehg (Cambridge: Polity, 1996), 447–62; J. Habermas, *The Postnational Constellation* (Cambridge: Polity, 2001).

been the domain of domestic law. When regulation of areas that are much closer to citizens' interests is directly or indirectly controlled by international treaties and conventions, it creates demand for new forms of authority in international law. Second, ambitious human rights conventions are improving the quality of the legal authority and legitimacy of international law. International human rights support the role of citizens and citizens' organisations as part of the basis for new forms of international law. Third, environmental and climate change, as well as new forms of global political conflicts, have led to increased pressure for international regulations. Cross-boundary dynamics require legitimate inter- and transnational law and competent authorities to solve problems. Additionally, domestic law will be too limited in its scope and does not, by itself, have the required capability, validity or authority to deal with cross-boundary dynamics.

Fourth, a growing number of international organisations, courts and dispute-settlement bodies have emerged with widely different legal mandates and forms and bases of legal authority. International non-governmental organisations (INGOs) and transnational corporations (TNCs) develop different private-law forms of regulation. Delegated competence from international organisations to various councils, committees, tribunals, courts and agencies contribute to creating a rather diverse map of international organisations with different forms and substantive mandates of authority. This includes decision making and adjudication, with direct or indirect effects, and negotiations, recommendations and standardization. The formal and societal forms of legitimacy vary correspondingly. Regulations and decisions are issued by delegated competence and interpretation of general and under-defined treaty texts. There may be initially legitimate formal legal authority in the form of state consent, but extensively applied wide delegations and under-defined legal standards to secretariats and expert environments create organisational and procedural structures that are hard to define in those terms.

Fifth, international experts and bureaucrats in law and other fields will have significant *de facto* power operating under treaty texts, with a pressure to make decisions, in the absence of democratic structures of international organisations and under lacking or unclear forms of legal authority. International law is extended in terms of legal areas, actors and procedures. What the basis of its authority and legitimacy are in the various fields is, however, not always clear. International law has been extended by political will and international organisations, but the normative and legitimacy aspects of the extensions have not always been accounted for. International law functions on many dimensions, but its legal authority is not always explained in a normative sense. This problem will be discussed later on in this chapter.

Since 1945, and increasingly over the last twenty to thirty years, international cooperation has expanded to a number of fields, resulting in more international treaties, conventions and agreements and the creation of different types of organisations, courts and dispute-settlement bodies. Even if the classical legal forms of legislative, treaty-making and adjudicative legal authority in international law are still essential, they offer an insufficient account of the factual emergence of new international law and its authority and legitimacy. Under-defined treaties, adjudication of general standards, delegated powers, private forms of legislation, standardisation, INGOs, contracting and so on play vital roles in the evolution of inter- and transnational law in ways that may be effective but are often based on unclear forms of legal authority and legitimacy.

In the following sections, I argue that international law emerges in a variety of ways, previously from international organisations, negotiations and treaties based on state consent initially, but now also from organisations exceeding their formal mandates. Thus international organisations function increasingly autonomously. Their secretariats, expert environments, tribunals, courts and dispute-settlement bodies will, in many cases, develop their legal mandates beyond the texts and intentions of treaties. International networks of diplomats and independent experts will often be the drivers of negotiations. INGOs, TNCs and other international economic actors may be significantly influential. Additionally, there may be strong political and economic pressure, with uncertain democratic basis, for the enactment of new treaties and other agreements in areas with significant international dynamics and interdependence. General mandates may be developed beyond intentions.

New legal concepts, principles and norms emerge and change as part of formal legal processes and broader societal expressions and interpretations of justice, norms and social values.[2] International human rights have evolved in a complex interplay among states, international organisations, courts, INGOs and citizen movements. It has arguably included

---

[2] K. Tuori, M. Maduro and S. Sankari, eds., *Transnational Law: Rethinking European Law and Legal Thinking* (Cambridge: Cambridge University Press, 2014); G. Teubner, *Constitutional Fragments: Societal Constitutionalism* (Oxford: Oxford University Press, 2012); C. Thornhill, *A Sociology of Constitutions* (Cambridge: Cambridge University Press, 2011), ch. 1.

a form of legitimacy in itself, adding to other accepted forms of authority and legitimacy of international law. Environmental protection and climate change treaties concern international purposes that require global cooperation. They may also add to the authority and legitimacy of international law.

Law evolves not only as specific decisions but also as interpretive and institutional patterns and through complex and contingent legal and political processes with a variety of actors.[3] Formal legal regulations are often unavoidably general and under-defined.[4] The evolution over time of the adjudication by the Court of Justice of the European Union (CJEU), the European Court of Human Rights (ECtHR) and the World Trade Organisation (WTO) Dispute Settlement Body (DSB) are cases in point. The *interaction* between different legal authorities involves formal decisions and negotiation, delegation, competition, learning processes and so on.

Factors such as professional expertise, local knowledge, ethics, human rights and international cooperation contribute to *how* legal authority in international law is constructed based on the functions of law.[5] Legitimacy may additionally be based on the output or the (intended) consequences of legal decisions. Yet another form of legitimacy of law and legal authority is found in the substantive societal basis or the social purposes of law. Whether new forms of legal authority have the required legitimacy is a more complex and controversial question.[6]

In the following sections, I will explore examples of how legal authority emerges in international law. Different approaches to understanding the new forms of legal authority will be discussed in Section 1. In Section 2, different typologies of legal authority are described. In Sections 3 and 4, specific examples of legal authority and its legitimacy in various fields of international law will be described and normatively and theoretically assessed.

---

[3] A. Cassese, ed., *Realizing Utopia* (Oxford: Oxford University Press, 2012); C. Joerges, I. J. Sand and G. Teubner, eds., *Transnational Governance and Constitutionalism* (Oxford: Hart, 2004); I. Alvik, M. Emberland and C. Eriksen, eds., *The New International Law* (Leiden: Martinus Nijhoff, 2010), 1–14.

[4] R. v. Gestel, H. W. Micklitz and M. P. Maduro, 'Methodology in the New Legal World' (European University Institute Working Paper, 2012), 13.

[5] Thornhill, *Sociology of Constitutions*.

[6] Tuori, Maduro and Sankari, *Transnational Law*; M. Koskenniemi, 'International Law: Constitutionalism, Managerialism and the Ethos of Legal Education', *European Journal of Legal Studies* 1 (2007): 1–18.

1 Sociological and Normative Understandings of Changes in Legal Authority

In the situation of a more expansive, differentiated and effective international law, state sovereignty and state consent have become too narrow ways to describe the legal authority of international law. Different types of inter- and transnational organisations, courts, expert committees and so on participate in preparing and creating inter- and transnational law in ways that exceed the formal presumptions of how legal authority functions. Discretionary standards, societal purposes, powerful organisations, highly specialized expertise networks and pressure for a more effective international law all contribute to an increased variation and effectiveness in how international organisations work and how international law is developed.[7]

The argument put forward here is that the current dynamics of modern and international law evolves in the form of comprehensive interactions with different fields of political, societal, cultural, economic and technological semantics and processes. First, formal law and legal authority are increasingly dependent on other societal discourses, communications and actors in how legal norms, concepts and argumentation are substantively shaped. Several legal standards are taken directly from other societal semantics and discourses, such as sustainable development, economic competition, best interests of the child, polluter-pays and so on. Second, law is becoming more internally differentiated due to the many new regulatory tasks concerning climate change, environmental degradation, new bio- and information technologies, global trade and so on. Such new dynamics add societal purposes and logics to law that differ qualitatively from other principles and logics of law. Third, legislation, implementation and adjudication of different domestic, inter- and transnational *levels* of governance increasingly interact, interdepend and compete.

International treaties may define vital framework and principles of law but are unavoidably general and under-specified. Law is consequently additionally developed by a variety of international and domestic public law organisations, courts, tribunals and agencies with different forms of expertise, but these entities are below the level of treaty-making states. INGOs, TNCs and citizens will further influence the implementation of international law by their legal practices and cases brought before courts

---

[7] M. Koskenniemi, 'The Fate of Public International Law: Between Technique and Politics', *Modern Law Review* 70 (2007): 1–32.

and tribunals.[8] We need to describe, analyse and understand the larger societal context of international law and how it emerges, including the immense map of the many different legal authorities and institutions involved and the various political, societal, economic and technological trajectories and environments they refer to.

Several theoretical contributions have been made towards a better understanding of the new and more comprehensive forms of inter- and transnational law. Kaarlo Tuori has asked for *new conceptual tools* in order to come to terms with the many-faceted and pluralistic forms of transnational law in a new legal landscape.[9] Tuori accepts that new forms and procedures of law have emerged that differ from the classical hierarchical forms of domestic and international law and that may be labelled legal hybrids, transnational law, legal pluralism, legal perspectivism or interlegality.[10] Examples of the new forms of law are the extension of competition and contract law into public administrative law, resulting in new combinations that could transform the meaning of both public- and private-law principles; environmental law concepts such as sustainability and new legal areas such as bio-law, environmental law, sports-law and internet-law, which introduce highly specialized scientific or other semantics into the legal language and categories.

Tuori suggests that some of these new forms of law have not been developed by nation-state legislators.[11] They refer to social, economic and scientific transnational fields and have emerged as legal fields transnationally. They are representative of the semantics of new transnational societal dynamics such as new bio- and information technologies, environmental hazards, climate change and security. New social, scientific, ethical or economic norms and standards are developed first. Legal norms follow. The legal regulation of new biotechnologies, the internet, climate change and security often emerge on inter- and transnational arenas before becoming part of specific domestic legal patterns. They evolve through cross-disciplinary and polycentric legal sources and orders. Legal regulations are characterized by close connections to social, economic and technological semantics. Knowledge-based and technical standards are transferred into law. The result is a blurring of the boundaries between legal and social norms, which were previously seen as vital to the very rationality

---

[8] Tuori, Maduro and Sankari, *Transnational Law*; Teubner, *Constitutional Fragments*.
[9] Tuori, Maduro and Sankari, *Transnational Law*, ch. 1.
[10] Ibid., 15.
[11] Ibid., 16.

of modern law.[12] The legal regulation of biotechnology may be a case in point.[13] Innovations are used as arguments for new technologies and for the acceptance of technology-based standards in law, such as patents on biotechnological inventions, strictly evidence-based use of precaution, acceptance of new medical prenatal techniques and so on. Ethical and societal arguments may be left out. The transfer of technology-based standards into law may challenge the autonomy of law. The close connections between societal and technological discourses and law may be seen as a form of *hybridization* of law.[14] Concepts and normative standards are used interchangeably in factual and normative discourses.

Tuori further points to how European Union (EU), European Convention on Human Rights (ECHR) and WTO law can be described as transnational rather than international because they claim a certain autonomy in relation to international law, such as the Vienna Convention.[15] Constitutions and treaties regulate how nation-states and transnational authorities interact, but such formal regulations will often not cover all possible situations. In fact, domestic and inter- and transnational institutions will interact, overlap, combine and learn from each other in a number of ways that no hierarchical order can describe. Tuori uses the term *legal pluralism* to describe these forms of interaction but emphasizes that this refers to the legal pluralism of legal sources and orders, not legal systems such as specific sovereign nation-states.[16] There may be a plurality of legal orders within the legal system of a nation-state. There may be a competition between EU and domestic law, between non-state and state law, but these are not fatal conflicts. This does, however, refer to a more dynamic and open legal system than in previous nation-state models. Tuori prefers to use the concepts of *interlegality, judicial dialogue* and *perspectivism* to describe the new forms of legal pluralism and interaction between legal authorities. His view is that autonomy and dialogue between different legal authorities can be combined and are not necessarily contradictory.

---

[12] Ibid.; N. Luhmann, *Law as a Social System* (Oxford: Oxford University Press, 2012), 470.

[13] Cfr. Directive 98/44/EC on the Legal Protection of Biotechnological Inventions, *O.J. 1998* No. L 213/13; Directive 2001/18/EU, 12 March 2001, on the deliberate release of GMOs, OJ L 106.

[14] G. Teubner, 'Coincidentia Oppositorum: Hybrid Networks beyond Contract and Organization', in *Networks: Legal Issues of Multilateral Co-operation*, ed. G. Teubner and M. Amstutz (Oxford, Hart, 2009); I. J. Sand, 'Hybridization, Change and the Expansion of Law', in *Hybrid Forms of Governance*, ed. Å. Andersen and I. J. Sand (Basingstoke: Palgrave Macmillan, 2012).

[15] Tuori, Maduro and Sankari, *Transnational Law*; Luhmann, *Law as a Social System*, 19–21.

[16] Tuori, Maduro, and Sankari, *Transnational Law*, 25.

State and international courts can make decisions across the differences of legal orders. He finds support for this in Neil Walker and Paul Schiff Berman's contributions.[17] In contrast to these views, Kaarlo Tuori depicts 'radical legal pluralism' as represented by such diverse contributions as Hans Kelsen's *Stufenbau*, Martti Koskenniemi's critical legal theory and Niklas Luhmann's systems theory. Tuori considers these approaches as fragmented, closed and solipsistic forms of legal argumentation.[18] These theories are seen as expressions of legal conflict, not dialogue between the institutions involved.

In my view, Tuori's division between his own views on legal pluralism and the 'radical pluralists' is too strict. Most writers on this subject agree that the legal institutional landscape has changed – dramatically, to some extent. There is a plethora of legislative, executive and adjudicate institutions on domestic and inter- and transnational levels. They cooperate and build on each other, interact, overlap, compete and conflict. EU member states have legal systems that refer to and include both domestic and EU authoritative legislation and adjudication. There may be differences of opinion among courts about conflicting legislation that are not easily solved. For example, while some theorists would argue that each member state and the EU all have unified legal systems, others will argue that these legal systems should be seen as in continuous processes and with gaps and conflicts. The legal systems may be fragmented but still operative and working.

In my view, there is a wide range of relations between the various legal institutions and authorities in and between legal systems. This includes processes such as competition, learning processes, conflicts, conflict-of-law principles, mutual influence and judicial dialogue. There may be elements of unified coherence and deep conflicts of authority at the same time. The 'radical pluralists' have provided insight into vital aspects of the new landscape. Their contributions include perspectives of law as part of both continuous social change and complexity and differentiation. This does not exclude learning processes and judicial dialogue. Koskenniemi

---

[17] Ibid., 23–26; N. Walker, 'Beyond Boundary Disputes and Basic Grids: Mapping the Global Disorder of Normative Orders', *International Journal of Constitutional Law* Vol 6, no. 3–4 (2008): 3–4; P. S. Berman, *Global Legal Pluralism: A Jurisprudence of Law beyond Borders* (Cambridge: Cambridge University Press, 2012).

[18] Tuori, Maduro, and Sankari, *Transnational Law*, 34; Koskenniemi, 'International Law', 1–18; N. Luhmann, *Die Wirtschaft der Gesellschaft* (Germany: Suhrkamp Taschenbuch Wissenschaft, 1994), 344.

is realistic about the social function of law and how this influences the evolution of law, at times creating conflicts within law. Teubner has written extensively on transnational law and the many fields of law that are legislated, practiced or adjudicated outside of formal constitutional or public international organisations.[19] He emphasizes the significance of the UN Charter as international law, areas of law with relatively autonomous bodies and institutions of law such as labour law and areas that are regulated by transnational customary law or non-state agreements, such as *lex mercatoria*, *lex sportiva* and the International Organisation for Standardisation (ISO). He argues that several inter- and transnational treaties and institutions have constitutional qualities and structures. In his view, differentiation, complexity and fragmentation are unavoidable parts of modern law.

2 Different Forms of Authority in Inter- and Transnational Law

The most common way to define legal authority in public law today is through national democratic constitutions and state-consented international treaties. State consent has remained a standard of authority of international law, but international cooperation, human rights and autonomous courts and tribunals have been included as bases for the authority of international law. Sociological and political explanations of legal authority may be added to the normative.[20]

Thus international law cannot easily be described as one consistent and homogeneous regime or body of law; rather, it may be seen as a pluralistic regime consisting of a variety of treaties, conventions and principles that have emerged from different institutional contexts and for different purposes. This supports a *pluralistic, sociological* and *contextual* approach to what the authority of international law is.[21] International law has, over time, expanded to an increasing number of substantively different fields, such as trade and economic law (General Agreement on Tariffs and Trade [GATT], International Monetary Fund [IMF] and WTO); international cooperation and peacekeeping (e.g.,

---

[19] Teubner, *Constitutional Fragments*, 45, 51, 88, 110.

[20] Ibid.; Thornhill, *Sociology of Constitutions*.

[21] A. M. Slaughter, *A New World Order* (Princeton: Princeton University Press, 2004); Koskenniemi, 'Fate of Public International Law', 1–32; Tuori, Maduro and Sankari, *Transnational Law*; Thornhill, *Sociology of Constitutions*; Teubner, *Constitutional Fragments*.

the United Nations [UN]); human rights (Universal Declaration on Human Rights [UDHR], ECHR); environmental law (Stockholm and Rio declarations, UN Environment Programme [UNEP], Convention on Biological Diversity [CBD] Commission on Protection of the Environment and Sustainable Development); climate change (Kyoto Protocol); health, biotechnology and ethics (Bio-Safety Protocol, Universal Declaration on Bioethics and Human Rights, Universal Declaration on the Human Genome and Human Rights); criminal law (International Criminal Court [ICC]) and many more. These and other treaties and conventions are adjudicated internationally by different global organisations, courts and tribunals and domestically by nation-state authorities, with no unifying international court for cases cutting across different legal treaties.[22] The International Court of Justice (ICJ) decides only in legal conflicts between states and is not used if there are special treaty tribunals. The differentiation and fragmentation of international law raises questions in terms of what the legal authority of international treaty and transnational law is.

First, the conventions referred to previously are formally international obligations for states and governments. However, they are increasingly concerned with rights and regulations directed at citizens, organisations and corporations, which previously were seen as internal to states, but are now internationally regulated because they involve cross-boundary dynamics. Human rights, competition law, free movement, sustainable development and climate change regulations are all examples. The question is to what extent international law and organisations have legitimate authority to regulate themes that primarily concern the rights of citizens and corporations and may have social and cultural implications that local and democratic authorities may be better equipped to handle.

Second, the expansion of law has increased the *scope* as well as the *diversity* of international law. Economic, technological, environmental and human rights purposes and discourses dominate different treaties contributing to substantively significant variations in and conflicts between the values and purposes in law. One consequence of such fragmentation of international treaty law is a lack of international authorities with a mandate of balancing between potentially conflicting legal

---

[22] M. Koskenniemi, 'Fragmentation of International Law: Report of the Study Group of the International Law Commission', UN Doc A/CN4/L.682, 2006.

purposes and principles, such as between the economic efficiency of trade (EU, WTO or the Organisation for Economic Co-Operation and Development [OECD]) and environmental protection (e.g., the UN Development Programme [UNDP]).

Third, the expansion of international regulations has, in some areas, developed a highly specialized international law with declarations, recommendations guidelines, annexes and other forms of secondary legislation. WTO law may be a case in point, with several additional agreements, understandings and annexes. UNDP, with several declarations on biotechnology, health and ethics is another. The high degree of specialization may contribute to an increasing power of international expertise, both legal and non-legal.

Fourth, the diversity of international law reflects an equivalent diversity of international organisations representing and expressing different forms of legal authority. Some organisations are primarily secretariats for international negotiations. Others have emerged as *de jure* or *de facto* relatively autonomous organisations contributing significantly to treaty amendments and administrative and legal decision making and creating expert environments. NGOs play an increasingly vital role in some fields, supplementing the expertise of more official organisations run by experts and/or citizen activists.

International law is part of a pluralistic and complex institutional and legal landscape. Domestic, inter- and transnational law have become more and more interdependent. In new legal areas such as biotechnology, internet law, security, environmental protection and climate change, international treaties, declarations and agreements have become particularly vital. The question that emerges, however, is what the basis of the authority of new international treaties can be. One *sociological* answer might be that international cooperation over time delivers and is thus seen as contributing substantively to the legitimacy of law. A *political* answer might be that international treaties concern themes that are considered necessary and vital that require cross-boundary cooperation and expertise and that the involved states cannot deal with alone. The economic affairs of states are deeply interwoven and require some form of legal regulation. Human rights, environmental protection and climate change are seen as international themes contributing substantively to the legitimacy of law. On the other side are the arguments of the democratic deficit of international politics and law and of the cultural and social variations among regions.

3   New Forms of Authority of International Law: The Closer
     Interaction of International, Regional and Domestic Law

In this section, different themes of law with a different affinity to global
dynamics will be discussed in terms of the interaction between inter- and
transnational and domestic law and the relevant changes in the authority
of international law.

A   *The Authority of Individual and Human Rights:
     Local or Global Citizens?*

The authority and legitimacy of law in modern states has been based on
the institutions of citizenship, fundamental and universal freedom rights
and equality of rights, as well as sovereignty and democracy. With the UN-
initiated UDHR of 1948, the first significant, comprehensive and authoritative international declaration of human rights emerged, and with that,
the symbolic representation of all humans as global citizens with certain
inherent rights.[23] The declaration was not made operative and sanctionable law and has primarily had symbolic and political effects, but it was
a paradigmatic change with effects for international law and the starting
point for the following UN and regional human rights conventions.[24]
    The Geneva Conventions concerning the rights of the wounded and
sick of armed forces in military conflicts, the rights of prisoners of war and
the protection of civilian persons in time of war, followed in 1949–50. The
UN Convention Concerning the Status of Refugees, which gave a right to
seek asylum, came into force in 1954. These conventions concerned individual rights pertaining to situations of international conflict, an area that
on several dimensions would not be covered or secured by domestic law.
In 1966, the UDHR was followed by the preparation of more legally binding human rights conventions, first by the two UN Covenants on Civil
and Political Rights (CCPR) and on Economic, Social and Cultural Rights
(CESCR).[25] Thereafter followed the Convention on the Elimination of All
Forms of Racial Discrimination (CERD; 1969), the Convention on the
Elimination of All Forms of Discrimination against Women (CEDAW;

---

[23] P. Alston and R. Goodman, *International Human Rights* (Oxford: Oxford University Press,
      2013), ch. 2; M. Doyle, 'The UN Charter: A Global Constitution', in *Ruling the World*, ed.
      J. L. Dunoff and J. P. Trachtman (Cambridge: Cambridge University Press, 2009), ch. 4.
[24] S. Benhabib, *Another Cosmopolitanism* (Oxford: Oxford University Press, 2006).
[25] Alston and Goodman, *International Human Rights*, ch. 2.

1979) and the Convention on the Rights of the Child (CRC; 1989) – still without an international human rights court. Several UN committees on human rights have been established, with experts from member states, a States parties' reports system and certain more limited forms of individual complaints systems. The functions of the committees are to control, overview and respond to the comments of states and issue general comments. The procedures of the committees are more legal and administrative and less adjudicative than those of international courts.

Regional conventions on human rights and courts have emerged, in Europe with the ECHR (1950) and the ECtHR.[26] The ECtHR was created as part of the convention, but it took more time than anticipated to establish a functioning court for European citizens, which did not occur until the mid-1970s and 1980s.[27] In the early 1990s, the case load increased rapidly, and the general interest in the decisions of the court as legal sources and precedence escalated. From the mid-1990s, the ECtHR has been overburdened by an enormous backlog of cases, which the court is now dealing with. The many problems of the court notwithstanding, it has undoubtedly contributed significantly to the recognition and improvement of the application of human rights as a more active part of domestic law in a number of the member states and in European law. Human rights law has consequently emerged as transboundary law in Europe, even if disagreements on the adjudication of the convention still are significant. The American Convention on Human Rights and the Inter-American Court were enacted and in force from 1978. Similar conventions are emerging in other regions.

The International Labour Organisation (ILO) and its several conventions – particularly Convention No.98 on the Right to Organize and Bargain Collectively – have played an immensely important role in the dissemination of these rights and their normative structure, even if domestic implementation varies considerably. One of the consequences of the increasingly global economy is that work conditions, health and social welfare rights for workers are internationally relevant – for example, the ILO Convention on Freedom of Association and Protection of the Right to Organise (1950). Through comprehensive transnational economic trade and interdependence and the large number of TNCs, the conditions and rights of workers may be seen as a transnational legal responsibility.

---

[26] J. Christoffersen and M. R. Madsen, eds., *The European Court of Human Rights between Law and Politics* (Oxford: Oxford University Press, 2011).
[27] Ibid.

International human rights have recently been highlighted due to increased immigration, particularly internally and to neighbour states and to Europe from the Middle East and from certain Asian and African countries. The rights to asylum and humanitarian rights and aid concern a growing number of persons, albeit in quite different situations.[28] The right to asylum and refugee status is only given to persons who have, for example, a well-founded fear of persecution for reasons of race or religion in their home states. Further protection can be given for humanitarian reasons. Immigration may, however, occur for a number of different reasons – not only war and warlike situations but also hunger and other inhuman conditions, internal conflicts, ethnic- and religion-based conflicts and climate change and environmental degradation, which all are situations raising legal questions.

International criminal law, with rules and sanctions against crimes against humanity and stricter regulations of the personal responsibility of political leaders, can be seen as an additional internationally based strengthening of human rights, such as the Rome Statute of the ICC (2002).[29]

Whereas up until now, the state has been the sole constitutional guarantee and legislator – as well as implementer and executor of public law – concerning the legal position of citizens and other persons living on a territory, today international treaties and conventions play a vital role as guidelines and obligations for domestic legislation. International organisations, courts and tribunals are integral to supplementing the states and their institutions concerning authoritative interpretation and adjudication of citizens' rights.[30] Implementing international human rights conventions is a complex task involving conflicts between different traditions and cultures of law and different substantive conceptions of human rights. Due to the lack of a global human rights court, the international implementation is left to UN committees with state and expert representatives, land reports, general comments and complaint procedures but do not

---

[28] See Geneva Conventions I–IV (1950), Convention relating to the Status of Refugees (1954).

[29] Alston and Goodman, *International Human Rights*, ch. 15; J. Klabbers, *International Law* (Oxford: Oxford University Press, 2013), ch. 12.

[30] Klabbers, *International Law*, ch. 6; R. Domingo, *The New Global Law* (Cambridge: Cambridge University Press, 2010); M. Palma, 'The Possible Contribution of International Civil Society to the Protection of Human Rights', in *Realizing Utopia: The Future of International Law*, ed. A. Cassese (Oxford: Oxford University Press, 2012); Alston and Goodman, *International Human Rights*, chs. 13, 16.

offer proper judicial mechanisms.[31] The European and Inter-American Courts of Human Rights are looked to as examples by other regions and have improved the legitimacy and authority of international human rights law for citizens in many states and regions, even if their decisions are still controversial for several states.

Taking on the responsibility of citizens' rights changes the purpose and character of international law and of the relevant international organisations with effects for their legitimacy and authority. International human rights create legal connections between citizens and international organisations requiring the latter to address and take care of the former. Human beings are addressed directly as legal subjects by international human rights law; thus the boundaries between domestic and international law overlap, interact and become more complex.

B   The Basis of Authority of EU Law: Free Movement, Citizenship and Social and Human Rights

The EU treaties and institutions over the last fifty years have arguably represented the most comprehensive development of a new legal system on a regional and international level, with its combination of supremacy, direct effect, wide substantive competences and relatively effective adjudication. EU law builds on supranational treaties and constitutionally based state consent transferring significant legislative, executive and adjudicative competences from the member states to the EU institutions in economic, environmental, health and social protection, citizenship, justice, security, immigration and more areas of law. The CJEU adjudicates in cases between the EU and its member states, between member states and, in some cases, between EU citizens and state authorities. Additionally, the CJEU can give preliminary rulings at the request of member states' courts on the interpretation of EU law (on the basis of powers in Article 19, No. 3 of the Treaty of the EU). From the Rome Treaty, it has been emphasized that the EC/EU treaties are not only between the member states but also between 'the peoples of Europe', underlining its transnational character.[32] EU legislation has direct effect for citizens, and EU citizenship was included in the Maastricht Treaty (1992) to underline this particular

---

[31] 'Human Rights Complaint Procedure', Resolution 5/1 of the Human Rights Committee, 18 June 2007.
[32] Case C- 26/62 *Van Gend en Loos*, 1963.

quality of the treaties. EU citizens may use domestic courts and, in some situations, the CJEU to ensure their rights.

EU legislation on the free movement of goods, services, persons and capital has been an extremely effective mechanism in the harmonisation of European law for citizens and corporations, further strengthened by the dynamic interpretation by the CJEU of free movement as *rights* and the supplementing directives defining social and health rights. One of the most vital and expansive directives in relation to citizens' rights is the EC Directive 2004/38 'on the rights of citizens and their family members to move and reside freely within the territory of the Member States', guaranteeing a wide scope of social rights to EU citizens in other member states. Regulation (EC) No. 883/2004 includes further legislation on the coordination of social security systems based on the principle of non-discrimination.

In its adjudication, the CJEU has given primacy to the rights of free movement and competition law.[33] Fundamental and other rights representing legitimate public policies may justify restrictions to community law when based on overriding reasons for public interests and seen as non-discriminatory, necessary and proportional.[34] Through legislation and adjudication, EU law has created a complex hierarchy of rights distinct from but, in effect, part of domestic law.

The CJEU has addressed and referred to fundamental freedom and human rights long before the EU Charter on Human Rights was agreed on in 2000, but it was not until the Lisbon Treaty in 2009 that the charter was included in the treaties as valid EU law. Fundamental rights may be given priority above EU economic rights but must as far as possible be applied consistently with and not in violation of economic rights.[35] Citizens' rights in EU law were further strengthened by the introduction

---

[33] Some examples include Case C-29/69 *Stauder v. Stadt ulm*; Cases C-267 and C-268/91 *Keck and Mithouard*; Case C-372/04 *Watts*; Case C127/08 *Metock and Others*; Case C341/05 *Laval un Partneri*; Case C-85/96 *Martínez Sala v. Freistaat Bayern*; Case C-413/99 *Baumbast and R*; C-112/00 *Schmidberger*; Case C-36/02 *Omega*.

[34] Case C-341/05, *Laval un Partneri*, ECR 2007, I-11767, para. 110; Case C-438/05 *The International Transport Workers' Federation and the Finnish Seamen's Union v. Viking Line ABP and OÜ Viking Line Eesti*, ECR 2007, I-10779; Case C-346/06 *Rüffert*; Case C-372/04, *Watts*.

[35] Case C-112/00 *Schmidberger*, ECR 2003, I-5659, para. 74; Case C-36/02, *Omega*, ECR 2004, I-9609, para. 33; Joined cases C-402/05 P and C-415/05 P, *Yassin Abdullah Kadi and Al Barakaat International Foundation* ECR 2008, I-6351; Case C-341/05, *Laval un Partneri Ltd.*, ECR 2007, I11767, paras. 90–94, 110; Case C-438/05, *International Transport Workers' Federation* ECR 2007, I-10779 and Case C-346/06, *Rüffert*, ECR 2008, I-1989.

of EU citizenship in the 1992 Maastricht Treaty.[36] It connects to and underlines the rights given to EU citizens and their families by the free movement of persons, including the additional regulations and directives. In a recent CJEU decision concerning the right to education, EU citizenship is described in the following way: 'Union citizenship is destined to be the fundamental status of nationals of Member States, enabling ... the same treatment in law irrespective of their nationality.'[37] This underlines the specific character of the authority of EU law as an international legal regime in relation to domestic law and member state citizens.

The authority of EU law is built on state consent and the transferal of comprehensive supranational competences. EU institutions thus have been endowed with a different type of legal authority than under general international law. The EU treaty institutions work with mandates from the treaties but with a considerable degree of autonomy within that framework and the purposes laid down in them. The EU has been described as a *sui generis* institution and constitution. EU citizenship and the extensive rights to free movement underline the active inclusion of citizens contributing to the authority EU law, even if its legitimacy is contested, as documented by several referendums.

C   Who Has the Authority to Define International Environmental Law?

Environmental protection and climate change are two of the most urgent global challenges and political and legal international responsibilities of our time. The scope and consequences of environmental degradation and climate change are truly global, but they are complex, uneven, hard to assess and, to some extent, in the future. The most vital principles of environmental law have been initiated at the international level.[38] There remains, however, a dramatic lack of international legal authorities and mechanisms for environmental law implementation, compliance and sanctions. There is no international organization or legal authority taking a comprehensive and overarching responsibility for a more effective environmental law regime, and there are still serious disagreements as to the level of adequate protection. The UN Framework Convention on

---

[36] P. Craig and G. de Burca, *EU Law: Texts, Cases and Materials*, 4th ed. (Oxford, Oxford University Press, 2008); P. Craig and G. de Burca, *EU Law: Texts, Cases and Materials*, 5th ed. (Oxford, Oxford University Press, 2011).

[37] Joined Cases C-523/11 and C-585/11, *Prinz and Seeberger*.

[38] N. de Sadeleer, *Environmental Principles: From Political Slogans to Legal Rules* (Oxford: Oxford University Press, 2002).

Climate Change reached an agreement in Paris in December 2015 to keep global warming at a level below two degrees Celsius.[39] The agreement is currently being implemented, despite the current US president's efforts. New technologies support the political and legal processes.

The UN conferences in Stockholm (1972) and Rio (1992) were crucial in setting international agendas and developing standards for environmental protection. In the Stockholm Declaration (Principle 21), the sovereign right to exploit natural resources, but also the responsibility to protect, is emphasized.[40] The transboundary responsibilities were, however, without sufficient clarification. The Brundtland World Commission on Environment and Development (WCED) was appointed to continue the work to combine environmental protection and the right to development on the global level.[41] Sustainable development was suggested as the answer to a principle and standard for the combination of the protection and development of human and natural resources, and the report from the commission was seen as the first authoritative formulation of the principle. The general support of the principle was reinforced by the Rio Conference on Environment and Development (UNCED) in 'Agenda 21', which is a comprehensive program for the sustainable protection of all types of natural resources, combined with actions to alleviate poverty and strengthen sustainable development. The Rio Declaration included the precautionary principle (Principle 15) after it had been affirmed by other declarations.[42] The precautionary principle has achieved the status of a vital principle of (international) environmental law, but it remains insufficiently defined, implemented and sanctionable internationally.[43] The Rio Conference additionally led to the Framework Convention on Climate Change and the Convention on Biological Diversity (CBD; 1992).

The international process via the UN and several of its organisations – such as UNESCO, the Food and Agriculture Organisation (FAO), WHO, UNEP, UNDP, the UN Congresses on Environment and Development and the UN Framework Convention on Climate Change – have, since

---

[39] 'Paris Agreement: Essential Elements', United Nations Framework Convention on Climate Change, http://unfccc.int/paris_agreement/items/9485.php.

[40] http://staging.unep.org/Documents.Multilingual/Default.Print.asp?DocumentID=97&ArticleID=1503&l=en.

[41] 'Report of the World Commission on Environment and Development: Our Common Future', UN Documents, www.un-documents.net/wced-ocf.htm.

[42] P. Birnie, A. Boyle and C. Redgwell, *International Environmental Law* (Oxford: Oxford University Press, 2009), 41–43, 116–17.

[43] N. de Sadeleer, *Implementing the Precautionary Principle* (London: Earthscan, 2007).

the Brundtland Commission and Rio Declaration, enabled the promotion of sustainable development, the precautionary principle and biodiversity as principles of international law. Compared to the serious and transnational challenges of environmental degradation, there is still a lack of international organisations working effectively and with sanctionable and judicial mechanisms. Thus there is no clear institutional or legal operative authority of international environmental law. The existing organisations, conventions, NGOs and so on depend on state cooperation and international experts, administrations and diplomats. The existing legal authorities of environmental law are thus combinations of states, international organisations, NGOs and experts working under the pressure of necessity of change.

4 Understanding the New Forms of Authority of Inter- and Transnational Law

A *The Authority of Citizens in a Global Society: Universal Human Rights and Cosmopolitan Law*

The Kantian project of a cosmopolitan law was first embodied in the foundation of the UN in 1945 and the Universal Declaration of Human Rights (UDHR) of 1948 as an expression of human rights as inherent and universal for all. The implication is that human beings are not only citizens of a state but members of a global humanity with equal rights for all. The UDHR was followed by several legally binding UN human rights conventions such as those mentioned previously.[44] These have been implemented and incorporated as positive law in a large number of states and are actively adjudicated to various degrees domestically and internationally.[45] The UN conventions can be seen as the bases for a new form of international law incorporating the rights of citizens in principle irrespective of their domiciles. In practice, the legal authority of UN human rights committees still depend to a large extent on the participating member states, but their decisions are vital legal sources and are both politically and symbolically important. The conventions and the UN committees can be seen as a paradigmatic change for the authority of international law in defining the international society as one of citizens, not only states. A plausible perspective on this could be that this significantly enhances

---

[44] See pp. 172–73 above.
[45] See p. 173 above.

the legitimacy and the authority of international law, even if international human rights adjudication and accountability is very limited. The UDHR and UN conventions set an international standard of human rights law that can be used politically and legally and has contributed to a set of UN committees that interact and communicate with the member states, even if sanctions are lacking. International human rights are increasingly seen as an ethical and symbolic basis of law even if their legal implementation varies significantly. The acceptance of international human rights implies that other forms of international law can no longer be seen as sector law separate from the notion of a more comprehensive legal system and thus from human rights law. The UDHR and the UN conventions can be seen as the beginning of a form of constitutionalisation of international law and of a legitimacy of international law apart from state consent.[46] More and more, international courts and tribunals are taking human rights into consideration when relevant, including the ICJ.[47] The two regional courts, the ECtHR and the Inter-American Court of Human Rights, have significant legal functions in their regions and act as role models for other regions. This is not to underestimate the immense differences in the implementation and interpretation of human rights internationally. The Rome Statute and the ICC have further strengthened the international position of human rights with the possibility of holding state leaders responsible for crimes against humanity.

Habermas has continued Kant's argument by emphasizing human rights as global, not state based.[48] Freedom and self-determination are seen as universal rights and are better protected as such rather than linked to the nation-state and thus dependent on local political variations. The existing UN conventions on human rights and the idea of universal human rights are vital in contributing to a legitimacy of international law and a basis of humanity underneath the myriad economic treaties and agreements. Seyla Benhabib emphasizes the theory of a discursive ethics based on the unbounded quality of morality and ethics for humanity.[49]

[46] S. Gardbaum, 'Human Rights and International Constitutionalism', in Ruling the World, ed. J. L. Dunoff and J. P. Trachtman (Cambridge: Cambridge University Press, 2009); B. Fassbender, 'Rediscovering a Forgotten Constitution: Notes on the Place of the UN Charter in the International Legal Order', in Ruling the World, ed. J. L. Dunoff and J. P. Trachtman (Cambridge: Cambridge University Press, 2009).
[47] J. Klabbers, International Law, ch. 6, 116; Alston and Goodman, International Human Rights.
[48] J. Habermas, 'A Political Constitution for the Pluralist World Society', in Between Naturalism and Religion, by J. Habermas (Cambridge: Polity, 2008).
[49] Benhabib, Another Cosmopolitanism.

Every human being is seen as a moral actor who must be included in 'society'. Arguments for limiting membership in humanity to nation-state citizenships are highly problematic from this point of view. Information technologies such as the internet and social media contribute to creating communicative infrastructures which are global and to some extent independent of nation-states. New technologies can be seen as means to express a civil society across boundaries and thus to treat citizens as global. This strengthens the position of seeing human rights as universal.

B   The Authority of Transnational Law: Civil Society, New Technologies and Markets

Below the level of states and across boundaries, there is an immense transnational interaction: economically via markets and TNCs and culturally via the internet with social and mass media, migration and other forms of travelling, INGOs and their activities, scientific cooperation and dissemination and so on.[50] New formations of civil society on the global level have emerged through the use of new technologies and transnational institutions. Legal regulations of transnational dynamics emerge as combinations of public and private law, including agreements, standards and guidelines from transnational organisations such as ICANN (Internet Corporation for Assigned Names and Numbers) and the ISO. The legal authority of transnational actors may be viewed as in process, hybrid and uncertain and often as a result of demand and output more than legitimate input procedures.

The development of the internet and information technology has intensified transnational interactions. ICANN remains the transnational organisation with authority to issue domain names, in cooperation with national committees, but with an unclear form of organisation for such a powerful communicative infrastructure. There is still no international organization or treaty with a comprehensive competence to regulate the internet. The functioning regulation of the internet is an unclear combination of domestic, trans- and international law, with human rights, competition and contract law included.

Many TNCs are as economically powerful as many states and influence local labour markets and social rights, international financial

---

[50] Teubner, *Constitutional Fragments*, ch. 1; A. Cassese, 'Can the World Become a Global Community?', in *Realizing Utopia*, ed. A. Cassese (Oxford: Oxford University Press, 2012).

markets, intellectual property rights, environmental and climate change policies, dissemination of technologies and science and so on. The legal regulations of TNCs are combinations of their own contracts and internal regulations with domestic, trans- and international law. There may be disagreements concerning the impact of private regulations and litigation of TNCs and what type of legal authority they represent. Corporate owners, labour organisations, INGOs, local communities and states may have different perspectives on what role the different authorities involved should play.[51] Several forms of transnational, private law or hybrid legal regulations with different forms of legal authority may develop as a result, such as industrial standards, investment contracts, labour regulations and contracts, ethical and social guidelines and contracts between TNCs and local communities. Transnational law can be seen as a response to the lack of effectiveness of public international law in areas where transnational actors and trajectories have emerged. The legal authority of transnational law in the areas just referred to relies on the substantive input to society of the new technologies and of the internet and social media as emerging forms of a transnational civil society. The legitimacy depends on how the societal contributions are perceived.

C   The Legal Authority to Regulate the Environment and Climate Change: Under Conditions of Social and Economic Global Diversity

Environmental and climate change are unavoidably global and need to be regulated accordingly in order to solve the problems involved. There is a large number of international treaties, conventions, agreements and recommendations on environmental protection and climate change. Additionally, international treaties on trade such as the WTO may impact environmental protection. In environmental law, the cooperation and interaction among domestic, inter- and transnational law is both comprehensive and vital. There is no effective unitary international adjudicatory body in environmental law, but many of the principles and general norms of environmental law have emerged through international conventions and agreements, such as the Stockholm and Rio Conferences, the WCED, the CBD, the Kyoto Protocol and, currently, the Paris Agreement.

---

[51] C. Joerges, I. J. Sand and G. Teubner, eds., *Transnational Governance and Constitutionalism*, pt. 2, chs. 9, 11, 13, 14, 15, 16; B. de Sousa Santos and C. Rodriguez-Garavito, eds., *Law and Globalization from Below* (Cambridge: Cambridge University Press, 2005), chs. 2, 3, 4, 5, 7, 10.

Purposes, goals and principles have not only been agreed on internationally but also implemented domestically. The importance of international agreements should not be underestimated for the total situation of environmental law. The current circumstances would probably have been much worse without international environmental law, even if it is fundamentally flawed. Transnational agreements such as the Codex Alimentarius, Forest Principles, UNCED and other standardisations are part of inter- and transnational environmental law.[52]

Many actors are involved in developing international environmental law, public and private organisations, international conferences and committees, expert networks and so on.[53] TNCs develop private forms of legislation. Citizens and INGOs have been increasingly active in international conferences on climate change, trade and environmental protection. Even if it is hard to speak about a well-functioning global civil society, there are certainly aspects of it. International environmental law is plagued by an emphasis on effective trade and competition and the lack of international environmental courts. The close interaction between international treaties and conventions and domestic implementation is, however, crucial for improving environmental protection. International environmental and climate law deals with global dynamics and thus have a greater potential for legitimacy and authority than many other areas of legal regulation. International law and agreement on environmental principles are necessary for the coordination of domestic regulations in a fundamental way. International legal authority should be possible to establish not only through state consent but also based on the substantive purposes of environmental protection, possible outcomes and necessity of the regulations.

Democratic governance is difficult to replicate on the inter- and transnational levels. International treaties are often flawed by standards that are too general or compromises that are unclear, but they may, in terms of authority and legitimacy, be supplemented by internationally based substantive purposes, such as environmental protection and carbon dioxide reductions. Expert environments and INGOs may supplement the dissemination of knowledge and information to citizens and government agencies.[54] The diversity of actors and procedures may contribute to pluralism and a

[52] Forest Principles have been adopted by UNCED to define sustainable management of forests first in 1992 and later in 2007 as non-binding principles. The principles have been further specified in regional conferences.

[53] De Sousa Santos and Rodriguez-Garavito, *Law and Globalization*, ch. 2.

[54] O. Godard, 'Social Decision-Making under Conditions of Scientific Controversy' in *Integrating Scientific Expertise into Regulatory Decision-Making*, ed. C. Joerges, K.-H.

robustness of law. The asymmetry of international law that privileges economic law over environmental protection remains a serious problem.

The protection of the environment is closely linked to the application of new biotechnologies. Legally, the implication is that there will be interdependence between the regulation of trade, biotechnology and environmental protection with quite different and conflictual societal purposes and combinations of domestic and international law, but without legitimate balancing authorities. A theoretical approach solving the complex balancing of effective markets, risk technologies and environmental hazards has been Christian Joerges's proposal for 'deliberative supranationalism'.[55] His approach is based on Habermas's theories of a deliberative ethics, and the obligation of objective and intersubjective procedures, in legislation and adjudication. Supranational processes may be seen as having the advantage of excluding vested interests on the domestic level: more heterogeneous decision-making situations have more rational and transparent decision making compared to the domestic level. The experience so far is, however, that it seems as difficult to balance *economic, technological, environmental* and *ethical* standards on the international level as on the domestic level.[56]

D   *New Formations of Legal Authority: Interaction, Interdependence and Expertise Supplementing Sovereignty and Consent*

Today, international treaties, conventions and agreements regulate substantive areas of law: trade, competition, environmental protection, climate change and new technologies. Legal and non-legal international experts have significant influence in the formation of international treaties. The UN International Panel for Climate Change, the WTO secretariat, the UNDP, the UNHCR, the Office of the United Nations High Commissioner for Human Rights, the IMF, the European Central Bank, OECD and many more are international expert-based secretariats that are either decision makers in their own right or influential advisers who lay down the premises of international law, politics and economics. Democratically elected authorities depend on such experts. There is a general lack of transparency on how expert-based organisations, or networks, function and how they interact with more democratic authorities. For example, scientific data on

Ladeur and E. Vos (Baden-Baden: Nomos Verlagsgessellschaft, 1997); N. Luhmann, *Risk: A Sociological Theory* (Berlin: De Gruyter, 1993).

[55] C. Joerges, 'Good Governance through Comitology' in *EU Committees: Social Regulation, Law and Politics*, ed. C. Joerges and E. Vos (Oxford: Hart, 1999).

[56] C. Joerges, 'Unity in Diversity as Europe's Vocation and Conflicts Law as Europe's Constitutional Form' (LSE Europe in Question Discussion Paper No. 28, 2010).

climate change, economic statistics, development data, human rights law and international humanitarian law constitutes important expert information that is formative for international law and politics. The communication of expert knowledge occurs more in the form of interaction and interdependence than in hierarchy, sovereignty and consent. The relations between state and international authorities include both types of communicative form and, additionally, negotiations, dialogue, learning processes and cooperation. Vital decisions are made in ways that often lack mechanisms of accountability and transparency and also with a distance from, and lack of information to, citizens.[57]

E The Authority of Democracy and Accountability: How Can International Law Achieve Legitimacy?

The most serious problem with the expansion of international law to areas affecting the rights of citizens is its distance to these citizens and the lack of democratic institutions and procedures, transparency and accountability measures, and accessible civil-society spheres. International law is still predominantly created through inter- and transnational negotiations and complex decision-making procedures among elite institutions. There may be state consent from democratic states, but international negotiations are generally conducted by executive state authorities and take place behind closed doors, with insufficient public information and transparency provided to both parliaments and the general public. INGOs and social movements have, in some instances, been active in relation to international organisations and their meetings, organizing parallel meetings of their own (e.g., at Seattle, Doha and Paris), thus extending a more open form of authority to international negotiations.[58] The Lisbon EU treaty includes reforms allowing for member-state parliament members to regularly visit the European Parliament. The lack of democratic participation by parliaments and citizens and the lack of transparency remain fundamental problems of legitimacy for international law. International courts and tribunals are generally accessible only for states, except for regional human rights courts, which are accessible for citizens. International law can be seen as the result of political, judicial, economic and technocratic elites working within international organisations, corporations and

---

[57] C. Joerges and C. Glinski, eds., *The European Crisis and the Transformation of Transnational Governance: Authoritarian Managerialism versus Democratic Governance* (Oxford: Hart, 2014); Koskenniemi, *International Law*.

[58] Cassese, *Realizing Utopia*; Tuori, Maduro and Sankari, *Transnational Law*; Teubner, *Constitutional Fragments*.

INGOs, based on highly specialized political and legal discourses, and within institutional contexts where economic efficiency and technological optimism dominate.[59] Specialized technocratic discourse predominate lacking transparency and accessibility for the general public. The Paris Agreement is promising and an important step forward.[60] International law is unavoidably a much more complex program in legislation, as well as adjudication, than domestic law.

5   A More Sociological Understanding of Authority and a More Cosmopolitan International Law

New international political and legal orders are created partly with active and comprehensively legislating international organisations and partly with nation-states engaging in and relying on intensive and committed international cooperation.[61] Nation-states act based on not only self-interest but also the values of international cooperation. The political orders of national sovereignty now include more committed forms of international collaboration and respect for global concerns and values. Transnational actors and fields have become vital parts of global interaction, creating new spaces and 'frontier zones' irrespective of state authorities.[62] The universal status of international human rights and their impact on domestic law is part of this. The acceptance of such rights as universal by international law implies a more extended responsibility for citizens by international as well as domestic political authorities. Large TNCs with operations in many states and regions are difficult to control in terms of human rights.[63] The comprehensive international trade and global economic interdependence resulting in the exploitation of cheap labour and a lack of human rights in some exporting states is an additional argument for international implementation of human rights.[64]

Stephen Gardbaum has argued that international human rights conventions have created a new international constitutional system qualitatively different from previous forms of international law because they concern

---

[59]   Koskenniemi, 'Fate of Public International Law'.
[60]   See the Paris Agreement at https://unfccc.int/resource/docs/2015/cop21/eng/l09r01.pdf.
[61]   Slaughter, *New World Order*; Dunoff and Trachtman, *Ruling the World*.
[62]   S. Sassen, *Territory, Authorities, Rights* (Princeton: Princeton University Press, 2006), chs. 5, 8.
[63]   Ibid., ch. 5.
[64]   De Sousa Santos and Rodriguez-Garavito, *Law and Globalization*.

the rights of individual persons.[65] The UDHR and conventions that followed it are manifestations of human rights as inter- and transnational law, and they have been influential in the implementation of human rights in domestic law. International human rights have changed the character of international law and national sovereignty. An international or more pluralistic form of constitutionalism emerges.[66]

Several lawyers and philosophers have advocated for universal human rights. Seyla Benhabib argues for the necessity of a universal ethics and thus for universal human rights in a global society.[67] From her discursive ethical perspective, we are all human beings on an equal level, and we have an obligation to justify our actions in relation to all other human beings. National boundaries cannot be recognized as arguments in ethical discourse concerning moral boundaries for human rights; only the whole of humanity can be accepted as the purpose of ethical norms. Habermas reinforces this position by emphasizing how any delimitation of the scope of human rights must be justified by ethically valid reasons.[68] He refers to open and democratic procedures, accessible for all, and practical deliberation in order to test the qualities of ethical arguments. Discourse ethics must be practical and concrete while at the same time have universal aspirations.

The substantive arguments for this ethical position are arguably strengthened by our modern-day global interaction and interdependence economically, technologically, culturally and politically and so on.[69] Economic and social inequalities are, however, still significant aspects of global dynamics. So far, global markets have not decreased the enormous social and economic disparities or the problem of exploitation.[70] Economic treaties, including binding references to human and social rights and environmental protection, are necessary for improving global social justice in addition to international human rights. A more internationally based ethic and more effective inter- and transnational regulations of environmental protection and climate change measures are necessary for improving environmental global justice.

---

[65] S. Gardbaum, 'Human Rights and International Constitutionalism', in *Ruling the World*, ed. Dunoff and Trachtman (Cambridge: Cambridge University Press, 2009).
[66] Tuori, Maduro and Sankari, *Transnational Law*.
[67] Benhabib, *Another Cosmopolitanism*, 27.
[68] J. Habermas, 'Discourse Ethics', in *Moral Consciousness and Communicative Action*, by J. Habermas (1989; Cambridge, MA: MIT Press, 2006); J. Habermas, *Between Facts and Norms* (Cambridge: Polity, 1996), ch. 4.
[69] J. Habermas, 'The Postnational Constellation and the Future of Democracy' in *The Postnational Constellation*, Cambridge: Polity Press, 2001; Domingo, *New Global Law*, ch. 6; De Sousa Santos and Rodriguez-Garavito, *Law and Globalization*.
[70] J. Stiglitz, *Globalism and Its Discontents* (London: Penguin, 2002), ch. 1.

7

The Legitimate Authority of International Courts and Its Limits

A Challenge to Raz's Service Conception?

ANDREAS FOLLESDAL*

Introduction: On the Relationship between Authority and Legitimacy of International Courts

A   *The Puzzle*

Many international courts (ICs) and treaty bodies are criticized for several reasons. Protests against the free market ideology and Western bias of the World Trade Organisation (WTO) and its dispute-settlement mechanism and against the allegedly anti-African international criminal court (ICC) are *legio*.[1] States themselves disobey: the South African government refused to arrest Sudanese president Omar al-Bashir in public defiance of the ICC and its own high court. Some protests and disobedience against ICs may be wholly due to governments' intransigence, which they may seek to hide. But states sometimes deliberately draw public attention to their noncompliance. Thus, politicians in the United Kingdom (UK) and Russia challenge particular judgments of the European Court of Human Rights (ECtHR), defying the blanket ban on prisoners' right to vote or refusing to implement rulings that contradict their constitution.

---

* This article has benefited greatly from discussions at the iCourts conference on International Jurisprudence: Rethinking the Concept of Law in the Light of Contemporary International Legality, December 19, 2014, at a PDJ workshop at UiT the Arctic University of Norway, March 5, 2014, and at a workshop in Dublin January 13, 2017. I am especially grateful for constructive comments from Oran Doyle, Margaret Martin, Oisin Suttle and the editors.

[1] Including S. Joseph, 'Trade Law and Investment Law', in *The Oxford Handbook of International Human Rights Law*, ed. Dinah Shelton (Oxford: Oxford University Press, 2013), 841–70; K. Kulovesi, *The WTO Dispute Settlement System: Challenges of the Environment, Legitimacy and Fragmentation* (Alphen aan den Rijn: Kluwer Law International, 2011); J. Stiglitz, *Globalization and Its Discontents* (New York: Norton, 2002), 214.

Such very public challenges by state governments, legislatures, domestic or international courts, corporations, investors or civil society groups are often draped in terms of 'legitimacy'. The challenges provoke several questions. Why should such 'compliance constituencies'[2] defer to ICs' judgments at all? More precisely: When do ICs' judgments give such constituencies reason to act differently than they would otherwise – and when do they not? Answering these questions require us to first understand what reasons there are for states and other constituencies to defer – in various ways – to ICs. What are the scope conditions for ICs' legitimate claims to deference? How should states respond to ICs' judgments when they venture beyond that scope? And how should they respond when some states disobey? Indeed, such public noncompliance prompts the question of why and when other actors' beliefs about the ICs' legitimacy – their *social* legitimacy – and their *actual* compliance affect the reasons other actors have to defer. These questions are especially important regarding international law as compared to domestic acts of noncompliance due to the lack of enforcement mechanisms and the risk that parts of the international legal order might unravel as a result.[3]

This chapter will begin to address these issues from the perspective of an account of the legitimate authority of ICs. The starting point is Joseph Raz's influential 'service conception' concerning the legitimate political authority of the state.[4] This account helps discern arguments that may substantiate an IC's claims to be a legitimate authority and arguably helps delineate the scope of such claims. One of the (in)famous features of this interpretation is that it lays out strict requirements for when – if at all – claims to authority are legitimate. For our purposes, it is helpful because it sheds light on the complex relationships between normative and social legitimacy. It outlines the structure of arguments needed to show when and why the legitimate authority of an IC's judgment may depend on widespread beliefs about its legitimacy and actual compliance by most states and other compliance constituencies – and when it does not. A state

---

[2] X. Dai, 'Why Comply? The Domestic Constituency Mechanism', *International Organization* 59 (2005): 363–98.

[3] I am grateful to Oisin Suttle for underscoring this point. See also Henrik Palmer Olsen, 'International Courts and the Building of Legal Authority beyond the State', Chapter 3 in this volume.

[4] J. Raz, 'The Problem of Authority: Revisiting the Service Conception', *Minnesota Law Review* 90 (2006): 1003–44. For attempts to apply Raz to international law generally, see S. Besson, 'Theorizing the Sources of International Law', in *The Philosophy of International Law*, ed. S. Besson and J. Tasioulas (Oxford: Oxford University Press, 2010), 176.

may have reason to defer, even when the IC lacks legitimate authority for its judgment, due to the compliance of others.

The grounds for justified noncompliance may appear particularly challenging for an account based on Raz's service conception. That theory explains why a legitimate authority's command merits obedience somewhat *independent* of the substantive contents of the command. This chapter argues that states' disobedience may still be justified due to the substantive contents of the particular ruling by an IC.

Section 1 provides a brief sketch of Raz's 'service account' of legitimacy and addresses some criticisms relevant to our concerns. Section 2 brings this account to bear on ICs and lays out some of its distinguishing features by comparing it to the influential accounts of Daniel Bodansky and Yuval Shany.[5] Section 3 then considers how this account accommodates and even justifies cases of disobedience against ICs.

1   Legitimacy: The Service Conception of Authority

How can someone who commands us to do something thereby give us a reason to act differently, even imposing on us a moral duty to do so? This is the topic of Raz's account of legitimate authority.[6] On this account, an authority is a body that claims to have the power to impose moral duties on others.

A claim to authority is most striking when that body issues a directive or command that appears stupid, mistaken, or unjust to those subject to it: 'It is of the nature of authority that it requires submission even when one thinks that what is required is against reason. Therefore, submission to authority is irrational.'[7] Even then, there is an assumption that authority's command imposes a moral duty on the subjects to act differently than they otherwise would have reason to.

---

[5] D. Bodansky, 'The Concept of Legitimacy in International Law', in *Legitimacy in International Law*, ed. R. Wolfrum and V. Roben (Heidelberg: Springer, 2008), 309–17; D. Bodansky, 'Legitimacy in International Law and International Relations', in *Interdisciplinary Perspectives on International Law and International Relations: The State of the Art*, ed. J. L. Dunoff and M. A. Pollack (Cambridge: Cambridge University Press, 2013), 321–42; Y. Shany, 'Assessing the Effectiveness of International Courts: A Goal-Based Approach', *American Journal of International Law* 106 (2012): 225–70; Y. Shany, *Assessing the Effectiveness of International Courts* (Oxford: Oxford University Press, 2013).

[6] Raz, 'Problem of Authority', 1005.

[7] J. Raz, 'Legitimate Authority', in *The Authority of Law: Essays on Law and Morality*, ed. J. Raz (Oxford: Oxford University Press, 2009), 3.

This understanding of what it means to claim authority seems appropriate for our topic, the legitimacy of ICs. An IC is similar to other bodies that claim *authority*, not just naked power over others like the mafia might use. The IC claims that it has a *right* to rule – that is, to issue such a judgment that others *have a duty* to heed.[8]

A   Justifying Legitimate Authority: The Service Conception

What reasons do potential subjects have to defer to an IC as a legitimate authority? Raz's general argument is 'the normal justification thesis': 'The subject would better conform to reasons that apply to him anyway (that is, to reasons other than the directives of the authority) if he intends to be guided by the authority's directives than if he does not.'[9]

Note that Raz holds that the directive of the authority must *replace* some of the reasons for action of the subjects – this is what creates the apparent puzzle: 'Because the arbitrator is meant to decide on the basis of certain reasons, the disputants are excluded from later relying on them. They handed over to him the task of evaluating those reasons. If they do not then deny them as possible bases for their own action they defeat the very point and purpose of the arbitration. The only proper way to acknowledge the arbitrator's authority is to take it to be a reason for action which replaces the reasons on the basis of which he was meant to decide.'[10]

This requirement – that the actors' original reasons are *replaced* by the judgment of the authority – appears to challenge our concern with whether disobedience might ever be justified on this account. I will turn to that in Section 4.

Raz sketches a non-exhaustive list of five kinds of reasons that legitimate authorities may promote. These are five kinds of *service* the authority can provide to actors – hence the name 'the service conception of authority'. Note that each of these provides a necessary, but not sufficient, condition for legitimate authority. And it remains an open, partly empirical

---

[8]   Raz, 'Problem of Authority', 1005.
[9]   J. Raz, *The Morality of Freedom* (Oxford: Clarendon Press, 1986) and Raz, 'Problem of Authority', 1014.
[10]   Raz, *Morality of Freedom*, 42. For a similar view, also see D. Bodansky, 'The Concept of Legitimacy in International Law', in *Legitimacy in International Law*, ed. R. Wolfrum and V. Roben (Heidelberg: Springer, 2008), 325.

question as to whether a body that claims authority indeed does provide any such service. These are Raz's five kinds of service:

1. The authority is wiser and therefore better able to establish how the individual should act.
2. It has a steadier will less likely to be tainted by bias, weakness or impetuosity, less likely to be diverted from right reason by temptations or pressures.
3. Direct individual action in an attempt to follow right reason is likely to be self-defeating. Individuals should follow an indirect strategy, guiding their action by one standard in order better to conform to another. And the best indirect strategy is to be guided by authority.
4. Deciding for oneself what to do causes anxiety, exhaustion, or involves costs in time or resources the avoidance of which by following authority does not have significant drawbacks, and is therefore justified. [...]
5. The authority is in a better position to achieve (if its legitimacy is acknowledged) what the individual has reason to but is in no position to achieve.[11]

2   The Service Conception Brought to Bear on International Courts

Two main modifications are significant for the service conception to help bring together several of the legitimacy concerns regarding ICs and explain how they fit together.

First, my concern is not with 'commands' but rather with the judgment, view or opinion (hereafter, judgment) that an ICs issues. Of particular concern are cases where compliance constituencies – domestic courts or parliaments, judges of other ICs or civil society groups – regard this judgment as poor, unjust or the like.

Second, note that an IC's correct claim to authority does not entail that others have a moral duty to *comply*. A more appropriate term may be *deference*: ICs' judgments, views, comments or interpretations should influence a wide range of actions. Other courts or legislatures may be required to *take account* of the judgments, to take them seriously or give some weight to them, even if in the end, the subject still fails to comply. For instance, a state may be expected to present counter arguments if it fails

[11] Raz, *Morality of Freedom*, 75.

to comply with the views of a treaty body.[12] Thus such judgments do not always provide *exclusionary* reasons to the subjects.[13]

One straightforward application of the service conception is that a necessary condition for an IC to be a normatively legitimate authority is that it enables states or other compliance constituencies to better act on the reasons they have. Candidate reasons are the objectives of the states that prompted the treaty establishing the IC. Arguably, ICs *might* provide several of the five services Raz delineates. Again, whether they in fact do so for various compliance constituencies remains an open question. There is thus no presumption in favour of the view that ICs exercise legitimate authority: that must be argued.[14]

Some ICs may provide a 'less biased will'. States have established them to provide assurance of their commitment to let their treaty obligations override their domestic short-term interests, ranging from human rights and international criminal law to investment conditions. Other ICs can reduce the burdens of making decisions. Thus states often agree to treaties whose central terms are left vague, leaving it to the IC as a sufficiently independent third party to interpret the legal text. Such agreements save time and help states bypass disagreements.[15] ICs may also reduce or resolve various collective action problems among states – for instance, removing free rider problems from international trade agreements by monitoring violations or trigger sanctions.

Such broad-brush applications of 'service arguments' may indicate some reasons why ICs' judgments should *exclude* some of the reasons states otherwise have for acting: that is the point of the steadier will and the collective action arguments. Note that these indications of how the service conception *may* apply do not yet show that any IC in fact ever exercises legitimate authority. The service conception only indicates the sort of arguments that must be provided. Determining which particular

[12] C. Tomuschat, *Human Rights: Between Idealism and Realism* (Oxford: Oxford University Press, 2008), 220.

[13] I am grateful to Oran Doyle and Alan Brudner, who prompted this clarification.

[14] I am grateful to Oran Doyle for noting the need to make this clear.

[15] J. Pauwelyn and M. Elsig, 'The Politics of Treaty Interpretation: Variations and Explanations across International Tribunals', in *Interdisciplinary Perspectives on International Law and International Relations: The State of the Art*, ed. J. L. Dunoff and M. A. Pollack (Cambridge: Cambridge University Press, 2013); A. Stone Sweet and T. L. Brunell, 'Trustee Courts and the Judicialization of International Regimes: The Politics of Majoritarian Activism in the European Convention on Human Rights, the European Union, and the World Trade Organization', *Journal of Law and Courts* 1 (2013): 61–88.

judgments, and by which ICs, create duties for whom requires detailed specification and arguments.

To spell out some implications of this account, it is useful to consider how it avoids some criticisms often levelled against various accounts of legitimate authority. Apparently, some accounts hold that legitimate authorities make 'absolute' demands that must always be complied with. Hurd criticizes those: 'Legitimacy is widely defined in relation to rule compliance ... These approaches leave no room to understand a case where rules appear to be widely accepted as legitimate and are also subject to non-compliance by those who believe in their legitimacy. In other words, these approaches deny agents the capacity to think, act, and choose in the presence of a legitimate rule or norm.'[16]

Raz's account, sketched previously, differs in several ways: it allows that legitimacy may be a matter of degree – that is, an authority may *increase* its legitimacy insofar as it provides a greater service to the subjects by helping them comply even more with the reasons and objectives they have. The moral duty an IC creates by its judgment may also be *prima facie*, able to be 'balanced' or set aside by other reasons such as commands from other authorities. And finally, even though the judgments of a legitimate authority have a moral claim to be obeyed, there is no moral claim that these subjects must change their beliefs (e.g., that the judgment is counterproductive, flawed etc.).[17]

Some critics of legitimacy dismiss such terms as mere tools of manipulation to prompt subjects into unthinking compliance: 'The very notion of legitimacy is ideological inasmuch as [it] lets power redescribe itself as authority on its own terms.'[18] In contrast, Raz's account holds that there may be no moral duty to obey all laws or other claimed authorities. Rather, it lays out the requisite sort of arguments necessary for self-proclaimed authorities to be *correct* in their claims to be legitimate for particular subjects. Therefore, this account may arguably help *resist* manipulation and unthinking compliance. Raz holds famously that there appears to be no 'legal system in which the normal justification thesis

---

[16] I. Hurd, 'The International Rule of Law: Law and the Limits of Politics', *Ethics and International Affairs* 28 (2014): 39–51.
[17] I am grateful to Henrik Palmer Olsen for urging elaboration of this point.
[18] M. Koskenniemi, 'Legitimacy, Rights and Ideology: Notes Towards a Critique of the New Moral Internationalism', *Associations: Journal for Legal and Social Theory* 7 (2003): 349–74, esp. 367.

can be shown to hold for every person and for every law which the system has in fact generated."[19]

A   On Social Legitimacy and Normative Legitimacy

This account distinguishes the normative legitimacy of an IC from *social legitimacy*, understood as the *belief* that an IC is normatively legitimate. This understanding of social legitimacy, harking back to Weber, is 'parasitic on the conceptually prior idea of normative legitimacy'.[20] A body that claims authority thus typically claims that the social legitimacy it enjoys in the eyes of some compliance constituencies is based on true beliefs. Bodansky, Shany and many other scholars concerned with the legitimacy of ICs use *legitimacy* and *authority* in similar ways as this account. They are not concerned with all bodies who yield any sort of power – only bodies that claim the right to rule. Both Bodansky and Shany distinguish between normative and social legitimacy in a similar way.[21]

Social legitimacy is often thought to have motivating force because actors believe that the IC's judgment gives them reason to act. Thus, insofar as some subjects regard an IC as a *legitimate* authority, they are often thought to be somewhat more likely to defer in such ways. However, Bodansky notes that this assumption has seldom been tested rigorously.[22]

A focus on the subjective beliefs of those under authority is sometimes called the 'subjective' tradition.[23] The alternative 'objective' tradition is illustrated by Allen Buchanan's claim that a government should only be considered legitimate if it meets certain standards in the way it treats its citizens. This, in turn, is separate from whether the population *believes* that the government is legitimate.[24] Even though normative legitimacy plays no direct causal role, it clearly must be included in accounts about contestations of the legitimacy of ICs. Such disagreements are usually about normative legitimacy – which reasons actors actually have. The parties seldom disagree about social legitimacy – whether certain parties believe

---

[19] S. Perry, 'Law and Obligation', *American Journal of Jurisprudence* 50 (2005): 263–95, esp. 276; and Raz, 'Problem of Authority', 1008.

[20] M. Weber, 'Politics as a Vocation', in *From Max Weber: Essays in Sociology*, by M. Weber, ed. and trans. H. H. Gerth and C. W. Mills (Oxford: Oxford University Press, 1973), 77–128.

[21] Bodansky, 'Concept of Legitimacy'.

[22] Bodansky, 'Legitimacy in International Law', 323.

[23] Hurd, 'International Rule of Law'.

[24] A. Buchanan, *Justice, Legitimacy, and Self-Determination: Moral Foundations for International Law* (Oxford: Oxford University Press, 2004).

that they have reasons to act stemming from the IC's judgment. Rather, the parties disagree about which of these beliefs about ICs being legitimate are correct or well grounded (i.e., matters of normative legitimacy). On this account, at least three conditions need to be met for an IC to not only claim to be an authority but actually be a legitimate authority for various compliance constituencies. Firstly, the provision of a service is not sufficient. In particular, more must be said about when the authority puts others under an obligation to defer. Subjects may have several reasons to act that they nevertheless have no *obligation* to act on, and this may reduce the authority's claim on the agent. And several competing bodies may be able to bolster a subject's ability to act according to reasons the subject has, raising the question of how to determine which of them should be authoritative for the subject. Regarding ICs, some of these issues are settled – imperfectly – by requiring states' consent. The remaining two issues concern the kinds of reasons required and the significance of compliance.

B Reasons versus States' Objectives

The reasons ICs must help subjects act on are not subjective but objective in the sense that legitimacy requires that an IC is of service regarding 'whatever reasons correctly *apply* to the case, not reasons of which the agent is aware, or which serve his self-interest narrowly understood'.[25] Thus such reasons may be other-regarding, and they may be unknown to the subject. A state might be subject to a legitimate IC because that IC's judgments better promote the reasons the state actually has to act – even though the state rejects those reasons.

This focus on objective reasons prompts a concern: How do we understand and address various forms of disagreements about such objective reasons?[26] Several issues may be distinguished for future discussions. One philosophically salient issue is, of course, the challenge of mutually incompatible yet not irrational conceptions of the good, which may be thought to be an even greater problem among individuals globally than within a liberal society.[27] A second concern arises when there are (reasonable) disagreements about what *justice* requires – for example, regarding the

---

[25] M. Weber, 'Der Sinn der "Wertfreiheit" der Soziologischen und Ökonomischen Wissenschaften', *Logos* 7 (1917): 40. See also L. Green, 'Legal Obligation and Authority', in *The Stanford Encyclopedia of Philosophy*, ed. E. N. Zalta, https://plato.stanford.edu/archives/win2012/entries/legal-obligation; Raz, 'Problem of Authority', 1008n10.

[26] I am grateful to Oisin Suttle for suggesting that this point be expanded.

[27] J. Rawls, *A Theory of Justice* (Cambridge, MA: Belknap Press, 1971).

appropriate extent of equality or liberty individuals should be accorded or the value of democratic governance. 'Meta-coordination' among such alternatives may be one fruitful approach.[28] A third set of important issues arises when some important compliance constituencies hold certain objectives or values, though for clearly bad reasons – thus cases where autocratic rulers reject any international expressions of concern for ongoing mass slaughter for reasons of sovereign immunity. A fourth range of cases come to light when compliance constituencies are mistaken, but for plausible reasons. To illustrate, an IC may be illegitimate if it enables states to act more in accordance with its *mistaken* beliefs. This is one way to understand some criticism raised against the WTO regime – namely, that global trade liberalization is a mistaken objective of states, claims that this is not an objective states have reason to pursue, given the impact on vulnerable segments of their populations.[29] Similar accounts may be offered in discussions about the Transatlantic Trade and Investment Partnership (TTIP) between the European Union (EU) and the United States (US). Typical challenges concern the public health impact of TTIP[30] and the erosion of state sovereignty wrought by the Investor-State Dispute Settlement (ISDS) mechanism, whether TTIP will indeed promote jobs and economic growth and how fairly the burdens and benefits will be distributed.[31] If critics are right, states do not have reason to agree to such a treaty, and a treaty body that faithfully adjudicates the treaty or investor-state disputes will *not* be legitimate on this account – even if the IC carries out its mandate diligently and impartially.

The upshot for the purposes of justifiable principled noncompliance with IC judgments is that some sources of disagreements render such noncompliance hazardous and may reduce support for international law in general. Others may remain unconvinced of the rationale offered by the protesters or suspect that the justification is a sham. Such not unreasonable risks may constrain the acceptable grounds for noncompliance.

A separate but related set of criticisms against an IC arise when the IC prevents states from acting on the other reasons they have. For instance,

---

[28] A. Buchanan, *The Heart of Human Rights* (Oxford: Oxford University Press, 2013), 179.

[29] Inter alia R. L. Howse, 'From Politics to Technocracy – and Back Again: The Fate of the Multilateral Trading Regime', *American Journal of International Law* 96 (2002): 94–117; J. Pauwelyn, *Conflicts of Norms in Public International Law* (Cambridge: Cambridge University Press, 2008), 33.

[30] N. Bennet, 'Health Concerns Raised over EU-US Trade Deal', *The Lancet* 384 (2014): 843–44.

[31] For an overview, see 'TTIP: Top 5 Concerns and Criticism', Atlantic-Community, 26 February 2014, www.atlantic-community.org/-/ttip-top-5-concerns-and-criticism.

if the overall effects of the set of ICs are detrimental to states' abilities to promote and protect the interests of their citizens, we may question whether the IC is indeed providing services that states have reason to value. To illustrate, consider the arguments that ICs that effectively promote free trade or foreign direct investment may severely restrict states' abilities to respect and promote citizens' human rights or secure their basic needs. John Ruggie has argued that such international commitments may have rendered states unable to alleviate and redistribute the social adjustment costs wrought by open markets and increased foreign investment.[32]

In such cases, if the criticisms are sound, the IC is an authority that claims its judgments create reasons for others – but it is not a *legitimate* authority regarding this matter on Raz's account. Note that this understanding of legitimacy allows critical and nuanced development of Shany's goal-based understanding of the effectiveness of international courts. Shany assumes that the effective pursuit of states' objectives in setting up ICs grants the ICs legitimacy: 'Mandate providers delegate to courts the powers to act as their "long arm" or as independent guardians of their collective interests ... on the presumptive ability of state representatives to speak and act on behalf of nations and their citizenry – which confers a significant degree of legitimacy on international courts. By the same token, the goals established through this legitimacy-conferring process need to be afforded some priority over the goals identified by the courts' own judges.'[33]

He notes that this focus must be supplemented: 'It fails to capture unintended or unexpected results, and it does not specifically take into account the costs invested in attaining the intended or expected goals.'[34] In contrast, the present account does *not* assume that state representatives speak on behalf of the interests of their citizens. Indeed, Raz's service conception also (and originally) applies to states – denying the presumption that states are legitimate authorities. States may fail to act on the reasons they actually have and instead establish an IC with flawed objectives – to the detriment of the normative legitimacy of both.

---

[32] J. G. Ruggie, 'International Regimes, Transactions and Change: Embedded Liberalism in the Postwar Economic Order', *International Organization* 36 (1982): 379–415. See also Shany, *Assessing the Effectiveness*, 237.

[33] Shany, *Assessing the Effectiveness*, 241.

[34] Ibid., 224.

C   On Legitimacy and General Compliance

A further requirement is that the IC must actually provide the service claimed. To secure this, very often, actual compliance by many subjects may be crucial. Consider an IC that is set up to assure that a state will honour its obligations, such as trade agreements or human rights treaties. The IC only provides such services insofar as enough relevant compliance constituencies comply or defer so as to bring about the coordination or assurance of benefits. For instance, if states continue to free ride on free trade agreements, the IC does not reduce the collective action problem, and the IC is an illegitimate authority. Arguably, human rights ICs are less dependent on general compliance: they can provide helpful services to some states and their individuals by providing credible monitoring of legislation and policies even though some other states systematically ignore the judgments. However, the role of human rights ICs as a 'self-binding' device may suffer. They can serve to make a state's human rights commitments more credible toward their own population, or toward other compliance constituencies, only if the IC is generally complied with. If many states continue human rights violations unabated, such attempts at self-binding no longer enhance states' commitment. So actual compliance by a significant proportion of the constituency may be a condition for an IC to be a legitimate authority. This account thus provides one explanation for why 'an institution could not be normatively legitimate if no one thought it so'.[35]

Note that this also limits the possible disparities between objective and subjective reasons: if an IC was to attempt to promote states' abilities to act according to objective reasons that they currently fail to accept, it is very unlikely that the states would indeed comply. Hence the IC would not promote its objective and would thus be illegitimate:

> There are independent reasons for thinking that someone or some body can be an authority only if the fact that the two conditions are met can be known to its subjects. The point of being under an authority is that it opens a way of improving one's conformity with reason. One achieves that by conforming to the authority's directives, and (special circumstances apart) one can reliably conform only if one has reliable beliefs regarding who has legitimate authority, and what its directives are. If one cannot have

---

[35] Bodansky, 'Legitimacy in International Law', 327.

> trustworthy beliefs that a certain body meets the conditions for legitimacy, then one's belief in its authority is haphazard, and cannot (again special circumstances apart) be reliable. Therefore, to fulfil its function, the legitimacy of an authority must be knowable to its subjects.[36]

Persistent free riding among state signatories thus challenges the normative legitimacy of the IC, especially if noncompliers impose excessive burdens onto compliers. Therefore, this account challenges rather than promotes unthinking general compliance. Indeed, when discussing domestic legitimate authorities, Raz notes that 'one crucial condition which, in the case of political authorities governing sizeable societies, is necessary to establish their [normative] legitimacy, does not obtain. That is the ability to co-ordinate the actions of members of the society in case in which they have reason to co-ordinate their actions, and the ability to do so better than they can. That ability requires effective power over them.'[37]

This limit to legitimate authority notwithstanding, a further important role of general deference by other compliance constituencies is that such deference may independently give subjects a reason to defer. The reasons may be out of fairness to those who defer – though they defer on mistaken grounds – and to avoid being a free rider on practices that the subject benefits from.

3   Can Noncompliance Be Justified?

Arguably, a theory of legitimate authority should help identify its own limits of application – and indeed, how to act in such borderline cases. Can this account of the legitimacy of ICs, drawn from Raz's service conception, permit a state to not defer with a judgment of a generally legitimate IC? Might it even permit a state to engage in some form of international 'civil disobedience' against judgments it finds beyond the bounds of acceptability? Such an account will also show that such legitimacy talk is not designed as a tool of manipulation to entice compliance constituencies to defer. However, the pedigree of this account from Raz's 'service conception' would seem to render it impossible to permit wilful noncompliance that is due to the *content* of the judgment. Such noncompliance would seem to contradict the whole point of having an authority,

---

[36]   Raz, 'Problem of Authority', 1025.
[37]   Raz, *Morality of Freedom*, 75–76.

since acceptance of the IC as a legitimate authority entails that the subject can no longer rely on the reasons that the IC's judgments exclude.[38]

On the face of it, Raz's account of legitimate authority might not be thought to provide such explanations or justifications of noncompliance against legitimate authorities. Deference is required even when the IC makes a mistake: 'There will be other cases, for example, cases in which the directive issued by authority is mistaken or unjustified ... This can be consistent with the directive being binding on us. Even legitimate authorities make mistakes. In such cases, we should conform with the directive, and the ideal case is one in which we do so because we are required to by the authority and not because of the other reasons that support the action.'[39]

Such claims may be why Arthur Applbaum argues that Raz's account cannot accommodate 'civil disobedience': 'If legitimate authority entails a dispositive duty to obey, civil disobedience disappears as a poignant moral phenomenon. If the authority is legitimate, disobedience is not justified. If, by assumption, disobedience is justified, then the authority that is disobeyed cannot have been legitimate.'[40]

In response, consider two kinds of non-compliance. First, subjects may recognize the legitimate authority of the IC but hold that *other* reasons override the authority's decision. Such arguments may be similar to those Franck might have in mind when he described the non-authorized NATO intervention into Kosovo as a morally mandatory act of international civil disobedience.[41] That description is challenged on several counts, including whether the case may be accepted as *sui generis* without setting precedence or whether this creates a slippery slope of nonauthorized exceptions by states with mixed motives. Thus the German Constitutional Court has refused to comply with an ECtHR judgment due to concern for *other* affected parties than those involved in the case.[42] Arguably, similar and more difficult issues may arise when there is disagreement about whether the foetus should be accorded a right to

---

[38] Ibid., 42.
[39] Raz, 'Problem of Authority', 1022–23, my emphasis.
[40] A. Applbaum, 'Legitimacy without the Duty to Obey', *Philosophy and Public Affairs* 38 (2010): 215–39, esp. 220; Bodansky, 'Legitimacy in International Law', 327.
[41] T. M. Franck, 'Lessons of Kosovo', *American Journal of International Law* 93 (1999): 857–60.
[42] *Görgülü [Gorgulu]*, 2 BvR 1481/04, paras. 1–72 (German Federal Constitutional Court, 2004).

life.[43] This fits with Raz's insistence that 'authoritative directives are not always conclusive reasons for the conduct they require. They can be defeated by conflicting reasons, or by conflicting directives. The reasons that can defeat them are those they do not exclude'.[44]

The second form of non-compliance may be understood as an extreme corrective measure within a legal or political system that is not fully just. John Rawls has argued that in such legal orders, some noncompliance may serve as an ultimate attempt to urge the authorities to change their directives to avoid serious injustice and to improve the system as a whole.[45] In such cases, an authority such as an IC may be generally legitimate in that it can create moral duties, but it does not do so always – namely, when its judgments fail to satisfy the 'normal justification' requirements in a particular case.

One type of example was mentioned previously: when general compliance is not to be expected. Another kind of case arises when the IC transgresses its domain of legitimate authority. There may be two kinds of such transgressions. First, the decisions may concern matters outside the IC's proper scope. Such cases may arise if the IC makes serious mistakes in its 'dynamic interpretation' of the treaty. We might include the 'Solange' mechanism as an example of this, where a domestic apex court warns that it will not automatically comply if, in its own view, the IC violates its proper domain.[46] Raz would appear to grant as much when he limits the kinds of reasons that the authority's judgment pre-empts: 'The pre-emption thesis claims that the factors about which the authority was wrong, and which are not jurisdictional factors, are pre-empted by the directive'.[47]

The compliance constituencies may thus have several other reasons to act that remain in force even when the IC's judgment pre-empts some reasons. Indeed, Raz may allow that when one judgment of a legitimate authority is clearly wrong, compliance constituencies may not defer to it: 'Even if legitimate authority is limited by the condition that its directives are not binding if clearly wrong, and I wish to express no opinion on

---

[43] I am grateful to Oran Doyle for this observation.
[44] Raz, 'Problem of Authority', 1023.
[45] J. Rawls, A Theory of Justice (Cambridge, MA: Harvard University Press, 1971).
[46] Bundesverfassungsgericht, 'Solange I: Internationale Handelsgesellschaft v. Einfuhr Und Vorratsstelle Für Getreide Und Futtermittel', BVerfGE 37, 271 (1974); and E. Petersmann, 'Human Rights, International Economic Law and "Constitutional Justice"', European Journal of International Law 19 (2008): 955–60.
[47] Raz, Morality of Freedom, 61.

whether it is so limited, it can play its mediating role. Establishing that something is clearly wrong does not require going through the underlying reasoning. It is not the case that the legitimate power of authorities is generally limited by the condition that it is defeated by significant mistakes which are not clear.'[48] Second, the IC may fail profoundly in procedures – for instance, where it is deemed by a state or other compliance constituency to depart drastically from legal methods but instead draws arbitrary or highly biased conclusions.

In these two cases, if less confrontational means of protest have been unsuccessful, the state might avail itself of public, reasoned disobedience to urge the IC that it must change its mode of operation. Such disobedience must be duly constrained and presented in ways to convey credibly to other compliance constituencies and to the IC that the state generally accepts the legitimate authority of the IC but believes there is no such obligation in the present case. The challenge for the disobedient state is thus to signal that it believes the IC to generally enjoy legitimate authority, but not in particular cases such as these. While noncompliance might usually be taken to express a desire to reject the IC's authority, the state here seeks not to reject the IC but to improve it. Note that this task is especially difficult when it comes to ICs and international law, where compliance is precarious and the different compliance constituencies may have differing, often conflicting, values and objectives.

In such cases, the state does not deny that the judgment of an IC acting within its appropriate domain with appropriate methods pre-empts a set of reasons for actions that the state otherwise had concerning the case in question. The noncompliance is primarily based on other reasons the state has, concerning whether the service conception applies to this particular case and how to best improve the IC. In these circumstances, one may want to claim that the authority is still legitimate in general but that subjects have no duty to comply with a particular command. Thus Applbaum appears mistaken in his claims quoted previously. On Rawls's account – which Applbaum appears to otherwise follow – civil disobedience is defined in part as actions that express a belief that the authority is *usually* legitimate: 'The law is broken, but fidelity to law is expressed by the public and nonviolent nature of the act, by the willingness to accept the legal consequences of one's conduct. This fidelity to law helps establish

[48] Ibid., 63.

to the majority that the act is indeed politically conscientious and sincere, and that it is intended to address the public's sense of justice. To be completely open and nonviolent is to give bond of one's sincerity, for it is not easy to convince another that one's acts are conscientious, or even to be sure of this before oneself.'[49]

What might be judgments by ICs that could fit such an account – so that noncompliance should be regarded as and assessed as acts of civil disobedience? Such a theory might support Lord Mance, who, when considering the possibility of the domestic court refusing to follow the ECtHR, held that 'it would then have to involve some truly fundamental principle of our law or some most egregious oversight or misunderstanding before it could be appropriate for this Court to contemplate an outright refusal to follow Strasbourg authority at the Grand Chamber level'.[50]

The account sketched previously may not appear to be completely consistent with the quotes from Raz's works so far presented. If so, I submit that this is a plausible correction. Moreover, elsewhere, Raz might seem prepared to accept such forms of noncompliance:

> Human judgment errs. It falls prey to temptation and bias distorts it. This fact must affect one's considerations. But which way should it incline one? The only general answer which I find persuasive is that it depends on the circumstances. In some areas and regarding some people, caution requires submission to authority. In others, it leads to denial of authority. There are risks, moral and other, in uncritical acceptance of authority. Too often in the past, the fallibility of human judgment has led to submission to authority from a misguided sense of duty where this was a morally reprehensible attitude.[51]

Thus this account of legitimate authority provides several grounds to resist deference to ICs.

4   Conclusion

Why and when should a judgment by an IC give others a reason to act differently than they would otherwise – be it domestic parliaments when drafting a new law or a domestic court interpreting such laws? Raz's famous

---

[49] Rawls, *Theory of Justice*, 366.

[50] P. Mahoney, 'The Relationship between the Strasbourg Court and the National Courts', *Law Quarterly Review* 130 (2014): 568–86.

[51] Raz, *Morality of Freedom*, 351.

account of legitimate authority helps frame answers to these questions. The account indicates systematic modes of argument about ICs' claims to be legitimate authorities and explains why actual compliance may sometimes be required for ICs to be normatively legitimate. A strength of this account is that it also helps explain why and when these authorities are mistaken about their claims to compliance. Indeed, this interpretation of the legitimate authority of ICs even allows for cases of justifiable disobedience. Such cases may seldom be justified due to the precarious state of parts of international law and widespread divergence of values. Still, public, reasoned disobedience may be urgently needed when considering how to improve the legitimate authority of present-day international courts within a not fully just multi-level legal and political order.

8

Consent, Obligation and the Legitimate Authority of International Law

RICHARD COLLINS

Introduction

Until relatively recently, international lawyers tended to worry little about the question of the legitimate authority of the object of their study. Having been plagued for a long time by scepticism and ontological self-doubt, the discipline had been rather more concerned with proving a more fundamental question about the very existence of international law in the first place.[1] In their effort to defend its reality in the face of such scepticism, many international lawyers have just presumed that if inter-national law can be shown to be law on the same terms as its domestic counterpart, its authority over states (and other actors) would be proven. On this account, the authority of international law is equated simply with its normativity, which is, in turn, presumed to follow from a norm's validation in accordance with the broadly consensual criteria included amongst its doctrine of sources (including treaties, customary interna-tional law and, to a lesser extent, subsidiary sources such as general prin-ciples of law). This kind of morally neutral, either/or assessment – what Başak Çali has recently termed the 'standard view' of the authority of international law[2] – seems unconcerned with questions of legitimacy. At best, such questions are seen as important but still tangential and, in contrast to legal normativity, necessarily beset by a certain 'fuzziness and indeterminacy'.[3]

---

[1] See, e.g., R. Collins, 'No Longer at the Vanishing Point? International Law and the Analytical Tradition in Jurisprudence', *Jurisprudence* 5 (2014): 265–98.

[2] See B. Çali, *The Authority of International Law: Obedience, Respect and Rebuttal* (Oxford: Oxford University Press, 2015), ch. 1. I will return to discuss this understanding in the following sections.

[3] J. Crawford, 'The Problems of Legitimacy Speak', *Proceedings of the American Society of International Law* 98 (2004): 271. See also, for similar concerns, M. Koskenniemi, 'Miserable Comforters: International Relations as New Natural Law', *European Journal*

Today, however, in international law's 'post-ontological' era,[4] it seems increasingly difficult to completely separate these two modes of enquiry.[5] Whilst it might well be the case, as Louis Henkin once argued, that most states obey most of the rules of international law most of the time,[6] this sociological explanation is surely not sufficient to show that states necessarily feel a genuine sense of obligation in doing so, nor that this sense of obligation follows simply from the existence of law *per se*. After all, it might well be the case, as others have contended, that compliance – and, in the inverse, non-compliance – with international law results from rational self-interest,[7] or from an overall assessment of the fairness,[8] or procedural justness,[9] of specific rules operating in certain circumstances.

The existence of such 'alternative' understandings of the authority of international legal rules does not, of course, disprove the 'standard view' outlined previously, but it does suggest that we cannot simply take it for granted. In fact, there are two reasons why I believe we need to think more deeply about international law's claim to authority (if indeed it makes such a claim at all). First, the view of international law as an autonomous legal system grounded in a stable set of social sources that is arguably presumed by this standard view is not something natural or intrinsic to the relations between states. Rather, this view has been deliberately constructed by states, international lawyers and other professionals to reflect a particular – that is, not incontestable – view of its overall legitimacy.[10] Specifically, the emergence and growing dominance of legal

---

of International Relations 15 (2009): 395–422, esp. 409–10. And see discussion in C. A. Thomas, 'The Uses and Abuses of Legitimacy in International Law', *Oxford Journal of Legal Studies* 34 (2014): 729–58, esp. 731–32.

[4] T. Franck, *Fairness in International Law and Institutions* (Oxford: Oxford University Press, 1995), 6.

[5] S. Besson, 'The Authority of International Law – Lifting the State Veil', *Sydney Law Review* 31 (2009): 343–80, esp. 346–48.

[6] L. Henkin, *How Nations Behave: Law and Foreign Policy*, 2nd ed. (New York: Columbia University Press, 1979), 47.

[7] See, e.g., A. T. Guzman, *How International Law Works: A Rational Choice Theory* (Oxford: Oxford University Press, 2008); J. L. Goldsmith and E. A. Posner, *The Limits of International Law* (Oxford: Oxford University Press, 2005).

[8] See, e.g., Franck, *Fairness in International Law*.

[9] See, e.g., J. Brunée and S. J. Toope, *Legitimacy and Legality in International Law: An Interactional Account* (Cambridge: Cambridge University Press, 2010).

[10] '[The systemic view] cannot be understood as reaffirming something that already "exists" before the systemic effort itself. *There is no single legislative will behind international law.*' International Law Commission, 'Fragmentation of International Law: Difficulties Arising from the Diversification and Expansion of International Law', Report of the Study Group

positivism from the nineteenth century onwards has reflected the influence of a broadly liberal view of political legitimacy that seeks to mediate
the intersubjective reasoning of international politics by means of a distinctly artificial, or institutional, form of legal reasoning.[11] On this view,
a systemic understanding of international law reflects, at least in part, a
commitment to the kind of procedural justice inherent in the rule of law,
specifically by purporting to reconcile and justify the binding authority of
international legal norms independently of any subjective assessment of
their specific content.[12]

Second, and more fundamentally, even if we can offer up a justification
for the aforementioned 'standard view', it is increasingly apparent that the
image of international law it projects is subject to challenge, particularly as
a result of the growing institutional complexity of the international legal
order in an age of so-called global governance. With an increasing number of autonomous international institutions, regimes and more informal
inter- and trans-national governance structures, one witnesses a growing
array of laws, rules, standards and norms that are very difficult to reconcile neatly with the kind of source-based legal validity that is presumed
on the 'standard view' of international law's authority. More and more, it
seems to be the case that the kind of 'relative' normativity presumed by

of the International Law Commission, finalised by M. Koskenniemi, UN Doc. A/CN.4/
L.682, 13 April 2006, 23, para. 34, emphasis added, available at http://legal.un.org/ilc/
documentation/english/a_cn4_l682.pdf.

[11] For discussion, see *inter alia*, M. Koskenniemi, 'The Politics of International Law',
European Journal of International Law 1 (1990): 4–32, esp. 4–7; A. Carty, *The Decay of
International Law: A Reappraisal of the Limits of Legal Imagination in International Affairs*
(Manchester: Manchester University Press, 1986), 1–11 *et seq.*; and R. Collins, 'Classical
Legal Positivism in International Law Revisited', in *International Legal Positivism in a Post-
Modern World*, ed. J. Kammerhofer and J. d'Aspremont (Cambridge: Cambridge University
Press, 2014), 28–36.

[12] As Samantha Besson has claimed, there are 'normative grounds for positing international law and adopting a positivist approach to the sources of international
law, and these are in particular grounds of global justice and peaceful cooperation
among equal international subjects whose conceptions of justice diverge'. S. Besson,
'Theorizing the Sources of International Law', in *Philosophy of International Law*, ed.
S. Besson and J. Tasioulas (Oxford: Oxford University Press, 2010), 166. On the distinction between 'normative' and 'methodological' positivism and the applicability of
the former to international law, see P. Capps, *Human Dignity and the Foundations of
International Law* (Oxford: Hart, 2009), 53–59, 83–84; and, generally, B. Kingsbury,
'Legal Positivism as Normative Politics: International Society, Balance of Power and
Lassa Oppenheim's Positive International Law', *European Journal of International Law*
13 (2002): 401–37.

this form of postnational rule-making,[13] often increasingly removed from the consent of states, requires another kind of justification altogether. With this background in mind, this chapter has three core ambitions. First, it aims to clarify a concept of legitimate authority that we might apply to make sense of the specific institutional structure of the international legal order – that is, one that is broadly reflective of Çali's 'standard view' but that nonetheless can be normatively justified as legitimate and coherent in the context of the particular political conditions of international relations. From now onwards, I shall refer to this as the justified standard view (JSV). Second, I will reflect on the role of consent in this context in an attempt to disprove certain misconceptions of the function that consent plays in either validating or legitimating international legal rules. Whilst I aim to defend a broadly consensual understanding of international law as crucial to its legitimacy in practice, I argue that the role of consent in international law acts as a necessary check on a legal system that is binding irrespective of whether states have consented to it any meaningful sense. Third, and finally, I reflect on an emerging challenge to the adequacy or sufficiency of this justification in grounding the authority of international law in the age of global governance. Whilst I believe that the growth in institutional complexity of the international legal order reflects a need to 'relativize' and take a critical disposition towards the apparent authority of global governance institutions,[14] I argue that a continued defence of the JSV, and specifically the consensual validation and formal binding / non-binding binary it presumes, is necessary for this very purpose. In other words, rather than argue that the doctrine of sources should be modified or expanded to encompass and account for the 'post-national' normative influence of the actors of global governance, I argue instead that this increasingly informal – or *deformalized* – form of normativity has to be considered aside from and held up against our more formal mode of international legality presumed by the JSV. In this respect, this more traditional – but nonetheless still justifiable – account of international legal authority continues to provide an important principle of accountability in the increasingly 'post-national' nature of international relations. Before seeking to defend this claim further, however, I

---

[13] See R. Collins, 'Mapping the Terrain of Institutional "Lawmaking": Form and Function in International Law', in *The Actors of Postnational Rule-Making: Contemporary Challenges of European and International Law*, ed. E. Fahey (Abingdon: Routledge, 2015), 27–46.

[14] For a similar argument for a more relative concept of the authority of international legal institutions, see N. Roughan, 'Mind the Gaps: Authority and Legality in International Law', *European Journal of International Law* 27 (2016): 329–51.

will first attempt to clarify how best to understand and defend an account of authority along the lines of the JSV.

1   Practical Authority and Legal Normativity: Some Initial Considerations and Questions

Despite a degree of philosophical controversy over the concept, there appears to be a sufficiently broad consensus that political authority acts as a form of practical rather than theoretical authority – that is, it is concerned with creating obligations or imposing duties, rather than simply persuading through expertise.[15] As such, we might speak of political authority in a descriptive sense as related to those institutions or bodies actually in a position of ruling over others, but to speak of *legitimate* authority in this context is also to pose the normative question as to a particular institution or body's *right to* rule.[16] However, as Tom Christiano argues, it is probably neither possible nor useful to determine a generalizable concept of authority applicable to all forms of political community, though in this context, we might still hold out a kind of focal or ideal concept of authority, which in its fullest iteration substantiates 'a moral power to impose a set of rules by which the others must regulate their conduct'.[17] In other words, a perfect form of legitimate (as opposed to *de facto*) political authority – at least in the state context – would give rise to a moral right on behalf of the ruler to command obedience, as well as a moral reason (perhaps even duty) on behalf of subjects to conform to the ruler's command.[18]

This view of political authority prompts a number of questions, not least of which is the question of the cogency of this understanding of authority when applied to the seemingly non-hierarchical political context of international relations. I will return to this issue again shortly, but it is worth returning to Christiano's aforementioned point insofar as he suggests that

---

[15] On the many ideas of authority, including what makes such authority legitimate, see T. Christiano, 'Authority', in *The Stanford Encyclopedia of Philosophy*, spring 2013 ed., ed. E. N. Zalta, http://plato.stanford.edu/archives/spr2013/entries/authority/.

[16] Les Green asserts that 'political authority, of which legal authority is one species, is normally seen as a right to rule, with a correlative duty to obey'. L. Green, 'Legal Obligation and Authority' in *The Stanford Encyclopaedia of Philosophy*, winter 2012 ed., ed. E. N. Zalta, http://plato.stanford.edu/archives/win2012/entries/legal-obligation/.

[17] T. Christiano, 'The Legitimacy of International Institutions', in *The Routledge Companion to Philosophy of Law*, ed. A. Marmor (New York: Routledge, 2012), 381.

[18] J. Tasioulas, 'Human Rights, Legitimacy, and International Law', *American Journal of Jurisprudence* 58 (2013): 1–25, esp. 9.

the ideal form of authority might not always be fully present, nor fully appropriate, ultimately depending on the kind of political relationship in play, as well as the type of body or institution holding out authority over us. For instance, an authority might be legitimate to the extent that it gives rise to a right to coerce, without necessarily grounding any correlative obligation to obey. Similarly, legitimate authority might give a reason for compliance without that reason necessarily amounting to an obligation in any pre-emptive sense.[19] In principle, therefore, it seems at least possible to imagine legitimate forms of political authority – courts, institutions, other actors – that are realisable in, and sensitive to the structural conditions of, the international context. Before taking up this discussion, however, I want to first consider a more fundamental question as to whether law itself claims authority (and relatedly, what such a claim might mean).

The first thing one might say in response is that this question may well be, as Scott Shapiro suggests, something of a 'banal' enquiry.[20] He may well be right in this regard. Whilst not all rules are constituted in the form of an obligation, it is surely not feasible to engage the concept of law or legal system without also considering the concept of obligation.[21] However, if this statement is indeed true, it only invites reflection on the question of what this claim to authority necessarily entails. In particular, perhaps the most important question in this context is whether law makes a distinctly moral claim on us – that is, whether it claims the legitimacy sufficient to ground a *moral obligation* of compliance.

The view that law does make such a claim has been a central component of certain legal positivist accounts – though not only such accounts[22] – that seek to isolate an *a priori* reason for compliance with the law, independent of any substantive moral or political assessment of the value of following individual legal norms.[23] In other words, on this view, it follows that if law claims authority over us, then we have a reason for compliance independent of our agreement or otherwise with the particular content of any given legal rule.[24] Whilst we might understand this kind of 'content-independent' normativity

---

[19] See, generally, Christiano, 'Authority', sec. 1.
[20] S. Shapiro, 'Hart's Way Out', in *Hart's Postscript: Essays on the Postscript to the Concept of Law*, ed. J. Coleman (Oxford: Oxford University Press, 2001), 149–50.
[21] Green, 'Legal Obligation and Authority'.
[22] This view is also supported by John Finnis. See J. Finnis, *Natural Law and Natural Rights*, 2nd ed. (Oxford: Oxford University Press, 2011), 148, 260 and *passim*.
[23] See, e.g., B. van der Vossen, 'Assessing Law's Claim to Authority', *Oxford Journal of Legal Studies* 31 (2011): 481–501.
[24] See, e.g., S. Shapiro, 'Authority', in *Oxford Handbook of Jurisprudence and Philosophy of Law*, ed. J. Coleman and S. Shapiro (Oxford: Clarendon Press, 2002), 390–91.

in a number of different ways – a point to which I will return later on – and although not universally accepted as an adequate or sufficient explanation of law's authority, this core notion of 'content independence' has become 'part and parcel of the conceptual vocabulary of legal theorists'.[25] In its most attenuated form, it would suggest that the validity of a legal norm not only offers us a *reason* to comply independent of any other reason we might have for compliance but also necessarily trumps or excludes these other reasons. As Les Green explains, 'Legal obligations are content-independent reasons that are both categorical and pre-emptive in force. The mark of their content-independence is that their force does not depend on the nature or merits of the action they require: in most cases, law can impose an obligation to do *X* or to refrain from doing *X* ... That they are pre-emptive means that they require the subject to set aside his own view of the merits and comply nonetheless. That they are categorical means that they do not condition their claims on the subject's own goals or interests.'[26]

The most prominent adherent to this view of law's authority is probably Joseph Raz, even though Raz himself is sceptical as to how many legal systems in force will succeed in actually substantiating such a moral claim. In other words, whilst Raz denies that we *actually do have* a moral obligation to obey the law in all instances – a decision to adhere to the law depending, ultimately, on whether the claim to authority is justified – he argues that it is part of law's very nature, conceptually speaking, that it must *necessarily* make such a claim.[27]

Raz's argument follows from his broader commitment to an 'exclusive' form of legal positivism. Specifically, he rejects the possibility, left open by H. L. A. Hart, that the rule (or rules) of recognition of a legal system may incorporate moral evaluation as part of the criteria for validating legal norms.[28] For Raz, law seeks to offer pre-emptive reasons (*second-order reasons*) that trump, or at least *exclude*, other reasons we have for acting (*first-order reasons*) and can do so only by holding out such a claim to authority.[29]

---

[25] N. Gur, 'Are Legal Rules Content-Independent Reasons?', *Problema* 5 (2011): 175–210, esp. 175.

[26] Green, 'Legal Obligation and Authority'.

[27] See J. Raz, *Ethics in the Public Domain: Essays in the Morality of Law and Politics*, rev. ed. (Oxford: Clarendon Press, 1994), 215.

[28] Hart concedes this point in the postscript to the second edition of *The Concept of Law*. See H. L. A. Hart, *The Concept of Law*, 2nd ed. (Oxford: Clarendon Press, 1994), 250, 253.

[29] See J. Raz, *Practical Reason and Norms* (London: Hutchinson, 1975); J. Raz, *The Authority of Law*, 2nd ed. (Oxford: Oxford University Press, 2009), 16–27, 30–33.

Nevertheless, Raz's argument has not escaped controversy, particularly amongst proponents of more 'inclusive' forms of legal positivism, many of whom not only raise empirical doubts about whether such a claim can be substantiated by reference to any legal system actually in force but also question the conceptual truth of the view that law is ever capable of displacing our subjective judgement as moral agents in this way.[30] In fact, certain theorists, including most prominently Ronald Dworkin,[31] have even gone so far as to question the cogency of the idea that a legal system, as a 'non-propositional abstract object', is even capable of making any such claims on us.[32] Whilst this latter criticism likely does sting in literal terms, we might nonetheless get around this conceptual stumbling block insofar as the practices of a legal system's agents or officials hold out such a view of the legal enterprise, thus at least substantiating the claim in a figurative and indirect sense.[33]

This qualified claim seems persuasive when considered in reference to familiar domestic legal systems, but the introduction of a hierarchical institutional context itself raises a fresh set of concerns for our current enquiry, not least of which is what would appear to be a *prima facie* incompatibility between such an account and the nature of the international legal system. Given the apparent absence of any ostensible distinction between legal officials and subjects at the international level,[34] are we simply to deny the authority of international law on these grounds? And if we are, then could we not simply relocate the question of legitimate authority from the legal to the political realm – specifically, to the prior question of the legitimacy of the official institutions that purport to rule over subjects in a domestic context? Perhaps, but such a move would seem to drain law of any independent normative content.

A way out of this bind might simply be to refine our account of law's authority so that we take seriously many of the criticisms of the inclusive legal positivists. Specifically, I believe that if we understand the notion of content-independent normativity in a less 'pre-emptive' or exclusionary

---

[30] See, e.g., K. E. Himma, 'Law's Claim to Legitimate Authority', in *Hart's Postscript: Essays on the Postcript to the Concept of Law*, ed. J. Coleman (Oxford: Oxford University Press, 2001), 277–80.

[31] See, principally, R. Dworkin, 'Thirty Years On', *Harvard Law Review* 115 (2002): 1655–87, esp. 1666–76.

[32] Himma, 'Law's Claim', 278.

[33] See, e.g., J. Gardner, *Law as a Leap of Faith* (Oxford: Oxford University Press, 2012), 127–28.

[34] On this point, see R. Collins, *The Institutional Problem in Modern International Law* (Oxford: Hart, 2016), chs. 3, 4.

sense, then law's claim to authority would just be to recognize a presumption that its rules are valid and should structure our inter-relations
and – so far as possible – guide our conduct. Such a view, I believe, does
not necessarily require law to displace or set aside our normal process
of reasoning as rational agents, but it does mean that there would be a
presumption of compliance unless there is a better, more compelling reason for doing otherwise.[35] With this point in mind, it might be useful to
distinguish between different – both weaker and stronger – forms of content-independent normativity. As Noam Gur has recognized, the notion
of content independence in a weaker sense might suggest a reason for
compliance with norms based simply on the recognized legitimacy of the
issuer of the norm or, alternatively, the accepted procedure by which a
norm comes into being, which exists apart from any substantive reasons
that we might have for compliance.[36] In the stronger, more 'exclusionary'
sense in which Raz employs the notion of content independence, however, the claim is that law must necessarily purport to pre-empt or exclude
these other reasons. Whilst it might be a plausible argument that Raz's
pre-emption thesis pertains to the determinations of specific officials,
particularly judges, it is clearly possible to imagine a functioning legal
system in the absence of such a binding judicial function at the constitutional level – international law being the primary example and, indeed,
my central concern here. Thus I believe that we have good *prima facie*
reasons to doubt the plausibility of the pre-emption thesis at the core of
Raz's argument, though I will return again to consider Raz's account in
more detail in the following section.[37]

   For now, I believe it is conceivable to reach a preliminary conclusion
that law, including international law, does claim authority in the sense
suggested, whilst recognizing that such a claim will not always give rise to
a corresponding duty of compliance.[38] In order to more fully substantiate
this argument, however, we need to look a little closer at the underlying

---

[35] Roughan makes a similar point in response to the pluralist challenge to an exclusionary
account of authority, which seems to raise doubts about many of the more demanding elements of Raz's claim set out previously. See Roughan, 'Mind the Gaps', 334.

[36] Gur, 'Are Legal Rules Content-Independent Reasons?', 178–81. See also the discussion
in A. van Mulligen, 'Framing Deformalisation in International Law', *Transnational Legal
Theory* 3–4 (2015): 635–60.

[37] Perry comes to a similar conclusion in S. R. Perry, 'Second Order Reasons, Uncertainty,
and Legal Theory', *Southern California Law Review* 62 (1989): 913–94, as does S. Bertea,
The Normative Claim of Law (Oxford: Hart, 2009).

[38] See, e.g., A. I. Applbaum, 'Legitimacy without the Duty to Obey', *Philosophy and Public
Affairs* 38 (2010): 215–39.

rationale for such authority – that is, what reasons there are to defer to legal authority amongst members of a political community.

2 Justifying the Authority of Law: The 'Service Conception' and Its Limits

My somewhat quick dismissal of the pre-emption thesis might seem surprising given certain well-rehearsed beliefs about the function of law within political communities. Indeed, for many – including Raz – the pre-emptive or exclusionary nature of legal rules logically follows from the social mediation and coordination function that is often ascribed to law.[39] On these terms, in fact, we might argue that a justified legal order is one that successfully mediates the circumstances of political disagreement and moral pluralism by offering pre-emptive reasons that exist apart from and exclude our other reasons for acting or refraining from acting in any given set of circumstances. Raz, for instance, argues that this mediatory function offers a number of advantages, including that it enables people to plan ahead 'through an advance commitment to a whole series of actions, rather than by case to case examination' and that it fosters a 'pluralistic culture ... [that] enables people to unite in support of some 'low or medium level' generalizations despite profound disagreements concerning their ultimate foundations.[40] In arguing for this function of law, Raz is telling a somewhat familiar and, to some extent, quite uncontroversial story – a 'creation myth', perhaps[41] – of how law establishes a 'limited domain' of practical reasoning that, through its apparent autonomy from the moral and political realm, is able to offer a basis for successful social coordination under conditions of moral and political disagreement.[42]

In one form or another, this explanation of law's function stretches back through a long lineage of legal and political philosophers, uniting figures

---

[39] This view of law would seem to unite legal positivists and modern natural lawyers. Compare, for instance, G. J. Postema, 'Coordination and Convention at the Foundations of the Law', *Journal of Legal Studies* 11 (1982): 165–203; and Finnis, *Natural Law and Natural Rights*, 276–77 and *passim*. See discussion in K. Ehrenberg, *The Functions of Law* (Oxford: Oxford University Press, 2016), ch. 8.

[40] J. Raz, *The Morality of Freedom* (Oxford: Clarendon Press, 1986), 58. And see the discussion in M. Mian, 'The Curious Case of Exclusionary Reasons', *Canadian Journal of Law and Jurisprudence* 15 (2002): 99–124, esp. 100–102.

[41] See M. Martin, *Judging Positivism* (Oxford: Hart, 2014), 2, and further in Collins, *Institutional Problem*, ch. 6.

[42] See, principally, G. Postema, 'Law's Autonomy and Public Practical Reason', in *The Autonomy of Law*, ed. R. George (Oxford: Clarendon Press, 1996), 79–118.

as diverse as Hobbes and Kant with more modern jurists, including – in addition to Raz (and likely Hart) – natural lawyers such as John Finnis.[43] It has been common, particularly in the past, to attempt to ground a justification for this view of law's function in terms of constituent or participant consent. A consensual justification purports to reconcile the autonomous will of individual agents with a system of coercive political institutions, finding its most common expression – historically, at least – in the idea of the social contract.[44] To speak of consent in this context is not to suggest voluntarism in the context of individuated decision making. Instead, as Green has claimed, consent features 'as a part of the constitution rule that sets up the political community in the first place'. In this context, in fact, Green argues that consent provides the 'normal justification for political authority'.[45]

Nevertheless, it is perhaps no exaggeration to say that consent has fallen out of favour as an adequate or sufficient grounding for the legitimate authority of political institutions, whether in actual empirical terms or from a more principled normative stance.[46] To counter such concerns, much contemporary political theory, whilst not giving up on the importance of a respect for moral autonomy in principle, has attempted to reformulate the contractual metaphor into a more *aprioristic* normative justification. This has ranged from an explanation of legitimate authority in terms of the associative obligations of political community,[47] to making a more prudential or moral claim grounded in social necessity (the need for coordination, perhaps)[48] or some more rationalistic account of justice or fairness.[49] Whilst these alternative rationales appear more convincing in what they do not presume (consent), the more fundamental problem is that they arguably remain threatening to the concern for moral autonomy

---

[43] See, e.g., Capps, *Human Dignity*, ch. 6.
[44] There are numerous formulations of the contract idea. For a good, relatively recent overview, see the collection of essays in D. Boucher and P. J. Kelly, eds., *The Social Contract from Hobbes to Rawls* (Abingdon: Routledge, 2005).
[45] Green, 'Legal Obligation and Authority', original emphasis.
[46] For criticisms, see, e.g., Finnis, *Natural Law and Natural Rights*, 247–49; and Hart, *Concept of Law*, 224. For a discussion, see A. J. Simmons, *Moral Principles and Political Obligations* (Princeton: Princeton University Press, 1979), 57–100
[47] For example, R. J. Dworkin, *Law's Empire* (Oxford: Hart, 1998), 195–202 *et seq*. For critical engagement, see A. J. Simmons, 'Associative Political Obligations', *Ethics* 106 (1996): 247–73.
[48] See, e.g., D. Estlund, *Democratic Authority* (Cambridge: Cambridge University Press, 2007).
[49] The most obvious example being J. Rawls, *A Theory of Justice* (Cambridge, MA: Harvard University Press, 1971).

that propelled them in the first place – constantly at risk of substantiating a form of enlightened tyranny under the rationale of moral autonomy. As such, we seem either to be left with only a very thin normative claim to authority, which remains potentially unstable in practice and contestable in principle,[50] or caused to find some means to defer to moral agency once more.

It is from this perspective that we can better understand the scope (and appeal) of Raz's account of authority, which he purports to ground in an instrumental rationale that he terms the 'service conception'.[51] The service conception of authority is not, of course, the only alternative understanding of legitimate authority, but it is arguably the most influential non-consensual account of legitimate authority in the modern era.[52] Furthermore, insofar as there has been a recent focus on the question of the legitimate authority of international law in response to the perceived inadequacies of consensual explanations, Raz's approach has proved quite compelling as a way of legitimizing international legal rules (irrespective of the adequacies of state consent).[53] I will return to the question of the legitimacy of international law's claim to authority again shortly. For the moment, it is worth spending some time engaging with Raz's theory, even if I will also outline its inherent weakness in doing so.

Raz constructs the service conception of authority as an accumulation of three interconnected theses, each of which follows from an effort to explain why autonomous moral agents would have reason to comply with binding legal rules. He begins one of his earliest essays on the topic by seeking to distinguish *de facto* from *legitimate* authority and uses the example of the appointed arbitrator to illustrate this point.[54] The arbitrator's authority is seen to depend on her ability to justify a decision by reference to reasons that apply to the parties to the dispute in question. Nevertheless, the final award of the arbitrator, although based on or reflecting such reasons, also purports to replace or pre-empt these reasons. In other words, when we comply with the arbitrator's decision, we

---

[50] Indeed, this seems to be Simmons's conclusion, who looks for some salvageable moral obligation to rescue an account of political authority. Simmons, *Moral Principles*, 136–42.

[51] See J. Raz, 'Authority, Law and Morality', *Monist* 86 (1985): 295–324, though similar claims have been reiterated consistently in Raz's work since: See, e.g., Raz, *Morality of Freedom*; as well as, more recently, J. Raz, 'The Problem of Authority: Revisiting the Service Conception', *Minnesota Law Review* 90 (2006): 1003–44.

[52] See, e.g., N. Roughan, *Authorities: Conflicts, Cooperation, and Transnational Legal Theory* (Oxford: Oxford University Press, 2013), ch. 1.

[53] See, e.g., Besson, 'Authority of International Law'; Tasioulas, 'Human Rights'.

[54] Raz, 'Authority, Law and Morality', 297–98.

do so because we accept her authority to decide the matter, not because the decision might also accord with our own view of the right outcome. From this, therefore, we get two of the three interconnected theses: what Raz calls the 'dependence thesis' – that authority is justified insofar as it is based on reasons that apply to us independently anyway – and the 'pre-emption thesis', insofar as the very point of appointing the arbitrator would be undermined if the parties remained free to determine for themselves the right outcome following the award.[55]

When considered on their own, these two theses might be understood as applying only to the special case of arbitration – or, at best, adjudicative institutions in general – and might therefore follow from a process of consensual deferral. However, Raz also wants to make the case that this kind of rationale can be applied to legitimise the authority of political institutions in general, whether or not we have consented to them in any meaningful sense – for instance, legislative, executive and other organs of the state. He does so by conditioning their authority by reference to their ability to help us better conform to reasons that apply to us anyway. As such, we have the final and arguably most significant of the three theses that are taken to underpin the service conception of authority: the 'normal justification thesis' (NJT), which provides that the citizen or subject is 'likely better to comply with reasons which apply to him (other than the alleged authoritative directives) if he accepts the directives of the alleged authority as authoritatively binding, and tries to follow them, than if he tries to follow the reasons that apply to him directly'.[56]

On these terms, then, the service conception explains legitimate authority by reference to the capacity of a political institution to aid us to be good moral agents. The grant of authority is clearly conditional, in other words, though it does raise a concern over how to identify those matters over which it is better to defer to authority compared to those that it is not. In this respect, however, particularly in later iterations of the service conception, Raz arguably refines the thesis further by reflecting on the question of why in certain areas we might not wish to defer to authority – for instance, when we believe that we have a greater expertise on a particular matter – and instead retain our freedom as moral agents to decide for ourselves. Although Raz had hinted at this distinction in earlier works, in his last major elaboration of the topic, he explicitly defines

---

[55]   Ibid., 298.
[56]   Ibid., 299.

this distinction as the *independence condition*,[57] which requires that 'the matters regarding which the [NJT are] met are such that with respect to them it is better to conform to reason than to decide for oneself, unaided by authority.'[58]

Taken together, these underlying and interlinked theses explain authority in a way that attempts to defer judgement to an institution over individuated decision making in certain areas, but in a way that keeps such a deferral, as well as the matters over which we make such a deferral, under critical review. If this reconciliation is indeed possible, it would appear that there are a number of virtues underpinning Raz's approach as an alternative to grounding authority in consent, not least of which is the completeness of his justification: the NJT and the independence condition together provide a seemingly good reason, if fulfilled, as to why law might justifiably pre-empt the other reasons we might have for acting (or refraining from acting) in certain circumstances. In fact, as Adam Tucker has argued recently, many of Raz's critics tend to miss the important interrelation between these theses when attacking his account.[59] At the same time, however, in better defining the ambit of Raz's theory, I would suggest that this observation reveals more clearly its central weakness. The independence condition purports to restrict the assessment of the NJT to matters over which it is better to defer to authoritative judgment, but it seems to presuppose that such assessments are stable within any given polity.[60] Insofar as the independence condition restricts the basis of assessment to the substance (rather than procedure) of decision making, it provides no *substantive* basis – moral content – for making the assessment as to which matters meet the conditions of the independence condition. In other words, the form of conceptual analysis applied by Raz *describes the problem of justifying* authority rather than actually providing the substance of the justification itself.[61] Furthermore, in setting up the problem in the way that he does – and thus focussing attention on the justification for deferral of moral reasoning – Raz's account seems to preclude (or at least subjugate to a secondary level) those non-instrumental factors that we might have for rejecting the legitimacy of certain institutions: we might deem them to be substantively unjust, for instance, in

[57] See A. Tucker, 'The Limits of Razian Authority', *Res Publica* 18 (2012): 225–40, esp. 232–33.
[58] Raz, 'Problem of Authority', 1014.
[59] Tucker, 'Limits of Razian Authority'.
[60] I owe this observation to conversations with Margaret Martin.
[61] See Tucker, 'Limits of Razian Authority', 234.

terms of either the values to which they are committed, the way they were constituted, or how they sustain their dominance over us.[62]

Of course, this criticism does not show that Raz's thesis is necessarily wrong. Rather, it demonstrates that it is, at best, only a partial or incomplete vision of authority. However, the problem also runs deeper. Even on its own terms, Raz's account seems beset by an irresolvable tension in the individuated, instrumental rationale that underpins it and at the same time constantly threatens its internal coherence. This problem is well described by Margaret Martin in a sustained critique of Raz's theory, where she notes how this tension plays out in the way that the pre-emption thesis, on the one hand, and the NJT, on the other, seem to pull Raz in conflicting directions. Specifically, the pre-emption thesis presupposes that participants are excluded from reflecting on reasons that apply to them anyway through their prior acceptance of authority, whilst the NJT – and, I would add, the independence condition also – seems to require a constant review and reflection on the question of deferral to authority.[63] One might counter this argument by suggesting that it simply misunderstands the nature of the normative assessment contained in the NJT, which is not a matter for participant reflection in relation to individuated decision making. However, if this is the case, then a more fundamental problem is established, for the normative assessment required under the NJT can only really reflect that of the detached, 'external' theorist rather than the 'internal', self-reflexive attitudes of legal subjects themselves.[64] If we reject this conclusion, however, then we also must admit that 'the recognition of the authority becomes a process involving continuing reflection, judgement and qualification.'[65] This point is also forcefully made by Mian, who suggests that the only way to unpick the tension in Raz's account is to reject the pre-emption thesis – that is, to suggest that the acceptance of legal authority might well provide particularly weighty reasons for compliance but that as moral agents, it is never fully justified to set aside our reasoning and reflection on the right course of action in most circumstances.[66]

[62] See, generally, T. Christiano, 'The Authority of Democracy', *Journal of Political Philosophy* 12 (2004): 266–90, esp. 277–80.
[63] See, generally, Martin, 'Judging Positivism', ch. 4.
[64] See, on this point in particular, D. Dyzenhaus, 'Consent, Legitimacy, and the Foundation of Political Authority' (unpublished manuscript).
[65] Mian, 'Curious Case of Exclusionary Reasons', 114.
[66] Ibid., 121 *et seq.*

In all, the service conception fails to provide an adequate answer to the problem that Raz seems to want to answer and that is necessarily definitive of the role of law in political communities – namely, the fact of legitimate disagreement between moral agents, and the need to subjugate individual moral decision making by some rightful procedure. At the same time, however, it also fails to see that such a deferral to right procedure is not to impose some kind of pre-emptive restraint that subjugates our capacity for individual moral and political reflection. Rather, it suggests only that the best way to respect individual moral autonomy is through designing and instantiating better sorts of *public* political institutions. In the circumstances of disagreement that beset political community, the most legitimate form of decision making is arguably one where the *a priori* deferral is kept under constant scrutiny by a balanced procedural model, requiring checks and balances and accountability inputs into the decision-making process through which those in positions of authority must act. In other words, it would seem that some kind of argument from democracy would offer an intuitively more plausible justification for authority, at least within the state context. On such an account, respect for moral autonomy both provides a rationale for the substantive exercise of coercive authority and suggests the need for some procedural check on the exercise of public power by instantiating a form of democratic oversight.[67] This is not to say that democracy is a sufficient condition for the legitimate authority of the state, or of all the political institutions within it, but only that it offers one means of keeping the competing demands of individual liberty and the collective interest in check.

I will return again to this consideration in the final section. My more immediate concern is that this democratic 'way out' seems to be unavailable or precluded by the particular institutional characteristics of the international legal order as a decentralized legal system.

It is for this reason that we might well re-engage the role of consent in the processes of international law as a legitimate system, not as a replacement for democracy, but as a consequence of the circumstances of disagreement and moral pluralism as they pertain to such a decentralized legal system. Nevertheless, as I seek to show in the following section, the role of consent in international law is very often misunderstood.

---

[67] Christiano, 'Authority of Democracy', 280–84.

3 Justifying the Authority of International Law: The Discontinuity Thesis and the Argument from State Consent

On the basis of the foregoing discussion, it might well be possible to postulate that rules of international law validated in accordance with its source criteria purport to be authoritative in the sense that they claim to bind states and other actors independently of any assessment of the substantive merits of these rules. Put simply, insofar as rules are validated by reference to international law's doctrine of sources, one might simply argue that there arises a content-independent reason for compliance. Without making the stronger claim that such reasons necessarily amount to pre-emptive obligations in the sense suggested by Raz, I will still proceed on the assumption that international law does indeed claim authority in the way described. In the introduction, I referred to this view as the JSV. In this section, I seek to understand exactly how we might ground this justification, taking account of the particular nature of international political relations.

It has commonly been argued in this context that the consent of states has been key to the legitimacy of international law, at least in its most 'classical' form – a view that is often simply equated with the rise to dominance of legal positivism from the nineteenth century onwards.[68] Indeed, considered in line with the rise of liberal political theory from this time, it does seem plausible and quite familiar to conceive of the legitimacy of international law according to a similar kind of 'creation myth' explanation as outlined in the previous section – that is, by referencing the kind of political theory that underpins the social contract tradition.[69] Indeed, understood figuratively rather than literally or empirically, the kind of (broadly consensual) reasoning that has been applied to justify forms of hierarchical governance at the state level can also be – and indeed, often has been – applied in the abstract to understand and attempt to justify the institutional structure of the international legal order.[70] Historically speaking, this kind of domestic analogy was explicit in the works of theorists such as Rousseau or Kant, but it is arguably also more pervasive

---

[68] See, e.g., Collins, 'Classical Legal Positivism'.
[69] Koskenniemi, 'Politics of International Law', 4–6.
[70] P. Capps, 'The Rejection of the Universal State', in *Transnational Constitutionalism*, ed. Nicholas Tsagourias (Cambridge: Cambridge University Press, 2007), 17. For the more pervasive use of domestic analogies in structuring thought on international relations, see also H. Suganami, *The Domestic Analogy and World Order Proposals* (Cambridge: Cambridge University Press, 1989).

in the implicit structuring of core international law doctrines. As Martti Koskenniemi has claimed, 'This is a theory which identifies itself on two assumptions. First, it assumes that legal standards emerge from the legal subjects themselves. There is no natural normative order. Such order is artificial and *justifiable only if* it can be linked to the concrete wills and interests of individuals. Second, it assumes that once created, social order will become binding on these same individuals. They cannot invoke their subjective opinions to escape its constraining force. If they could, then the point and purpose of their initial, order-creating will and interest would be frustrated.'[71]

As such, following the logic of something like the social contract, we can see also how international law claims to offer an objective basis for law's normative force from a broadly consensual model of associative politics. As Patrick Capps puts it, in both forms of justification, the concepts of 'consent, obligation and institutional form, are mutually supportive and logically parasitic upon each other'.[72] Of course, the idea of consent here would not be an empirical account of the founding of the international legal order, or even a justification for legal obligation in a more immediate sense,[73] but rather acts as *part of* the overall legitimacy claim underpinning and structuring the core doctrines of the international legal system.[74] In other words, the consensual justification should not simply be equated with voluntarism in political obligation. In fact, it was precisely this kind of voluntarist argument that was rightfully castigated for being an unworkable theory of obligation by inter-war jurists like Lauterpacht and Brierly and has remained largely unpalatable for many international lawyers and theorists since.[75] In this sense, it seems clear that, just as in the social contract tradition, the reason for international law's authority over states cannot be that they have actually given their consent to be bound by the system itself.

---

[71] M. Koskenniemi, *From Apology to Utopia: The Structure of International Legal Argument* (Cambridge: Cambridge University Press, 2005), 21–22. See also Carty, *Decay of International Law*, ch. 1.

[72] Capps, 'Rejection of the Universal State', 17.

[73] For (critical) discussion, see F. Kratochwil, 'The Limits of Contract', *European Journal of International Law* 5 (1994): 465–91, esp. 477–86.

[74] For instance, Philip Allott uses this kind of justification to explain the nature of customary international law, reconciling the idea of consent with a systematic explanation of legal obligation. P. Allott, 'The Concept of International Law', *European Journal of International Law* 10 (1999): 31–50, esp. 39.

[75] For discussion, see Collins, 'Classical Legal Positivism', 28–36.

At the same time, however, there is another sense in which consent is commonly taken as a more central aspect of the legitimacy of binding legal rules at the international level. Specifically, one might say that there is a sort of normative disjuncture in the chain of reasoning that leads from moral autonomy, through the social contract (or other normative rationale) to some form of hierarchical, centralized institutions characteristic of domestic society. Few theorists (or, indeed, international lawyers) who justify international law in this way also advocate anything like a universal state as an ideal institutional form for international law. Capps calls this the 'discontinuity thesis', a normative rationale explaining why the kind of reasoning that justifies the institutional form of the state at the domestic level does not (necessarily) justify the centralisation of authority at the international level.[76] On this basis, we might have reason to re-engage state consent as a more meaningful aspect of the legitimacy of international legal rules.

There are numerous reasons why this discontinuity might occur, including pragmatic motivations (e.g., that it is simply not feasible to subjugate states to a higher command), but also, and more importantly, those of principle (essentially, that it would be *illegitimate* to impose such a centralized command upon a pluralistic international society).[77] If we can accept, therefore, that there may well be a good reason for the specific institutional form of international law, we can also see how consent can re-enter our picture of the authority of international law as a central component of the legitimacy of binding legal rules.[78] In other words, it is not that the 'constitution rule' of international law can be grounded in consent – though it clearly is supported and sustained by the consensual practices of states – but rather that this rule itself predicates the acceptability, recognition and applicability of specific international legal norms, at least in part, on the consent of states (however indirect or strained such a justification might appear in empirical terms).

This constitution rule finds its expression in the doctrine of sources, particularly as expressed in Article 38 of the Statute of the International Court of Justice,[79] which, in the absence of the kind of centralized

---

[76] Capps, 'Rejection of the Universal State', 21.
[77] Ibid., 28–40. See also Capps, *Human Dignity*, 215–41.
[78] See, e.g., Collins, 'Classical Legal Positivism'.
[79] Article 38 includes as the sources to be applied by the ICJ: 'International conventions, whether general or particular, establishing rules expressly recognized by the contesting states ... international custom, as evidence of a general practice accepted as law ... the general principles of law recognized by civilized nations ... [and] judicial decisions and

constitutional architecture found at the state level, is often accepted as a kind of proto-'rule of recognition' for the international system as a whole.[80] By purporting to answer the epistemological question of law's origin and the ontological question of law's validity at the same time, the doctrine of sources has to revert back to the subjects of the system – states – on the question of the operative validity of the principal sources of new international norms: custom and treaties.[81] In a continuation of our incomplete or fractured analogy, we might thus follow Phillip Allott in describing international legal order as a 'permanent negotiation of a social contract, the forming and re-forming of a legal basis of social co-existence from day to day, with a necessary and inherent deep-structural mutuality of legal relationships'.[82]

Nevertheless, recognizing that state consent does and should play such a role in a legitimate international legal order is still not to suggest that consent is the reason for international law's binding force. As Samantha Besson has recently argued, consent is neither what ultimately validates international legal norms nor what initially justifies the criteria by which such norms are validated.[83] This might sound counter-intuitive, but it is necessary to understand that the reversion to state consent occurs according to criteria within a broader system of rules, to which states simply could not have consented in any meaningful sense. Thus if there is a good reason for having a system of binding international law – and let us postulate that there is a compelling *a priori* justification for such a system based on the circumstances of moral pluralism and political disagreement evident in international society – then this reason not only is, but must also necessarily be, independent of state consent.

---

the teachings of the most highly qualified publicists of the various nations, as subsidiary means for the determination of rules of law.'

[80] Allott, 'Concept of International Law', 35.

[81] See, e.g., T. Skouteris, *The Notion of Progress in International Law Discourse* (Hague: TMC Asser Press, 2010), 147; Koskenniemi, *From Apology to Utopia*, 303 *et seq.* As Oscar Schachter puts it, the conditions for the validity of legal norms 'are the observable manifestations of the "wills" of states as revealed in the *processes* by which norms are formed'. O. Schachter, 'The Nature and Process of Legal Development in International Society', in *The Structure and Process of International Law: Essays in Legal Philosophy, Doctrine, and Theory*, ed. R. St J. Macdonald and D. M. Johnston (Hague: Martinus Nijhoff, 1983), 762.

[82] Allott, 'Concept of International Law', 44. For a similar rationale, see also I. Hurd, 'The International Rule of Law and the Domestic Analogy', *Global Constitutionalism* 4 (2015): 365–95, esp. 367.

[83] S. Besson, 'State Consent and Disagreement in International Law Making: Dissolving the Paradox', *Leiden Journal of International Law* 29 (2016): 289–316, esp. 298–302.

This is an important distinction that is often missed in contemporary reflections on the functioning of international law, which tend to suggest not only empirical difficulties in actually finding state consent for international norms in any meaningful factual sense but also normative reasons why state consent is simply not an adequate or sufficient way of legitimizing contemporary international law, particularly with the emergence and proliferation of increasingly autonomous institutions, regimes and other forms of global governance. Both critiques – that consent is neither necessary to explain nor sufficient to justify the legitimate authority of international law – are each in their own way quite correct. However, as I have suggested, and as I now seek to demonstrate more clearly, both substantially misunderstand the role that consent (or, at least, consensualism) plays in structuring a legitimate international legal system.

4   Consent as an *Unnecessary* Condition for the Legitimacy of International Law? The Role of the Sources

It is perhaps now trite to suggest that consent is increasingly derided for both its explanatory and justificatory potential in grounding the authority of modern international law in any meaningful sense.[84] This reflection arises most often in relation to the contemporary functioning of international law's doctrine of sources. It is perhaps an obvious observation vis-à-vis the subsidiary sources listed in Article 38, such as general principles, judicial decisions or academic writings. However, even in the case of the two-principal, more deliberative and more paradigmatically 'consent-based' sources of international law – treaty and custom – the consensual justification often seems somewhat spurious.

To take the example of modern treaty practice to begin with, it is true that binding treaty rules follow from state consent as expressed through signature and ratification. However, since the codification of many of the constitutive rules of treaty law in the form of the 1969 Vienna Convention on the Law of Treaties, a significant limit has been placed on states' 'contractual freedom', particularly with regard to their inability to 'opt out' of what are deemed peremptory norms of international law.[85] Furthermore, many of the large-scale multilateral treaty drafting processes have taken on

---

[84] See J. I. Charney, 'Universal International Law', *American Journal of International Law* 83 (1993): 523–53.

[85] On the applicability and effect of *jus cogens* norms, see Articles 53 and 64 of the Vienna Convention on the Law of Treaties, 1969.

a more informal and 'quasi-legislative' function, either because the subject matter of the treaty is such as to have de facto impacts on the interests of third states[86] or, more directly, because the treaty is taken either to reflect existing, or generate new norms of customary international law.[87]

As soon as one turns to look at the customary law-making process itself – arguably the central motor for the creation of generally binding legal norms in international law[88] – it becomes even more difficult to speak of state consent in any meaningful sense. Indeed, it is in relation to customary international law where scholars have most often struggled with the 'paradox' of consensual validation.[89] This tends to occur in particular where the *opinio juris* element in the formation of custom is understood as a process of consensual validation of the legally binding character of certain state practices.[90] Such a view bears little relation to the way in which customary law is found and argued in practice, and from a theoretical perspective, it creates a certain paradox as soon as one considers how custom actually forms and changes over time.[91] Indeed, there would seem to be an inherent difficulty in any source criteria that simply defer back to state participants on the question of the existence or scope of the law binding them (particularly because questions as to the applicability or otherwise of customary international law most often arise in cases where opinion and practice is fundamentally divided).[92] It is because of the practical difficulties of reconciling the source requirements of customary

---

[86] The most seminal study in this regard of recent years is probably M. Fitzmaurice, 'Third Parties and the Law of Treaties', *Max Planck Yearbook of United Nations Law* 6 (2002): 37–137.

[87] See Charney, 'Universal International Law', 547–49. An obvious example of this would be the 1982 UN Convention on the Law of the Sea, many provisions of which, such as in relation to the Exclusive Economic Zone (EEZ), began to be identified as customary international law (e.g., in cases like *Continental Shelf [Libyan Arab Jarnahiriya/Malta]* [Judgment] (1985) ICJ Rep. 13) very swiftly after the Convention's drafting and long before it had entered into force.

[88] As Ian Brownlie states, 'Custom is not a special department or area of public international law: it *is* international law'. I. Brownlie, *The Rule of Law in International Affairs: International Law at the Fiftieth Anniversary of the United Nations* (Hague: Martinus Nijhoff, 1998), 18, original emphasis.

[89] See, e.g., C. L. Lim and O. A. Elias, *The Paradox of Consensualism in International Law* (Hague: Martinus Nijhoff, 1998).

[90] See, e.g., G. G. Fitzmaurice, 'The General Principles of International Law considered from the Standpoint of the Rule of Law', *Recueil des Cours* 92 (1957): 1–227, esp. 97.

[91] This is often referred to as the 'chronological paradox', or simply as the '*opinio juris* paradox'. See, e.g., M. Byers, *Custom, Power, and the Power of Rules: International Relations and Customary International Law* (Cambridge: Cambridge University Press, 1999), 130–33.

[92] See, e.g., Koskenniemi, *From Apology to Utopia*, 422–24.

international law that modern judicial practice seems to take necessary shortcuts, often giving rise to a more fluid (and by no means uncontroversial) form of reasoning that tends to either smudge state practice and *opinio juris* together or prioritize one element over the other.[93] In practice, very few judgments of the ICJ, for example, are able to convincingly demonstrate proof of both elements.[94] If the existence of a binding rule of customary international law is not just postulated without presenting any corresponding evidence to this effect, we see often the *opinio* being merely inferred from the practice[95] or, *vice versa*, inconsistent state practice can be side-lined altogether (such as in the controversial *Nicaragua* judgment[96]) in favour of relying on public statements, resolutions of international organisations or treaty practice as sufficient evidence for the existence of a custom.[97] This 'modern' approach to customary international law looks for a much looser form of social consensus, perhaps derived from the 'soft' normative output of international institutional *fora*, such as the UN General Assembly (UNGA) or – as noted previously – the prior existence of a multilateral treaty, which though not seen as binding in lieu of consent is clearly seen as relevant practice and/or *opinio*.[98]

Recognizing the difficulty of actually applying the source criteria in any coherent way, a number of commentators have suggested the need to discard the additive – that is, 'two-element' – theory of customary international law altogether.[99] Even if not necessarily leading international lawyers

---

[93] Ibid., 418 and *passim*. See also A. E. Roberts, 'Traditional and Modern Approaches to Customary International Law: A Reconciliation', *American Journal of International Law* 95 (2001): 757–91; and F. L. Kirgis Jr., 'Custom on a Sliding Scale', *American Journal of International Law* 81 (1987): 146–51.

[94] Koskenniemi, 'From Apology to Utopia', 428–29.

[95] Indeed, this seems to be the conclusion of the International Law Association in its study on the topic of the formation of customary international law. See International Law Association, 'Final Report of the Committee on Formation of Customary (General) International Law', 2000, 31–32, www.ila-hq.org/download.cfm/docid/A709CDEB-92D6-4CFA-A61C4CA30217F376.

[96] *Military and Paramilitary Activities in and Against Nicaragua (Nicaragua v United States)* (Merits) [1986] ICJ Rep. 14, at *inter alia* 99–100.

[97] Roberts, 'Traditional and Modern Approaches', 758–59. On the problem of international criminal tribunals applying custom without sufficient practice, see N. Arajärvi, *The Changing Nature of Customary International Law: Methods of Interpreting the Concept of Custom in International Criminal Tribunals* (Abingdon: Routledge, 2014).

[98] A. Boyle and C. Chinkin, *The Making of International Law* (Oxford: Oxford University Press, 2007), 225–29.

[99] For convincing theoretical criticisms of the coherence of the two-element (or 'additive') approach to customary international law, see, e.g., G. Postema, 'Custom in International Law: A Normative Practice Account', in *The Nature of Customary Law: Legal, Historical*

to abandon the idea of custom as possessing any inherent authority and normative influence – though there are perhaps some exceptions[100] – some have suggested the need to understand custom as a much less formal and looser form of discursive normative practice,[101] whilst others still have suggested the need to incorporate moral evaluation as part of the source criteria or test of pedigree for the creation of new customary norms.[102]

These are persuasive critiques in many respects, but the problem would seem to lie more in how the twin elements of custom are perceived – that is, insofar as they are seen as validating criteria that can simply be applied to a state of affairs in order to determine binding norms. In fact, it is not at all clear that this rather more complicated picture of customary international lawmaking in practice necessarily undermines the consensual justification underlying the JSV as I have outlined it in this chapter. The empirical critique of spurious consent misses the point that the consensual justification is intrinsic to the structure of the system of international law itself in its deferral back to state participants in the absence of any other institutional hierarchy. The fact that any international tribunal's view of the existence or otherwise of any given customary norm cannot be taken as 'final' on the matter suggests the continuing relevance and vitality of the broadly consensual view of international law's legitimate authority. The point is not whether it is easy to meet the source requirements of customary international law in any real, objective sense but rather that what they require from authorized decision makers in terms of reasoning and argumentation continues to express a particular view of international law's overall institutional legitimacy. Even if moral judgement is required in the process of ascertaining customary international norms, the point is both that it would be illegitimate for any decision maker to pronounce the existence of custom on the basis of moral utility alone and that any such pronouncement cannot be the final say. In other words, that the contemporary realities of international lawmaking are now in many senses more

and *Philosophical Perspectives*, ed. A. Perreau-Saussine and J. B. Murphy (Cambridge: Cambridge University Press, 2007), 279–306; and E. Voyiakis, 'Customary International Law and the Place of Normative Considerations', *American Journal of Jurisprudence* 55 (2010): 163–200.

[100] See, e.g., A. T. Guzman, *How International Law Works: A Rational Choice Theory* (Oxford: Oxford University Press, 2008).

[101] See, e.g., G. Postema, 'Custom in International Law: A Normative Practice Account', in *The Nature of Customary Law: Legal, Historical, and Philosophical Accounts*, ed. J. B. Murphy and A. Perreau-Saussine (Cambridge: Cambridge University Press, 2007), 279–306.

[102] See, e.g., Voyiakis, 'Customary International Law'.

complicated is not sufficient to undermine the deep structural mutuality of international relations insofar as this complexity is, if anything, only really a reflection of that structural condition.

At the same time, the previous discussion perhaps masks or disguises a more fundamental objection to the contemporary relevance of our 'standard view' of international legal authority, specifically by overplaying the relevance or significance of customary international law in an age of 'global governance'. In an increasingly institutionalized international legal order, lawmaking, broadly defined, seems to encompass much more than the cumbersome, formal processes of treaty negotiation and customary law formation. An array of formal and informal regimes, institutions and other clusters and constellations of sub-state and non-state actors are perceived to be involved in variegated forms of rule-making, standard setting and the exercise of more informal normative influence in what might be termed an increasingly 'post-national constellation' of legal normativity.[103] This wide range of actors, standards and rules presents a challenge to the JSV, not least because the normative influence of many such institutions and practices appears quite difficult to reconcile on the basis of state consent. In fact, in their myriad forms and effects – both formal and informal – such institutional processes seem to call into question the kind of binding/non-binding binary opposition that is arguably central to the model of consensual legitimacy underpinning the JSV.

5   Consent as an *Insufficient* Condition for the Legitimate Authority of International Law: The Age of Global Governance

The phenomenon of 'global governance' appears, therefore, *prima facie* unsettling and destabilizing for the aforementioned picture of legitimate authority in international law. The range of normative practices, standards, acts and directives – in addition to formal legal rules – which we might draw together under the umbrella of 'postnational rule-making', creates a complicated picture of legal normativity, calling into question the explanatory potential of a formal, source-based account of legal validity. Indeed, we might place these institutionalized normative practices and forms of rule-making on a spectrum that moves increasingly away from the kind of formal, source-based validity justified under the JSV.

For instance, at one extreme, we find ourselves in the realms of traditional 'institutional law' broadly defined (e.g., EU law, WTO law), which

---

[103]   See, e.g., Collins, 'Mapping the Terrain'.

might be quite easy to reconcile – albeit indirectly – with the consensual validation of the organisation's constituent treaty. However, related to this body of institutional law are those binding determinations (as opposed to general legal rules) that are underpinned by formal legal authority (e.g., decisions of the ICJ, resolutions of the UN Security Council or rulings of the WTO Dispute Settlement Body). Again, it is possible to explain these determinations as legally valid due to the underlying treaty obligation; however, to the extent that they seem to have quite considerable 'legislative' purport – for example, the Security Council assuming authority to mandate international criminal tribunals[104] – the functional effect might come closer to a kind of general law-making power. Whilst it is not impossible to explain this kind of normativity in terms of the traditional sources of international law, one must accept that sources doctrine will neither tell us very much about the normative compliance pull of many of these practices nor provide a meaningful way to legitimize them in most instances.[105]

Perhaps more troubling, however – both in a conceptual and, at times, a moral sense – is the increasing use of (or reliance on) 'soft' forms of regulatory output, such as UNGA resolutions or the guidelines and codes of conduct of bodies like the UN Environment Programme (UNEP) or International Labour Organization (ILO). Further along the spectrum, we also find an increasing reliance on the 'soft' normative output of non-treaty or non-governmental organizations (e.g., codifications/reports of bodies such as the International Committee of the Red Cross) or indeed policy agreements, guidelines and other instruments produced by informal transnational networks of actors operating below the level of inter-state diplomacy.[106] And at perhaps the furthest extreme, we might also include the 'soft' normative output of 'soft' international actors, which might include private interest groups, multinational corporations and informally constituted meetings of heads of states outside of traditional UN or other forms of institutionalized diplomacy (e.g., meetings of the G20 or G7/8).[107]

---

[104] For discussion, see, e.g., W. Sandholtz, 'Creating Authority by the Council: The International Criminal Tribunals', in *The UN Security Council and the Politics of International Authority*, ed. B. Cronin and I. Hurd (Abingdon: Routledge, 2008), 131–53.

[105] I. Venzke, *How Interpretation Makes International Law: On Semantic Change and Normative Twists* (Oxford: Oxford University Press, 2013), 6 and *passim*.

[106] See, principally, A.-M. Slaughter, *A New World Order* (Princeton: Princeton University Press, 2004).

[107] See, e.g., J. Klabbers, 'Institutional Ambivalence by Design: Soft Organizations in International Law', *Nordic Journal of International Law* 70 (2001): 403–21; J. Petman,

The normative force and impact of this range of standards, instruments, decisions and so on will obviously vary greatly, not only vis-à-vis state officials, but also beyond the state, in impacting and limiting the normative choices of individuals and other sub- and non-state actors. As such, in the absence of any (convincing) means by which to validate this kind of 'post-national' normativity at source, or by some other form of 'right procedure', such normative practices seem to lack any *a priori* – that is, content-independent – authority over international legal participants (broadly defined). In this context, to speak in terms of 'softness' or another gradated, or 'relative', form of legal normativity remains deeply problematic, jarring uneasily with the kind of rule-of-law values that are presumed under the JSV, at least as I have defended it in this chapter.[108]

Whilst some international lawyers have suggested that the normative impact of this kind of institutionalized lawmaking should simply be assessed on the basis of any given norm's ability to effect compliance,[109] this kind of assessment seems to essentially deny the authority of such rules altogether (at least considered in terms of content independence).[110] The question of the legitimate authority of international law cannot simply be reduced to a sociological enquiry into what is accepted in practice, *ex post facto*, but should instead act as a counter-factual normative judgement of whether to comply with an institution's command.[111] In this context, then, one might well pose the question of whether there might be some alternative means of legitimizing this exercise of such proto-authority at the global level.

It is perhaps no surprise that the phenomenon of global governance has given rise to concerns over the need for greater democratic mediation within and between international institutions.[112] Notwithstanding some spirited defences to the contrary,[113] however, Christiano is probably

'Deformalization of International Organizations Law', in *Research Handbook on the Law of International Organizations*, ed. J. Klabbers and Å. Wallendahl (Cheltenham: Edward Elgar, 2011), 398–430.

[108] See, e.g., criticisms of J. Klabbers, 'The Redundancy of Soft Law', *Nordic Journal of International Law* 65 (1996): 167–82.

[109] See, e.g., J. E. Alvarez, *International Organizations as Lawmakers* (Oxford: Oxford University Press, 2005).

[110] For a discussion, see J. d'Aspremont, *Formalism and the Sources of International Law: A Theory of the Ascertainment of Legal Rules* (Oxford: Oxford University Press, 2011), ch. 4.

[111] See, on this distinction, Besson, 'Authority of International Law', 345, 371.

[112] See, e.g., discussion in E. Stein, 'International Integration and Democracy: No Love at First Sight', *American Journal of International Law* 95 (2001): 489–534.

[113] See, e.g., S. Wheatley, *The Democratic Legitimacy of International Law* (Oxford: Hart, 2010).

correct as to the unlikelihood of any meaningful and authentic democratic processes emerging that are sufficient to either legitimize the broad spread of institutionalized normative practices that characterize contemporary global governance or bestow legitimacy on many such regimes or institutions individually.[114] Indeed, whilst there have been well-meaning attempts to find some means of democratic legitimisation at the international level (though perhaps more amongst political scientists than international lawyers),[115] many of these proposals remain far from persuasive.[116] With direct forms of political representation at the universal level something of a chimera, the only plausible prospect appears to be to enhance the participatory role and normative influence of non-governmental organisations (NGOs) and other non-state actors as a nascent form of 'global civil society'.[117] Nevertheless, with long-standing concerns about the accountability and representative credentials of many NGOs,[118] the idea that this nascent civil society could serve to legitimize the kind of power and influence exercised by many global actors seems to drain democracy of much of its meaning, being ultimately premised on a decidedly 'pre-modern' idea of constituent power.[119]

The question thus becomes whether we might instead formulate a more instrumental form of justification, perhaps by recasting or reaching beyond the traditional doctrine of sources by seeking some conditional assessment of the 'public' credentials of candidate international legal norms. In other words, might it be possible to return to the initial *a priori*

---

[114] Christiano, 'Legitimacy of International Institutions', 382; and further in T. Christiano, 'Democratic Legitimacy and International Institutions', in *Philosophy of International Law*, ed. S. Besson and J. Tasioulas (Oxford: Oxford University Press, 2010), 119–38. See also J. H. H. Weiler, 'The Geology of International Law – Governance, Democracy and Legitimacy', *Zeitschrift für Ausländisches Öffentliches Recht und Völkerrecht* 64 (2004): 547–62, esp. 561–62.

[115] See, e.g., D. Held, *Models of Democracy*, 3rd ed. (Cambridge: Polity Press, 2006), 275–81, 304–8. For a push for a deliberative democratic approach to international law, see Wheatley, 'Democratic Legitimacy'; and A. von Bogdandy, 'Globalization and Europe: How to Square Democracy, Globalization, and International Law', *European Journal of International Law* 15 (2004): 885–906, esp. 904–5.

[116] See, e.g., Weiler, 'Geology of International Law', 560–61.

[117] See, e.g., the discussion of J. A. Scholte, 'Civil Society and Democratically Accountable Global Governance', *Government and Opposition* 39 (2004): 211–33.

[118] See, e.g., J. Friedrichs, 'The Neomedieval Renaissance: Global Governance and International Law in the New Middle Ages', in *Governance and International Legal Theory*, ed. I. F. Dekker and W. G. Werner (Leiden: Martinus Nijhoff, 2004), 11–16.

[119] A. Somek, 'The Owl of Minerva: Constitutional Discourse before Its Conclusion', *Modern Law Review* 71 (2008): 473–89, esp. 487–89.

justification for authority – the kind of liberal-constitutionalist principle that seeks to restrain power in the service of moral autonomy – in order to substantively assess an actor's authority to influence behaviour? Recent years have seen a range of such alternative perspectives emerging, often grounded in a concern for the rule of law and the apparent 'publicness' of the actor[120] or instrument involved.[121] This is exemplified by the 'Global Administrative Law' project, in which a specific class of institutional practice is distinguished and seen to be mediated by its 'public' character,[122] as well as – more extensively – much of the 'global constitutionalist' literature, which seeks to operationalize a value-based assessment of constitutional compliance as a compensatory response to the perceived impacts of global governance activities on the rule of law at the domestic level.[123]

As well-meaning as many of these efforts are, there is an ironic movement apparent here, insofar as the concern to bring legitimacy through some formal 'gatekeeper' requirement – to proceduralize – causes a push towards an informal mode of substantive normative assessment. Such an assessment would seem to be very much in tension, therefore, with the same rule-of-law concerns that propelled these approaches in the first place. As noted previously, insofar as the doctrine of sources is premised on a view of international law's legitimate authority expressed through content-independent normativity, many of these perspectives end up justifying the formalisation of criteria that are, by their very nature, *content dependent* rather than independent.

In this context, whilst I would venture that there is a great deal more empirical work required to understand the kinds of factors that shape and condition the normative influence of global governance institutions and actors, from a more normative perspective, it might well be the case that we simply have to deny any *a priori* authority other than what can be

---

[120] See, most recently, M. Goldmann, 'A Matter of Perspective: Global Governance and the Distinction between Public and Private Authority (and Not Law)', SSRN, 15 January 2015, http://ssrn.com/abstract=2260293, in which legitimate international public authority is identified on the basis of whether 'the actor may reasonably claim to act on behalf of a community of which the affected person or entity is a member, or a member of such member' (18).

[121] M. Goldmann, 'Inside Relative Normativity: From Sources to Standard Instruments for the Exercise of International Public Authority', *German Law Journal* 9 (2008): 1865–1908.

[122] B. Kingsbury, 'The Concept of "Law" in Global Administrative Law', *European Journal of International Law* 20 (2009): 23–57, esp. pp. 31–33.

[123] See, e.g., A. Peters, 'Compensatory Constitutionalism: The Function and Potential of Fundamental International Norms and Structures', *Leiden Journal of International Law* 19 (2006): 579–610, esp. 585.

traced back to a formal source or justified on a case-by-case assessment. In this framework, the *a priori* practical authority of global governance institutions is likely to diminish the further along the aforementioned spectrum it sits – that is, the more tenuous its link to the formal sources of international law. The more it does so, the greater is the need for it to appeal to more substantive – that is, *content-dependent* – justifications in order to ground its authority in many instances. This is not to deny the obvious normative influence of many of these institutions, actors and regimes, but only to stress the importance of retaining the ability to judge each case on its merits, so as not to pre-suppose an authority that an institution might not possess.[124]

This might sound like a defeat for or a diminishment of the relevance of international law in its most contemporary form; however, as I argued above, if we move away from the idea that international law's content-independent normativity necessarily implies a kind of coercive pre-emption, we might well be less alarmed by the fact that normative choices are determined only partly by the existence of formally binding legal rules. We should certainly not be surprised that we might have many good content-dependent reasons to accept or reject the normative influences of purported authorities and that one's capacity to make such decisions when necessary requires precisely that we *should not pre-empt* our other reasons by a spurious legitimisation of the authority of others to act on our behalf. On these terms, it would seem far from novel that there are, in effect, content-independent and content-dependent modes of normative assessment at play and in tension in the discursive processes of reasoning and action at the global level, even if the range of normative influences at play are now more varied and complex.[125]

As such, I believe that there are good reasons to leave certain 'sources' of post-national legal normativity outside of international law's formal criteria of validity.[126] To the extent that many of these normative practices remain contested and controversial, the ability to decry their 'non-legality' by reference to agreed-upon criteria that do not invoke the very

---

[124] I've made this argument elsewhere, not least in Collins, *Institutional Problem*, ch. 9; but also Collins, 'Mapping the Terrain'.

[125] Although not exactly the same in scope and justification, Roughan makes a similar call for a more relativized concept of authority to apply to the plural range of international legal institutions – broadly defined – where authority is not only dependent on the strength or weakness of competing claims but also on the interaction between those claims. See Roughan, *Authorities*, esp. chs. 5, 8.

[126] Collins, 'Mapping the Terrain'.

same values that may well be the source of conflict in the first place still seems important to the legitimate authority of the system of international law overall. Whether and to what extent these post-national normative standards are accepted as legitimate may well depend on an evaluative assessment of their content as such and not their source, pedigree or other rightful – that is, authoritative – procedure. However, the point is that the judgment required in making such determinations is not susceptible to public promulgation without a concomitant acceptance of some agreed-upon procedure or institution with the ability to determine authoritatively what such values might mean in any given situation.

6　Conclusion

On the basis of what I have just argued, then, it remains still plausible to defend a formal source-based account of international law as an important reflection of respect for moral autonomy and political pluralism through the requirement of a broadly consensual decision-making process. As I have sought to show, that this view does not equate with the reality of how normative influences actually shape the practices of states and other actors is irrelevant to the more principled question of what kind of legal system is justified, and how it is justified, at the international level. That there is a range of other normative practices and influences that require another kind of justification is, on this view, not a reason to revisit or reconstruct the JSV but rather to use that disjuncture between ideal and reality to exercise a cautious scepticism in questioning and, if necessary, challenging those who purport to claim an authority for themselves that cannot be legitimized in the same way. In other words, there is a benefit to retaining a formal, institutional perspective as a mirror against which we can highlight the informal nature of, as well as power imbalances potentially perpetuated by, much of the rule-making that takes place outside of or beyond our inherited yet still important legal world view.[127]

---

[127] See, on this point, A. Somek, "The Concept of "Law" in Global Administrative Law: A Reply to Benedict Kingsbury', European Journal of International Law 20 (2010): 985–95, esp. 993–94.

9

The International Criminal Court

The New Leviathan?

MARGARET MARTIN*

> International criminal justice cannot create by fiat a world that would make
> sense of its existence. It must make sense of its existence in the world as it is.
>
> Frédéric Mégret

When international criminal law (ICL) was born, its creators lauded its transformative potential. Many hopes were thrust upon the newest addition to the international law family. ICL was going to alter international relations, holding powers accountable to a newly enacted set of international legal norms. Not only would legal justice be brought to places that seem to need it most; the hope that ICL could deter would-be perpetrators was also an intoxicating thought. Politics would no longer be a wholly lawless affair.

Over time, however, the limits of the enterprise have become increasing visible. Now-familiar complaints that legal proceedings interfere with domestic peace processes, or amount to little more than 'victor's justice', began to emerge.[1] One line of response was to insist that we were in the early, infantile stage of the life of the International Criminal Court (ICC).[2]

* I would like to extend sincere thanks to Patrick Capps and Henrik Palmer Olsen for their dedication to this project and their careful commentary at every stage. I would also like to thank Jakob v. H. Holtermann, James Gallen and the participants at both workshops for their incisive comments. I am also grateful for the excellent interventions offered by François Tanguay-Renaud, Michael Guidice, Timothy Fowler and the participants at the Legal Philosophy Between State and Transnationalism seminar, hosted by Osgoode Hall Law School in fall 2016 and at the University of Bristol Legal and Political Theory Seminar Series in March 2016. Finally, I wish to extend a special thanks to Alan Brudner, Richard Collins and Stuart Toddington for their detailed feedback and ongoing support.

[1] For a discussion of the multiplicity of complaints, see F. Mégret, 'The Anxieties of International Criminal Justice', *Leiden Journal of International Law* 29 (2016): 197–221.
[2] I will discuss the ICC and various *ad hoc* tribunals. My critique applies to both, even though there are salient differences.

Only in time, and with perseverance, would its latent potential be realized. Former prosecutor Luis Moreno Ocampo urged practitioners to hold their nerve in the face of mounting criticism: only with an unwavering commitment to the project would ICL bear the fruits promised.[3] Other defenders of the enterprise adopted a different strategy: they stressed the value of realizing a single goal, such as bringing an end to impunity.[4] ICL, after all, is but one tool; why would we expect it to do everything in every context? It is unclear, however, if ICL can be justified on such narrow grounds. Indeed, it is highly doubtful that the ICC would have come into being if it was believed that its potential was this limited.

Interestingly and tellingly, a new approach to ICL, and ICL scholarship, has recently emerged – one that is marked by a radical hopelessness. It is as if our teenager has become so unwieldy that we can do no more than throw up our hands. Darryl Robinson, for instance, argues that everything that legal practitioners do is the subject of valid criticism. Robinson illustrates this point by demonstrating the cogency of Martti Koskenniemi's well-known critique of international law. Koskenniemi argues that the ICC can be criticized for being utopian when the law reflects ideals that are too idealistic to carry practical import, or it can be criticized for being too political when there is no perceivable distance between the interests of power and legal norms.[5] If one works to ensure that the enterprise is not overly utopian, it quickly looks like mere politics, sacrificing any claim to normative legitimacy. Likewise, if practitioners create distance between existing practices and the law, the charge of utopianism can be quickly launched. Robinson refers to this as the 'Goldilocks principle'. But in contradistinction to the famous fairy tale, in the world of ICL, Robinson maintains that it is impossible to get things 'just right'.[6]

Robinson's assessment seems benign, as he has donned the hat of a reporter rather than a critic. Despite his modest aims, a normative message is easily gleaned: if it is impossible to adjust current practice to placate the critics, international lawyers will be tempted to 'solider on'. After all, if one can never satisfy every critic, then what is the point in trying to

---

[3] L. Moreno Ocampo, 'Address to the Assembly of States Parties' (14 November 2008) ICC, 2–11, esp. 6.

[4] For a detailed critical assessment of this move, see K. Engle, 'Anti-impunity and the Turn to Criminal Law in Human Rights', *Cornell Law Review* 100 (2015): 1069–1127.

[5] D. Robinson, 'Inescapable Dyads: Why the ICC Cannot Win', *Leiden Journal of International Law* 28 (2015): 323–47. Robinson notes that while Koskenniemi has an 'emancipatory agenda', Robinson himself is mainly interested in 'patterns of discourse' (325n9).

[6] Ibid., 325.

satisfy any critic?[7] This point is magnified when placed in the context of Koskenniemi's critique: altering law to placate one set of critics will make the practice vulnerable to the worries of a different set of critics. Moreno Ocampo's initial call to soldier on – to hold one's nerve – was direct and idealistic; here, the push to persevere is indirect and rooted in existential despair. But, interestingly, the despair does not translate into a call for radical change.[8]

While I agree with Robinson that practitioners may not be able to get things 'just right', he is wrong to assume that practitioners cannot do better. In order to determine what 'better' amounts to, a normative framework is required. This is a point that Robinson concedes,[9] but he fails to acknowledge that an account of ICL that relies on such a framework will lead to judgements that are incompatible with his quasi-descriptive 'report' of the status quo. An evaluative framework allows for a nuanced diagnosis of the current situation: the most pressing critiques become readily identifiable, whilst other vocal critics can be quickly disarmed.

Consider one example that illustrates this point. Robinson treats the claim that international law is 'too political' as normatively equivalent to the claim that ICL is problematic when it interferes with peace processes.[10] Upon inspection, it becomes apparent that these two familiar criticisms are not on par, normatively speaking.[11] If, for instance, the apolitical ideal is unattainable in a given instance, the charge that the ICC is acting in a manner that is too political may prove to be a judgement that is generated by false expectations. Conversely, I will argue that the most pressing moral

[7] Robinson flags this worry but claims he is contributing to a 'textured discourse', adding that we should not fear that his approach will lead to nihilism or paralysis. See ibid., 332. As my chapter indicates, I am unconvinced that the danger has been averted.
[8] Also see Mégret, 'Anxieties of International Criminal Justice', 219. Mégret is a vocal critic of ICL in this article, but he suggests that one of the strengths of the enterprise is that practitioners opt to soldier on despite the problems he identifies: 'But it is also true that anxieties do not necessarily doom international criminal justice. Dilemmas are, paradoxically, a source of its resilience. For all its frailties, international criminal justice as a normative enterprise nevertheless presses on, steering a path through its chronic angst.'
[9] Ibid., 346n4.
[10] Ibid., 334–35. Robinson is right to note that the charge that the ICC is 'too political' can be launched from a variety of perspectives, thereby masking disagreement (331–32). Robinson, however, treats all these arguments as valid, whereas I do not make this assumption.
[11] Robinson also fails to consider the possibility that the politicisation of ICL may be normatively required. Henrik Palmer Olsen explores the possibility in reference to international law in general in Chapter 3 of this volume, 'International Courts and the Building of Legal Authority beyond the State'.

obstacle facing the ICC is its impact on vulnerable populations, including victim populations. This can occur when legal proceedings interfere
with local peace processes. But there are other ways the application of
ICL can have a negative impact on vulnerable populations. The actions of
the ICC can have regrettable consequences that are unintended but foreseeable. I will suggest that such consequences should be included in the
moral calculus that the ICC performs when determining the next course
of action and that we perform when we assess the moral authority of the
institution. More specifically, I will argue that the ICC should render con-
textualized judgements that place the interests of the victims (and vulnerable populations more generally) at the forefront of the decision-making
process. The ICC continually refers to victims in an attempt to justify its
work – this appeal rings hollow unless their interests are taken seriously.[12]

I will turn to the evaluative framework of Thomas Hobbes to illuminate the precise contours of the moral obstacles that ICL encounters.
I will not look to Hobbes to inform a realist account of international
relations, but rather to offer a sober reminder about what people have
reason to do when faced with unrelenting risks to their survival. The
brilliance of Hobbes's theory, political theorist John Dunn explains, is
that it anchors an account of sovereign authority in human vulnerabili-
ties. The need for personal survival underpins and justifies the decision
to acquiesce to authority: 'The justification of state power, if it is to rest
anywhere stable at all, must depend finally upon the peculiar urgency
for every human being of meeting this particular need: on a mutual relation between protection and obedience.'[13] Hobbes, of course, did not
contemplate the possibility of an ICC. He was primarily concerned with
preventing civil wars. Nevertheless, the fundamental question remains
salient: What institutional arrangements is it rational for individuals to
commit to insofar as they are interested in securing the conditions that
make survival more likely?

---

[12] For an illuminating discussion of the gap between the ICC's rhetoric and the realities of
practice, see S. Nouwen and S. Kendall, 'Representational Practices at the International
Criminal Court: The Gap between Juridified and Abstract Victimhood', *Law and
Contemporary Problems* 76 (2013): 235–62.

[13] J. Dunn, *The History of Political Theory and Other Essays* (Cambridge: Cambridge University
Press, 1996), 69. I will be offering a fairly conventional interpretation of Hobbes's theory.
For an alternative view see D. Dyzenhaus, "Hobbes on the authority of law" in *Hobbes and
the Law*, ed D. Dyzenhaus and T. Poole (Cambridge: Cambridge University Press, 2012),
186–209.

For Hobbes, it is rational to consent to obey the sovereign precisely because survival is more likely once peace is secured.[14] Of course, the ICC is not a sovereign in the typical sense, not least because it does not have its own sword. This may tempt us to frame the question of the authority of the ICC in a particular fashion. In the world of ICL, we are dealing with the indirect submission of individuals to the law: states – not individual agents – consent to be bound by ICL. This means that it may be sensible to think of the authority of the court along three interrelated planes: (1) What authority does the ICC have over states? (2) What obligations do states take on under the principle of complementarity?[15] and (3) What direct authority does the ICC have over individuals in a given set of circumstances? These questions arise in this way if we look through the lens offered by ICL. I propose to access the question of normative authority via a different route. Specifically, I wish to explore the exercise of power by institutions, regardless of whether we are dealing with the executive of the legislative branch of government and whether individuals or states are in a position to give consent.

Again, while the lenses offered by Hobbes and ICL are clearly different, the moral issue of how power is utilized remains salient. The world the ICC has imagined for itself is one where the institution is only responsible for the *legal* consequences of the decisions it makes. Domestic law holds individuals responsible for the foreseeable consequences of their actions and, while the ICC presents itself as a good global citizen, it does not take responsibility for the foreseeable but unintended consequences of its own actions. The ICC has become a sovereign power in this sense (albeit one that is dependent on the power of sovereign states, or the Security Council), and a potentially dangerous one, or so I shall argue. Hobbes is useful in highlighting the plight of the vulnerable and underscoring the unbounded nature of the power that the ICC currently enjoys.

Thus we can reframe Hobbes's fundamental question in at least two ways. As mentioned previously, we can ask what institutional arrangements individuals should consent to, even if they are never in a position to give consent. The ICC does, after all, take away a certain amount of sovereign power from states, so it still makes sense to ask what institutional arrangements are best suited to enable survival and, potentially,

---

[14] T. Hobbes, *Leviathan*, ed. E. Curley (Indianapolis: Hackett, 1994), ch. 14.
[15] The principle of complementarily states that ICL only has authority over the accused if the relevant state(s) itself is 'unwilling or unable' to prosecute the accused.

flourishing for vulnerable populations. In *Leviathan*, Hobbes acknowledges that individuals are rarely in a position to consent to authority,[16] but they can rebel and disrupt authority. Civil war is the realization of the power of an aggregate of individuals over that of the state. Obedience, Hobbes famously maintains, is preferable, since peace is the most promising pathway to survival and human flourishing. Can the same be said about obedience to the ICC? This question is all the more pressing once we recognize that vulnerable populations have very little (if any) power to rebel against the actions taken by the ICC.

The second way to phrase the question takes us further away from Hobbes's framework but closer to the institutional structure of the ICC. The Hobbesian inquiry can be tailored to reflect this institutional reality that rulers, not individuals, consent to be bound by the ICC: Is it rational for rulers to consent to be bound by the ICC? In what follows, I will argue that benevolent rulers would be wise to withdraw their consent to be bound by ICL.[17] It is simply not clear in advance whether the ICC will in fact work to forward the basic interests of the populace. To be clear, my point is not that ICL is never able to help bring peace and create the conditions for personal security; rather, my claim is that in many instances, it is difficult to predict if ICL will contribute to these ends, which speaks to the risk assessment one must undertake before consenting to be bound by the Rome Statute.

When exploring the actions of the ICC (and the *ad hoc* tribunals), we can begin to distinguish between the features that are essential to the enterprise and those that are contingent exercises of power. I am concerned with both dimensions of the use of ICL, partly because there is not always a clear line between the two. The prosecutor, for instance, exercises discretion when deciding if and when to issue arrest warrants. Any decision is contingent (given that any particular offender need not be pursued by the court); however, the act of issuing arrest warrants is an essential feature of the enterprise. In Section 1, I will focus on the impact such decisions can have on vulnerable populations. I will suggest that the discretionary power should be utilized in a manner that helps, not hinders, the security interests of vulnerable populations. In other words, the office of

---

[16] Hobbes, *Leviathan*, ch. 15.
[17] The OP can operate without the consent of states insofar as the instructions have been given by the Security Council. While I focus on consent, my critique also calls into question the moral salience of this practice.

the prosecutor (OP) should consider the political context prior to acting and not simply the 'legal' variables.[18]

In Section 2, I will focus on interpretive practices of the court in order to highlight problems that arise when so-called universal norms are applied in particular contexts. At times, the court has its own narrow institutional goals, which may or may not coincide with the needs of particular communities. Why, I will ask, should a ruler agree to subsume the needs of the populace to the ICL's own institutional ends? Indeed, rulers who are interested in doing what is best for their communities have reason to be wary of ICL. On the other hand, rulers who are interested in solidifying power may have very good reasons to join forces with ICL. These political realities raise grave moral concerns for the legitimacy of ICL, or so I shall argue.

In Section 3, I will claim that the power exercised by the ICC is more worrisome than the near all-encompassing power bestowed upon the sovereign in Hobbes's *Leviathan*. When, for instance, the court aligns itself with oppressive leaders in order to pursue a select few perpetrators, the power of ruthless leaders can be solidified, often at the expense of vulnerable populations within the state. Significantly, the exercise of power in Hobbes's world is visible, and intentionally so. The power exercised in the name of ICL is all too often covert and indirect and thus all the more dangerous.

Hobbes's ideas can also help us identify worrying utopian elements that infect the ICC's project. While Section 3 focuses primarily on Hobbes's *Leviathan*, in order to explain its applicability in greater detail, Section 4 will explain what ICL practitioners can learn from Hobbes. Hobbes tries to understand the human condition as it is in the hopes of transforming it; the ICC tries to transform it without first understanding it. This point becomes startlingly clear when the International Criminal Tribunal for the former Yugoslavia's (ICTY) first decision, *Prosecutor v. Erdemović*, is explored. The policy-based justification offered by the ICTY does not pay heed to the familiar human impulse to survive – the very impulse on which Hobbes erects his grand intellectual edifice. *Erdemović*, I will argue, represents the peak of utopian reasoning, which renders it both morally questionable and practically ineffective.

---

[18] This is possible, from a doctrinal perspective, given that Article 53(c) of the Rome Statute allows the OP to consider the 'interests of justice' when deciding whether to initiate legal proceedings.

If ICL hopes to enjoy an acceptable degree of legitimate authority in the future, a radical rethinking of the project is required. The shift that I am calling for is seismic, as it would require a level of restraint that few practitioners would want to exercise. While I reject Robinson's pessimism (i.e., that we cannot do better), my brand of optimism may prove to be unpalatable to many in the ICC community. 'Doing better', according to the victim-centred account being offered here, may require the OP to not act in many instances. It may also require a shift in focus towards the victim and away from the broader long-term goals with which the ICC is often associated. The ICC will have to become self-consciously political for this vision of its authority to be realized.

I will begin my discussion with a comparison between domestic and criminal law. The message that ICL practitioners should simply soldier on is delivered, once again, by Robinson when he forwards the claim that Koskenniemi's critique applies to *all* forms of law, domestic and international.[19] Why, after all, should we get rid of ICL and leave untouched other kinds of law, including domestic law, if both suffer from the same defects? The problem with Robinson's comparison is that it fails to address important differences between domestic law and ICL. Domestic law is on much stronger normative footing, not least because it is a proven component in peaceful states. While the rhetoric surrounding the ICL project may make it appear as if there is no downside, a closer look at the realities of the practice reveals the dark underbelly of this venture.

1   Peace, Justice and the Criminal Law

In the world of ICL scholarship, one discovers that ICL has a curious relationship with domestic criminal law. At times, critics insist that international law is wholly different from its domestic counterpart: it should not be viewed as a lesser version simply because it does not (and often cannot) work in the same way.[20] Nevertheless, defenders frequently appeal to the purposes of domestic criminal law in the hopes of legitimizing ICL. The difficulty with this tactic becomes clear quite quickly. In the domestic context, the purposes that are thought to underpin criminal law are often mutually reinforcing, and together they serve the security interests of the

---

[19] Robinson, 'Inescapable Dyads', 326.
[20] There have been some useful comparative analyses carried out, however. See S. Bibas and W. W. Burke-White, 'International Idealism Meets Domestic-Criminal-Procedure Realism', *Duke Law Journal* 59 (2010): 637–704.

victims and the community more generally. Conversely, in the international context, certain goals like peace and security are often sacrificed for the sake of legal justice.[21]

Consider the familiar purposes that are thought to underpin, and justify, the existence of criminal law: retributivism, expressivism and deterrence. Retributivist accounts focus on the wrong committed in order to justify punishment.[22] Expressivist theories focus on the normative message sent to would-be perpetrators and the community more broadly.[23] Finally, deterrence-based accounts focus on how the act of punishment works to protect the community in the future by influencing behaviour going forwards.[24] To see how all three purposes are intertwined, consider the practice of incarceration in the domestic context. When criminals are incarcerated, a number of stated goals are served simultaneously. First, any surviving victims are spared from future attack, while the community as a whole is also safer as a result of this practice (at least temporarily). Second, incarceration sends a message to would-be offenders that this is the fate they may face if they partake in similar behaviour. The hope, of course, is that the punishment of offenders will deter others (including the offender) from engaging in such conduct. Not only are these purposes mutually reinforcing (to a degree); more important still, the achievement of any or all of these particular functions is rarely at the expense of the security interests of the populace. All three dimensions of the practice help in some way to secure and maintain peace and security.

It is significant that theorists who reflect on the nature of criminal law usually attempt to make sense of a pre-existing system. They are dissecting and analysing features of an existing legal regime as a way to understand law and often as a ground to advocate for reform. Criminal law, in the

---

[21] It is worth noting that the inverse is also likely: legal justice is sacrificed for peace. For reasons discussed in this chapter, I generally find this option more palatable in many instances.

[22] See A. Brudner, *The Unity of the Common Law: Studies in Hegelian Jurisprudence* (Berkeley: University of California Press, 1995). Also see M. Berman, 'Two Types of Retributivism', in *The Philosophical Foundations of Criminal Law*, ed. R. A. Duff and S. P. Green (Oxford: Oxford University Press, 2011).

[23] M. M. deGuzman, 'Choosing to Prosecute: Expressive Selection at the International Criminal Court', *Michigan Journal of International Law* 33 (2012): 265–320, esp. 302. For a useful critique of expressivism, see H. Hurd, 'Expressing Doubts about Expressivism', *University of Chicago Legal Forum* 1 (2005): 405–35.

[24] For a deterrence-based account of ICL, see J. v. H. Holtermann, 'A "Slice of Cheese" – a Deterrence-Based Argument for the International Criminal Court', *Human Rights Review* 11 (2010): 289–315.

domestic context, is not a free-standing enterprise: it is not up to criminal law alone to secure peace and bring about justice. Domestic criminal law works alongside other kinds of law that, of course, operate within particular socio-economic contexts. Care must be taken not to idealize the workings of domestic criminal justice systems in modern Western states, but nevertheless, the features of these systems that potentially endow them with moral legitimacy are often glaringly absent in the international realm. This is precisely why efforts must be made to keep the needs of the vulnerable people, including victims, in focus: meeting their needs is not a by-product of the work of criminal law in the international context.

ICL occupies a markedly different space than its domestic counterpart. The time-sensitive nature of the tribunals points to the limited power they have in transforming societies. The notion that international legal justice would be a required element for a lasting peace is certainly an assumption that is frequently made,[25] but it is not an assumption that holds, regardless of context. Moreover, peace is a goal for which ICL is ill-suited. These trials do not address the causes of war; hence it is not surprising that they are often unable to help establish peace and security.[26] Only if we think of law in abstraction from context does the international legal context become thinkable; only if law *is* just a set of rules and procedures will the project succeed.[27] But when we turn our attention to the workings of ICL, the limits of criminal law (and by extension, the limits of legal positivism[28]) become apparent. The failure to realize the stated goals of the project, in whole or in part, also illustrates the limits of our own abilities to bring about the imagined world where law rules.

A proponent of ICL might point out that the ICC (and the *ad hoc* tribunals) can work alongside other organizations, like the United Nations

---

[25] See Amnesty International, 'Angola: A New Cease-Fire – a New Opportunity for Human Rights', Amnesty International, 5 April 2002, www.amnesty.org.uk/press-releases/angola-new-cease-fire-new-opportunity-human-rights. Amnesty International takes the following position: 'While acknowledging the difficulties in reaching a cease-fire agreement, Amnesty International maintains that there can be no reconciliation, and therefore no lasting peace, without both truth and justice.'

[26] For a discussion of the aftermath of the ICTR in Rwanda, see M. A. Drumbl, 'Juridical and Jurisdictional Disconnects' (Washington & Lee Public Law Research Paper No. 02-02), 2003.

[27] For a discussion about the manner in which the a-contextual, positivist assumptions informed early thinking about ICL, see E. Borgwardt, *A New Deal for the World: America's Vision for Human Rights* (Cambridge, MA: The Belknap Press of Harvard University, 2005), 215.

[28] For a critique of legal positivism, see M. Martin, *Judging Positivism* (Oxford: Hart, 2014).

(UN) and human rights bodies. Together all these institutions can help bring about positive change, and thus we should judge ICL according to its collaborative successes (or failures). Unfortunately, however, the ICC can and has worked against the interests of human rights organizations. Consider one recent example of the ICC's pursuit of legal justice, which had grave consequences for vulnerable peoples.

In 2008, the OP stated its intention to issue an arrest warrant for sitting president of Sudan, Ahmad al-Bashir (Bashir). Bashir warned the ICC that there would be repercussions for following through with its stated intention – namely, aid agencies would be expelled from the country. When the arrest warrant was issued in 2009, Bashir responded as promised:

> In March 2009, the ICC issued an arrest warrant for Bashir, prompting the GoS [Government of Sudan] to expel 13 international aid agencies and terminate the licenses of three national organisations that it alleged were providing evidence to the ICC. After the expulsions, the security situation for those aid agencies that remained in the country worsened; notably, the first kidnap of an international staff member occurred shortly after the expulsions. By 2011, there was consensus that the GoS wanted all international aid workers out of Darfur, and all humanitarian organisations out of rebel and contested areas. According to a UN Secretary-General report in late 2011, all attempts by humanitarian organisations to gain access to west Jebel Marra had been blocked by the GoS, leaving 'an estimated 300,000 vulnerable people' beyond the reach of the humanitarian community.[29]

While the expulsion of humanitarian workers was an unintended consequence of the actions taken by the ICC, it was foreseeable. In this instance, the ICC eventually withdrew the arrest warrant, but serious damage had already been inflicted. While the legal impact was negligible and temporary, the political fallout of the OP's decision was not. It has proven to be difficult for aid workers to resume their work in Darfur, given that the bonds of trust between the locals and foreign aid workers had been significantly impaired.[30]

When the decision was made to issue the arrest warrant for Bashir, despite the clear risks to vulnerable people, it became clear that the world of ICL is a world of trade-offs. Such calculated trade-offs are often thought of as the stuff of 'dirty' politics – the very thing that ICL was supposed to

---

[29] J. Loeb, 'Talking to the Other Side: Humanitarian Engagement with Armed Non-state Actors in Darfur' (Humanitarian Policy Group Working Paper), 2013, 1–48, esp. 25, footnotes omitted.

[30] Ibid., 26.

transcend.[31] The choice to issue an arrest warrant for a sitting leader is all the more troubling given the known limits of the enterprise. The hope that OP could act without the help of local governments was mere wishful thinking – a sign that the prosecutor's understanding of what was possible was dangerously askew. The utopian impulse to impose the world one wants onto the world that is had tragic consequences in this particular case.

Notice that the gap between 'mere politics' and the lofty 'utopian' justifications does not simply identify an intellectual conundrum over which academics can puzzle; this gap is the space where new victims are created or old ones are re-victimized by the institution that was created, at least in part, to help them. The pursuit of a purely legal mandate (which excludes considerations related to peace and security) means it will be luck, and not intentional decision making, that will result in on-the-ground improvements for the vulnerable. And when such luck is absent, the ICC is not merely a neutral force; it can and does exacerbate suffering in a multiplicity of ways. It is, after all, remarkably difficult to ameliorate the precarious situations of vulnerable peoples when international organizations intentionally work to achieve this end. When the ICC knowingly works against this end, what we are witnessing is yet another man-made atrocity.

One might point out, however, that such acts of hubris can be avoided in the future. The ICC can and should refrain from trying to arrest sitting leaders when the cost in terms of human suffering is so great. However, this is not the only situation where the work of the ICC places vulnerable people at risk. The worry that the ICC will interfere with peace processes is an old one.[32] Not only has the ICC explicitly excluded considerations of peace from their decision-making process,[33] but international lawyers have also taken a hard line against blanket amnesties.[34] This is the official consensus, despite the fact that amnesties have been used in certain

---

[31] For a defence of an a-political understanding of ICL, see H.-P. Kaul, 'The International Criminal Court: Current Challenges and Perspectives', *Washington University Global Studies Law Review* 6 (2007): 575–82, esp. 578–79.

[32] D. G. Newman, 'The Rome Statute, Some Reservations concerning Amnesties, and a Distributive Problem', *American University International Law Review* 20 (2004): 293–357.

[33] The express mandate of the OP excludes such considerations. See International Criminal Court, Office of the Prosecutor, 'Policy Paper on the Interests of Justice', September 2007, www.icc-cpi.int/NR/rdonlyres/772C95C9-F54D-4321-BF09-73422BB23528/143640/ICCOTPInterestsOfJustice.pdf, 8. The Rome Statute does, however, allow considerations that are in the 'interests of justice' to enter into the decision-making process. See Article 53 of the Rome Statute.

[34] See, for instance, M. C. Bassiouni, 'Accountability for Violations of International Humanitarian Law and Other Serious Violations of Human Rights', in *Post-conflict Justice*, ed. M. C. Bassiouni (New York: Transnational, 2002), 3.

contexts to end wars and establish relatively peaceful and prosperous societies.[35]

Of course, those advocating peace over justice have pressed these points before. But this does not mean the problem has been, or can be, wholly resolved. Perhaps it is precisely for this reason that the dichotomy between 'peace' and 'justice' has hardened into a cliché. In literary circles, clichés are problematic, as they signal that the writer has become lazy – communication is hampered when ideas are expressed in pre-formulated phrases that do not prompt the reader (or indeed, the writer) to think deeply.[36] Serious concerns, like 'victor's justice' or 'show trials', are transformed into pre-bundled ideas that, through the sway of language, can be reduced to mere irritants that are as annoying as the cliché itself.[37] Notice that the same worry that infects Robinson's critique is present here as well: if the problems captured in these well-worn clichés cannot be overcome, then the international lawyers should simply soldier on. This is a dangerous message that should be countered.

Observe how language can conceal the moral hazards that accompany the work of the ICC. The well-worn dichotomy between peace and justice can actually work to buttress the status quo. If we accept this dichotomy, it appears as though we are witnessing a battle between two forces for good: we can simply choose a side and cheer happily for our preferred moral gladiator. But the ICC is not always on the side of the good. Sometimes, as we saw previously, when the OP prioritizes the pursuit of legal justice over peace and security, the ICC itself becomes an instrument of grave injustice. In the international context, the central virtue of a court of law – the ability to hold perpetrators to account – can quickly become a vice.

Victims and vulnerable people may not be better off as a result of the actions of the ICC. Not only are the peace dividends unpredictable; in many contexts, they are unlikely precisely because the ICC is often indifferent to such considerations. Unless the ICC consistently and intentionally acts in a way that is consistent with the basic needs of the victim population (or vulnerable populations more generally), it is simply too

---

[35] Consider the case of Angola. See J. v. Wijk, 'Amnesty for War Crimes in Angola: Principled for a Day?', International Criminal Law Review 12 (2012): 743–61.

[36] N. Frye, The Educated Imagination (Concord: House of Anansi Press Limited, 1993), 61.

[37] For a discussion of 'victor's justice' and 'show trials', see M. Martin, 'Reflections on Punishment from a Global Perspective: An Exploration of Chehtman's The Philosophical Foundations of Extraterritorial Punishment', Criminal Law and Philosophy 8 (2014): 693–712, esp. 705–11.

risky to give up autonomy to this particular authority. History tells us that justice is not needed for stable peace to exist, and the kind of justice that is promised is partial and all too often unsatisfactory (even on a purely legal standard). If a given ruler is interested in working for the good of his people, he should be concerned with personal and collective security in addition to justice. And if these are the primary concerns (rather than, say, selfish political gain), a benevolent ruler should *not* consent to be bound by the Rome Statute. Again, it may very well be irrational to give up a degree of autonomy for such unpredictable gains.

Problems are not only encountered when the OP issues arrest warrants: attention must also be given to the interpretive choices made by the ICC or any of the *ad hoc* tribunals. When rendering decisions, judges can and must make important interpretive choices. The nature of these choices, explored in the following section, signals the importance of a shared interpretive context. I will suggest that if legal justice is going to be realized – even in part – the court must work to make sense of the atrocity in the context in which it has occurred. If victim communities are reduced to a mere means through which ICL practitioners pursue institutional ends, it is questionable whether benevolent rulers should consent to be bound by ICL.

2   Interpreting Justice

If we turn to the institutional workings of the ICC, it becomes clear that the interests of a given society and the interests of the court may diverge in important ways. The big question, 'Who is the ICC for?', is one that continually arises. This question is salient once again when one explores the interpretive practices employed by the judiciary. I will suggest that if a state is going to consent to be bound by ICL, it should do so only if it can expect that justice will be done in a manner that both serves and is understood by the particular community in question. There is, of course, no guarantee that a given community will perceive proceedings (or their outcomes) as just, but when the court prioritizes institutional interests and/or its own understanding of legal justice, we can begin to see why states might be wise to reject ICL.

Consider, for instance, the case of *Prosecutor v. Ndahimana*.[38] The International Criminal Tribunal for Rwanda (ICTR) indicted Grégoire Ndahimana, the bourgmestre of Kivumu, accusing him of committing

---

[38] Summary of Judgement, *Ndahimana*, ICTR-01-68-T, ICTR, 17 November 2011.

genocide and crimes against humanity, in large part because of his role in the Nyange Parish massacre, in which more than two thousand Tutsi refugees were slaughtered. Ndahimana received a sentence of fifteen years in prison after being convicted. The reason for the comparatively light sentence was that the ICTR had great difficulty determining the requisite level of individual agency. Mark Drumbl argues that the crux of the problem is not necessarily a failure of law (although there were many fact-finding failures in this case) but the paradox that underlies the act of genocide itself:

> Simply put, Ndahimana lacked the level of agency that might otherwise be expected of a bourgmestre. His descent into genocide was rapid – a matter of days; it was coaxed, if not cajoled – perhaps even compelled; and, in the majority's own words, it was 'belated' – almost as if the genocide accosted him or otherwise happened to him. In sum, then, herein lies the curious criminality of mass atrocity, in which 'mere presence' implicates while 'the scale of the operation' mitigates.[39]

For Drumbl, it was the lack of agency that speaks to a problem that is inherent in the nature of international crimes. Nevertheless, it is odd for someone convicted of what is considered to be one of the most serious of crimes in history to receive such a lenient sentence. While in general, Drumbl's point is insightful, it is unclear that it applies easily in this instance. The problem is not simply that Ndahimana was found guilty and the punishment does not match the severity of the crime. The problem, as I will show, is that it is a matter of dispute as to whether the accused had a reduced level of agency because of the circumstances.

Not surprisingly, the length of Ndahimana's sentence was heavily criticized by Rwandan authorities. Martin Ngoga, Rwanda's chief prosecutor, chastised the ICTR for being 'too lenient in sentencing', adding that 'the judgment does not fully appreciate the role in the genocide of local authorities like Ndahimana, who were very instrumental in the killings'.[40] The problem identified by Ngoga is not one inherent to the nature of genocide itself but one that rests on the nature of cultural understandings: the judiciary failed to grasp local conceptions of

---

[39] M. A. Drumbl, 'The Curious Criminality of Mass Atrocity: Diverse Actors, Multiple Truths, and Plural Responses' (*Washington & Lee Legal Studies Paper* No. 2012–33), 4 October 2012, https://papers.ssrn.com/sol3/papers.cfm?abstract_id=2156512, 27.

[40] Ibid., 29. For the primary source, see J. Kron, 'Rwandan Is Convicted in 1994 Killings', *New York Times*, 17 November 2011, www.nytimes.com/2011/11/18/world/africa/former-rwandan-mayor-convicted-in-tutsi-massacre.html?_r=0.

authority.[41] Given Ndahimana's position of authority, everyone present during the slaughter, including Ndahimana himself, would have understood the power he wielded, even if it was unclear to those reared in the Western tradition.

In this instance, the judiciary was faced with a choice. The decision rendered could reflect the norms of the local community. Alternatively, the judiciary could opt to create precedents that reflect Western norms. Even if the idea of a 'universal standard' is a mere fiction, it remains a useful one: the court knows that deference to local standards produces local jurisprudence. The law that emerged would be contextual and piecemeal, thereby undermining the goal of creating a body of law that could be applied to future offenders. (And, of course, only if such a body of norms is generated can the charge of 'ex post facto application of law' be dealt with.)

A proponent of ICL might add that the justices are not simply prioritizing their institutional goal of generating norms; they are doing what they believe justice requires in the case at hand. After all, a turn to the local threatens to relativize the very idea of justice and, as a result, another deep tension will emerge in the project: the ICC is premised on the idea that justice can transcend context; thus recognition that justice is local would potentially undermine the legitimacy of the enterprise.[42] Notice, however, that the worry articulated by Ngoga does not call into question the understanding of legal justice in full: all parties are interested in assessing culpability. The turn to local norms is required in order to gauge culpability and deliver legal justice.

Also notice that the charge that the ICTR would be acting in a political, and hence illegitimate, fashion if it opted to be guided by local norms is misplaced. That charge presupposes that there is a single neutral standpoint that the court can adopt. Instead, Ndahimana exposes a flaw in this assumption and the related assumption that law is best understood as a set of a-contextual norms whose meaning can wholly transcend spatial and temporal boundaries. Neutrality is likely impossible in this context, and while the ICTR's decision is understandable, it is also worrying. If the hope was that ICL was going to fill a void in lawless communities or that ICL would be able to heal fractured societies, this is only

---

[41] Ibid. Drumbl does not, however, identify the tension between his understanding of the paradox that underlies genocide and the problem generated by cultural conceptions of authority.

[42] Again, there is no 'just right': placating one set of criticisms will make the enterprise vulnerable to another.

possible (if it is possible) insofar as practitioners prioritize local needs over institutional goals.

The victim-centred account I am championing will often require the needs of the community to take priority over other institutional goals. Again, it is not clear that a leader should consent to be bound by ICL if the relevant population will be treated as a mere means through which the court is able to forward its own ends, regardless of the desirability of those ends. Significantly, the feature of the practice explored here is a contingent one: judges can work to reflect local norms if they chose to do so. But for this change to occur, one of the central goals of the ICC – establishing universally applicable precedents – must give way to the needs of the local community.

This is not a minor shift in orientation for ICL. After all, the decision to create universal precedents is connected to a broader aim of the ICL project: to create a world where law rules. Establishing 'universal' norms is essential if the ICC is going to create a set of global norms that, in time, will have a transformative effect. We can now identify a utopian element in the project: insofar as the ICC had to choose between competing conceptions of authority, the dream of a settled set of rules that govern all is revealed to be fantastical. The very fact that the institutional forward-looking goal of transforming the world requires the sacrifice of another institutional goal – healing fractured societies – signals the existence of a fundamental problem. The norms are supposed to apply universally, but it is already apparent that they are not culturally appropriate for the very community where the Ndahimana's trial occurred.

The brittleness of the notion of a single common good for all humanity is underscored once it becomes apparent that the appeal to the abstract category of 'humanity' is often made after the category itself has already been splintered. The intrinsic appeal of the idea of a single common good helps veil the fault line, albeit thinly. The ICC asks us to put faith in projected long-term gains and overlook short-term losses. But the long-term gains are speculative and, as I argued previously and elsewhere, all too often, the goals are unattainable.[43]

If we really want to bring about the best possible future world order, we cannot easily dismiss Raymond Geuss's provocative thought

[43] M. Martin, 'International Criminal Law: Between Utopian Dreams and Political Realities', in *Rethinking Criminal Law Theory: New Canadian Perspectives in the Philosophy of Domestic, Transnational, and International Criminal Law*, ed. F. Tanguay-Renaud and J. Stribopoulos (Oxford: Hart, 2012), 249–66.

experiment: if 'there is to be a feasible common good for the world, it might require that some of us, some individuals and some types of individuals, say the 600 million or so over-privileged consumers of the developed world, simply did not exist'.[44] The point is not that Geuss's proposal should be considered; rather, it is the opposite. His point illuminates the radical nature of any claim that involves following the utilitarian calculus that the interests of a given group should be sacrificed for the betterment of humanity. While this kind of calculus may be inevitable in some circumstances (e.g., in the context of certain wars), it is not inevitable in this case. The ICC does not have to issue an arrest warrant if the well-being of 300,000 people would be placed at greater risk by so doing. Nor does the court have to prioritize 'universal' conceptions of authority over local ones, especially if doing so will likely exacerbate tensions in a war-torn country. Serving the 'human community' does not serve any of the particular communities, thereby threatening to empty the term 'legal justice' of meaningful content in a given context. The court can 'do better', even if perfection is out of reach.

One might argue that insofar as deterrence is prioritized as a goal of ICL, notable sacrifices will likely be required. In the aforementioned case, the goal of deterrence may well be served by rendering tough sentences, but in other cases, vulnerable people generally may have to be sacrificed in the pursuit of a world where such tragedies are less frequent. Consider a tempting analogy: the decision to refuse to negotiate with hostage takers involves the deliberate decision to sacrifice the hostages to the longer-term goal of reducing the prevalence of this practice.

The difference between the two scenarios is noteworthy, however. Hostages are used as human bargaining chips; if they are not recognized as such, the bargaining power of the hostage takers disappears, as does the point of taking hostages in the first place. War, and international relations more generally, does not typically involve this simple incentive structure. There are many reasons for war and, consequently, the utilitarian calculation involved is more complex, and the goods secured are far less certain. But notice that even if the gains were clear and predictable, it is still unclear why a benevolent leader would allow her citizens to be treated as sacrificial lambs. In other words, even if prosecutions would be able to deter future perpetrators, rulers will still have a good reason to withhold consent. Moreover, notice that the role of the OP is not replicated in the typical hostage scenarios. Officials must react to hostage situations: the

---

[44] R. Geuss, *Public Goods, Private Goods* (Princeton: Princeton University Press, 2001), 102–3.

victims have been chosen by the hostage takers. Conversely, in the world of ICL, the OP decides when to act and who will be sacrificed. In short, while the analogy with hostage taking seems promising, it oversimplifies the variables that are morally relevant for an accurate assessment of the authority of ICL.

With these worries in mind, let us return to one of the central questions under consideration: Is it rational for well-intentioned rulers to consent to be bound by ICL? I will look to the work of Hobbes to shed further light on the question and, indeed, my answer.

3 Beyond War and Peace: Why Consent to Be Bound by ICL?

Consent is often viewed as a powerful legitimizing tool in international law circles. States are bound by the terms of the contract (treaty) signed. It is the distance between the self-interests of states and the requirements of law that serves as an indication of the reality of international law – and often, its perceived legitimacy.[45] International law is meant to act as a check on the unbridled self-interests of states. Not surprisingly, Hobbes is often cited as an authority for the idea that consent legitimizes the workings of international law. But for Hobbes, it is not the mere act of will that makes law legitimate; rather, it is the ends that motivate the decision to consent that are foundational. For him, the primary good that justifies consent is the attainment of peace.[46] When faced with persistent threats to personal security, which includes ongoing threats to one's bodily integrity and life, he argues that it is rational to do what one can to escape such conditions.

The state of nature, which is itself a state of war, is characterized by the persistence of fear and insecurity: life without a common power to keep our natural appetites in check promises to be 'solitary, poor, nasty, brutish, and short'.[47] Famously, Hobbes thinks it is rational 'to lay down this right to all things' in order to create the conditions that make long-term survival more likely.[48] Thus we consent to be bound by the sovereign rule, which is the only route through which the goods of peace and survival can be attained. The price for peace is absolute obedience:

---

[45] S. R. Ratner, *The Thin Justice of International Law: A Moral Reckoning of the Law of Nations* (Oxford: Oxford University Press, 2015), 55–56.
[46] Hobbes, *Leviathan*, ch. 14.
[47] Ibid., ch. 13.
[48] Ibid., ch. 14.

> For by this authority, given him by every particular man in the common-
> wealth, he hath the use of so much power and strength conferred on him
> that by terror thereof he is enabled to conform the wills of them all to
> peace at home and mutual aid against their enemies abroad.[49]

The populace is frightened into submission, but this is preferable to living in fear outside of a state.

In the voluntary act of exiting the state of nature via a social contract, Hobbes maintains that the multiplicity of voices is unified. The subjects have authorized the sovereign to speak on their behalf. This is how Hobbes generates the idea that it is unjust to go against the will of the sovereign, and hence he who breaches the command of the sovereign is the author of his own punishment.[50] We consent to obey authority in such circumstances precisely because it is rational for us to choose the conditions that will allow us to live in peace.[51] Hobbes acknowledges that conditions rarely arise where individuals have the option to consent to be bound; rather, rulers frequently come to power via acts of conquest. He insists that the same logic applies: whether we are dealing with commonwealths that arise out of consent or acquisition, obedience is rational insofar as peace is secured.[52]

One might argue that Hobbes can help, not hurt, the cause of ICL. After all, not all people enjoy the protection of the state. ICL is needed to fill the gaps left when sovereignty breaks down. If rulers abuse their power, neglect their responsibilities or lose control completely, ICL can fill this void.[53] Most governments are in a position to punish non-governmental actors, but no one is in the position to punish state actors – except, of course, for the ICC (and other international tribunals).

While it is true that it is a blind spot in Hobbes's project, it is not a void that the ICC is equipped to fill in most instances. The ICC arrives on the scene only after the atrocity has occurred; in an important sense, it arrives much too late. Moreover, it is more common for the ICC to be used to punish perpetrators who are not governmental actors than to punish government leaders themselves. The ICC needs the cooperation of states to execute arrest warrants and hold trials. The practical upshot of this reality is that the ICC

---

[49] Ibid., ch. 17.

[50] Ibid., ch. 18.

[51] This is also so for 'commonwealths of acquisition', which come about via conquest. Ibid., ch. 17. For an illuminating discussion of our obligation to the state, see J. Dunn, 'Contractualism', in *The History of Political Theory and Other Essays*, ed. J. Dunn (Cambridge: Cambridge University Press, 1996), 50–53.

[52] Hobbes, *Leviathan*, ch. 17.

[53] See A. Chehtman, *The Philosophical Foundations of Extraterritorial Punishment* (Oxford: Oxford University Press, 2010).

frequently must align itself with oppressive regimes in order to secure arrests. There are many worrisome outcomes that have been documented: the victims recognized by the court are those terrorized by rebel groups, not the government. Often, the kind of legal justice delivered is partial.

The problems run deeper still. In such instances, the ICC is not simply aligning itself with governments that mirror Hobbes's Leviathan; it is aligning itself with oppressive regimes that are much scarier than the dark portrait of the state crafted by Hobbes. In Hobbes's world, the state, governed by an all-powerful sovereign, is constructed in order to ensure individual survival. Michael Oakeshott, commenting on Hobbes, maintains that 'this alleged apostle of absolutism would, more than others, appear to be in danger of making civil association a hell by conceiving it as a heaven'.[54] If Hobbes's vision straddles this divide, my worry is that the ICC can, at times, operate on the wrong side of it.

In the real world, rulers often systematically threaten the security, and even the survival, of certain groups. When the ICC makes such unsavoury alliances, it becomes a dangerous player in the game of politics, and its own claim to moral authority is undermined. After all, if one shudders in the face of the *Leviathan*, where security of all citizens is paramount, one should recoil all the more when the ICC (or an *ad hoc* tribunal) supports rulers who intentionally create conditions of insecurity for minority groups residing within the state. Asad Kiyani draws attention to political consequences of the work of the ICC in Uganda:

> The civil war that installed Museveni in 1986 was marked by ethnic-based conflict and atrocity, which transformed into the present-day conflict with the LRA [Lord's Resistance Army]. The ICC's unwillingness to cross this ethno-political divide reifies it by passively legitimating UPDF [Uganda People's Defence Force] practice through non-prosecution, and by representing itself as politically aligned with the government.[55]

The court decides who is on the right side of the war (which is itself a political judgement) and then helps legitimize the actions of one group while demonizing the actions of their opponents. Kiyani adds that 'this pattern repeats itself in other situations, where group-based selectivity often favours a repressive regime in the context of ethno-political conflict'.[56] The oppressive regimes receive official sanction while, and their

---

[54] M. Oakeshott, *Rationalism in Politics and Other Essays* (Indianapolis: Liberty Fund, 1991), 293.

[55] A. G. Kiyani, 'Group-Based Differentiation and Local Repression: The Custom and Curse of Selectivity', *Journal of International Criminal Justice* 14 (2016): 939–57.

[56] Ibid.

political enemies demonized, precisely because it is assumed that the ICC is on the side of 'good'.

There is another unintended, but foreseeable, consequence of the work of the ICC: instead of deterring leaders from committing crimes, the ICC can also send the message that rulers are wise to hold on to power at all costs. It is more desirable to work with the court against political enemies than to be out of power and a potential target of the ICC. And further, the ICC can prove to be an invaluable political instrument to be wielded by ruthless leaders who aim to solidify their power base domestically and internationally.

Of course, from a Hobbesian perspective, strengthening a leader's grip on power may not be problematic insofar as the leader is able to maintain peace. But as mentioned, Hobbes is *not* thinking in terms of systematic oppression of groups. This surely constitutes a blind spot in his account, but it is an informative one. Hobbes assumes that with peace comes personal security, but history has demonstrated that a sovereign can maintain a stable peace and a thriving economy without providing security for all identifiable groups or classes. American inner cities are one obvious example;[57] the Jewish community under national socialism is another. In these cases, there is a de-coupling of peace and security. If the ruler fails to provide protection, the duty to obey breaks down.[58] Whilst peace is often required for security to exist, insecurity can persist in peaceful society. Echoing Hobbes's understanding of a state of nature where war is understood as actual war in addition to 'a tract of time wherein the will to contend by battle is sufficiently known',[59] it should be noted that a state of insecurity is not a state where one is actually impoverished, but instead where the fear of future impoverishment is ever present and real.

Furthermore, insecurity need not only be the result of intentional oppressive actions on the part of the sovereign; it can also be the result of other familiar means: the breakdown of community bonds, the instability of pension schemes, precarious employment and the rise of the global property market are all variables that can contribute to a state of uncertainty and insecurity within a peaceful and wealthy state. While the ICC cannot be expected to bring all citizens out of a state of insecurity, we should worry that the actions of the court directly contribute to the

---

[57] J. Dunn, *Political Theory*, 80. See also Q. Skinner in T. Hobbes, *Writings on Common Law and Hereditary Right*, ed. A. Cromartie and Q. Skinner (Oxford: Clarendon Press, 2005), 163.

[58] Ibid.

[59] Hobbes, *Leviathan*, ch. 13.

continued oppression of groups. Leaders who are fundamentally interested in forwarding the interests of their subjects should be wary about
consenting to be bound by ICL, given past practice. By way of contrast,
self-interested, ruthless rulers may be wise to consent, at least if they
can reasonably anticipate the cooperation of the ICC. Hobbes's theory
does not categorize rulers in this fashion, and thus his theory is able to
illuminate some, but not all, of the moral obstacles facing ICL. This is not
Hobbes's only blind spot.

As stated previously, a concern about group oppression is outside
the reach of Hobbes's program, and self-consciously so. The communal
aspect of group oppression is invisible if one views the world through the
lens Hobbes offers. He conceives of the human condition as an aggregate
of isolated individuals who enjoy relative equality. He abstracts away the
very characteristics that would be relied on to distinguish groups within
society. Hobbes, no doubt, is well aware of the power of difference and
the way rulers can and do treat such differences. His project is a self-
conscious effort to place an end to religious wars. The vision of radical
equality articulated in his many works is intentional. It undercuts conventional assumptions of the divine right of kings, along with the constructed
(and false) sense of superiority taught to all of the faithful. Erasing difference was itself part of the nation-building project – a project that was
underpinned by the social goal of peace. Hobbes is not passively reflecting
on the human condition; he is prompting us to re-imagine ourselves in
the hopes of transforming society.

Dunn, once again, makes an eloquent contribution on a related point.
The bonds that bind people together into groups often prove to be very
disruptive to the political order as a whole. Hobbes's theory of political
obligation re-imagines these bonds in order to ensure that people are
more loyal to the state than to any one group:

> Religious and social solidarity, so far from being the solution to the prob-
> lems of political instability, were virtually the source of that instability.
> The point of political obligation was precisely to contain, to bring under
> rational and human control, the diffuse but vivid menace which these
> wider imaginative bonds represented.[60]

Hobbes harnesses a familiar feature of human existence in order to make
transformation both plausible and possible – namely, the fact that most fear
death more than they fear other things. ICL, by contrast, is not conceiving

---

[60] Hobbes, *Leviathan*, 71.

of the world in terms of social bonds, security or peace. Rather, practitioners tend to think of bringing about legal justice, regardless of the impact it
has on social bonds or the conditions required for mere survival. The narrow confines of this legal lens are coming into focus, as are the sacrifices
that the OP is willing to make for the sake of the realization of this vision.

The possibility of triggering social transformation turns on the skill of
the architect: she must both understand and harness familiar impulses,
appetites and motivations. Hobbes is one of the masters. He offers viable
reasons for action that tap into existing human motivations. One cannot
create radically new reasons for action if one hopes to transform society,
even in part. This, I shall argue, is yet another failure of the project of ICL,
at least in certain contexts.

4 Imagining Change: Articulating New Reasons for Action?

The legitimacy problems that plague ICL extend beyond the issues can-
vassed in the previous sections. Thus far, I have been worried about the
foreseeable but unintended consequences and the variables that impact
(or fail to impact) assessments of individual culpability. I have also discussed the manner in which the court can align itself with unsavoury
rulers. In this final discussion, I hope to underscore how questions of
individual responsibility intersect with questions of the purposes of the
enterprise in ways that are potentially morally problematic. I also aim to
illuminate the hidden acts of power that complicate any account of the
moral authority of ICL.

In *Erdemović*,[61] the utopian dreaming of ICL practitioners reaches an
apex, and ICL is stuck in the dangerous world of wishful thinking. Hobbes
understands what the justices at the ICTY failed to: if you wish to alter
people's reasons for action, you must utilize pre-existing motivations. In
Erdemović, the court seeks to create new reasons for action that are wholly
disconnected from the human condition. Hence the only other plausible
reading of this case is that the actual reasons offered by the court are not
the real reasons driving the decision: the aim is to ensure that they can
generate as many guilty verdicts as possible. In what follows, I will explore
both readings of the case in order to illuminate the utopian and utilitarian
elements that collide and, taken separately and together, undermine the
moral authority of the institution.

---

[61] Judgement, *Prosecutor v. Erdemović*, Case No. IT-96-22-A (ICTY, Appeals Chamber, 7
October 1997), www.icty.org/case/erdemovic/4.

Drazen Erdemović was a low-ranking soldier in the Serbian army. He participated in the massacre at Srebrenica in July 1995. On 31 May 1996, he pleaded guilty to murder as a crime against humanity. The ICTY accepted as fact that if Erdemović had chosen not to kill, he himself would have been killed; nevertheless, he was convicted of committing a crime against humanity. The fact that he participated in the slaughter under duress was a mitigating factor that was considered during the sentencing phase of the proceedings.[62] By untangling the legal and political dimensions of this case, the utopian bent of the decision is revealed.

The central legal question in this case was whether duress is able to serve as a full defence to the charges of genocide and crimes against humanity. Judge Antonio Cassese, in his dissent, articulates an understanding of what tasks law is best suited for. Demanding that people die in order to be in compliance with the demands of ICL is not something we can or, rather, should do. Law, Cassese argues, is based on what 'society can reasonably expect of its members', and thus the question becomes whether we can expect people to sacrifice their own lives in order to live law-abiding lives. Cassese insists that international law 'should not set intractable standards of behaviour which require mankind to perform acts of martyrdom, and brand as criminal any behaviour falling below those standards'.[63] By siding with Cassese on this point (and with Hobbes), I do not simply wish to underscore the importance of survival as a basic good; rather, I wish to highlight the failure of the ICTY to pay sufficient attention to basic features of the human condition. This failure deems this decision morally problematic and practically inert, at least if the ICTY hopes to create new reasons for action, which they claim that they do.

In the domestic context, the criminal law sets a low watermark for acceptable moral conduct. Refraining from acts of cruelty and revenge are necessary if we are to co-exist in the crowded conditions of modern life. When citizens live in compliance with the moral standards articulated in criminal law, they are often simply conforming to basic moral norms. We rarely praise people for their ability to refrain from stealing or murdering each other. Conversely, in *Erdemović*, the plurality opinion by Judges McDonald and Vohrah uses the law to demand martyrdom. In this case,

---

[62] Sentencing Judgement, *Prosecutor v. Erdemović*, Case No. IT-96-22-Tbis (ICTY, Trial Chamber, 5 March 1998), www.icty.org/x/cases/erdemovic/tjug/en/erd-tsj980305e.pdf.

[63] Separate and Dissenting Opinion of Judge Antonio Cassese, *Prosecutor v. Erdemović*, Case No. IT-96-22-A (ICTY, Appeals Chamber, 7 October 1997), www.un.org/icty/erdemovic/appeal/judgement/erd-adojcas971 007e.htm, para. 47.

an attempt is made to use law in order to transform exceptional behaviour into normal behaviour. Failing that (and that project will fail), the decision operates as a mere tool by which to generate guilty verdicts that serve the interests of the enterprise. And, of course, we should not forget that the ICTY was certainly anxious to convict the first person to be tried in connection to the massacre at Srebrenica, who happened to be Erdemović.

One might reply that ICL is not substantively different from the law in many familiar jurisdictions. The United Kingdom (UK), for instance, does not allow duress to serve as a full defence to the killing of innocents. This is a point that the plurality use to buttress their argument.[64] But why should the ICTY prioritize the UK's common-law jurisprudence over, for instance, civil-law jurisdictions?[65] This point is particularly pressing when relevant differences between domestic and international law are considered. In the domestic context, this defence would only be relevant in rare instances. Gang members might benefit, surely, but few others would (in all likelihood) need to use this defence. Conversely, in the countries ravaged by war, the tragic choice that Erdemović faced is fairly commonplace. It is precisely for this reason that the stakes – both moral and legal – are so high. Moreover, notice that the ruling is laced with hypocrisy that is magnified by context: it is highly unlikely that the justices who penned the prevailing decision will ever find themselves in Erdemović's predicament. Those living privileged lives are laying down norms for those living through war. The shadow of imperialism looms.

When considering whether duress is a complete defence, the plurality opinion by Justices McDonald and Vohrah declare that ICL is unclear on the issue and that clarity should be brought via an appeal to policy considerations. This controversial move has numerous implications. Recall that one of the central assumptions that informs the work of ICL is that it both *is* and *should be* distinct from politics.[66] We are now told by Justices McDonald and Vohrah that 'it would be naive to believe that international law operates and develops wholly divorced from considerations of social and economic policy'.[67] The neutrality that the international lawyers covet is not available: 'Even if policy concerns are entirely ignored, the law will nevertheless fail in its ambition of neutrality', given that every

---

[64] Joint Separate Opinion of Judge McDonald and Judge Vohrah, *Prosecutor v. Erdemović*, Case. No. IT-96-22-A (ICTY, Appeals Chamber, 7 October 1997), para. 71–72.

[65] Justice Cassese accuses Justice McDonald and Justice Vohrah of 'cherry picking', paras. 20–39.

[66] See Moreno Ocampo, 'Address to the Assembly', 6.

[67] Ibid., para. 78.

legal decision has 'political and social consequences'.[68] For this reason, 'there is no avoiding the essential relationship between law and politics'.[69] Intellectually, I am sympathetic to the claim that neutrality does not exist; I am less sympathetic, however, to their appeal to policy considerations in this instance.

The plurality justified its appeal to political ends by reminding its audience that it was not dealing with 'the actions of domestic terrorists, gang-leaders and kidnappers'; rather, they were addressing 'the most heinous crimes known to humankind'.[70] At this juncture, the presupposition is that the nature of the charges warrants an appeal to political considerations. But, of course, the question that they must answer is whether Erdemović deserves the label of 'international criminal'. Erdemović's individual culpability is not the centre of gravity in this decision. The ICTY unapologetically and explicitly shifts attention away from the accused, focusing instead on the court's role as 'norm creator':

> Our view is based upon a recognition that international humanitarian law should guide the conduct of combatants and their commanders. There must be legal limits as to the conduct of combatants and their commanders in armed conflict. In accordance with the spirit of international humanitarian law, we deny the availability of duress as a complete defence to combatants who have killed innocent persons. In so doing, we give notice in no uncertain terms that those who kill innocent persons will not be able to take advantage of duress as a defence and thus get away with impunity for their criminal acts in the taking of innocent lives.[71]

The law is supposed to guide the actions of combatants and their commanders; in addition, it is supposed to ensure that criminals cannot escape liability. Also notice that the plurality is assuming (or asserting) that taking the lives of innocents is a criminal act, but this is only so if duress cannot serve as a complete defence. Curiously, they do not even consider the possibility that the defence of duress can act as an excuse rather than a justification, which signals that Erdemović is still morally culpable but not criminally responsible.

Also notice that the two stated aims – creating a new normative order and ensuring that all 'loopholes' are closed – sit in tension with each other. If the new normative order changes behaviour, the loopholes

[68] Ibid.
[69] Ibid.
[70] Ibid., para. 75.
[71] Ibid., para. 80.

would be irrelevant. After all, anyone who finds himself in Erdemović's predicament and opts to adhere to the requirements of ICL will be dead. Those who are dead are unable to 'take advantage' of this defence. Only the living – those who chose to disobey ICL – will potentially end up in the courtroom. In all likelihood, the real goal is to ensure that individuals who carried out the orders of their commanders cannot access this defence. The real goal, then, appears to be institutional: the court wants to be able to generate guilty verdicts.[72] The court is no longer focusing on Erdemović but on future would-be perpetrators. Erdemović appears to be the sacrificial lamb.[73] Is Erdemović really worse than a gang leader, a kidnapper or a domestic terrorist, as Justices McDonald and Vohrah suggest?

Consider Erdemović's stated motivations. In addition to his desire to survive, Erdemović claims that part of the reason he chose to kill rather than to be killed is that he was responsible for the well-being of both his wife and his young child.[74] He explained that he quickly weighed these responsibilities against his own (accurate) assessment of his predicament: any act of self-sacrifice would be virtually meaningless, given that it was highly unlikely that any lives would have been spared.[75] In short, Erdemović was motived by love and fear – two strong impulses that are remarkably difficult to overcome, particularly if there are no clear benefits that he could secure via an act of self-sacrifice. We do not, after all, even know the name of Erdemović's colleague who was executed when he refused to obey orders.

It is precisely because most people in Erdemović's situation would act as he did that we are led to judge outliers as martyrs. The ability to override the strong impulse to survive and return to loved ones is rare, and thus such sacrifices are deserving of praise. The ICTY, insofar as it hopes to alter our reasons for action, aims to turn all of us into heroes, but very strange ones. If its imagined world came to be, people would be dying for the sake of ICL; after all, if the moral norm was strong enough to motivate behaviour on its own,

---

[72] Notice that this decision can be criticized for being too political (insofar as it is interested in institutional ends rather than the contours of the current case) and too utopian.

[73] Not everyone is troubled by this. Daryl Lim Tze Wei sees the court as a 'vehicle through which the international community expresses its outrage at the atrocities committed in the former Yugoslavia'. See D. L. T. Wei, 'Rethinking *Erdemović*: Beyond the Clash of Laws', *Singapore Law Review* 23 (2003): 71–84, esp. 83.

[74] 'Testimony of the Accused Drazen Erdemović', International Criminal Tribunal for the Former Yugoslavia, www.icty.org/x/cases/erdemovic/trans/en/960531ID.htm

[75] Ibid.

the ICTY would not have needed to attempt to alter the normative land-scape with a new norm. Citizens of this strange global community would be more committed to the norms of international law than they would be to one another, or even to their own lives.

The ICTY seems to want ICL to be a new religion, but religions harness love and fear in order to motivate behaviour. This is precisely why the actions of believers are intelligible to non-believers, even if non-believers are bewildered by the belief system itself. Dying for God makes sense if one believes in an afterlife, for instance; any suffering in this life will be rewarded eternally. Consider another example. The US Marines have a creed that sets out a hierarchy of values: 'God, Country, Corps'. The commitment is comprehensible because it is yet another expression of love for community. The soldiers' fear of dying is overcome for the sake of love for country. They are also committed to each other – their corps – as their collective aim to protect the objects of love can only be achieved if work is carried out as a unit. Even if it is hard for one to imagine becoming a Marine, it is easy to understand why some people choose to do so. Conversely, dying to be in compliance with ICL makes very little sense. If this particular precedent is meant to guide conduct, then it will likely fail. The justices have failed to work with basic features of the human condition in this instance, thus rendering the understanding of the brave new world where ICL will guide our conduct as an absurd one. While lawyers are often viewed as practical agents who help create or re-enforce reasons for action, it is the philosopher Hobbes who occupies a more practical space.

Hobbes also wants to create a new version of religion, but unlike the justices who penned *Erdemović*, he understands that to create a mortal god, he must channel the impulses that would otherwise be directed towards the Immortal God. Hobbes is also keenly aware of the fact that he cannot rid people of their belief in God – he can only tame it.[76] His aim is to ensure that religion does not operate as a force that contributes to instability and war. One cannot will away the desire to act out of love and fear; one can only hope to use these pre-existing levers to alter behaviour. People are to fear the sovereign in the same way that they fear God.[77] Even if they do not love the sovereign, they should be grateful to her: she bestows many tangible goods while removing the worst kind of earthly evils. If international lawyers want tangible practical results, they

---

[76] For a discussion of the 'seeds' of religion in *Leviathan*, see Hobbes, *Leviathan*, ch. 11.
[77] See R. Harrison, *Hobbes, Locke and Confusion's Masterpiece* (Cambridge: Cambridge University Press, 2003), 45.

too must understand and respect the impulses and desires that lead people to act. Until lawyers come to understand the human condition, the
results of the work of ICL will be tragic rather than emancipatory. If ICL
wants to enjoy the moral authority it claims, it cannot sacrifice vulnerable
people, or relatively powerless actors, to its cause.

When we return to consider Erdemović's fate, we can see clearly what
a tragic figure he has become. He is guilty of 'crimes against humanity'
in large part because the justices used this opportunity to deter future
would-be criminals (or, more plausibly, to generate guilty verdicts) rather
than assess his situation in full. After all, if Erdemović and people like him
are going to die if they abide by the law, it is not clear that their failure in
this regard should make them guilty of the most unimaginable crimes.
Moreover, unlike domestic terrorists and rapists, Erdemović does not
pose a danger to his community, so his incarceration cannot be justified
on those grounds.

When we broaden the lens to consider the actions and inactions of
global superpowers, we can see precisely how blinkered ICL's lens is. Not
only is ICL easily manipulated with interpretive manoeuvres employed to
serve the interests of the enterprise itself; it is a lens that leaves out salient information about agency and responsibility. Once the curtains are
pulled back on the global politics that led to the massacre at Srebrenica,
the full scope of the catastrophe is exposed. Erdemović was a low-ranking
soldier who was a reluctant participant in the massacre, yet he is branded
as an 'international criminal'. He was almost powerless, unlike the global
superpowers, many of whom played a direct role in this atrocity (and who
fund the ICTY).

It is well known that the Dutch abandoned the safe zone, leaving the
Muslim men, women and children to be dealt with by Slobodan Milošević
and his troops. But in a recent tell-all written by Florence Hartmann,
the role of high-ranking officials in the US, UK and UN is revealed.[78]
Hartmann explains that the policy adhered to the US, UK, France and the

---

[78] See the following article, written by E. Vulliamy and F. Hartmann, which is based
on Hartmann's book (only published in French): 'How Britain and the US Decided to
Abandon Srebrenica to Its Fate', *The Guardian*, 4 July 2015, www.theguardian.com/world/
2015/jul/04/how-britain-and-us-abandoned-srebrenica-massacre-1995. Hartmann was
subsequently arrested and imprisoned by the ICC for revealing confidential information
in her book. See 'French Journalist Florence Hartmann Jailed by War Crimes Tribunal', *The
Guardian*, 26 March 2016, www.theguardian.com/law/2016/mar/26/french-journalist-
florence-hartmann-jailed-by-war-crimes-tribunal--srebrenica-massacre.

UN – 'peace at any price' – played a key role in the unfolding of events.[79] The road to peace involved letting Milošević and his troops do whatever they thought necessary to secure it. It was also revealed that the CIA watched the slaughter in almost 'live time' and chose to do nothing to stop it.[80] The international community failed to act, and as mentioned, the very same international community funds the ICTY. Just as 'peace at all costs' is an extremely dangerous strategy, so is 'justice at all costs'. Those in power can and do use ICL to help legitimize their activities while veiling the role they play in any given atrocity. This is yet another reason to resist the narrative that ICL is primarily an apolitical mechanism that delivers justice.

David Luban argues that 'not even the so-called "likeminded" states who promote the ICL project are heretical enough to reject the religion of sovereignty'.[81] This may be so, but it is my contention that it is better to believe in the religion of sovereignty than the religion of ICL. The state has proven to be an indispensable arrangement for the protection of and the preconditions for human flourishing. Conversely, the international legal community cannot control all the variables that exacerbate human suffering, and too often it becomes the unwitting agent of the perpetuation of suffering. If the enterprise is ever going to enjoy a degree of the moral legitimacy it craves, practitioners must exercise authority in a manner that is sensitive both to the suffering of vulnerable groups and to the fact that some features of the human condition are not infinitely malleable. It is now clear that Mégret is correct in his observation that 'international criminal justice cannot create by fiat a world that would make sense of its existence'.[82] If the ICC is going to be an authority that is worthy of our obedience and respect, it must navigate the world as it is with greater care and measure.

---

[79] Vulliamy and Hartman, 'How Britain and the US Decided to Abandon Srenrenica to Its Fate'.
[80] Ibid.
[81] D. Luban, 'Fairness to Rightness: Jurisdiction, Legality, and the Legitimacy of International Criminal Law' (Georgetown Law Faculty Working Paper), 2008, https://papers.ssrn.com/sol3/papers.cfm?abstract_id=1154177.
[82] Mégret, 'Anxieties of International Criminal Justice', 221.

BIBLIOGRAPHY

Aalberts, T. *Constructing Sovereignty between Politics and Law* (London: Routledge, 2012).

Allan, T. R. S. *Constitutional Justice* (Oxford: Oxford University Press, 2001).

Allott, P. 'The Concept of International Law'. *European Journal of International Law* 10 (1999): 31–50.

The Health of Nations (Cambridge: Cambridge University Press, 2002).

Alston, P., and R. Goodman. *International Human Rights* (Oxford: Oxford University Press, 2013).

Alter, K. 'The New International Courts: A Bird's Eye View' (Buffett Center for International and Comparative Studies Working Paper Series No. 09-001, 2009).

The New Terrain of International Law: Courts, Politics, Rights (Princeton: Princeton University Press, 2014).

Alter, K., L. Helfer and M. R. Madsen. 'How Context Shapes the Authority of International Courts'. *Law and Contemporary Problems* 79 (2016): 1–36.

'The Variable Authority of International Courts'. *Law and Contemporary Problems* 79 (2016): 1–314.

Alvarez, J. E. *International Organizations as Lawmakers* (Oxford: Oxford University Press, 2005).

Alvik, I., M. Emberland and C. Eriksen, eds. *The New International Law* (Leiden: Martinus Nijhoff, 2010).

Anghie, A. 'Angola: A New Cease-Fire – A New Opportunity for Human Rights'. Amnesty International, 5 April 2002. www.amnesty.org.uk/press-releases/ angola-new-cease-fire-new-opportunity-human-rights.

'The Evolution of International Law: Colonial and Postcolonial Realities'. *Third World Quarterly* 27 (2006): 739–53.

Applbaum, A. 'Legitimacy without the Duty to Obey'. *Philosophy and Public Affairs* 38 (2010): 215–39.

Arajärvi, N. *The Changing Nature of Customary International Law: Methods of Interpreting the Concept of Custom in International Criminal Tribunals* (Abingdon: Routledge, 2014).

Arendt, H. *Human Condition* (Chicago: University of Chicago Press, 1958).

'What Is Authority?' In *Between Past and Future*, edited by H. Arendt and J. Kohn (New York: Penguin Books, 2006).

Armitage, D. *Foundations of Modern International Thought* (Cambridge: Cambridge University Press, 2013).

Austen, J. *Persuasion*. The World Classics, vol. 356 (Oxford: Oxford University Press, 1975).

Bassiouni, M. C. 'Accountability for Violations of International Humanitarian Law and Other Serious Violations of Human Rights.' In *Post-conflict Justice*, edited by M. C. Bassiouni (New York: Transnational, 2002).

Baum, L. *Judges and Their Audiences: A Perspective on Judicial Behavior* (Princeton: Princeton University Press, 2006).

Beitz, C. *The Idea of Human Rights* (Oxford: Oxford University Press, 2009).

Benhabib, S. *Another Cosmopolitanism* (Oxford: Oxford University Press, 2006).

Bennet, N. 'Health Concerns Raised over EU-US Trade Deal'. *The Lancet* 384 (2014): 843–44.

Bentham, J. *A Fragment on Government and an Introduction to the Principles of Morals and Legislation*, edited by W. Harrison (Oxford: Blackwell, 1967).

Benton, L., and L. Ford. *Rage for Order: The British Empire and the Origins of International Law, 1800–1850* (Cambridge, MA: Harvard University Press, 2016).

Benvenisti, E., and G. W. Downs. 'National Courts, Domestic Democracy, and the Evolution of International Law'. *European Journal of International Law* 20 (2009): 59–72.

Berman, M. 'Two Types of Retributivism'. In *The Philosophical Foundations of Criminal Law*, edited by R. A. Duff and S. P. Green (Oxford: Oxford University Press, 2011).

Berman, P. S. *Global Legal Pluralism* (Cambridge: Cambridge University Press, 2014).

'A Pluralist Approach to International Law'. *Yale Journal of International Law* 32 (2007): 301–29.

Bertea, S. *The Normative Claim of Law* (Oxford: Hart, 2009).

Besson, S. 'The Authority of International Law – Lifting the State Veil'. *Sydney Law Review* 31 (2009): 343–80.

'State Consent and Disagreement in International Law Making: Dissolving the Paradox'. *Leiden Journal of International Law* 29 (2016): 289–316.

'Theorizing the Sources of International Law'. In *The Philosophy of International Law*, edited by S. Besson and J. Tasioulas (Oxford: Oxford University Press, 2010).

Besson, S., and J. Tasioulas, eds. *The Philosophy of International Law* (Oxford: Oxford University Press, 2010).

Bibas, S., and W. W. Burke-White. 'International Idealism Meets Domestic-Criminal-Procedure Realism'. *Duke Law Journal* 59 (2010): 637–704.

Bingham, T. *The Rule of Law* (London: Penguin, 2011).

Birnie, P., A. Boyle and C. Redgwell. *International Environmental Law* (Oxford: Oxford University Press, 2009).

Bjorge, E. *The Evolutionary Interpretation of Treaties* (Oxford: Oxford University Press, 2014).

Bodansky, D. 'The Concept of Legitimacy in International Law'. In *Legitimacy in International Law*, edited by R. Wolfrum and V. Roben (Heidelberg: Springer, 2008).

'*Non Liquet* and the Incompleteness of International Law'. In *International Law, the International Court of Justice and Nuclear Weapons*, edited by L. de Chazournes and P. Sands (Cambridge: Cambridge University Press, 1999).

Borgwardt, E. *A New Deal for the World: America's Vision for Human Rights* (Cambridge, MA: Belknap Press of Harvard University, 2005).

Boucher, D., and P. J. Kelly, eds. *The Social Contract from Hobbes to Rawls* (Abingdon: Routledge, 2005).

Bourdieu, P. 'Authorized Language: The Social Conditions for the Effectiveness of Ritual Discourse'. In *Language and Symbolic Power*, edited by P. Bourdieu, translated by G. Raymond and M. Adamson (Cambridge, MA: Harvard University Press, 1999).

Entwurf einer Theorie der Praxis (Frankfurt am Main: Suhrkamp, 1996).

'The Force of Law: Toward a Sociology of the Juridical Field'. *Hastings Law Journal* 38 (1987): 814–53.

The Logic of Practice (Stanford: Stanford University Press, 1992).

Sozialer Sinn. Kritik der theoretischen Vernunft (Frankfurt am Main: Suhrkamp, 1987).

Boyle, A., and C. Chinkin. *The Making of International Law* (Oxford: Oxford University Press, 2007).

Brandom, R. 'Some Pragmatist Themes in Hegel's Idealism: Negotiation and Administration in Hegel's Account of the Structure and Content of Conceptual Norms'. *European Journal of Philosophy* 7 (1999): 164–89.

Brownlie, I. *The Rule of Law in International Affairs: International Law at the Fiftieth Anniversary of the United Nations* (Hague: Martinus Nijhoff, 1998).

Brudner, A. *Constitutional Goods* (Oxford: Oxford University Press, 2004).

The Unity of the Common Law: Studies in Hegelian Jurisprudence (Berkeley: University of California Press, 1995).

Brunée, J., and S. J. Toope. *Legitimacy and Legality in International Law: An Interactional Account* (Cambridge: Cambridge University Press, 2010).

Buchanan, A. *The Heart of Human Rights* (Oxford: Oxford University Press, 2013).

Justice, Legitimacy, and Self-Determination: Moral Foundations for International Law (Oxford: Oxford University Press, 2004).

Buckle, S. *Natural Law and the Theory of Property: Grotius to Hume* (Oxford: Oxford University Press, 1991).

Byers, M. *Custom, Power, and the Power of Rules: International Relations and Customary International Law* (Cambridge: Cambridge University Press, 1999).

Çali, B. *The Authority of International Law: Obedience, Respect and Rebuttal* (Oxford: Oxford University Press, 2015).

Capps, P. *Human Dignity and the Foundations of International Law* (Oxford: Hart, 2009).

  'Legal Idealism and Global Law'. In *Ethical Rationalism and the Law*, edited by P. Capps and S. D. Pattinson (Oxford: Hart, 2017).

  'The Rejection of the Universal State'. In *Transnational Constitutionalism*, edited by N. Tsagourias (Cambridge: Cambridge University Press, 2007).

Capps, P., and J. Rivers. 'Kant's Concept of International Law'. *Legal Theory* 16 (2010): 229–57.

Carruba et al., 'Judicial Behavior under Political Constraints: Evidence from the European Court of Justice'. *American Political Science Review* 102 (2008): 435.

Carty, A. *The Decay of International Law: A Reappraisal of the Limits of Legal Imagination in International Affairs* (Manchester: Manchester University Press, 1986).

Cassese, A., ed. *Realizing Utopia* (Oxford: Oxford University Press, 2012).

Charney, J. I. 'Universal International Law'. *American Journal of International Law* 83 (1993): 523–53.

Chehtman, A. *The Philosophical Foundations of Extraterritorial Punishment* (Oxford: Oxford University Press, 2010).

Christiano, T. 'Authority'. In *The Stanford Encyclopedia of Philosophy*, Spring 2013 ed., edited by E. N. Zalta. http://plato.stanford.edu/archives/spr2013/entries/authority/.

  'The Authority of Democracy'. *Journal of Political Philosophy* 12 (2004): 266–90.

  'The Legitimacy of International Institutions'. In *The Routledge Companion to Philosophy of Law*, edited by A. Marmor (New York: Routledge, 2012).

Christoffersen, J. *Fair Balance: A Study of Proportionality, Subsidiarity and Primarity in the European Convention on Human Rights* (Leiden: Martinus Nijhoff, 2009).

Christoffersen, J., and M. R. Madsen, eds. *The European Court of Human Rights between Law and Politics* (Oxford: Oxford University Press, 2011).

Collingwood, R. G. *An Essay on Metaphysics* (Oxford: Clarendon Press, 1940).

  An Essay on Philosophical Method (Oxford: Clarendon Press, 1933).

  The New Leviathan or Man, Society, Civilization and Barbarism (Oxford: Clarendon Press, 1942).

Collins, R. 'Classical Legal Positivism in International Law Revisited'. In *International Legal Positivism in a Post-Modern World*, edited by J. Kammerhofer and J. d'Aspremont (Cambridge: Cambridge University Press, 2014).

The Institutional Problem in Modern International Law (Oxford: Hart Publishing, 2016).

'Mapping the Terrain of Institutional "Lawmaking": Form and Function in International Law'. In *The Actors of Postnational Rule-Making: Contemporary Challenges of European and International Law*, edited by E. Fahey (Abingdon: Routledge, 2015).

'No Longer at the Vanishing Point? International Law and the Analytical Tradition in Jurisprudence'. *Jurisprudence* 5 (2014): 265–98.

Combacau, J., and S. Sur. *Droit International Public* (Paris: Montchrestien, 2010).

Coşeriu, E. *Synchronie, Diachronie und Geschichte. Das Problem des Sprachwandels* (München: Wilhelm Fink Verlag, 1974).

Cover, R. M. 'The Folktales of Justice: Tales of Jurisdiction'. *Capital University Law Review* 14 (1985): 179–203.

'Nomos and Narrative'. *Harvard Law Review* 97 (1983): 4–68.

Craig, P., and G. de Burca. *EU Law: Texts, Cases and Materials*, 5th ed. (Oxford: Oxford University Press, 2011).

Crawford, J. *The Creation of States in International Law*, 2nd ed. (Oxford: Oxford University Press, 2007).

'The Problems of Legitimacy Speak'. *Proceedings of the American Society of International Law* 98 (2004): 271.

d'Aspremont, J. *Formalism and the Sources of International Law: A Theory of the Ascertainment of Legal Rules* (Oxford: Oxford University Press, 2011).

Participants in the International Legal System: Multiple Perspectives on Non-state Actors in International Law (London: Routledge, 2012).

Dai, X. 'Why Comply? The Domestic Constituency Mechanism'. *International Organization* 59 (2005): 363–98.

de Chazournes, L. B., and P. Sands, eds. *International Law, the International Court of Justice and Nuclear Weapons* (Cambridge: Cambridge University Press, 1999).

de Goede, M. *Speculative Security: The Politics of Pursuing Terrorist Monies* (Minneapolis: University of Minnesota Press, 2012).

de Goede, M., and G. Sullivan. 'The Politics of Security Listing'. *Environment and Planning D: Society and Space* (2015): 67–88.

de Sadeleer, N. *Environmental Principles: From Political Slogans to Legal Rules* (Oxford: Oxford University Press, 2002).

Implementing the Precautionary Principle (London: Earthscan, 2007).

de Sousa Santos, B. *Toward a New Legal Common Sense* (Evanston, IL: Northwestern University Press, 2002).

de Sousa Santos, B., and C. Rodriguez-Garavito, eds. *Law and Globalization from Below* (Cambridge: Cambridge University Press, 2005).

de Vattel, E. *The Law of Nations*. Edited by B. Kapossy and R. Whitmore (Indianapolis: Liberty Fund, 2008).

DeGuzman, M. 'Choosing to Prosecute: Expressive Selection at the International Criminal Court'. *Michigan Journal of International Law* 33 (2012): 265–320.

Dezalay, Y., and B. G. Garth. *Dealing in Virtue: International Commercial Arbitration and the Construction of a Transnational Legal Order* (Princeton: Princeton University Press, 1998).

Dezalay, Y., and M. R. Madsen. 'The Force of Law and Lawyers: Pierre Bourdieu and the Reflexive Sociology of Law'. *Annual Review of Law and Social Science* 8 (2012): 433–52.

Domingo, R. *The New Global Law* (Cambridge: Cambridge University Press, 2010).

Dothan, S. *Reputation and Judicial Tactics: A Theory of National and International Courts* (Cambridge: Cambridge University Press, 2015).

Doyle, M. 'The UN Charter – A Global Constitution'. In *Ruling the World*, edited by J. L. Dunoff and J. P. Trachtmann (Cambridge: Cambridge University Press, 2009).

Drumbl, M. A. 'The Curious Criminality of Mass Atrocity: Diverse Actors, Multiple Truths, and Plural Responses' (Washington & Lee Legal Studies Paper No. 2012-33, October 4, 2012). https://papers.ssrn.com/sol3/papers .cfm?abstract_id=2156512.

'Juridical and Jurisdictional Disconnects' (Washington & Lee Public Law Research Paper No. 02-02, 2003).

Dunn, J. 'Contractualism'. In *The History of Political Theory and Other Essays*, edited by J. Dunn (Cambridge: Cambridge University Press, 1996).

The History of Political Theory and Other Essays (Cambridge: Cambridge University Press, 1996).

Dunoff, J. L., and J. P. Trachtmann, eds. *Ruling the World?: Constitutionalism, International Law, and Global Governance* (Cambridge: Cambridge University Press, 2009).

Dworkin, R. *Law's Empire* (Oxford: Hart, 1998).

'A New Philosophy for International Law'. *Philosophy and Public Affairs* 41 (2013): 2–30.

Taking Rights Seriously (Cambridge, MA: Harvard University Press, 1977).

'Thirty Years On'. *Harvard Law Review* 115 (2002): 1655–87.

Dyzenhaus, D. *Legality and Legitimacy* (Oxford: Clarendon Press, 1997).

Ehrenberg, K. *The Functions of Law* (Oxford: Oxford University Press, 2016).

Ehrlich, E. *Freie Rechtsfindung und freie Rechtswissenschaft*. Translated by I. Venzke (Leipzig, 1903). http://www.gleichsatz.de/b-u-t/can/rec/ehrlich1frei.html.

Fundamental Principles of the Sociology of Law (1913; London: Transaction, 2001).

Engle, K. 'Anti-impunity and the Turn to Criminal Law in Human Rights'. *Cornell Law Review* 100 (2015): 1069–1127.

Eschenburg, T. *Über Autorität* (Frankfurt: Suhrkamp, 1969).

Estlund, D. *Democratic Authority* (Cambridge: Cambridge University Press, 2007).

Fassbender, J. 'Rediscovering a Forgotten Constitution: Notes on the Place of the UN Charter in the International Legal Order'. In *Ruling the World*, edited by J. L. Dunoff and J. P. Trachtman (Cambridge: Cambridge University Press, 2009).

Finnis, J. *Natural Law and Natural Rights*, 2nd ed. (Oxford: Oxford University Press, 2011).

Fischer-Lescano, A., and P. Liste. 'Völkerrechtspolitik. Zu Trennung und Verknüpfung von Politik und Recht der Weltgesellschaft'. *Zeitschrift für Internationale Beziehungen* 12 (2005): 209–49.

Fitzmaurice, G. G. 'The General Principles of International Law considered from the Standpoint of the Rule of Law'. *Recueil des Cours* 92 (1957-II): 1–227.

Fitzmaurice, M. 'Third Parties and the Law of Treaties'. *Max Planck Yearbook of United Nations Law* 6 (2002): 37–137.

Flanders, C. 'Toward a Theory of Persuasive Authority'. *Oklahoma Law Review* 62 (2009): 55–88.

Flathman, R. E. *The Practice of Political Authority: Authority and the Authoritative* (Chicago: University of Chicago Press, 1980).

Franck, T. *Fairness in International Law and Institutions* (Oxford: Oxford University Press, 1995).

'Lessons of Kosovo'. *American Journal of International Law* 93 (1999): 857–60.

Friedrichs, J. 'The Neomedieval Renaissance: Global Governance and International Law in the New Middle Ages'. In *Governance and International Legal Theory*, edited by I. F. Dekker and W. G. Werner (Leiden: Martinus Nijhoff, 2004).

Fuller, L. L. *The Morality of Law*, rev. ed. (New Haven: Yale University Press, 1969).

Gardbaum, S. 'Human Rights and International Constitutionalism'. In *Ruling the World*, edited by J. L. Dunoff and J. P. Trachtman (Cambridge: Cambridge University Press, 2009).

Gardner, J. *Law as a Leap of Faith* (Oxford: Oxford University Press).

Geuss, R. *Philosophy and Real Politics* (Princeton: Princeton University Press, 2008).

Public Goods, Private Goods (Princeton: Princeton University Press, 2001).

Giddens, A. *Central Problems in Social Theory: Action, Structure and Contradiction in Social Analysis* (London: Macmillan, 1979).

Gillroy, J. M. *The Assent of Public Order Principles in International Law: Philosophical Method, G. W. F. Hegel and Legal Right through Recognition* (New York: Palgrave Macmillan, forthcoming).

An Evolutionary Paradigm for International Law: Philosophical Method, David Hume and the Essence of Sovereignty (New York: Palgrave Macmillan, 2013).

Justice and Nature: Kantian Philosophy, Environmental Policy and the Law (Washington, DC: Georgetown University Press, 2000).

'Justice-as-Sovereignty: David Hume and the Origins of International Law'. *British Year Book of International Law* 78 (2008): 429–79.

'Philosophical Policy and International Dispute Settlement: Process Principle and the Ascendance of the WTO's Concept of Justice'. *Journal of International Dispute Settlement* 53 (2012): 3.

Glenn, H. P. 'Persuasive Authority'. *McGill Law Journal* 32 (1986–87): 261–98.

Godard, O. 'Social Decision-Making under Conditions of Scientific Controversy'. In *Integrating Scientific Expertise into Regulatory Decision-Making*, edited by C. Joerges, K.-H. Ladeur and E. Vos (Baden-Baden: Nomos Verlagsgessellschaft, 1997).

Goldmann, M. 'Inside Relative Normativity: From Sources to Standard Instruments for the Exercise of International Public Authority'. *German Law Journal* 9 (2008): 1865–1908.

'A Matter of Perspective: Global Governance and the Distinction between Public and Private Authority (and Not Law)'. January 15, 2015. http://ssrn.com/abstract=2260293.

Goldsmith, J. L., and E. A. Posner. *The Limits of International Law* (Oxford: Oxford University Press, 2005).

Goodin, R. E. 'Enfranchising All Affected Interests, and Its Alternatives'. *Philosophy and Public Affairs* 35 (2007): 40–68.

Green, L. 'Legal Obligation and Authority'. In *The Stanford Encyclopaedia of Philosophy*, Winter 2012 ed., edited by E. N. Zalta. http://plato.stanford.edu/archives/win2012/entries/legal-obligation/.

Grotius, H. *On the Law of War and Peace*, vol. 1. Translated by G. L. Williams (Oxford: Clarendon Press, 1950).

Gur, N. 'Are Legal Rules Content-Independent Reasons?' *Problema* 5 (2011): 175–210.

Guzman, A. T. *How International Law Works: A Rational Choice Theory* (Oxford: Oxford University Press, 2008).

Habermas, J. *Between Facts and Norms* (Cambridge: Polity Press, 1996).

Between Naturalism and Religion (Cambridge: Polity Press, 2008).

Moral Consciousness and Communicative Action (1989; Cambridge, MA: MIT Press, 2006).

The Postnational Constellation (Cambridge: Polity Press, 2001).

Hachez, N., and J. Wouters. 'A Glimpse at the Democratic Legitimacy of Private Standards: Assessing the Public Accountability of GLOBALG.A.P'. *Journal of International Economic Law* 14 (2011): 677–710.

Hale, R. 'Our Equivocal Constitutional Guarantees'. *Columbia Law Review* 39 (1939): 563–94.

Halliday, M. A. K. *Language as a Social Semiotic: The Social Interpretation of Language and Meaning* (Baltimore: University Park Press, 1978).

Halliday, M. A. K., and R. Hasan. *Language, Context, and Text: Aspects of Language in a Social-Semiotic Perspective* (Oxford: Oxford University Press, 1989).

Harrison, R. *Hobbes, Locke and Confusion's Masterpiece* (Cambridge: Cambridge University Press, 2003).

Hart, H. L. A. *The Concept of Law* (Oxford: Oxford University Press, 1961).
Essays on Bentham (Oxford: Oxford University Press, 1983).
Hegel, G. W. F. *Encyclopedia of Philosophical Science V1: Logic*. Translated by W. Wallace (Oxford: Oxford University Press, 1975).
Encyclopedia of Philosophical Science V3: Philosophy of Mind. Translated by W. Wallace and A. V. Wallace (Oxford: Oxford University Press, 2007).
Natural Law. Translated by T. M. Knox (Philadelphia: University of Pennsylvania Press, 1975).
Outlines of the Philosophy of Right. Translated by T. M. Knox and S. Houlgate (Oxford: Oxford University Press, 2008).
The Phenomenology of Spirit. Translated by W. Wallace and A. V. Miller (Oxford: Oxford University Press, 1977).
The Philosophy of History. Translated by J. Sibree (New York: Dover, 1956).
Science of Logic. Translated by A. V. Millers (London: George Allen & Unwin, 1976).
Werke in 20 Bänden mit Registerband (Frankfurt: Surkamp, 1986).
Held, D. *Models of Democracy*, 3rd ed. (Cambridge: Polity Press, 2006).
Helfer, L. 'Redesigning the European Court of Human Rights: Embeddedness as a Deep Structural Principle of the European Human Rights Regime'. *European Journal of International Law* 19 (2008): 125–59.
Henkin, L. *How Nations Behave: Law and Foreign Policy*, 2nd ed. (New York: Columbia University Press, 1979).
Hernandez, G. *The International Court of Justice and the Judicial Function* (Oxford: Oxford University Press, 2014).
Higgins, R. 'Policy Considerations and the International Judicial Process'. *International and Comparative Law Quarterly* 17 (1968): 58–84.
Himma, K. E. 'Law's Claim to Legitimate Authority'. In *Hart's Postscript: Essays on the Postscript to the Concept of Law*, edited by J. Coleman (Oxford, Oxford University Press, 2001).
Hobbes, T. *De Cive* (Whitefish: Kessinger, 2004).
Leviathan. Edited by E. Curley (Indianapolis: Hackett, 1994).
Leviathan. Edited by M. Oakeshott (Oxford: Blackwell, 1957).
Writings on Common Law and Hereditary Right, edited by A. Cromartie and Q. Skinner (Oxford: Clarendon Press, 2005).
Holmes, O. W. 'The Path of the Law'. *Harvard Law Review* 10 (1897): 457–78.
Holtermann, J. v. H. 'A "Slice of Cheese" – a Deterrence-Based Argument for the International Criminal Court'. *Human Rights Review* 11 (2010): 289–315.
Hovell, D. 'Kadi: King-Slayer or King-Maker? The Shifting Allocation of Decision-making Power between the UN Security Council and Courts'. *Modern Law Review* 79 (2016): 147–82.
Hume, D. *An Enquiry Concerning the Principles of Morals*, 3rd ed. Edited by L. A. Selby-Bigge and P. H. Nidditch (Oxford: Oxford University Press, 1975).

A Treatise of Human Nature, 5th ed. Edited by L. A. Selby-Bigge and P. H. Nidditch (Oxford: Oxford University Press, 1978).

Hurd, H. 'Challenging Authority'. *Yale Law Journal* 101 (1991): 1611–77.

'Expressing Doubts about Expressivism'. *University of Chicago Legal Forum* 1 (2005): 405–35.

'The International Rule of Law and the Domestic Analogy'. *Global Constitutionalism* 4 (2015): 365–95.

'The International Rule of Law: Law and the Limits of Politics'. *Ethics and International Affairs* 28 (2014): 39–51.

International Criminal Court, Office of the Prosecutor, 'Policy Paper on the Interests of Justice'. September 2007. https://www.icc-cpi.int/NR/rdonlyres/772C95C9-F54D-4321-BF09-73422BB23528/143640/ICCOTPInterestsOfJustice.pdf.

International Law Association, 'Final Report of the Committee on Formation of Customary (General) International Law'. 2000. http://www.ila-hq.org/download.cfm/docid/A709CDEB-92D6-4CFA-A61C4CA30217F376.

International Law Commission. 'Fragmentation of International Law: Difficulties Arising from the Diversification and Expansion of International Law'. Report of the Study Group of the International Law Commission. UN Doc. A/CN.4/L.682. Geneva, 13 April 2006. http://legal.un.org/ilc/documentation/english/a_cn4_l682.pdf.

Jabloner, C. 'Verrechtlichung und Rechtsdynamik'. *Zeitschrift für öffentliches Recht* 54 (1999): 261–78.

Jansen, N. *The Making of Legal Authority* (Oxford: Oxford University Press, 2010).

Joerges, C. 'Good Governance through Comitology'. In *Committees: Social Regulation, Law and Politics*, edited by C. Joerges and E. Vos (Oxford: Hart, 1999).

'Unity in Diversity as Europe's Vocation and Conflicts Law as Europe's Constitutional Form'. LSE Europe in Question Discussion Paper No. 28, 2010.

Joerges, C., and C. Glinski, eds. *The European Crisis and the Transformation of Transnational Governance: Authoritarian Managerialism versus Democratic Governance* (Oxford: Hart, 2014).

Joerges, C., I. J. Sand and G. Teubner, eds. *Transnational Governance and Constitutionalism* (Oxford: Hart, 2004).

Joseph, S. 'Trade Law and Investment Law'. In *The Oxford Handbook of International Human Rights Law*, edited by D. Shelton (Oxford: Oxford University Press, 2013).

Kammerhofer, J., and J. d'Aspremont, eds. *International Legal Positivism in a Postmodern World* (Cambridge: Cambridge University Press, 2014).

Kant, I. *The Metaphysics of Morals*. Translated by M. Gregor (Cambridge: Cambridge University Press, 1991).

Kaul, H.-P. 'The International Criminal Court: Current Challenges and Perspectives'. *Washington University Global Studies Law Review* 6.3 (2007): 575–82.

Keller, R. *Sprachwandel* (Tübingen: Francke, 2003).

Kelsen, H. *Law and Peace in International Relations* (Cambridge, MA: Harvard University Press, 1942).

Kendall, S. 'Commodifying Global Justice: Economies of Accountability at the International Criminal Court'. *Journal of International Criminal Justice* 13 (2015): 113–34.

Kingsbury, B. 'International Courts: Uneven Judicialization in Global Order'. In *Cambridge Companion to International Law*, edited by J. Crawford and M. Koskenniemi (Cambridge: Cambridge University Press, 2011).

'Legal Positivism as Normative Politics: International Society, Balance of Power and Lassa Oppenheim's Positive International Law'. *European Journal of International Law* 13 (2002): 401–37.

'The Concept of "Law" in Global Administrative Law'. *European Journal of International Law* 20 (2009): 23–57.

Kirgis, F. L. Jr. 'Custom on a Sliding Scale'. *American Journal of International Law* 81 (1987): 146–51.

Kiyani, A. G. 'Group-Based Differentiation and Local Repression: The Custom and Curse of Selectivity'. *Journal of International Criminal Justice* 14.4 (2016): 939–57.

Klabbers, J. 'Institutional Ambivalence by Design: Soft Organizations in International Law'. *Nordic Journal of International Law* 70 (2001): 403–21.

International Law (Oxford: Oxford University Press, 2013).

'The Redundancy of Soft Law'. *Nordic Journal of International Law* 65 (1996): 167–82.

Klabbers, J., A. Peters and G. Ulfstein. *The Constitutionalization of International Law* (Oxford: Oxford University Press, 2009).

Koh, H. H. 'Transnational Legal Process'. *Nebraska Law Review* 75 (1996): 181–207.

Kolb, R. 'Repères historiques dans l'évolution de l'occupation de guerre'. *The Global Community: Yearbook of International Law and Jurisprudence* (2007): 65–102.

Koskenniemi, M. 'Between Commitment and Cynicism: Outline for a Theory of International Law as Practice'. In *Collection of Essays by Legal Advisrers of States, Legal Advisers of International Organizations and Practitioners in the Field of International Law*, edited by United Nations (New York: United Nations Publication, 1999).

'The Fate of Public International Law: Between Technique and Politics'. *Modern Law Review* 70 (2007): 1–32.

'Fragmentation of International Law: Report of the Study Group of the International Law Commission'. UN Doc A/CN4/L.682, 2006.

From Apology to Utopia: The Structure of International Legal Argument (Cambridge: Cambridge University Press, 2005).

The Gentle Civilizer of Nations (Cambridge: Cambridge University Press, 2001).

'International Law: Constitutionalism, Managerialism and the Ethos of Legal Education'. *European Journal of Legal Studies* 1 (2007): 1–18.

'Legitimacy, Rights and Ideology: Notes towards a Critique of the New Moral Internationalism'. *Associations: Journal for Legal and Social Theory* 7 (2003): 349–374.

'Miserable Comforters: International Relations as New Natural Law'. *European Journal of International Relations* 15 (2009): 395–422.

The Politics of International Law (Oxford: Hart, 2011).

Krahmann, E. *States, Citizens and the Privatization of Security* (Cambridge: Cambridge University Press, 2010).

Kratochwil, F. 'The Limits of Contract'. *European Journal of International Law* 5 (1994): 465–91.

Krisch, N. *Beyond Constitutionalism: The Pluralist Structure of Postnational Law* (Oxford: Oxford University Press, 2010).

Kron, J. 'Rwandan Is Convicted in 1994 Killings'. *New York Times*, 17 November 2011. www.nytimes.com/2011/11/18/world/africa/former-rwandan-mayor-convicted-in-tutsi-massacre.html?_r=0.

Kulovesi, K. *The WTO Dispute Settlement System: Challenges of the Environment, Legitimacy and Fragmentation* (Alphen aan den Rijn: Kluwer Law International, 2011).

Lewis, D. *Conventions: A Philosophical Study* (Oxford: Wiley-Blackwell, 2002).

Lim, C. L., and O. A. Elias. *The Paradox of Consensualism in International Law* (Hague: Martinus Nijhoff, 1998).

Lincoln, B. *Authority: Construction and Corrosion* (Chicago: University of Chicago Press, 1991).

Llewellyn, K. 'What Price Contract? An Essay in Perspective'. *Yale Law Journal* 40 (1931): 704–51.

Loeb, J. 'Talking to the Other Side: Humanitarian Engagement with Armed Non-state Actors in Darfur'. Humanitarian Policy Group Working Paper, 2013, 1–48.

Luban, D. 'Fairness to Rightness: Jurisdiction, Legality, and the Legitimacy of International Criminal Law'. Georgetown Law Faculty Working Paper, 2008. https://papers.ssrn.com/sol3/papers.cfm?abstract_id=1154177.

Luhmann, N. *Das Recht der Gesellschaft* (Frankfurt am Main: Suhrkamp, 1993).

Die Wirtschaft der Gesellschaft (Germany: Suhrkamp Taschenbuch Wissenschaft, 1994).

Law as a Social System (Oxford: Oxford University Press, 2012).

Legitimation durch Verfahren (Frankfurt: Suhrkamp, 1983).

Risk: A Socological Theory (Berlin: De Gruyter, 1993).

Maduro, M. P. *We, the Court: The European Court of Justice and the European Economic Constitution* (Oxford: Hart, 1998).

Mahoney, P. 'The Relationship between the Strasbourg Court and the National Courts'. *Law Quarterly Review* 130 (2014): 568–86.

Martin, M. 'International Criminal Law: Between Utopian Dreams and Political Realities'. In *Rethinking Criminal Law Theory: New Canadian Perspectives in the Philosophy of Domestic, Transnational, and International Criminal Law*, edited by F. Tanguay-Renaud and J. Stribopoulos (Oxford: Hart, 2011).

Judging Positivism (Oxford: Hart, 2014).

'Reflections on Punishment from a Global Perspective: An Exploration of Chehtman's *The Philosophical Foundations of Extraterritorial Punishment*'. *Criminal Law and Philosophy* 8.3 (2014): 693–712.

Mashaw, J. L. 'Recovering American Administrative Law: Federalist Foundations, 1787–1801'. *Yale Law Journal* 115 (2006): 1256–1344.

McDougal, M. 'International Law, Power, and Policy: A Contemporary Conception'. *Recueil des Cours* 82 (1954): 137–259.

Studies in World Public Order (New Haven: Yale University Press 1960).

Mégret, F. 'The Anxieties of International Criminal Justice'. *Leiden Journal of International Law* 29 (2016): 197–221.

Meidinger, E. 'The Administrative Law of Global Private-Public Regulation: The Case of Forestry'. *European Journal of International Law* 17 (2006): 47–87.

Merleau-Ponty, M. *Die Abenteuer der Dialektik* (Frankfurt am Main: Suhrkamp, 1968).

Merrills, J. 'International Adjudication and Autonomy'. In *International Organizations and the Idea of Autonomy: Institutional Independence in the International Legal Order*, edited by R. Collins and N. D. White (New York: Routledge, 2011).

Mian, M. 'The Curious Case of Exclusionary Reasons'. *Canadian Journal of Law and Jurisprudence* 15 (2002): 99–124.

Mommsen, T. *Römisches Staatsrecht*, vol. 3 (Cambridge: Cambridge University Press, 2010).

Moyn, S. *The Last Utopia* (Cambridge, MA: Belknap Press, 2010).

Murphy, C. 'The Dynamics of Transnational Counter-terrorism Law: Towards a Methodology, Map, and Critique'. In *Constitutionalism across Borders in the Struggle against Terrorism*, edited by F. Fabbrini and V. Jackson (London: Edward Elgar, 2016).

Musielak, H. J., and K. Schurig, eds. *Festschrift für Gerhard Kegel* (Berlin: Kohlhammer, 1987).

Neff, S. *Justice among Nations* (Cambridge, MA: Harvard University Press, 2014).

Neuhouser, F. *Rousseau's Theodicy of Self-Love: Evil, Rationality, and the Drive for Recognition* (Oxford: Oxford University Press, 2008).

Newman, D. G. 'The Rome Statute, Some Reservations Concerning Amnesties, and a Distributive Problem'. *American University International Law Review* 20.2 (2004): 293–357.

Nouwen, S., and S. Kendell. 'Representational Practices at the International Criminal Court: The Gap between Juridified and Abstract Victimhood'. *Law and Contemporary Problems* 76 (2013): 235–62.

Nouwen, S., and W. Werner. 'Doing Justice to the Political: The International Criminal Court in Uganda and Sudan'. *European Journal of International Law* 21 (2011): 941–65.

Oakeshott, M. *Rationalism in Politics and Other Essays* (Indianapolis: Liberty Fund, 1991).

Olsen, H. P. 'Fidelity to International Law: On International Law and Politics'. In *Ethical Rationalism and the Law*, edited by P. Capps and S. D. Pattinson (Oxford: Hart, 2017).

'International Courts and the Doctrinal Channels of Legal Diplomacy'. *Transnational Legal Theory* 6 (2015): 661–80.

Olsen, H. P., and S. Toddington. 'The End of an Era: Static and Dynamic Interpretation in International Courts'. *International Criminal Law Review* 14 (2014): 1–26.

Orakhelashvili, A. *Peremptory Norms in International Law* (Oxford: Oxford University Press, 2006).

Palma, M. 'The Possible Contribution of International Civil Society to the Protection of Human Rights'. In *Realizing Utopia. The Future of International Law*, by A. Cassese (Oxford: Oxford University Press, 2012).

Pattinson, S. D. 'The Human Rights Act and the Doctrine of Precedent'. *Legal Studies* 35 (2015): 142–64.

Pauwelyn, J. *Conflicts of Norms in Public International Law* (Cambridge: Cambridge University Press, 2008).

Pauwelyn, J., and M. Elsig. 'The Politics of Treaty Interpretation: Variations and Explanations across International Tribunals'. In *Interdisciplinary Perspectives on International Law and International Relations: The State of the Art*, edited by J. L. Dunoff and M. A. Pollack (Cambridge: Cambridge University Press, 2013).

Payandeh, M. 'The Concept of International Law in the Jurisprudence of H. L. A. Hart'. *The European Journal of International Law* 21 (2011): 967–91.

Peat, D., and M. Windsor. 'Playing the Game of Interpretation: On Meaning and Metaphor in International Law'. In *Interpretation in International Law* (Oxford: Oxford University Press, 2015).

Pelc, K. 'The Politics of Precedent in International Law: A Social Network Application'. *American Political Science Review* 108 (2014): 547–64.

Perry, S. R. 'Law and Obligation'. *American Journal of Jurisprudence* 50 (2005): 263–95.

'Second Order Reasons, Uncertainty, and Legal Theory'. *Southern California Law Review* 62 (1989): 913–94.

Peters, A. 'Compensatory Constitutionalism: The Function and Potential of Fundamental International Norms and Structures'. *Leiden Journal of International Law* 19 (2006): 579–610.

Peters, B., and J. K. Schaffer. 'The Turn to Authority beyond States'. *Transnational Legal Theory* 4 (2013): 315–33.

Petersmann, E. 'Human Rights, International Economic Law and "Constitutional Justice"'. *European Journal of International Law* 19 (2008): 955–60.

Petman, J. 'Deformalization of International Organizations Law'. In *Research Handbook on the Law of International Organizations*, edited by J. Klabbers and Å. Wallendahl (Cheltenham: Edward Elgar, 2011).

Pettit, P. *Republicanism: A Theory of Freedom and Government* (Oxford: Oxford University Press, 1999).

Postema, G. J. 'Coordination and Convention at the Foundations of the Law'. *The Journal of Legal Studies* 11 (1982): 165–203.

'Custom in International Law: A Normative Practice Account'. In *The Nature of Customary Law: Legal, Historical, and Philosophical Accounts*, edited by J. B. Murphy and A. Perreau-Saussine (Cambridge: Cambridge University Press, 2007).

'Law's Autonomy and Public Practical Reason'. In *The Autonomy of Law*, edited by R. George (Oxford: Clarendon Press, 1996).

Pound, R. 'Law in Books and Law in Action'. *American Law Review* 44 (1910): 12–36.

Ragazzi, M. *The Concept of International Obligations Erga Omnes*, ed. (Oxford: Oxford University Press, 1997).

Ratner, S. R. *The Thin Justice of International Law* (Oxford: Oxford University Press, 2015).

Rawls, J. *The Law of Peoples* (Cambridge, MA: Harvard University Press, 1999).

A Theory of Justice (Cambridge, MA: Harvard University Press, 1971).

Raz, J. 'Authority, Law and Morality'. *Monist* 86 (1985): 295–324.

The Authority of Law (Oxford: Clarendon Press, 1979).

The Authority of Law, 2nd ed. (Oxford: Oxford University Press, 2009).

Ethics in the Public Domain: Essays in the Morality of Law and Politics, rev. ed. (Oxford: Clarendon Press, 1994).

'Legitimate Authority'. In *The Authority of Law: Essays on Law and Morality*, edited by J. Raz (Oxford: Oxford University Press, 2009).

The Morality of Freedom (Oxford: Clarendon Press, 1986).

Practical Reason and Norms (London: Hutchinson, 1975).

'The Problem of Authority: Revisiting the Service Conception'. *Minnesota Law Review* 90 (2006): 1003–44.

Reisman, M. 'International Lawmaking: A Process of Communication'. *American Society of International Law Proceedings* 75 (1981): 101–20.

'Unilateral Action and the Transformations of the World Constitutive Process: The Special Problem of Humanitarian Intervention'. *European Journal of International Law* 11 (2000): 3–18.

Rivers, J. 'Proportionality and Variable Intensity of Review'. *Cambridge Law Journal* 65 (2006): 174–207.

Roberts, A. E. 'Traditional and Modern Approaches to Customary International Law: A Reconciliation'. *American Journal of International Law* 95 (2001): 757–91.

Roberts, S. 'After Government? On Representing Law without the State'. *Modern Law Review* 68 (2005): 1–24.

Robinson, D. 'Inescapable Dyads: Why the ICC Cannot Win'. *Leiden Journal of International Law* 28 (2015): 323–47.

Roughan, N. *Authorities: Conflicts, Cooperation, and Transnational Legal Theory* (Oxford: Oxford University Press, 2013).

'Mind the Gaps: Authority and Legality in International Law'. *European Journal of International Law* 27 (2016): 329–51.

Ruggie, J. G. 'International Regimes, Transactions and Change: Embedded Liberalism in the Postwar Economic Order'. *International Organization* 36 (1982): 379–415.

Rundle, K. *Forms Liberate: Reclaiming the Jurisprudence of Lon L. Fuller* (Oxford: Hart, 2012).

Sand, I. J. 'Hybridization, Change and the Expansion of Law'. In *Hybrid Forms of Governance*, edited by Å. Andersen and I. J. Sand (Basingstoke: Palgrave Macmillan, 2012).

Sandholtz, W. 'Creating Authority by the Council: The International Criminal Tribunals'. In *The UN Security Council and the Politics of International Authority*, edited by B. Cronin and I. Hurd (Abingdon: Routledge, 2008).

Sassen, S. *Territory, Authorities, Rights* (Princeton: Princeton University Press, 2006).

Schachter, O. 'The Nature and Process of Legal Development in International Society'. In *The Structure and Process of International Law: Essays in Legal Philosophy, Doctrine, and Theory*, edited by Macdonald, R St. J and D. M. Johnston (Hague: Martinus Nijhoff, 1983).

Schatzki, T. R. 'Introduction: Practice Theory'. In *The Practice Turn in Contemporary Theory*, edited by T. R. Schatzki, Centina K. Knorr and von E. Savigny (London: Routledge, 2001).

Schauer, F. 'Authority and Authorities'. *Virginia Law Review* 94 (2008): 1931.

Scholte, J. A. 'Civil Society and Democratically Accountable Global Governance'. *Government and Opposition* 39 (2004): 211–33.

Schöndorf-Haubold, B. 'The Administration of Information in International Administrative Law: The Example of Interpol'. *German Law Journal* 9 (2008): 1719–52.

Schrijver, N. *The Evolution of Sustainable Development in International Law: Inception, Meaning and Status* (Leiden: Nijhoff, 2008).

Sciaraffa, S. 'On Conent-Independent Reasons: It's Not in the Name'. *Law and Philosophy* 28 (2009): 233–60.

Shany, Y. *Assessing the Effectiveness of International Courts* (Oxford: Oxford University Press, 2013).

'Assessing the Effectiveness of International Courts: A Goal-Based Approach'. *American Journal of International Law* 106 (2012): 225–70.

Shapiro, S. 'Authority'. In *The Oxford Handbook of Jurisprudence and Philosophy of Law*, edited by J. Coleman, K. Himma and S. Shapiro (Oxford: Oxford University Press, 2004).

'Hart's Way Out'. In *Hart's Postscript: Essays on the Postscript to the Concept of Law*, edited by J. Coleman (Oxford: Oxford University Press, 2001).

Shklar, J. N. *Legalism* (Cambridge, MA: Harvard University Press, 1964).

Simmons, A. J. 'Associative Political Obligations'. *Ethics* 106 (1996): 247–73.

Moral Principles and Political Obligations (Princeton: Princeton University Press, 1979).

Skouteris, T. *The Notion of Progress in International Law Discourse* (Hague: TMC Asser Press, 2010).

Slaughter, A.-M. *A New World Order* (Princeton: Princeton University Press, 2004).

Somek, A. 'The Concept of "Law" in Global Administrative Law: A Reply to Benedict Kingsbury'. *European Journal of International Law* 20 (2010): 985–95, esp. 993–94.

'The Owl of Minerva: Constitutional Discourse before Its Conclusion'. *Modern Law Review* 71 (2008): 473–89.

Sorel, J. M., and V. B. Eveno. 'Article 31'. In *The Vienna Conventions on the Law of Treaties: A Commentary*, edited by O. Corten and P. Klein (Oxford: Oxford University Press, 2011).

Stein, E. 'International Integration and Democracy: No Love at First Sight'. *American Journal of International Law* 95 (2001): 489–534.

Stewart, R. 'Remedying Disregard in Global Regulatory Governance: Accountability, Participation, and Responsiveness'. *American Journal of International Law* 108 (2014): 211–70.

Stiglitz, J. *Globalization and Its Discontents* (New York: Norton, 2002).

Stone Sweet, A., and T. Brunell. 'Trustee Courts and the Judicialization of International Regimes: The Politics of Majoritarian Activism in the European Convention on Human Rights, the European Union, and the World Trade Organization'. *Journal of Law and Courts* 1 (2013): 61–88.

Suganami, H. *The Domestic Analogy and World Order Proposals* (Cambridge: Cambridge University Press, 1989).

Sullivan, G., and M. de Goede. 'Between Law and the Exception: The UN1267 Ombudsperson as a Hybrid Model of Legal Expertise'. *Leiden Journal of International Law* 26 (2013): 833–54.

Swart, M. 'Judicial Lawmaking at the Ad Hoc Tribunals: The Creative Use of the Sources of International Law and "Adventurous Interpretation"'. *Zeitschrift für ausländisches öffentliches Recht und Völkerrecht* 70 (2010): 459.

Tams, C. *Enforcing Obligations Erga Omnes in International Law* (Cambridge: Cambridge University Press, 2005).

Tasioulas, J. 'Human Rights, Legitimacy, and International Law'. *American Journal of Jurisprudence* 58 (2013): 1–25.

'The Legitimacy of International Law'. In *The Philosophy of International Law*, edited by S. Besson and J. Tasioulas (Oxford: Oxford University Press, 2010).

Taylor, C. 'To Follow a Rule …' In *Bourdieu: Critical Perspectives*, edited by C. Calhoun, E. LiPuma and M. Postone (Chicago: University of Chicago Press, 1993).

Teubner, G. 'Coincidentia Oppositorum: Hybrid Networks beyond Contract and Organization'. In *Networks: Legal Issues of Multilateral Co-operation*, edited by G. Teubner and M. Amstutz (Oxford, Hart, 2009).

Constitutional Fragments: Societal Constitutionalism (Oxford: Oxford University Press, 2012).

Law as an Autopoietic System (Oxford: Blackwell, 1993).

'Substantive and Reflexive Elements in Modern Law'. *Law and Society Review* 17 (1983): 239–86.

Thomas, C. A. 'The Uses and Abuses of Legitimacy in International Law'. *Oxford Journal of Legal Studies* 34 (2014): 729–58.

Thornhill, C. *A Sociology of Constitutions* (Cambridge: Cambridge University Press, 2011).

Tomuschat, C. *Human Rights: Between Idealism and Realism* (Oxford: Oxford University Press, 2008).

Torrance, M. 'Persuasive Authority beyond the State: A Theoretical Analysis of Transnational Corporate Social Responsibility Norms as Legal Reasons within Positive Legal Systems'. *German Law Journal* 12 (2011): 1573–1636.

Tucker, A. 'The Limits of Razian Authority'. *Res Publica* 18 (2012): 225–40.

Tuori, K., M. Maduro and S. Sankari. *Transnational Law. Rethinking European Law and Legal Thinking* (Cambridge: Cambridge University Press, 2014).

v. Gestel, R., H. W. Micklitz and M. P. Maduro. 'Methodology in the New Legal World'. European University Institute Working Paper, 2012, 13.

v. Jhering, R. *Der Kampf um's Recht* (1913; Frankfurt am Main: Klostermann, 1948).

v. Wijk, J. 'Amnesty for War Crimes in Angola: Principled for a Day?' *International Criminal Law Review* 12.4 (2012): 743–61.

van der Vossen, B. 'Assessing Law's Claim to Authority'. *Oxford Journal of Legal Studies* 31 (2011): 481–501.

Van Hoof, G. J. H. *Rethinking the Sources of International Law* (Deventer: Kluwer, 1983).

van Mulligen, A. 'Framing Deformalisation in International Law'. *Transnational Legal Theory* 3–4 (2015): 635–60.

Venzke, I. 'Between Power and Persuasion: On International Institutions' Authority in Making Law'. *Transnational Legal Theory* 4 (2013): 354–73.

 How Interpretation Makes International Law: On Semantic Change and Normative Twists (Oxford: Oxford University Press, 2013).

 'Is Interpretation in International Law a Game?' In *Interpretation in International Law*, edited by A. Bianchi et al. (Oxford: Oxford University Press, 2015).

 'Legal Contestation about "Enemy Combatants": On the Exercise of Power in Legal Interpretation'. *Journal of International Law & International Relations* 5 (2009): 155–84.

Venzke, I., and J. Von Bernstorff. 'Ethos, Ethics, and Morality in International Relations'. In *Max Planck Encyclopedia of Public International Law*, edited by R. Wolfrum (Oxford: Oxford University Press, 2010).

Verdirame, G. 'A Normative Theory of Sovereignty Transfers'. *Stanford Journal of International Law* 49 (2013): 371–424.

 'Rescuing Human Rights from Proportionality'. In *Philosophical Foundations of Human Rights*, edited by R. Cruft, S. M. Liao and M. Renzo (Oxford: Oxford University Press, 2014).

von Bogdandy A. 'Globalization and Europe: How to Square Democracy, Globalization, and International Law'. *European Journal of International Law* 15 (2004): 885–906.

von Bogdandy A., M. Goldmann and I. Venzke. 'From Public International Law to International Public Law: Translating World Public Opinion into International Public Authority'. *European Journal of International Law* 28 (2017): 115–45.

von Bogdandy, A., and I. Venzke. *In Whose Name? A Public Law Theory of International Adjudication* (Oxford: Oxford University Press, 2014).

Voyiakis, E. 'Customary International Law and the Place of Normative Considerations'. *American Journal of Jurisprudence* 55 (2010): 163–200.

Vulliamy, E., and F. Hartmann. 'How Britain and the US Decided to Abandon Srebrenica to Its Fate', *The Guardian*, 4 July 2015. www.theguardian.com/world/2015/jul/04/how-britain-and-us-abandoned-srebrenica-massacre-1995.

Walker, N. 'Beyond Boundary Disputes and Basic Grids: Mapping the Global Disorder of Normative Orders'. *International Journal of Constitutional Law* 3–4 (2008): 373–396.

Weber, M. 'Der Sinn der "Wertfreiheit" der Soziologischen und Ökonomischen Wissenschaften'. *Logos* 7 (1917): 40.

 Economy and Society. Edited by G. Roth and C. Wittich (Berkeley: University of California Press, 1978).

'Politics as a Vocation'. In *From Max Weber: Essays in Sociology*, by M. Weber, translated and edited by H. H. Gerth and C. W. Mills (Oxford: Oxford University Press, 1973).

Wei, D. L. T. 'Rethinking *Erdemović*: Beyond the Clash of Laws'. *Singapore Law Review* 23 (2003): 71–84.

Weiler, J. H. H. 'The Geology of International Law: Governance, Democracy and Legitimacy'. *Zeitschrift für Ausländisches Öffentliches Recht und Völkerrecht* 64 (2004): 547–62.

Wheatley, S. *The Democratic Legitimacy of International Law* (Oxford: Hart, 2010).

Willaschek, M. 'Which Imperatives for Right? On the Non-prescriptive Character of Juridical Law in Kant's Metaphysics of Morals'. In *Kant's Metaphysics of Morals: Interpretative Essays*, edited by M. Timmons (Oxford: Oxford University Press, 2002).

Winkler, M. 'Die Normativität des Praktischen'. *Juristenzeitung* 64 (2009): 821.

Wittgenstein, L. *Philosophical Investigations*. Translated by G. E. M. Anscombe (Oxford: Blackwell, 1958).

Wolfrum, R. 'Legitimacy of International Law and the Exercise of Administrative Functions: The Example of the International Seabed Authority, the International Maritime Organisation (IMO) and the International Fisheries Organizations'. *German Law Journal* 9 (2008): 2039–59.

INDEX